Democratic Brazil Revisited

PITT LATIN AMERICAN SERIES

Catherine M. Conaghan,
Editor

Democratic Brazil Revisited

Edited by

Peter R. Kingstone

and Timothy J. Power

UNIVERSITY OF
PITTSBURGH PRESS

Published by the University of Pittsburgh Press, Pittsburgh, Pa., 15260

Manufactured in the United States of America
Printed on acid-free paper
10 9 8 7 6 5 4

Library of Congress Cataloging-in-Publication Data

Democratic Brazil revisited / edited by Peter R. Kingstone and Timothy J. Power.
p. cm. — (Pitt Latin American series)
Includes bibliographical references and index.
ISBN-13: 978-0-8229-4354-9 (cloth : alk. paper)
ISBN-10: 0-8229-4354-9 (cloth : alk. paper)
ISBN-13: 978-0-8229-6004-1 (pbk. : alk. paper)
ISBN-10: 0-8229-6004-4 (pbk. : alk. paper)
1. Brazil—Politics and government—2003– 2. Democracy—Brazil. 3. Political participation—Brazil. I. Kingstone, Peter R., 1964– II. Power, Timothy J. (Timothy Joseph), 1962–
JL2431.D46 2008
320.981—dc22

2008030190

Contents

Figures and Tables

Figures

Tables

Preface

THIS COLLECTION OF ESSAYS is a sequel to *Democratic Brazil: Actors, Institutions, and Processes*, a volume which we coedited some eight years ago. The earlier volume was a product of a rich collaborative experience among a group of young scholars who had conducted fieldwork in Brazil in the early 1990s and had recently defended their dissertations in the United States. Many of these dissertations had been supervised by senior scholars who had first come to know a Brazil that was authoritarian, but in the midst of an economic miracle. By contrast, our cohort first came to study a Brazil that was newly democratic, but in the midst of a powerful economic crisis. The Brazil of the late 1980s and early 1990s endured a dizzying inflationary spiral, with all its attendant social and economic perversities. Our encounter, then, was with a Brazil struggling to make democracy work against terrific odds, and the objective of *Democratic Brazil* was to carefully parse the evidence for signs of progress, regress, and stagnation. What the team of researchers found was a mixed pattern that spoke to the complexity of democratic politics and the challenge of theorizing about actors, institutions, and processes.

Democratic Brazil Revisited takes up chronologically from where *Democratic Brazil* left off, at the end of the first presidential term of Fernando Henrique Cardoso in 1998. But, the current project reflects two important differences as well. The first is that the group contributing to *Democratic Brazil Revisited* is more diverse than the original, in terms of generation as well as nationality. In addition to drawing on emerging scholars, the group also includes senior colleagues such as Barry Ames and Janice Perlman. Ames was the author of a major early study of Brazil's defunct dictatorship, *Rhetoric and Reality in a Militarized Regime* (1973), and Perlman here revisits *The Myth of Marginality* (1976), her landmark study of Rio's poor. This volume also draws on the insights of a group of Brazilian scholars, both established and junior. In certain areas of research on Brazilian democracy—particularly on political institutions and on social policy—it is sometimes observed that foreign analysts of Brazil ("Brazilianists") have displayed more pessimism and criticism than their Brazilian colleagues. Such distinctions often fail to appreciate the diversity of the scholarship that is being produced, both in the North and in the South, but in any case we hope that an inclusive volume such as this one will force both optimists and pessimists to look carefully and critically at their own assumptions. We take up this theme further in the introduction to the present volume.

The second important difference from the first volume has to do with the objective performance of Brazil's democracy. The country's political system has made impressive and important advances since the original *Democratic Brazil* was conceived in the mid-1990s, including the peaceful and historic presidential succession of former labor leader and one-time socialist Luiz Inácio Lula da Silva, who won both the 2002 and 2006 elections. January 1, 2007, when Lula was sworn in for a second time, marked the first time in Brazil's history that a democratically elected president (Cardoso) had turned over power to a democratically elected successor (Lula) who was then able to serve a complete term in office. The economy has made considerable advances, and Brazil stands out for some of the world's most innovative social policymaking. In short, many of the gravest concerns articulated by earlier studies of Brazilian democracy have proven less intractable than expected. To be sure, *Democratic Brazil Revisited* still finds a mixed pattern of advances and setbacks—much like the original *Democratic Brazil*. But the concerns about Brazilian democracy in 2008 are now couched in terms of policy challenges rather than existential threats. In particular, the more critical views in *Democratic Brazil Revisited* address dilemmas of profound social inequality and its attendant violence, and the weaknesses of the rule of law as evidenced by Brazil's crime rate and recurrent corruption scandals. The focus here is not on the *survival* of democracy, but rather on the *quality* of democracy, and the objective here is to assess this quality via collaborative research.

Like its predecessor, this volume grew out of linked panels presented at the meetings of the Latin American Studies Association, this time in held in San Juan, Puerto Rico, in March 2006. The authors benefited greatly from the lively participation of numerous sunburned audience members, many of whom sat on the floor for up to four hours (we would like to thank the San Juan fire marshal for not inspecting our meeting room that day). As with the original volume, all the contributors benefited from the input, comments, and insights of a large and thriving community of scholars working on Brazilian democracy—both in the United States and Brazil. We are particularly grateful to the University of

Pittsburgh Press for their ongoing enthusiasm and support for this project. We would particularly like to thank Peter Kracht and Cynthia Miller.

Peter Kingstone would like to thank the University of Connecticut for its support for research related to this volume through the Large Grant and Small Grant programs, as well as the Center for Latin American and Caribbean Studies, and the Hewlett Foundation. Timothy Power would like to thank the Centre for Brazilian Studies at Oxford University and the Helen Kellogg Institute for International Studies at the University of Notre Dame for their valuable support.

Finally, as in all our endeavors, we would like to thank our families, Lisa, Ben, and Lara Kingstone, and Valéria Carvalho Power, for their unflagging love and support.

Acronyms

Abong	Associação Brasileira de ONGs
ANA	Agência Nacional de Águas
ANATEL	Agência Nacional de Telecomunicações
ANCINE	Agência Nacional do Cinema
ANEEL	Agência Nacional de Energia Elétrica
ANP	Agência Nacional de Petróleo
ANS	Agência Nacional de Saúde Suplementar
Antaq	Agência Nacional de Transportes Aquáticos
ANTT	Agência Nacional de Transportes Terrestres
ANVISA	Agência Nacional de Vigilância Sanitária
ARENA	Aliança Renovadora Nacional
BNES	Brazilian National Election Study
BPC	Benefício de Prestação Continuada
CDES	Conselho de Desenvolvimento Econômico e Social
CFEMEA	Centro Feminista de Estudos e Assessoria
CPF	Cadastro de Pessoa Física
CNBB	Conferência Nacional dos Bispos do Brasil
Conlutas	Coordenação Nacional de Lutas
CUT	Central Única dos Trabalhadores
FBO	Fórum Brasileiro do Orçamento
FNB	Brazilian Black Front
FPM	Fundo de Participação dos Municípios
FSE	Social Emergency Fund
GMO	genetically modified organisms
IBASE	Instituto Brasileiro de Análises Sociais e Econômicas
IGP	Índice Geral de Preços
IMF	International Monetary Fund
IPCA	Índice Nacional de Preços ao Consumidor Amplo
LGT	General Law of Telecommunications

MDB	Movimento Democrático Brasileiro
MESA	Ministério Extraordinário para a Segurança Alimentar e Combate à Fome
MNU	Unified Black Movement
MP	medida provisória
MST	Movimento dos Trabalhadores Rurais Sem-Terra
OECD	Organization for Economic Co-operation and Development
OLPR	open-list proportional representation
PCdoB	Partido Comunista do Brasil
PCC	Primeiro Comando da Capital
PDT	Partido Democrático Trabalhista
PESB	Pesquisa Social Brasileira
PFL	Partido da Frente Liberal
PL	Partido Liberal
PMDB	Partido do Movimento Democrático Brasileiro
PNSP	National Plan for Public Security
PP	Partido Progressista
PPB	Partido Progressista Brasileiro
PPS	Partido Popular Socialista
PRN	Partido de Reconstrução Nacional
Pronasci	Programa Nacional de Segurança Pública e Cidadani
PSDB	Partido da Social Democracia Brasileira
PSOL	Partido Socialismo e Liberdadc
PSB	Partido Socialista Brasileiro
PSTU	Partido Socialista dos Trabalhadores Unificado
PT	Partido dos Trabalhadores
PTB	Partido Trabalhista Brasileiro
RVM	Renda Mensal Vitalícia
SEDEPRON (later changed to **SEAFRO**)	Secretaria Extraordinária de Defesa e Promoção das Populações Negras
SENASP	Secretaria Nacional de Segurança Pública
SEPPIR	Secretaria Especial de Politicas de Promoção da Igualdade Racial
SUSP	Sistema Único de Segurança Pública
TEN	Black Experimental Theater
TSE	Tribunal Supremo Eleitoral

Democratic Brazil Revisited

1

Introduction

Peter Kingstone and
Timothy J. Power

On January 1, 2007, Luiz Inácio Lula da Silva celebrated the inauguration of his second term as president of Brazil. His reelection in October 2006 was an impressive achievement for the young democracy: more than one hundred million voters cast their vote in the largest turnout in the history of Latin America. Lula drew 61 percent of the second-round vote—a reflection of his ability to claim credit for a widespread improvement in the country's economic performance and a general increase in living standards, especially for the poorer segments of Brazilian society. The vote, the fifth direct election since the restoration of democracy in 1985, occurred without fraud, coercion, or any other irregularities that might call into question the legitimacy of the process. The earlier 2002 election, which involved the smooth transition from the centrist government of Fernando Henrique Cardoso (1995–2002) to the leftist Lula, is another illustration of how stable Brazilian institutions have become. Even members of the military and the business community accepted the legitimacy of the election of a figure who had been anathema to them as little as ten years earlier.

The Brazilian Puzzle

For many observers of Brazilian politics, the achievement of a considerable degree of institutional and economic stability is cause for some puzzlement. In the late 1980s and into the early 1990s, scholars, politicians, and policymakers voiced serious concerns about Brazil's volatile economy and chaotic political system, describing the situation with adjectives such as "drunk," "ungovernable," or "feckless." A variety of indicators suggested that Brazil was among the least likely to "consolidate" among Latin America's nascent democratic regimes. This pessimism stands in sharp contrast to the situation as of 2007. Today, there is widespread consensus that Brazil is not at risk of an authoritarian retrogression. In many ways, Brazilian democracy looks considerably stronger than democratic rule in many other Latin American nations.

The Brazilian story is not, however, one of continuous and unblemished success. A range of persistent and seemingly intractable problems have plagued Brazil historically and continue to cast shadows over what was initially called the "New Republic." Among them, corruption has been a particularly troubling issue that has tainted every government since the transition to democracy in 1985. The Lula government and the Workers' Party (Partido dos Trabalhadores or PT), longstanding champions of clean government, transparency, and accountability, were themselves caught in a web of corruption and scandal beginning in 2005 that traced back into the upper echelons of the party.

In addition to corruption, Brazilian democracy also continues to suffer from problems of deep inequality and rising violent crime and lawlessness. More than two decades after the restoration of democracy, Brazil remains among the world's most unequal societies. These inequalities manifest themselves economically, socially, and politically and correlate with gender, race, and geography. The challenges stemming from deep socioeconomic inequality have been exacerbated by pervasive and steadily worsening violent crime. With 3 percent of the world's population, Brazil is responsible for 11 percent of its homicides; in the time since we published our earlier volume *Democratic Brazil* in 2000, more than three hundred thousand Brazilians have been murdered. Governments at all levels have done little to stem the extreme violence of Brazilian society, and the poor, in particular, suffer from both fear of crime and fear of ineffectual and often corrupt police. Moreover, successive public opinion surveys have shown that Brazilians have been unusually disappointed by and disaffected from democratic politics over this same period of relative political and economic stability. In fact, Brazilian support for democracy is near the very bottom among Latin American nations, along with Guatemala, which has only recently emerged from a brutal civil war characterized by savage abuses of human rights. Thus, the Brazilian case offers a particularly striking contrast for students of Latin America and democratization: an intriguing mixture of positive and negative aspects, of progression and of regression, of stagnation and stasis. The challenge, then, is what to make of this complex portrait.

In the original *Democratic Brazil*, a group of young U.S.-based scholars examined various dimensions of politics and society, asking what effect democracy had had on their area of study and in turn how their chosen dimension had affected democracy. The project intentionally avoided applying any single, uniform conceptualization of democratic rule. The result was a subtle and nuanced portrayal of a moving target. One of the central lessons from the original project was that change appeared to be progressing at different rates in different areas of Brazil's polity and society. On some criteria, things seemed to be improving, while on others, things were stagnant or even backsliding. Observing this pattern led to an overarching question: was Brazilian democracy "still standing," or was it "standing still"? This question is still relevant a decade after the original project began. The contributors to *Democratic Brazil Revisited* find the same complex pattern: progress and stagnation, promise and disappointment, success and failure. Ultimately, the answer to the question of how Brazilian democracy is performing seems to depend on who is answering and on their specific issue or area of study.

In short, the passage of time has not pushed Brazilian democracy clearly in one direction or another. *Democratic Brazil Revisited* takes up the challenge of evaluating democracy's performance anew, asking two broad questions. First, what is the significance of 2002? In other words, how has the historic election of Lula and the Workers' Party affected Brazil? The election of former metalworker Lula, the first president drawn from the popular classes, is a fascinating development. The Workers' Party is the most important and successful labor-based party in Latin America and the most significant leftist party in Brazilian history. It has stood for clean government, transparency, redistributive social policy, an end to the egregious clientelism of Brazilian politics, and a return to nationalist and state-led economic growth policies. The very fact of Lula's successful election and inauguration is a critical moment for Brazilian democracy. Yet many observers question the degree to which the PT, which since 2003 has formed the core of a heterogeneous multiparty coalition and adopted centrist economic policies, has remained true to its traditional profile and platform. The original *Democratic Brazil* noted the PT's special role in Brazil politics and identified it as an actor with unique possibilities to effect change in the political system. In that sense, the contributors to the earlier volume conformed to the expectations of virtually every observer of Brazil in the 1990s: that Brazil under PT rule would somehow be fundamentally different from the Brazil that we witnessed during the two decades of the PT's oppositional role. But with Lula's victory in 2002, Brazilian democracy had finally cycled through all of the main political parties—every major tendency has now had a chance to govern the country, and there is no longer an untested savior lurking in the wings. The clear message of post-2002 Brazil was that continuity trumped change: the PT, by all accounts, has made only the smallest of dents in Brazil's elitist political culture, and "politics as usual" prevails. Thus, *Democratic Brazil Revisited* approaches the question of Lula and the PT with a greater sense of realism about what may or may not be possible in the Brazilian political system.

The second question is: how has Brazilian democracy performed in different crucial areas? The chapters that address this question have particularly focused on the contrast between macro-level institutional and policy performance on the one hand, and micro-level attitudes and behaviors of citizens on the other. As with the original *Democratic Brazil*, there is no uniform, legislated definition or standard of democracy, and once again the result is a complex portrait of Brazilian democracy in which progress in some areas is offset by stagnation in others. But *Democratic Brazil Revisited* also reveals important disjunctures and contradictions, not only in differing paces of change, but also in scholarly interpretations of key aspects of Brazilian politics and society. Most importantly, the *Democratic Brazil Revisited* project encompasses important internal debates over the evaluation both of Brazil's political institutions as well as of citizens' attitudes. The nuances and complexities of evaluating Brazil's democracy operate within three distinct analytic dimensions: in contrasts between macro-level and micro-level assessments, in differing speeds of change across different areas of Brazilian politics and society, and in differing interpretations of important institutional and attitudinal dimensions of Brazilian democracy.

Brazilian Democracy and Reflections on the State of Democratic Theory

In the original *Democratic Brazil*, each author asked how their specific area of study had been affected by democracy and in turn how democracy had affected it. We left open the definition of democracy so that each author relied on his or her own preferred standard. We wanted to avoid imposing a uniform definition on an "essentially contested" concept. But that decision was also justified theoretically by the claim that democracies are made up of multiple constituent parts or dimensions and that the rate of change can and does vary dramatically among them. In short, we embraced the call from scholars such as Guillermo O'Donnell (1996), Philippe Schmitter (1992), and Ben Ross Schneider (1995) to disaggregate the concept of democracy. O'Donnell and others argued that democratization theory of the 1990s was suffering from a host of problems, including tautology, teleology, and the undertheorization of the large category of intermediate cases between authoritarianism and consolidated democracy.

Nearly a decade later, the state of democratic theory continues to be underdeveloped. The third wave of democratization that began in Portugal in 1974 and swept through the Americas produced multiple stages of theorizing, beginning with transition studies, then consolidation studies, and settling in recent years on the issue of quality. The first two stages generated a great deal of theory, but much of it was criticized and ultimately abandoned as scholars moved on to new questions. The current emphasis on democratic quality seems more focused on assessment than on causation.

Thus, as of 2008, we still lack the theoretical tools to account for the pace and extent of change in Brazilian democracy, and we still cannot answer the question of how and why a new democracy becomes a fully *liberal* democracy. Facing the daunting issues of a moving target and of multiple causation, we once again rely on an analytical strategy that is explicitly disaggregative. The question continues to be important, because *Democratic Brazil Revisited* reveals the same pattern as *Democratic Brazil*: Some dimensions of democratic governance have improved rapidly and dramatically, while some have improved very little or not at all. Some aspects of political life are shadowed by authoritarian legacies, while others seem relatively unencumbered by the past. An additional problem for theorizing about democratization in Brazil is that the aspect that once generated the most concern about the future of Brazilian democracy has been subjected to important revisionist interpretations. In the early years of the "New Republic," both Brazilian scholars (notably Bolívar Lamounier) and U.S. scholars (led by Scott Mainwaring and Barry Ames) identified serious concerns about the functioning of Brazilian political institutions and their ability to generate governability. Yet, as of 2007, institutional performance is viewed positively—or at the very least, not negatively—by a growing number of scholars, both Brazilian and Brazilianist. This gap between expectations and outcomes highlights limits to our understanding of how new democracies evolve.

Offering our own theories of democratization is beyond the scope of this project, but the contributions to *Democratic Brazil Revisited* do support three promising lines of theorizing. First, the chapters in this volume strongly support O'Donnell's notion of a fuzzy middle category of regimes that blend democratic, undemocratic, liberal, illiberal, and traditional/clientelistic practices. Brazilian democracy in 2008 features globally recognized and admired social policies, sound macroeconomic management, and increasingly stable patterns of party competition alongside ugly and large-scale corruption, lawlessness, and injustice, and deep-seated alienation of much of the voting public. Thus, *Democratic Brazil Revisited* echoes Schmitter's (1992) call for disaggregation of the concept of democracy and separate causal hypothesizing about each component "partial regime."

The gap between institutional performance and changes (or lack thereof) experienced by average citizens echoes recent work by O'Donnell (2001, 2004). In his ongoing efforts to push the conceptual and theoretical envelope, O'Donnell has articulated a conception of democracy predicated on *citizens* as the central defining element of this regime type. In this conception, citizenship is the core aspect of democratic society, and thus the quality of democracy (and causal hypothesizing) should revolve around the factors that shape the capacity of citizens to fully participate in society. This is a particularly rigorous standard that goes well beyond traditional emphases on electoral participation, partisan competition, and alternation in power. O'Donnell includes questions of economic rights, social rights, and public security among other elements that affect citizens.

O'Donnell's formulation was a tentative, first step towards developing new theory, but it does highlight an issue that seems to be supported by the contributions to *Democratic Brazil Revisited.* Specifically, the volume suggests that full and meaningful participation of citizens is the most daunting challenge for new democracies. The set of social and economic rights that allow citizens to authentically participate, and the quality of rule of law as experienced by citizens directly on the ground, are much harder to address than mainstream institutional and policy problems. Thus, Brazilian elites have been able to figure out how to navigate even slippery institutional contexts: the first two decades of democracy showed them to be artful dodgers of continual crises. But the profound social and political injustices that have characterized Brazil will require more time and more gradual, incremental (perhaps even generational) changes.

This last point leads to a final speculation: perhaps our expectations about democratic deepening and quality have been too high, and not enough time has passed to make definitive statements about democratization. One of the notable points that emerges in a number of contributions (for example, on social policy, affirmative action, and even public security) is the extent to which political competition and accountability have played positive roles in promoting change and deepening democratic governance. John Gerring et al. (2005) have argued that democracy's influence develops over time (as an accumulating stock), as opposed to being an immediate consequence of regime type. Thus, while *Democratic Brazil Revisited* finds the same complex and disaggregated pattern as the original *Democratic Brazil*, mixing positive with negative aspects, the present volume lends itself to a plausible and tentatively more optimistic prognosis, even if we do not yet fully grasp the precise causal mechanisms at work. Some may find this frank admission unsatisfactory, but it is high time that comparative social scientists admitted that we do a far better job of *describing* the unevenness of democratization than we do of *explaining* it.

Overview of the Book

Part I of the book explores the rise of the Workers' Party. The PT's 2002 electoral victory was a watershed moment for Brazilian democracy, but it was also one of the most important contemporary achievements of the Left in Latin America. As various scholars have noted, the Left in Latin America is not monolithic (Schamis 2006; Corrales 2006), and the PT was widely seen as embodying a more democratic, responsible, and moderate version of progressive politics. But, as Wendy Hunter documents in chapter 2, the PT's experience in national power since 2003 has raised important questions about the extent to which it is still a party of the Left. Hunter traces the PT's evolution from a principled leftist opposition to a more opportunistic party and considers the implications of the PT's conversion for Brazilian democracy. In chapter 3, Kathryn Hochstetler explores the PT's long-term allegiance with the civil society organizations (CSOs) that emerged during the process of democratization. Together the PT and CSOs championed participatory and inclusive forms of politics, and for much of its history the PT was able to count on the CSOs to mobilize voters, which helped compensate for the party's financial disadvantages. As a result of the shift in the PT chronicled by Hunter, however, the PT-CSO alliance no longer functions as the dynamic axis of the Brazilian Left, and the PT is no longer the automatic umbrella party for sectors of progressive civil society. For many CSOs, the question "what is the significance of 2002?" has an uncomfortable answer: it was a brief, euphoric celebration followed by a sobering reality check. The CSOs of the post-2002 era are more cautious and are returning to their independent roots. They offer both a profound critique of representative democracy as well as alternative channels of political participation for disaffected Brazilian citizens.

Part II takes up one the central debates about Brazilian democracy over the past twenty years: the role of political institutions. Analyses of Brazilian institutions date back to work by scholars such as Scott Mainwaring and Bolívar Lamounier who expressed concern about the ability of the country's institutions to function effectively. These early studies inspired a large number of critiques focused on different aspects of the system's character and performance. In turn, the criticism led to a spirited defense of the country's institutions, led primarily by Argelina Figueiredo and Fernando Limongi's landmark revisionist study, *Executivo e legislativo na nova ordem constitucional* (1999). Others offered analyses that tried to reconcile the two rival images of the performance of the country's political institutions (Castro Santos 1997; Kingstone 2000, 2003; Amorim Neto 2002; Armijo and Faucher 2002). *Democratic Brazil* tended to emphasize the more critical elements, as shown in Timothy J. Power's rather pessimistic contribution to that volume. As of 2007, however, Brazil's political institutions appear to have performed better than the more skeptical views would have predicted.

In chapter 4, Fabiano Santos and Márcio Grijó Vilarouca provide an overview of the most important concerns raised about the performance of Brazil's political institutions and an analysis of the reasons for the system's relative successes. They argue that despite the system's shortcomings, signs of institutionalization, stability, and coherence have emerged that help account for effective governability. Perhaps most importantly, the authors show that the system is characterized by a reasonable degree of ideological coherence and consistency. One crucial consequence is that voters can generally identify the ideological profile of parties and vote appropriately. In stark contrast to Power's essay in the original *Democratic Brazil,* Santos and Vilarouca argue that there is little need for the kind of significant political reforms often called for among both scholars and policymakers.

In chapter 5, Power provides further evidence of the growing coherence of the political system by tracing the evolution of party views on key policy issues over the past two decades. He relies on a series of surveys of elected officials in the legislature, focusing on three critical cleavages that defined political conflicts immediately after the 1985 redemocratization: economic policy, the role of the military, and the reform of political institutions. In contrast to the highly polarized period right after democratization, Power shows a significant and growing degree of attitudinal convergence among elites. While he does not claim that all ideological disputes have vanished, Power argues that the fading of early postauthoritarian cleavages has contributed to a strengthening of democracy's durability and has freed up political capital to focus on other pressing policy issues in Brazil, such as poverty.

Barry Ames, Andy Baker, and Lucio Rennó take up another indicator of the growing institutionalization of the political system. In chapter 6, these authors examine voting behavior to determine why voters decide on particular candidates. Like Santos and Vilarouca, the authors note the defects of the system, but they also find important and encouraging indicators of coherence. Ames, Baker, and Rennó differentiate among four reasons for voting: clientelistic private exchanges, pork-barrel neighborhood or district-level exchanges, pageantry, and issue voting. Early studies of voting behavior in Brazil argued that much of what goes on is purely clientelistic exchanges—in short, vote buying—an indicator of low-quality democratic behavior. By contrast, the authors' survey finds high levels of issue voting—a strong indicator of much higher quality democracy, given the high levels of political information and attention required to vote for candidates and parties based on their position on key issues. Thus, like Santos and Vilarouca, the authors express cautious optimism about the ability of Brazil's political institutions to facilitate effective democratic governance.

While part II suggests that Brazil's political institutions have been more capable of generating effective democratic governance than earlier studies had predicted, part III puts this view to the test by exploring the outputs of Brazil's political institutions: public policies. The various chapters in this part of the volume present a more varied portrait about Brazilian performance (although they generally do not blame institutions). However, they do lend credence to Power's argument that the declining relevance of traditional ideological cleavages is allowing governments to begin focusing on other pressing issues: in particular, competitiveness and micro-level development, social policy, crime, and affirmative action.

In chapter 7, Aline Diniz Amaral, Peter Kingstone, and Jonathan Krieckhaus ask to what extent the PT was constrained in its choice of economic policies. The authors note that Lula and the PT campaigned explicitly on a platform that called for a reversal of the market-oriented reforms championed by Fernando Henrique Cardoso. However, on both macroeconomic policy and on regulatory policy, the Lula administration was constrained by the need to maintain foreign-investment inflows. Thus, the Lula administration veered sharply to the right on macroeconomic policy even before taking office. On regulatory policy, the government spent its first year developing and beginning to implement a leftist/nationalist reform. By the end of the first year, though, the need to attract new foreign investments led the administration to back off its plans and ultimately to shelve any effort at reforms. Brazil has undoubtedly prospered under a stable, consistent macroeconomic policy. But, it has come at the expense of the PT's ideological consistency and of a coherent micro-level strategy for promoting competitiveness and development.

Marcus André de Melo's examination of social policy in Brazil (chapter 8) provides a much more positive assessment of policy performance. Melo directly addresses the institutional debate and notes that contrary to pessimistic scholarly expectations, Brazil has managed to develop and implement social policies that are internationally recognized for their quality and innovation. He shows how political responsiveness and accountability led politicians to converge on a shared approach to addressing difficult challenges of poor access to health care and education. In particular, he shows how political competition between the PT and Cardoso's Brazilian Social Democracy Party (Partido da Social Democracia Brasileira, PSDB) led both parties to copy each other's successes in an effort to claim credit for a set of highly salient and remarkably successful policies. In short, institutional arguments that focus on the fragmentation, incoherence, and unresponsiveness of the political system have systematically underestimated the capacity of Brazil's institutions to produce high-quality policies.

By contrast, Anthony Pereira's chapter 9 offers a much more critical view of another policy dilemma: public security and crime. Whereas Melo's work on social policy demonstrates the responsiveness of the system, Pereira's analysis of public security highlights one of the most critical areas of unresponsiveness. Pereira notes that public insecurity is a worsening phenomenon in Brazil, is one of the most salient and pressing concerns of voters, and constitutes a significant threat to the quality of democracy and the rule of law. Yet, politicians at all levels of politics have largely failed to respond to growing demands for political action. For Pereira, the principal culprit is an "institutional sclerosis" rooted in federalism, intergovernmental relations, and related conflicts over jurisdiction and resource allocation. These are amplified by political and bureaucratic tensions among the various agencies responsible for public security. In a context of crippling bureaucratic turf wars, politicians have been reluctant to address an apparently intractable problem.

Finally, Ollie Johnson turns, in chapter 10, to one of Brazil's most enduring and puzzling social challenges: racial inequality. Traditionally, Brazilian elites propagated the myth of racial democracy so successfully that the issue of racism lay politically dormant for most of the country's history. Johnson notes, however, that in recent decades, a very small number of leading black figures—intellectuals and politicians—worked strenuously to put the issue of racism and white dominance on the table for public debate. These efforts met with little success until finally, under presidents Cardoso and Lula, concrete policy responses emerged to the problems of racism and racial inequality. As Johnson notes, however, these incipient efforts to promote affirmative action continue to face powerful objections from policymakers and intellectuals.

Part IV offers a solution to the gap between Brazil's institutional performance and the low levels of public support for democracy and democratic institutions discussed earlier in this chapter. In chapter 11, Alberto Almeida updates Roberto DaMatta's famous characterization of Brazilian society, addressing democracy at the micro level. In *Carnival, Rogues, and Heroes: An Interpretation of the Brazilian Dilemma* (1991 [1978]), DaMatta interprets the characteristic Brazilian phrase "do you know who you are talking to?" as revealing a deeply hierarchical and undemocratic impulse ingrained in a wide range of social interactions. Almeida, drawing on recent public-opinion survey work, makes an important qualification to DaMatta's characterization. Almeida shows that due to rising educational levels, Brazilian society is changing rapidly, and at present it is more accurate to describe the country as being divided between an "archaic" mass and a growing "modern" sector. The latter group displays a range of attitudes that are significantly more tolerant, egalitarian, and democratic than DaMatta's classic portrayal. The archaic group, however, continues to reveal hierarchical, undemocratic, and intolerant attitudes—including deeply racist views. While this archaic group still accounts for the numerical majority of Brazilians, Almeida argues that expanding access to education promises democratic and egalitarian change.

The final chapter gives the clearest evidence of the gap between elites and the poor. Janice Perlman returns to her landmark 1976 study of the urban poor, *The Myth of Marginality*. In her earlier work, Perlman showed that the urban poor were not a marginalized, fringe group (i.e., parasites on the economy). Instead, they were integral to the workings of that economy and systematically and actively excluded from its economic and political benefits—in short, they were integrated into the system on a highly unequal and asymmetrical basis. Perlman returns to the same favela dwellers she studied in the 1960s, as well as both their children and grandchildren, and finds that democratization has not changed this fundamental condition of unfairness and social injustice. While the new generation of slum dwellers expresses greater belief in and awareness of democratic principles, skepticism, disappointment, alienation, and very low levels of belief in political efficacy characterize all three generations. Although many of the chapters in this volume point to surprising and encouraging levels of success in Brazil's new democracy, Perlman's study of the urban poor demonstrates the great distance left to resolve the country's deepest injustice.

Altogether, the Brazilian case offers a particularly striking contrast for students of Latin America and democratization: an intriguing mixture of positive and negative aspects, of progression and of regression, of stagnation and stasis. The challenge, then, is what to make of this complex portrait.

PART I

The Workers' Party in Power

2

The Partido dos Trabalhadores: Still a Party of the Left?

Wendy Hunter

THE LARGEST LEFTIST PARTY in Latin America, the Partido dos Trabalhadores (Workers' Party, PT) has attracted much attention in the academic literature and popular press. It played an important role as an opposition party from its founding in 1980 until the election of its candidate, Luiz Inácio Lula da Silva, in 2002, following his fourth bid for the presidency. Noted for being different in many important respects from most of its catchall counterparts, the PT focused on programs rather than on patronage and personalities, notwithstanding Lula's highly visible public image. It also maintained internal organizational norms and characteristics—such as an emphasis on discipline, loyalty, and cohesion—that distinguished it in the landscape of Brazilian parties. Over time, the party started to adapt and become more mainstream in character. Its accommodation to global economic trends and to the institutional pressures of Brazilian politics accelerated in the second half of the 1990s and took an especially sharp turn upward in Lula's 2002 presidential campaign.

With Lula's victory, the PT completed the cycle: all leading Brazilian parties have now been in both the opposition and the government in the period since the country returned to democracy in 1985. Yet, rather than transforming Brazil's social and economic landscape, which the PT had promised to do for many years in opposition, the first Lula government (2003–2006) oversaw considerable continuity. The government's commitment to maintaining market reform and the social status quo has been highly marked. Its increasing resemblance to other Brazilian parties has extended to the serious allegations of corruption with which it has been charged starting in 2005. Lula owed his re-election in October 2006 in large part to voters who had never supported the PT's ideological project (and did not vote concurrently for the PT in lower house elections) but who benefited from concrete (more conventional) measures that Lula pushed through with the benefit of executive power. Reinaugurated in January 2007, Lula and the PT-led government will need to navigate their way among a myriad of conflicting demands until 2010. We will know only then whether these pressures have induced the PT to converge even more with its catchall counterparts or whether it can still be rightfully regarded a party of the Left.

It is important to consider what is at stake in the PT's status as a leftist party, how the party's distinctiveness has impacted Brazil's political system, and what might be lost if the PT assimilates to more conventional party politics over time. By examining the PT's trajectory from opposition to government, we can place the party in a broader context by comparing it with leading competitors. For various reasons, the party began a process of normalization in the second half of the 1990s, and Lula's race for the presidency in 2002 accelerated this trend. During the PT's first term, divergences between Lula and his party grew, and the popularity of the former surged vis-à-vis the latter, as revealed starkly in the elections of 2006 for the presidency and the Chamber of Deputies.

Is the PT Still a Party of the Left, and What Is at Stake with the Question?

In the words of Herbert Kitschelt, parties that are left wing in the socialist tradition "affirm solidarity and equality and reject the primacy of markets and allocative efficiency as the final arbiters of social development and justice." Like the Green parties of Western Europe, however, this focus may be combined with "calling for a society in which individual autonomy and citizen participation in public affairs have high priority" (Kitschelt 1989, 2). The PT could unequivocally be seen as a party of the Left for most of its existence in the opposition. Committed to addressing the striking inequalities in income and human development prevalent in Brazil, the party advanced clear platforms about using the central state to redistribute the country's considerable wealth. It also promoted greater citizen participation through programs like participatory budgeting. The PT's emphasis on programs to ameliorate poverty extended to innovative schemes designed and implemented on the local level, such as microcredit programs and the *Bolsa Escola*, an income subsidy for lower-income families who agree to keep their children enrolled in school. Beyond its quest to enact sweeping economic transformation and to boost societal participation, the PT sought to differentiate itself on political dimensions as well. In stark contrast to most major parties in Brazil, it demanded strong discipline, loyalty, and cohesion from its ranks.

As an opposition party on the Left, the PT had a varied but mainly positive impact on Brazilian politics. In the predecessor to the current volume, William R. Nylen argued that the PT contributed to the consolidation of Brazilian democracy by acting within the boundaries of a democratic "loyal opposition," using the opportunities provided by formal democracy to openly oppose social and economic exclusion and the practices that perpetuate them and to champion more inclusionary practices and policy outcomes, and providing a nonviolent channel of participation for political activists and potential activists who reject Brazil's traditional fare of nonideological, patrimonial, and organizationally diffuse parties (Nylen, 2000). Indeed, the PT used the mechanisms provided by formal democracy to promote alternative economic programs (more radical in the 1980s and more social-democratic in character in the 1990s) and more-participatory forms of politics, the best known of these being the Orçamento Participativo, or participatory budgeting practices. This was true at the national level within the Chamber of Deputies and Senate, as well as at the state and local levels. It helped to channel social movements, even quite radical ones like the largest and most active landless movement in Latin America, the Movimento Sem Terra. In these ways, the PT worked within the system and thus constituted a vocal but loyal opposition. That the PT's delegation in the lower house of Congress grew from sixteen seats in 1986 to ninety-one in 2002 (equivalent to 3.3 percent and 17.7 percent of all seats, respectively) and that the PT went from governing 36 cities in 1988 to 187 in 2000 (representing 17.5 percent of the Brazilian population) suggest that the party became not only a vital alternative but also a leading competitor within Brazilian politics.

Analysts who approached the question of the PT's impact through the framework of political parties saw positive effects as well. Focusing on the programmatic character of the PT in a political-party system in which personalism and clientelism, rather than programmatic appeals, are thought to dominate politics (Ames 2001, Mainwaring 1999), various analysts maintained that the strong positions the PT staked out over the course of the 1980s and 1990s induced other parties to respond on a similar basis and in turn become more programmatic themselves (e.g., Rosas and Zechmeister 2000). Others contended that the PT played an important role in the institutionalization of the political system. Brazil witnessed the emergence of a more-institutionalized party system in the 1990s (Panizza 2000). The PT grew and became hegemonic within the once highly fragmented Left. Whereas the PT's share within the bloc of Left parties in the Chamber of Deputies was 26.1 percent in 1982, it was 54.7 percent in 2002. At the very least, by bringing together forces within the Left, the PT helped to lessen fragmentation within the system overall.

Analysts who examined the PT in relation to the issue of partisanship in Brazil regarded the party as a positive force as well (Carreirão and Kinzo 2004; Samuels 2006). This literature took as a point of departure the notion that higher levels of partisanship can help strengthen political parties, especially if partisanship entails attachment to a party organization and its values, and not just (or even especially) its personal leaders at any given time. In the 1980s and 1990s, only the PT could count on as large a base of partisan identifiers. Identification with the PT was estimated to reach approximately 22 percent of the electorate by 2002 (that it reached nearly that in 2000 suggests the figure was not simply a reflection of the euphoria and momentum of Lula's winning campaign). And while Lula was always more popular than the party organization as such (Samuels 2006), being a PT partisan did not rest on a strong attachment to the party's effective leader. On both these counts—the rate of partisan identification and the non-personalistic basis of it—the PT compared highly favorably with its more catchall counterparts. From these various perspectives, the PT provided a ray of hope for those who wished to see a strengthening of Brazil's system of weak and inchoate political parties. By the same logic, if the PT were to become more similar to other parties in the system and not be replaced by any viable contender, such hopes would be diminished.

From Opposition to Government, 1980–2002

What, in fact, has been the trajectory of the PT in recent years? Does it still represent a programmatic alternative in Brazilian politics? Can it still serve as a voice against corruption in Brazilian politics? Does it continue to be a source of cohesion and inspiration for those on the Left? Do social movements retain enough confidence in the PT's leadership to work with the party? Finally, how has the partisan following and electorate of the PT changed over time? Has it become more or less party oriented (as opposed to personalistic) in recent years?

In the twenty-two years that the PT spent in the national opposition (1980–2002), it underwent significant changes. The mid-1990s constituted an important point of inflexion toward greater moderation and assimilation overall. Until the mid-1990s, the PT was distinguished both by the substance of its programmatic commitments as well as by the organizational forms and strategies to which it adhered. Holding economic and political positions considerably to the left of most other parties, the PT placed basic ideological principles above the goal of immediate power acquisition. Notwithstanding internal debate over what emphasis to place on the promotion of core ideological principles versus more immediate electoral goals, party leaders promoted and adhered to the PT's strong programmatic commitments.

Economic Position: Redistribution and State-Led Development

Central to the PT's substantive commitments was the redistribution of Brazil's wealth through the implementation of major structural reforms such as land reform. The PT also called for a significant diminution of foreign control over the Brazilian economy by pushing back the influence of international financial institutions like the International Monetary Fund (IMF) and the World Bank. At a time that saw the emergence of market advocates favoring privatization, diminished trade barriers, and state reform, the PT strongly opposed the privatization of state enterprises and public services. It also fought against labor "flexibilization" (facilitating the hiring and firing of workers) and measures designed to enhance fiscal efficiency in the social sectors.

The PT projected its statist economic orientation in a variety of ways. It supported prolabor positions in the Constituent Assembly (1987–1988), called for socialism in Lula's 1989 presidential bid, opposed President Fernando Collor's (1990–1992) pursuit of market reforms, and rejected out of hand most of the neoliberal reforms attempted under the governments of Fernando Henrique Cardoso (1995–2002). Complementing behavioral evidence of the PT's economic orientation are data from legislative surveys conducted in 1987 and 1997; in both years, not a single PT deputy professed liberal economic views (Rodrigues 1987; Power 1998a).

Notwithstanding its open calls for socialism prior to the mid-1990s, the PT rejected centralism and bureaucratic socialism in favor of a more participatory model. For example, it instituted a number of participatory decision-making procedures, such as the Orcamento Participativo, and supported some instances of social service decentralization (e.g., the Programa Saúde Família and greater school autonomy in the state of Minas Gerais) and other measures aimed at increasing the autonomy of citizens vis-à-vis state supervision.

Political Position: Party-Oriented Politics

In a country noted for the weakness of its political parties, the PT stood out as uniquely well organized and unified, notwithstanding internal debates among its various factions. Notable were the high rates of cohesion, discipline, and loyalty displayed by its legislative delegation. Of all the parties, PT representatives manifested one of the highest levels of agreement with one another on a range of issues.[1] Moreover, they voted together and remained within the party at much higher rates than other parties.[2] And when asked to rank their commitments, it was PT deputies who expressed the greatest willingness to support the party's program and label over their individual interests and the districts they represented (Hagopian 2005). Similarly, they reported spending the highest percentage of their time on "policy analysis" instead of activities like "attending to lobbies or requests from individuals."[3]

The PT also stood out for the predominance of its national-level organization and project in a system where many parties are mere collections of regional machines and where local political considerations are subordinated to the national ones, evident in such practices as forming alliances at the local level with little correspondence to alliances at the national level. The PT national directorate exercised authority over state and local directorates and sought to impose uniformity on such dimensions as alliance formation.

In line with this profile, the PT observed a restrictive alliance policy, joining exclusively with parties on the left in the 1989 and 1994 elections.[4] While from time to time subnational party authorities were tempted to enhance their immediate electoral fortunes by allying with nonleft parties, with frequency the national directorate rejected their proposals to do so. The PT's hardline alliance policy separated the PT not only from major parties on the Right, such as the PFL (Liberal Front Party), but also in crucial ways from its main competitor on the Left, the PDT (Democratic Labor Party).

Perhaps nothing encapsulates the commitment of PT politicians to the party better than their willingness to undergo a serious process of scrutiny before being admitted and to donate to the party thereafter a tithe of 10–30 percent, depending on the specific position held within the party. In short, beyond its adherence to a unique economic program, the PT stood out for its party orientation, as manifested concretely in everything ranging from the strength of its national-level organization to its strict alliance posture and the cohesion, discipline, and personal sacrifices displayed by its politicians to the party. Engagement in activities to combat clientelism and corruption contributed further to the PT's distinctive political profile. Beyond working to expose and hold guilty parties accountable in specific corruption scandals at the national level, PT politicians at the municipal level developed and implemented practices aimed at making government decision making more transparent to the public. In short, "clean government" became a cornerstone of the PT's program.

Comparisons with Other Parties

The unique niche occupied by the PT prior to the mid-1990s is perhaps best appreciated by reference to how other parties lined up on these same dimensions.

The PFL

The PFL constituted a key point of contrast for the PT, given the former's economic and political profile. The PFL was the largest party in the Congress by the second half of the 1990s. Its delegation strongly supported President Collor's market-reform agenda and later the Cardoso government's economic reforms. Its representatives also displayed a pronounced tendency to identify themselves as economic liberals.[5] The only party ranking higher than the PFL in behavioral and subjective indicators of economic liberalism was the much smaller and far more ideological PPB (Brazilian Progressive Party).

While adherence to economic liberalism gave the PFL a programmatic pillar of cohesion and identity, other aspects conformed to a more traditional political profile.[6] The conduct of PFL deputies vis-à-vis the electorate, within the legislature, and towards the executive revealed a political machine aptly described as a *partido de sustentação* or support party. "A collection of clients whose patron is the president but who are also patrons themselves in their states, regions, and municipalities" (Power 2000a, 184), the PFL typically backed the government of the day and received resources in turn. When asked to describe what role a congressional representative should fulfill, PFL deputies frequently chose patronage-oriented rather than program-oriented activities (Hagopian 2005).

The PDT

The PDT (Partido Democrático Trabalhista or Democratic Labor Party) shared the PT's statist orientation, yet differed strikingly in its political style. Its economic nationalism gave the party a "moderately leftist" cast (Ames 2001, xiii), but the PDT eluded simple classification on a left-right scale due to the personal prominence and populist style of its leader for decades, Leonel Brizola. Brizola built the party's following in two states, Rio de Janeiro and Rio Grande do Sul, where its support was concentrated. On key dimensions such as loyalty, the PDT lacked a party-oriented profile. PDT deputies switched parties at high rates, and when they did, they moved all across the political spectrum. The PT stood out as being far less personalistic, better organized, and more national in its reach than the PDT.

The PMDB and PTB

It was easy for the PT to distinguish itself from these classic catchalls. The broad-based PMDB (Partido do Movimento Democrático Brasileiro or Party of the Brazilian Democratic Movement) was arguably the most opportunistic and internally diverse of Brazilian parties. Often divided between government and opposition supporters, PMDB members were notorious for switching in and out of the party according to what served them best at the time. Due to the large size of its delegation and the flexibility of its members' programmatic commitments, the PMDB was often sought out as a governing ally. Similar to the PMDB, although smaller and somewhat more conservative, was the Partido Trabalhista Brasileiro (PTB).

The PSDB

The PSDB (Partido da Social Democracia Brasileira or Brazilian Social Democratic Party) was the PT's main competitor in the presidential elections of 1994, 1998, 2002, and 2006. Like the PT, it adhered (for the most part) to programmatic politics, but it came to differ strikingly from the PT on the economic positions it embraced. Created by seasoned yet socially committed politicians who broke away from the PMDB in 1988, the PSDB supported statist positions in the late 1980s but by 1993 had begun to advocate market reforms.[7] Reforms pursued under the successive administrations of Fernando Henrique Cardoso consolidated the party's promarket profile. The percentage of PSDB representatives who professed a liberal affiliation doubled between 1987 and 1997, rising from 31 percent to 60 percent (Power 1998a, 58).

The PSDB was similar to the PT in the considerable degree of programmatic cohesion and esteem for the party label its deputies displayed throughout the 1990s.[8] Yet the former's character was more reformist and technocratic, and the latter's more radical and activist. There was also a certain class difference between the two. For example, in greater São Paulo, the PT received the concentration of its vote in the periphery, whereas the PSDB captured the middle class in the central districts. Also, actions taken by the PSDB leading up to the 1994 election—namely, forging an electoral alliance with the barons of the PFL—muddied the party's principled image. In its struggle to overcome notable disadvantages against the more mainstream party, the PT launched a vociferous public campaign against these measures. The hope was to give itself an exclusive claim to principled politics.

The Accommodation of the PT

If the PT was at its most distinctive before the mid-1990s, thereafter it began to accommodate more to various pressures and began to adopt some important characteristics of catchall parties in Brazil. In a determined effort to win the presidency, the PT's programmatic differences became less pronounced. So did its style of politics. Lula's winning campaign of 2002 punctuated the trend towards convergence. The reasons for the PT's ideological moderation and assimilation on other dimensions are complex and treated at length elsewhere (Samuels 2004; Hunter 2007a). Suffice it to state here that there are two basic approaches to understanding this issue. The first, articulated well by Samuels (2004), emphasizes factors endogenous to the party that led the PT to abandon its position on the far left of the political spectrum, namely, the rise of pragmatists following the party's governing experiences at the local level and its success in mayoral elections, and the flexibility for adaptation permitted through specific internal rules. The second, put forth by Hunter (2007a), emphasizes forces external to the party that induced and sustained its assimilation. The two most important exogenous factors concern global economic changes, which made adherence to market reform virtually impossible to avoid, and an unwieldy set of political institutions, which forced Lula to gather support from a majority of voters in his candidacies, in the context of an extremely fragmented electorate and party system.

Indeed, reinforced by Lula's strong desire to become president and the sway that his faction exerted on the party as a whole, these factors led the PT to make significant modifications beginning in the second half of the 1990s. Regardless of why exactly it moved toward the center ideologically and diminished some of its other differences, its adjustment assumed the following forms. Notably, the party broke with the past and publicly acknowledged the benefits of adapting to international market trends. This first occurred with Lula's third run for the presidency, in 1998, and became even clearer in the 2002 campaign. Beyond omitting the word *socialism* from the party program, the most notable sign of moderation on the economic dimension was the promise to adhere to Brazil's existing agreements with the IMF. The party did, however, advocate market-conforming policies that would enhance the welfare of poorer Brazilians, such as job creation and even a minimum income provision.

Similarly, the leadership began to consider alliance partners that it would have rejected earlier.[9] By the mid-1990s, Lula was busy trying to convince militants of the need to loosen the party's restrictive alliance policy in order to have a chance of capturing an electoral majority. These efforts helped pave the way for a stark concession to pragmatism that the party made in 2002 in the form of an alliance with the Liberal Party (PL), known for its unusual leadership mix of evangelical pastors and affluent businessmen.[10] The alliance was thought to be opportune for various reasons. Evangelicals, an anti-PT group historically, constitute a sizable and growing percentage of Brazil's population, roughly 15 percent, and enjoy a growing share of control over various media outlets (Freston 2001). The PL's stronghold, Minas Gerais, is the state with the second-largest electorate. That so many of these come from impoverished rural areas of the state, a weak point of the PT historically, merely added to the calculation. Furthermore, it was hoped that the strong connections the party's president had to business leaders would diminish their fears about the prospect of a Lula-led government.

The party also shifted its stance on political marketing. Whereas it had previously felt it to be more important to clarify the substance of its programs and convince people to embrace the party's ideals, various electoral losses led party pragmatists to accept the importance of style and image and to advocate the hiring of professional consultants and publicists to bring the PT more in line with what appealed to the average Brazilian voter.

By 2002, Lula had hired Brazil's best-known and most expensive publicist to run his campaign, Duda Mendonça, who had earned a reputation for successfully advising a number of prominent politicians from the Right. One of Mendonça's main objectives was to remake the image of the party and its candidate, embodied in everything from giving Lula a more typically "presidential" physical appearance to formulating catchy yet unobjectionable slogans like "Lula, paz e amor" (Lula, Peace, and Love) and "O PT: para um Brasil decente" (The PT: For a Decent Brazil).

Pragmatism also prevailed with respect to trying to overcome the party's financial shortfalls. The PT had always been handicapped by material shortages, in a country where political campaigns—especially those for president—are noted for their extraordinarily high expense. In the end, the single-minded determination to win the presidency subjected the party to financial pressures and temptations that it had previously withstood. Behind-the-scenes efforts to fill the party's campaign coffers through questionable means were revealed in 2005, halfway into Lula's first presidential term. Apparently, underpinning the 2002 campaign (and mostly likely that of 1998) was an intricate and illegal scheme whereby PT mayors extracted kickbacks from private and public firms seeking municipal contracts; they then diverted this money into a secret campaign slush fund. Paulo de Tarso Venceslau, a former secretary of finance employed by two important municipal PT administrations (Campinas and São José dos Campos) had denounced financial irregularities he had discovered as far back as 1995.[11] The PT expelled him in 1997 and managed to keep further damage from being done until the informational floodgates broke years later with a major corruption scandal involving the Lula government's buying of legislative votes, discussed below.

The party as a whole did not advocate or even accept all of the decisions that resulted in these modified tactics. It was mainly Lula and his pragmatic faction, the Articulação, that paved the way for change. Lula tried to persuade the skeptical and was even known to engage in heavy arm-twisting when he encountered resistance (e.g., the decision to ally with the PL was extraordinarily controversial within the party). When he could not get the results he wanted, he sought autonomy from the party. One important example of this was the refuge he found since 1996 in the Instituto Cidadania, a think tank where he met with private business people in an effort to gain their support against the objections of the most radical sectors of the party. Another was the issuance—completely independent of the party—of the "Carta ao Povo Brasileiro" in June of 2002. In this "Letter to the Brazilian People," Lula assured the electorate (and perhaps more importantly, the domestic and international financial community) that he would honor all of Brazil's debts, contracts, and other outstanding financial obligations. Indeed, with presidential victory as his goal, Lula undertook a process to separate himself and his candidacy from the party organization. Nevertheless, many of the new tactics devised to help Lula win presidential office came to be associated with the PT as a whole.

The PT in Government, 2003–2006

If the PT was induced to change in order to win the presidency in 2002, its experience in government brought on new challenges and pressures that for the most part reinforced its assimilation. In the end, the continuities that Lula's first government oversaw were more pronounced than any shifts that it brought about. This held true for macroeconomic policy as well as social policy. Moreover, the corruption scandals that surfaced during this time made the PT appear more like a "normal" Brazilian political party. Lula's increasing distance from more militant sectors of the party, and the privileging of more mainstream elements within it, accentuated the impression that the PT had begun to descend into "politics as usual." Perhaps the most telling image of the Lula presidency was seeing him side by side with Fernando Collor, with the two mutually praising each other.

Conformity with market reform and fiscal stability marked the first Lula government's economic policy. The high degree of continuity observed with the previous Cardoso governments reflected, in part, the economic team's concern that foreign investors and multilateral institutions would fail to support a government that had only a decade before called for radical change. To allay such potential fears, the government observed high interest rates and fiscal tightness, even going so far as to surpass the fiscal-surplus target agreed upon between the Cardoso government and the International Monetary Fund. In the opposition, the PT had long criticized such austerity. The stated justification to party militants for the turnaround was that any antipoverty programs the party might introduce would depend on economic growth and stability.

Efforts to further a structural-reform agenda proceeded along with overseeing continuities in macroeconomic policy. The most outstanding accomplishment in this area was the successful passage of a pension reform bill at the end of Lula's first year in office. The new legislation, while watered down greatly from the initial proposal, was aimed at addressing grave deficits in the country's special pension system for government employees. It was also intended as a further signal to the foreign investment community and to international financial institutions that the Lula government was committed to multiple elements of the neoliberal package. The resulting law raised the effective minimum retirement age, reduced survivor benefits, limited benefit ceilings, and called for taxes to be levied on pensions and benefits for the most affluent. The government's proposal did not even try to reverse the previous administration's successful efforts to attach a minimum age requirement to the previous time-of-service provision for paid retirement. Also, it went against the PT's own prior attempts to exempt retired people from more affluent brackets from having to contribute to the system. The reform was especially controversial with the PT's congressional delegation because it reduced the privileges of civil servants, an important and longstanding component of the PT's support base. Cardoso had launched a similar effort years before, yet his measure was defeated, in no small measure because of the PT's obstructionism (Kingstone 2003). In the end, Lula carried the day, but only after applying heavy pressure to members of his own party, ultimately having four of them expelled for voting against the government's proposal: Senator Heloísa Helena, and deputies Luciana Genro, Raúl Font, and João Batista (more commonly referred to as Babá). The four went on to form the PSOL (Partido Socialismo e Liberdade or Party of Socialism and Liberty), which albeit still very small seems to have become the new repository of old-style PT radicalism in the Chamber of Deputies.

Social policy under the first Lula government assumed a remarkably mainstream character. Land reform, one of the central programs that the PT had promoted in the opposition, did not take off and gain the momentum that many had expected. No doubt Lula was concerned about the negative implications that a major redistribution of land might well have for future business investment (Ondetti 2006). The challenge was to balance efficiency concerns (maintaining high levels of productivity in Brazil's booming agribusiness sector) with historic PT concerns (commitment to the landless via land reform). He thus created two ministries for agriculture, staffing one with personnel oriented towards agribusiness and the other with historic figures involved with land reform (Hippolito 2005, 52–54). The Movimento Sem Terra, however, has been less than satisfied with what the latter ministry has produced in the way of concrete results. Its increasing tendency to pursue political strategies outside of the PT and the weak support shown toward Lula at the time of his re-election bid were striking for a social movement long associated with the PT.

The Lula government's biggest mark in the area of social policy was made vis-à-vis the Bolsa Família (Family Stipend), a conditional cash transfer program of the kind promoted by the World Bank to secure social support for economic adjustment and market reform. The Bolsa Família, the core idea of which was developed and implemented by PT governor Cristovam Buarque in Brasília, was designed to give low-income families a minimum income provided they keep their young children (ages six to fifteen) enrolled in school and see that they receive basic medical care. Pregnant women are also required to receive prenatal care and attend classes on maternal and childhood health. Eligibility for funds hinges on a family earning less than R$120 per month. The main contribution of the first Lula government was to unify into the Bolsa Família what had been four separate programs and to extend its coverage dramatically over time. By December 2006, the BF served 11.1 million families. However successful the program has been with regard to poverty reduction and the generation of important political support for Lula, the Bolsa Família departs significantly from the kind of structural social reforms that the PT called for when it was a radical left party. The highly targeted, means-tested program is very cost effective and fits exceedingly well within a market framework. Not a product of collective mobilization, it is administered in a top-down fashion by the Ministry of Social Development in conjunction with municipal governments in the country (Hall 2006; Soares et al.) The rhetoric of "human capital development" that surrounds the program's official justification is distinctly not within the tradition of the PT.

Serious corruption charges came to taint the PT after July 2005. Although Lula ultimately managed to escape the worst of these allegations and win re-election in October 2006, the party itself has consequently lost much of its initial luster and reputation for staying above the fray. Presidential victory in 2002 shifted the structure of institutional pressures facing the PT from the electoral to the governing arena. The disjuncture between leading the government and controlling less than 20 percent of seats in the Chamber of Deputies was problematic, especially since Lula would need supermajorities to pass market-oriented constitutional reforms in areas like social security and taxation. The main dilemma concerned how the government would muster sufficient legislative backing without allocating an excessive number of ministerial positions to allied parties, especially those outside the Left, in exchange for their legislative support. A key method used to break this impasse was the "*mensalão*," monthly bribes amounting to several million dollars paid to legislators from these parties.[12] The *mensalão* scandal provided momentum for the surfacing of information about illegal PT campaign-financing schemes predating the Lula presidency, namely, the centrally organized networks developed with smaller businesses in cities where it governed (i.e., the party's *caixa dois*, or second set of accounting books, used to avoid taxes).

The corruption charges that erupted in 2005 were of an extremely serious nature. The *mensalão* and related malfeasance were far more systematic and sustained than anything President Fernando Collor had done. Corruption charges ultimately hurt the party more than they hurt Lula himself, tarnishing its image as the standard-bearer of ethics in politics. They led to the resignation of Lula's chief of staff and former party president, José Dirceu, as well as that of the presiding party president, José Genoíno, and of several other historic PT figures. That Lula himself escaped as well as he did and was not subject to impeachment attempts testifies to his "Teflon" character. It also reflects the demographics and political culture of large segments of the electorate. Public opinion research suggests that disenchantment with Lula and the party fell most markedly among citizens with higher levels of education and income and who live in urban areas of the South and Southeast. A relatively confined share of the electorate, these were precisely the sectors that had once provided the strongest support for the party's ideological program. By the same token, thanks in large part to executive power and the Bolsa Família program, Lula was able to buffer his candidacy by winning support from the huge numbers of citizens who occupy the lowest income and education brackets. They tend to reside in remote areas of the country, places that had never been PT strongholds and where Lula had been solidly defeated in previous elections (Hunter and Power 2007).

The concurrent elections of 2006 for the presidency and the Chamber of Deputies raised further concerns about the party's future. They also placed in stark relief some of the growing divergences between Lula and the PT. While Lula secured an impressive victory at the polls (61 percent of all valid votes versus 39 percent for his PSDB competitor, Geraldo Alckmin), the performance of PT candidates to fill all 513 seats in Chamber of Deputies was less positive. The national vote total for a given party's candidates in the Chamber of Deputies is arguably the best indicator of its electoral support in the country. The PT won only enough votes to secure 83 chamber seats, placing it second to the PMDB.

Yet in 2002, the PT had won 91 seats, making it the single largest party in the Chamber. In the Senate, the PT suffered a loss of 4 seats. This marked the first time in its history that the PT had not grown compared with its previous performance in national legislative elections. This reflected especially poorly on the party, given that it had held the presidency in the intervening four years and therefore should have enjoyed the advantages of incumbency, a situation that has helped governing parties historically. Obviously, the PT as a party has suffered a reputational setback.

Moreover, the demographic support base of the party (as indicated by seats in the Chamber of Deputies) and that of Lula are increasingly incongruent. In contrast to Lula, who has managed to gain cross-regional support, the party's stronghold remains concentrated in the more urban, industrialized areas of Brazil. A comparison of the PT partisan vote and the Lula presidential vote across Brazil's states in four successive elections suggests an increasing geographical spread between the two over time. The PT's lackluster legislative performance is indeed a cause of concern among PT partisans and militants. While fully aware that Lula's popularity was always greater than the party's ideological appeal, they accepted that fact as long as Lula worked in the service of the PT. In doubt is whether he has used his presidential office to advance the objectives they fought for while in the opposition. Beyond the fact that the policy positions endorsed by the Lula government have strayed so far from the party's historic concerns, PT followers wonder what will become of the party after Lula leaves the scene in 2010. Currently, there is no obvious individual from the PT that could be a winning presidential candidate and fill Lula's shoes. Rumors suggest that there is movement in some circles to have the constitution changed so that Lula could run again in 2010. In the absence of a constitutional change to such effect, there is nothing to prevent Lula from running again in 2014. Yet in any event, if the PT aspires to remain true to its original cause as a programmatic party on the Left, its future electoral trajectory cannot reasonably rest on the popularity of a personal leader.

The Future of the PT

The story of the PT in the last decade contains some elements of continuity and many of change. No doubt the PT retains programmatic inclinations and will not become a "*partido de sustentação*" any time soon. It also retains some of the organizational norms and behaviors (such as an emphasis on discipline and loyalty) that have distinguished it historically from other parties in the system. Yet the most notable trend within the PT in the last decade or so concerns the accommodations it has made to global economic developments and to the constraints of Brazilian politics. Most striking has been its ideological moderation, manifested most clearly in its acceptance of the market. Similarly, the party—especially the faction most closely associated with Lula—has begun to adopt the political tactics of catchall parties in Brazil, such as allying with parties from across the political spectrum, hiring publicists, and even doling out patronage. Its core militants have grayed and their enthusiasm has diminished greatly from the 1980s. It is doubtful that the party is replenishing its ranks with a new generation of supporters whose commitment parallels that of their predecessors. The PT of today is indeed very different from the party of the past.

The questions posed at the beginning of the chapter—of whether the PT is still a left party and what is at stake in the answer to this question—call for revisiting and reassessing several of the dimensions that once made the PT distinctive in the system of Brazilian parties. Does the PT continue to represent a programmatic alternative, allowing people to feel that formal democracy gives them real choices? Does the party still represent a point of coalescence within the political Left? Does it still work with a wide array of social movements, promoting but also channeling their demands? Has partisan attachment to the party continued to rise, experiencing the turn upward it has seen in every major election year? The answer to all of these questions is "much less so than before." With the PT's growing assimilation, its capacity to promote a programmatic orientation in the party system has undoubtedly diminished, as has its ability to bring the political Left together within one organizational umbrella. So too has the party ceased to provide the institutionalized mechanisms of political influence that it once did for various social movements. And while Lula may be gaining a personal following, the party as such is not growing stronger insofar as gaining partisan supporters is concerned. Thus, the PT's ability to strengthen the party system and help to legitimate Brazilian democracy has not continued to expand.

The question that lies ahead is whether the party will continue to assimilate further and adopt the ways of Brazil's conventional parties even more unequivocally than it has until now or whether it will undergo an internal process of criticism and reformulation, re-emphasizing values and practices that it previously embraced. That Lula was re-elected in October 2006 will undoubtedly influence the direction the party will take. The PT-led government finds itself up against conflicting pressures anew, and it is equipped with no greater congressional support than it enjoyed the first time around. At the same time, it presides over a growing economy, including a booming export market for many of Brazil's major agricultural commodities. The government may even be able to draw upon the discovery of new oil reserves. Backed by strong approval ratings, Lula's second-term government might well be able to tackle some of the challenges that it shied away from or failed to meet in its first term. These range from regulating privatized enterprises to accelerating the distribution of land to the landless.

By the same token, having Lula in the presidency no doubt diminishes the party's interest and capacity to undertake a process of internal criticism and reform. The inclusion into the cabinet of more members of the PMDB and other allied parties, combined with the party's failure until now to discipline its members who were involved in corruption activities, suggests that being in power unleashes countervailing forces that may well lead the party to converge more and more with its conventional counterparts. Doing so would leave Brazil's party system without a clear alternative to "politics as usual," and worse off because of it. Eventually, the PT will be returned to the opposition. Once out of government, the party might have a fighting chance of recovering some of the characteristics that once made it so distinctive. But reverting in full-fledged fashion to what the PT once was is unlikely. The party has become a fixture of the political mainstream. As part of the system, it cannot credibly be against it anymore. Nonetheless, on the sidelines of power the PT may regroup and establish a new niche for itself, albeit one closer to the political center than in years past.

3

Organized Civil Society in Lula's Brazil

Kathryn Hochstetler

In 1980, an alliance of unions, social movements, intellectuals, the progressive church, and other opponents to the military government chose to push forward the process of political change by forming the Workers' Party (Partido dos Trabalhadores or PT). A quarter century later, in 2003, the PT gained its first national president, Luiz Inácio Lula da Silva (Lula). The civil society organizations (CSOs)—a term used here to refer to a full array of nongovernmental, nonprofit voluntary associations, including social movements and unions—that had historically worked with the PT and now generally greeted Lula's election with enthusiasm.[1] Over his first term, their initial approval gave way to a growing sense of disappointment with how the Lula and the PT managed the challenges of governing Brazil.

A particular historic political project developed over several decades between the PT and CSOs, both inside and outside the party structure. I identify three phases in the deteriorating relationship between CSOs and the Lula administration. In the first, which lasted less than a year, CSOs tried to use their mobilizing power to support Lula and nudge him closer to their shared historic agenda in the face of strong pressures for economic continuity with Cardoso's neoliberal policies. In the second stage, CSOs began to doubt that they did, in fact, share a political project with the PT's first national administration. Their substantive disappointment led them to begin to separate from the PT organizationally and to express doubts about the value of participating in the administration's consultative processes. Finally, after the PT was credibly accused of widespread corruption in 2005, CSOs formulated new critiques of representative democracy and party politics but still sought to protect Lula personally from impeachment.

The first Lula administration created a turning point in the political strategies of Brazilian CSOs, many of whom are on the political Left. Throughout the periods of democratic transition and consolidation, many CSOs prioritized building and supporting the PT's party organization, assuming that the party could and would carry their agenda forward if it could just reach national power.[2] The unfolding of the first Lula administration shook many of the bedrock expectations of its historic CSO allies. The end result is that the PT's monopoly as the political instrument of the Left for twenty years is now gone (Gebrim 2005–2006). The strong critiques of the second and third phases make it difficult to conclude, as some have, that CSOs have simply been co-opted by the PT (Flynn 2005, 1241). CSOs certainly have abandoned the presumption that a PT government will resolve all their problems and now are looking for alternative conceptions of how they might interject their views into national politics. After examining these shifts, it is important to reflect on what these developments mean for Brazilian democracy as a whole.

Political Parties and Civil Society Organizations

For the most part, academic literatures on political parties and CSOs tend to treat them separately, and they are, in fact, often quite distinct. Many CSOs operate well outside the world of electoral politics and prize their autonomy from it. By the same token, many political parties are not grounded in specific social organizations. The most common solidarity relations are between socialist parties and trade unions, and between conservative parties and business organizations, but these develop in idiosyncratic and country-specific ways (Thomas 2001). Close relationships between parties and social movements are quite a bit scarcer, with the Green Party phenomenon a notable exception. A political party like the

PT, with its strong foundation in both unions and an array of social movements, is thus highly unusual, but it provides a provocative case for thinking about the possibilities and limitations of close links between political parties and CSOs.

Although they are distinct forms of organization, political parties and CSOs perform partially overlapping functions in modern political systems. All are mediating institutions that link citizens and the state, turning individuals into collective actors and articulating their demands and values to political decision makers. Yet their functions only partially overlap. All of them can play the representational or social-input functions of parties: they articulate and aggregate interests and integrate and mobilize citizens (Bartolini and Mair 2001, 331). Only political parties have usually been able to play a second set of institutional roles, "including the recruitment of political leaders and the organization of parliament and government" (Bartolini and Mair 2001, 332). As a result, only political parties have access to authoritative decision-making spaces in most political systems, while CSOs are limited to the less-authoritative public sphere of deliberation and social practices.

The obvious problem for political parties is that they virtually always end up facing contradictions between their role in expressing societal values and their role in winning electoral campaigns and governing. CSOs do not face the dilemma themselves, but they do face the question of how to relate to party allies who do. Those party allies, for example, may be calculating whether they can electorally afford to support the demands of their associated social movements (e.g., Nylen 2000, 114). One of the few empirical generalizations that can be made about the relationship between parties and their allied social groups is that it is nearly always more conflictual when the party is actually in government, especially for leftist parties (Thomas 2001, 285). A party in legislative opposition can exercise its expressive role more freely, since it is not in a position of actually having to balance claims and create decisional majorities. Once electoral success places the party in the legislative majority or an executive position, governing concerns become paramount.

Partly for this reason, many parties grounded in CSOs engage in internal debates about whether to try to win elections if that means moving away from core movement or union principles to attract first a majority of electoral votes and then a majority of legislative support for proposals. The lure of organizing and leading authoritative decision making on central CSO agenda items—which might not even be discussed by less-sympathetic party leaders—is the primary argument in favor of making the necessary compromises. These dilemmas are especially acute for political systems of the presidential type, like Brazil, where executives are separately and directly elected by the population. Presidents represent their parties and their electorate, but they are also the head of state (Linz 1994, 24). If the executive is seen as too partisan or as speaking too much for a particular constituency, he or she will be seen as not fulfilling the head-of-state role, speaking for the entire population. Because of the symbolically central role of a national president, Lula's election heightened the potential contradictions and gains in the party-CSO relationship. These were present at lower levels of government, but in more diffuse ways.

A Historic Political Project: The PT Way of Governing

Since its origin in 1980, the PT has openly discussed these kinds of dilemmas, with party activists showing a keen understanding of the trade-offs between a party's expressive role and its electoral and governing roles. The party has struggled with different internal preferences for balancing the trade-offs. As the PT developed, these different preferences were ultimately expressed by formal internal party factions, which leaned either towards or away from electoral compromises. Lula's own Articulation faction favored vote-maximizing strategies, compared with other factions that are often grouped together as more leftist or radical factions. In addition, the PT gradually added concrete experience with balancing its dual identities; this tended to strengthen the more pragmatic, governing-oriented balances of its dual identities (Samuels 2004). The PT's experiences with subpresidential executive power are critical for understanding the new Lula administration. These experiences date to the election of the first PT mayoral candidates in 1982, reaching a peak of 411 mayoralties in 2004; as well, two PT governors were elected in 1994, and three in 1998.

These executive experiences were quite varied in terms of their levels of success and CSO approval (Baiocchi 2003b). In them, the PT developed a basic formula for its governing strategy, which the party itself refers to as *o modo petista de governor*, or the PT way of governing (Fundação Perseu Abramo 1997). The model reflects some moderation in the PT's aims and approaches over time. Entering into the twenty-first century, the PT way of governing included two essential priorities: a substantive commitment to pursue redistributive policies that favor the poor over the wealthy, and a procedural commitment to incorporating popular participation in decision making (Baiocchi 2003a; Nylen 2000; Nylen 2003). A third "good government" principle showcased the administrative achievements of the PT's better executive experiences. While not all of its subnational administrations were successful, many of them demonstrated unusually clean and innovative governance, including the well-known participatory budgeting process (Baiocchi 2003b). While the three principles are clearly related, they have made distinct contributions to helping the PT address the dilemmas of a political party with a strong base in CSOs.

The PT stands virtually alone in Brazil as a political party with a strong and specific substantive ideology. Over more than two decades, the exact content of that ideology has changed somewhat, as can be tracked by the varying definitions and prominence of the PT's commitment to socialism (Samuels 2004). Despite all the changes, the focus on redistribution toward the poor remained a bottom line. It has been the heart of the PT's appeal to its traditional constituency of organized unions and social movements. Nylen argues, "Ideology is fundamental to the very identity of the PT as a progressive party of the Left; it functions as the ideational glue for holding together its many factions and currents. The party *must* have a 'transformation project' that envisions an eventual transformation of the status quo into a more socially just (i.e., egalitarian) future, or it will lose the allegiance of its most expressive leaders and active membership" (Nylen 2003, 104). While maintaining this ideology is a sine qua non for the PT's organized base, it has sometimes helped the PT electorally as well, by allowing it to be seen as the clearest alternative to politics as usual.

The procedural commitment to participation performs a different role. It also plays well with the traditional base, especially social movements. Baiocchi traces the participatory vision of the PT to Brazil's urban social movements of the 1970s, which put such demands at the center of their challenge to the military government of the time (Baiocchi 2003a, 7). Brazilian CSOs have had an unusually strong and well-developed participatory vision that they link to the concept of citizenship (Dagnino 2004; Friedman and Hochstetler 2002). The PT has been a central support, but not the only party, in the development of this vision. Perhaps more important, however, has been the way that broad participation has helped the PT to mediate between its organized base and the larger population that it governs. "In terms of negotiating societal demands," relates Biaocchi, "it could create settings where claimants themselves could be part of the negotiations of demands; in terms of governance, broad-based participation could generate legitimacy for strategies of governance, if not improving governance directly" (2003a, 21). This was especially critical insofar as redistributing to the poor might well mean directing resources away from the comparatively privileged public-sector unions and middle-class social movements and intellectuals who form much of the PT's political base.

The PT has long identified itself as an ethical alternative to politics as usual, which in Brazil frequently means administrative corruption. Some of its local administrations have gone well beyond that minimal claim to actively creating global models of high-quality and innovative public administration. Most famously, the participatory budgeting process developed in the PT's Porto Alegre administration has been copied across Brazil and worldwide (Baiocchi 2003b). Commentators assume that this reputation was one element of Lula's electoral appeal in 2002 (Flynn 2005, 1222; Hunter and Power 2007), although no published survey data confirm or deny that argument. In fact, Samuels' study of partisanship in Brazil uses a 2002 survey to conclude that partisan supporters of Lula and the PT were not associated with any particular attitude toward corruption (Samuels 2006, 16, 19), although *voters* may still choose the party for reasons of probity.

As noted, this three-part model of governing and the dilemmas it seeks to resolve have their origins in the PT's political experiences at subnational levels. Not all PT administrations have been equally successful at putting the model into practice. One constantly cited reason for failure has been the backdrop of unsympathetic national governments with other priorities and practices. When the PT's Lula became national president in 2003, this backdrop finally changed. Lula won the presidency on a platform that continued to uphold the three priorities of redistribution, participation, and good government, and an ample majority of the Brazilian population (61 percent) chose him over the PSDB's (Partido da Social Democracia Brasileira) José Serra.

Civil Society Organizations in Brazil

In assessing Lula's first administration, it is interesting to evaluate how his government has managed the dilemmas of governing, from the perspective of the CSOs who have been an important part of the PT's social and political base. CSO responses can be divided in three phases based on an analysis of the documents and activities of a number of organizations that regularly joined with the PT in expressive mobilizations and organizations before it gained national office. These include the CNBB (Conferência Nacional dos Bispos do Brasil) and its allied organizations of the progressive Catholic Church, the CUT trade union (Central Única dos Trabalhadores), the MST landless movement (Movimento dos Trabalhadores Rurais Sem-Terra), and the Abong organization of NGOs (Associação Brasileira de ONGs), which have all been frequent partners with the PT. Thousands of smaller, grassroots organizations joined these better-known organizations in a variety of political mobilizations. Highlights of the historic PT-CSO alliance include the *diretas já!* (direct elections now!) campaign of the early 1980s, the millions-strong mobilizations for impeachment of then-president Collor in 1992, the annual marches of the excluded (*grito dos excluídos*), and the mass plebiscite on the repudiation of the national debt of 2000. CSOs have also joined in the more formal opportunities for participation with PT administrations at lower levels. Several dimensions of PT partisanship relate to this historic relationship: Lula's supporters were opposed to the suppression of political protest, and the PT's partisans were strongly inserted into social networks that led them to participate both in campaigns and a variety of movements (Samuels 2006).

In order to present a coherent account, I am stressing broadly shared positions of CSOs. When I do discuss specific movements or sectors, it is because they exemplify a phase in the relationship or signal a turning point in the overall phases. Identifying broadly shared positions is possible because Brazilian CSOs are unusually inclined to organize themselves into temporary or permanent networks that issue joint pronouncements and plan collective action (Hochstetler 2000). I call these regional- and national-level permanent networks "peak organizations," borrowing from terminology used to describe national labor confederations. Some of these networks conjoin a single kind of CSO, such as the CUT labor central or Abong, which groups only the larger, more formal organizations known as nongovernmental organizations (NGOs). Others are substantive networks that include many kinds of CSOs interested in a given issue, like the Brazilian Budget Forum (FBO—Fórum Brasileiro do Orçamento). There is even a peak organization of peak organizations, Inter-Redes (Between Networks), that joins thirty-three of the smaller networks for some purposes.

Each of these networks is grounded in a multitude of individual organizations, each with its own particularities. The MST counts hundreds of thousands of members and uses combative grassroots strategies like land occupations to pursue agrarian reform. The NGO IBASE (Instituto Brasileiro de Análises Sociais e Econômicas—Brazilian Institute of Social and Economic Analyses) sometimes joins in marches and demonstrations but also provides critical organizational infrastructure for other CSOs and CSO networks. Notably, IBASE brought electronic communication to Brazilian CSOs very early in the 1990s. Public-sector unions and intellectuals are two other groups that have been historic supporters of the PT, contributing strategies such as workplace strikes, as well as critical analyses of the political conjuncture. There are inevitable and sharp differences among these and the many other organizations that make up the PT's historic base. They disagree on the party's stated mission, and they have disagreed even more on how to put it into practice and how to judge the Lula administration as it actually did so. A different version of this chapter could have picked any one of these organizations or sectors and traced a somewhat different trajectory of its relationship with the PT and the Lula administration. Nonetheless, for most of them the overall outline would be the same. From an initial phase of trying to help the administration achieve the PT's historic goals, there would be a steady decline of satisfaction with the government and the party, culminating in deep questioning about how CSOs should relate to partisan, representative politics.

The Evolving Relationship between CSOs and the PT

Phase 1: Enabling Lula to Make the Right Choices

In late 2002, many CSO activists were elated by Lula's growing political strength, which culminated in his election as president. They believed that this represented a historic opportunity for significant change in Brazil—politically, economically, and socially. At the same time, they understood that there were powerful forces of continuity, exemplified by the "Letter to the Brazilian People" ("Carta ao Povo Brasileiro") which Lula wrote in June 2002 (Luiz Inácio da Silva 2005). This letter stressed the importance of continuing Cardoso's policy of fiscal equilibrium, albeit "not as an end, but as a means" to greater economic growth. Notwithstanding its title, the target audience of this letter was really the increasingly nervous international financial system that feared Lula's rise. Lula's promises of economic continuity helped calm financial markets but awakened new anxieties among his CSO allies. The period of Lula's election and first months in office were thus characterized by a CSO strategy of putting sufficient counterpressure on Lula to help him withstand conservative pressures and pursue their historically shared substantive agenda. At the same time, CSOs looked forward to a time when they would achieve greater participation in decision making.

As noted above, the PT's substantive baseline has been economic distribution to the poor. The "Letter to the Brazilian People" continued to make many such promises, along with those about continuing the previous government's economic stabilization policies. CSOs girded themselves in this first phase to create the political conditions through which Lula would be able to direct more resources and attention to the former over the latter. MST leader João Pedro Stédile, speaking in a public lecture in Toronto at the end of 2003, was typical in seeing social mobilization as key to achieving social change: "It is not so much a question of Lula's will as it is of the balance of power. We in the MST believe that if the people really got involved and got behind the popular project, we could make a real leftist out of Lula" (Stédile 2004, 13).[3]

Lula's first months in power consequently saw CSOs turning to extensive protest strategies intended to *support* the PT's historic agenda and the Lula administration. Land occupations, for example, jumped to 222 in Lula's first year, compared to 103 in 2002 and 158 in 2001 (*Folha de São Paulo*, May 28, 2004).

This "supportive mobilization" strategy reflected CSOs' conviction that expressive politics continued to be relevant after their party allies occupied the government and could even overwhelm the electoral and governing logics that would otherwise push the administration to unacceptable substantive compromises. Normatively, this view reflected the CSO's self-conception that they speak for a true majority interest and the public good (see, for example, Fernandes 1994), which is frequently undermined by minority interests who manipulate party and governing mechanisms to undermine that good—the "elites," as they are often called by CSOs and the PT alike. In their preferred expressive/participatory logic, CSOs would magnify the popular demand for change and economic redistribution through their street protests and other participation, enabling the administration to act as an additional amplifier for the popular mandate; collectively, they would simply drown out the voices for continuity (see, for example, Projeto Mapas 2005). The PT's participatory budgeting process actually follows this logic, a fact that is often poorly understood. The participatory process does not generate final budgets, but only gives PT municipal and state administrations budget projects that they can then take through the normal budgetary process. The strong weight of popular participation behind the participatory budgets often has, in fact, successfully pressured legislatures to adopt them, but this was not necessarily the case, especially outside the prototype in Porto Alegre (Nylen 2003).

Not all CSOs were as sure of the administration's substantive intentions as this analysis suggests, even in the early days of the first phase. One group of CSOs formed the Brazilian Budget Forum in August of 2002, before the election, after none of the parties was willing to support their budget proposals. The FBO's priorities included more social spending and transparency of information and procedures surrounding the federal budget. They have monitored proposed budgets and actual spending, analyzing the budgets and lobbying for alternatives. For example, the FBO has distributed more than thirty thousand copies of a booklet meant to explain the meaning and implications of the primary budget surplus (*superávit primário*) (Fórum Brasileiro do Orçamento 2004). The FBO had "somewhat higher hopes" that the PT would support their proposals than other parties, but at least some of its members were disillusioned even before Lula's term began.[4]

All CSOs, both those hopeful and those skeptical about the administration's substantive commitments, continued to put their faith in its procedural opportunities for participation in the new government in the first phase. These were seen as additional channels for expressing citizen input that could supportively pressure the Lula government and thus overcome more traditional political forces. IBASE was so sure that the PT administration would open up innovative participatory processes that it even sought and received funding for a project to monitor the expected radicalization of democracy. The PT "way of governing" at lower levels inspired this expectation (Projeto Mapas 2005, 3).[5] The PT administration did initiate a number of participatory consultative processes once in office, but they were largely extensions of existing participatory models (Friedman and Hochstetler 2002; Hochstetler 2000) rather than clear innovations.

Perhaps the most ambitious of its new consultative mechanisms is the Economic and Social Development Council (CDES—Conselho de Desenvolvimento Econômico e Social). Its orienting commitment—"a good government is a government that shares the act of governing with society"—reflects the participatory vision of the PT and its historic CSO allies.[6] Broadly corporatist in its structure, CDES has just twelve governmental representatives, plus the president and ninety civilian members. Most of these are from peak business and labor organizations, although other CSOs are also represented, including those of indigenous and disabled populations. The CDES is intended to be a forum for cross-sectoral social dialogue and has been given specific tasks such as drafting proposals for pension, tax, and labor-reform bills. It reports consensual conclusions, which the administration has committed to working into its own legislative projects. It is worth noting that even in this first phase, there were clear signs that CSOs found the CDES's dialogues inadequate: when Lula took the pension and tax bills to Congress with an entourage of all the country's governors and his entire cabinet, he had to be driven the block from the executive building because of hostile union protesters—including CUT members—in the streets (*Latin American Weekly Report*, May 6, 2003, 197). In addition, the Congress made numerous and large changes in the proposed bills, notwithstanding the consultations (and the documentation now available concerning bribes paid by the government).

The CDES was only the most prominent of thirteen new national councils, deepening Brazil's "council democracy" (Alvarez 1997). In addition, the government supported more-episodic consultation processes on other issues. CSOs counted that almost two million CSO members had participated in the administration's consultative processes in its first three years (*Reforma Política* 2006, appendix 3), on topics such as urban, environmental, and food-security issues. Two CSO peak organizations, Inter-Redes and Abong, joined in partnership with the federal government in the first half of 2003 to coordinate discussions in every state capital on the *Multiyear Plan 2004–2007: A Brazil for Everyone* (Fórum Brasileiro do Orçamento 2004, 31–32). Minister Luiz Dulci wrote in the process' final report that "a change-oriented government is interested not just in having civil society participation be all that it already is, but in having it be much bigger, wider, deeper, and more diversified" (quoted in Inter-Redes 2004).

Similar ideas were expressed through much of the government, all the way to the top. Lula has had tremendous personal charisma and credibility among the PT's allied CSOs, and his appointment book as president made significant room for them. In his first months in office, the country's main newspapers reported on his meetings with representatives of labor, business, indigenous, antipoverty, religious, and women's CSOs. With these meetings, Lula brought prominence to CSOs' agendas and leaders and had the opportunity to remind them of their shared purposes. With CSOs, Lula praised their work and expressed sympathy for their aims, urged them to join in supporting governmental projects like the Zero Hunger plan—and asked them for patience. Such meetings were effective even well into the administration. In September 2004, for example, Lula met with the executive council of Abong, and the Abong president later reported that the organization "left with a very positive sense that there is currently a stronger recognition, in the public sphere, of the role of NGOs. Evidence of this was the president's interest in the meeting, extending it and reacting with quite a lot of enthusiasm to the idea that NGOs have an important role to play in the process of South American integration as well" (quoted in *Informes Abong* 246, September 4–10, 2004).

The most systematic inclusion for CSOs came in the way the Lula government staffed the national administration. CSO leaders of all kinds now worked within the government on issues they formerly tried to influence from outside. Leaders of the CUT found themselves on the government side of salary negotiations in nine ministries, fifty-three secretariats, and thousands of second- and third-tier bureaucratic appointments (*Jornal do Brasil,* September 15, 2003). Other examples include the first head of the Incra land reform institute (Instituto Nacional de Colonização e Reforma Agrária), who had strong ties to the landless movement, and former Minister of Environment Marina Silva, who grew up in the rubber-tapper communities of the Amazon and has years of credibility as an environmental activist and legislator. This is a recruitment pattern familiar from the earliest PT administrations and has equally familiar tensions and allures for CSO activists. They are close to the center of power and able to make decisions but also find themselves limited by budgetary and bureaucratic constraints that often divide them from those still outside. Those CSO activists who remain outside see their ranks diminished by the exodus of leaders to the government.

In summary, the major unanticipated development in CSO-government relations in the first phase was the substantive direction of the Lula administration. CSOs had to strategize about how to help the administration confront pressures to continue the previous government's economic stabilization policies, choosing supportive mobilizations in this phase.

Phase 2: Procedural and Substantive Disillusionment

The transition from the first to the second stage took place gradually, at somewhat different times for different organizations and individuals. In the transition to the second stage, CSOs began to question whether they did, in fact, share a political project with the PT government. Many of their meetings were dominated by open arguments about this question, with evidence accumulated for and against (Projeto Mapas 2005). As CSOs concluded they did not share a political project with the government, they withdrew from some of its participatory opportunities and established new parallel expressive spaces. While the PT and Lula had often been part of such spaces in the past, they were no longer welcome. The administration responded with some concern to these developments, but the government did not change economic and social policies as CSOs hoped, and no other response was acceptable to CSOs. As they distanced themselves from the government, CSOs explicitly rejected the compromises and consensus the PT was willing to adopt to be part of the governing experience.

Given the importance of the CDES to the administration's participatory strategy, developments in August of 2003, just eight months into the new administration, mark a point of inflection. In this month, many of the PT's traditional movement and union allies, including the CUT and MST, formed a new Coordination of Social Movements (Coordenação dos Movimento Sociais) that did not include the PT, to discuss similar issues to those raised in the CDES, especially unemployment, and to prepare jointly for its meetings. They did so questioning whether consensus with promarket actors is actually possible or desirable at all, a fundamental critique of consultation of this kind. Abong's director of institutional relations, José Antônio Moroni, raised this question after a September meeting of the council's Special Secretariat: "Is consensus possible in a society as complex and divided as ours, where the only form of communication between classes is currently violence? What consensus would that be?" (quoted in *Informes Abong* 248, Oct. 1–Sept. 25, 2003).

The organizations in the Coordination of Social Movements still argued in September that "another Brazil is possible!" but they did not want the vision of Brazil's future that the CDES's meeting had "consensually" produced. Instead, they insisted on a return to the policy proposals they had much earlier shared with the PT in opposition to Cardoso: "nonrenewal of the agreement with the IMF; control of currency exchange rates and capital flows, suspension of the payments on the foreign debt and a review of the debt, following the Brazilian Constitution" (Coordenação dos Movimento Sociais 2003). It is worth noting that the PT had left such proposals out of its electoral platforms years before (Samuels 2004); CSOs' articulation of them now suggests that different participants in the CSO-PT alliance had had conflicting understandings of the purposes of such changes. The Coordination's February 2004 meeting produced a "Letter from São Paulo" that had lost the optimistic tone of its earlier communications, suggesting its participants were no longer sure that another Brazil was possible. Now in the second year of the administration, the Coordination concluded, "The current policy maintains a clear neoliberal slant and a perverse character, subordinated to financial capital and to the agreements with the IMF, which are harmful to the national interest" (Coordenação dos Movimento Sociais 2004). The letter set out a schedule of national mobilizations and protests increasingly conceived of as nonsupportive of the administration. In mid-2004, a number of CSOs were prepared to leave the CDES altogether, but were persuaded to stay by a change in its leadership (Projeto Mapas 2005, 13).

Environmentalists and their allies concluded first that the PT was not on their side. More than five hundred organizations sent a public letter to Lula on

October 20, 2003, which stands out as a highly personal rebuke to the president himself. "It is obvious that the government is not correctly evaluating the scale of the erosion that already affects Your Excellency, and that can still become much worse, in a short time, if the unfolding decision-making processes continue to disdain socioenvironmental variables."[7] The letter is not a rejection of the entire PT administration and was conceived in part as a means of support for the embattled minister of the environment against other parts of the administration. It singles out three areas of disagreement: the inclusion of numerous infrastructure projects for the Amazon region in the *Multiyear Plan 2004–2007*, lack of action on global climate change issues, and permission to plant genetically modified organisms (GMOs).

In addition to the actual content of the policies, environmentalists and their allies had procedural complaints as well. Some of them had been among the 2,200 NGOs who ostensibly helped shape the *Multiyear Plan*. The 170 NGOs who met with him to give their report on the *Plan*'s forums were told by Lula that there had never been a planning process with so much participation and were assured that the partnership would help them demand the results they wanted to see (*Informes Abong* 243, August 14–20, 2003). Yet the final *Plan* contained projects that directly contravened the input of socio-environmentalist NGOs and others. As environmentalists sent their letter, they were also engaged in preparations for the First National Conference on the Environment, which involved sixty-five thousand representatives of CSOs, many not normally related to the environment. That diverse crowd sent a very strong supporting message for environmentalists, making the prohibition on GMOs one of the four points of consensus coming out of the conference (*Informes Abong* 257, November 28–December 4, 2003). In response, the administration did significantly edit the legislative project on GMOs to give the Ministry of the Environment more control over them, but it then worked behind the scenes in the national Congress to restore a bill that matched the agribusiness vision of the Ministry of Agriculture, enraging environmentalists.[8]

A similar combination of substantive and participatory complaints drove an even more significant wedge between the PT and its historic allies. In March of 2004, some eighteen hundred union and social-movement activists joined to form the Conlutas (Coordenação Nacional de Lutas—National Coordination of Struggles), which was created to oppose the Lula administration's economic policies. While organizations of all kinds are welcome in Conlutas, its core is the public sector unions who resisted proposed social security reforms in the

CDES and then in the streets outside the congress building. In its own presentation of itself, Conlutas stresses that it is "an alternative for the struggles of workers, in the fact of the degeneration of the CUT, which has transformed itself into a '*chapa-branca*' ['white plate,' i.e., government sell-out, alluding to the color of the license plates on government vehicles] organization, preferring to support the government to defending workers" (Conlutas n.d.). Conlutas' anti-neoliberal agenda is shared with the new party PSOL (Partido Socialismo e Liberdade), which held its founding meeting in June 2004. PSOL's most prominent members are PT legislators who were expelled from the party for voting against the same social security reforms.

Another sign of the change in tone can be seen in the mobilizational choices of the MST. In October 2003, Stédile said that the MST had changed its occupation strategy with the PT in power: "We used to occupy the public offices of the agrarian reform agency, in the days when Cardoso was in power. But now we occupy roads, estates—there is a different focus because the government is no longer our enemy" (Stédile 2004, 18). This position gives special poignancy to MST leader João Paulo Rodrigues's announcement at the end of March 2004 that "the time limit has already ended." Just six months after Stédile's confident speech, the MST no longer assumed that the PT government was on its side The MST's new plans were "to invade estates, close roads, organize pickets in public buildings, march to Brasília, and to occupy agencies of the Bank of Brazil" (*Jornal do Brasil*, March 20, 2004). "Red April" 2004 saw the highest number of land occupations in any month ever counted, 109 (*Folha de São Paulo*, May 28, 2004).[9] Lula warned the MST that as union leader, he had lost every time he radicalized his demands, and the two traded barbs about following the applicable laws (*Folha de São Paulo*, April 20, 2004).

These examples out of the many that exist serve to illustrate the transition to the second phase. By mid-2004, CSOs had concluded that the Lula administration might welcome their participation and speak highly of them, but it had no intention of using CSOs' clearly stated preferences in formulating policies when they contradicted the administration's own preferences (as these could no longer be attributed to elites or the International Monetary Fund) for economic stabilization. The thirty-three networks that make up the meta-network group Inter-Redes spoke for their tens of thousands of member organizations in publicly breaking with the *Multiyear Plan* process in August 2004, noting that their contributions had not even become part of the congressional debate (Inter-Redes 2005). The smaller, but especially prominent, Projeto Mapas group decided unanimously in December 2004 to abandon their monitoring of all institutional public-participation spaces and wrote an epitaph for the administration's participation policies in April 2005: "In this meeting, the perception was solidified that the participatory style of governing, characteristic of the experiences of the Partido do Trabalhadores in municipal and state executives, was not part of the 'language' of the Lula government, which has contributed to the consolidation of a 'low-impact democracy' in Brazil" (Projeto Mapas 2005, 21).

In the Projeto Mapas group's analysis, the administration had ultimately opted for a parliamentary governing strategy based on building alliances with an array of political parties, rather than the one CSOs favored, a participatory governing strategy that used mobilized citizen support to push a radical new agenda over the resistance of political and economic elites. In a divided administration, ministries like the Ministry of Environment with strong ties to CSOs simply lost out to those like the Ministry of Agriculture, whose agro-exporting vision could garner congressional support and export dollars (Projeto Mapas 2005, 24–25). With the government turning its back on them at decision-making time, CSOs in the remainder of the second phase of realignment related to it largely as they had to earlier administrations—from the outside. The main difference, said a coordinator of the FBO, was that earlier CSOs had had the PT *with* them and had the hopes of a future PT administration that would someday make their vision of another kind of Brazil surge into reality.[10]

A return to earlier patterns of state-society relations did not mean a purely combative relationship. Through the 1990s, Brazilian CSOs had come to play larger roles in routine governance, notably carrying out various kinds of services for all levels of government. In 2003, CSOs received R$1.3 billion from the federal government (*O Globo*, May 3, 2004), and twenty-nine thousand organizations were expected to receive R$2 billion in 2004 (*Estado de São Paulo*, June 20, 2004). To give one example of the complexity of this kind of relationship, Lula faced a chorus of boos from CSOs at the 2005 World Social Forum, but his Ministry of Tourism and three other federal agencies gave Abong more than R$5 million to organize the forum (Associação Brasileira de ONGs 2005). CSOs also continued to participate in the many councils to which they had gained access since the 1980s; whatever environmentalists' dissatisfaction with the broader policies of the administration, their seats on the various environmental councils still gave them to power to carry on important work, such as approving environmental impact assessments. Some remained in the CDES, while others left. More combative CSOs like the MST returned to earlier patterns of periods of rapprochement and distancing from the administration, depending on the status of land-reform initiatives. The CUT was divided over economic reforms proposed by Cardoso (S. J. da Silva 2001) and continued to be when they were proposed by Lula.

What the developments of the second phase meant was that CSOs engaged in these kinds of activities without presuming they would share positions with the administration or that there would be significant new funds available for programs they defended. In other words, it was a phase of disillusionment with and diminished expectations for a national PT administration. Lula's honeymoon with these organizations had lasted only some eight months to a year before falling apart largely over substantive policy issues, reinforced by CSOs' inability to turn participatory opportunities into the substantive outcomes they wanted.

Phase 3: Representative Democracy Has Failed—But Don't Impeach Lula

CSOs continued in this mode until the corruption allegations of June to August 2005 immobilized the country and the administration. These allegations are detailed in other chapters, so my focus here is on the contradictory CSO response. CSOs, already disappointed with the administration, felt the corruption scandals confirmed their suspicions about the defects of representative democracy as practiced in Brazil. In its place, they urged more direct political mechanisms that could translate popular pressures directly into policy without the warping interference of electoral and party governance. On the other hand, they were reluctant to take strong negative stands against the administration, especially as these would have aligned them on the wrong side of the longstanding divide between the PT and the "elites" or the cleavage between the PT and the PSDB. Their hesitance to demand Lula's removal was part of what protected him from serious investigation and impeachment proceedings.

In one of the first responses from CSOs to the corruption allegations, a new "Letter to the Brazilian People" presaged all these positions. Organized by the Coordination of Social Movements, many of Brazil's most important CSOs signed this letter, dated June 22, 2005.[11] As the crisis continued, Lula himself initiated a turn to CSOs, going back to the ABC region of São Paulo, the industrial ring around the city core where he began his union activities, in order to receive their support in late July (*Estado de São Paulo*, July 25, 2005). Various organizations declared their willingness to defend Lula in the streets if the elite opposition tried to push him out early. The *Folha de São Paulo* newspaper interviewed fifty-seven leaders of civil society several weeks later and found that only thirteen of them supported an impeachment investigation (August 14, 2005). The CSM coordinated a march of about ten thousand people in mid-August, described in news reports as a march in support of Lula (*Estado de São Paulo,* August 17, 2005). One leader stressed, however, that it was a march in support of democracy rather than of Lula and a reflection of the CMS's conclusion that even the Lula government was better than returning to be in the political opposition. Their support had conditions: "[The CMS] was very strong in its meeting with Lula, telling him they would not continue to support him if he continued with Palocci [the finance minister]."[12] Two days later, the PT-dissident parties PSTU (Partido Socialista dos Trabalhadores Unificado) and PSOL, along with university professors and some social movements, led a march of the same size calling for Lula's ouster (*Estado de São Paulo,* August 20, 2005). In this context, six opposition parties met and concluded that the "political climate" needed to initiate impeachment did not exist (*Folha de São Paulo,* August 16, 2005). Across South America, almost a quarter of presidents since 1978 have been removed from office before the end of their term. All of the successful removal processes included mass popular protests demanding the president go early, so the absence of such protests was likely decisive in Brazil as well (Hochstetler 2006). It is worth noting that the mass protests that helped bring down President Collor in 1992 were much larger, including millions of participants.

The defense against his removal from office was not a free pass for Lula, however. CSOs criticized his government hard for its corrupt practices, made all the more bitter for them because the corruption was so closely linked to the parliamentary governing strategy they decried. In August, Abong called for all those guilty to be punished; the organization lamented the PT's failure to turn a twenty-year social project of democracy, social transformation, and social justice into an effective governing project and pointed to the need for mechanisms of direct and participatory democracy to replace representative democracy. Joining all CSOs and all social sectors in vast mobilizations was its overarching solution (*Informes Abong,* August 9–15, 2005). The two hundred thousand people who joined in September's "cry of the excluded" reached very similar conclusions in their manifesto (Grito dos Excluídos, 2005), as did an October 2005 Popular Assembly, organized by groups related to the Catholic Church. The Popular Assembly also sent a very critical and personal letter to Lula telling him that his failure to comply with his agrarian reform promises "is an affront to the families in camps and brings shame on your government" (*Jornal dos Trabalhadores Rurais Sem Terra* 256, October 2005).

In 2006, twenty umbrella organizations—whose members include thousands of CSOs—drafted a detailed set of reform proposals. The proposals cover reforms in direct, participatory, and representative democratic spheres, as well as communications and the judiciary (*Reforma Política*). They were discussed in April at the Brazilian Social Forum and received their final formulation at the end of November. The timing is noteworthy, since it ignored the Brazilian electoral calendar, with national elections in October; CSOs also did not seek endorsement from any candidates. Both the proposals and the process reflect themes of the third stage: notably, continued interaction with the representative democratic sphere mixed with a profound skepticism of it. To give just one concrete example, proposal 1.3 calls for both the national Congress and popular referendums to approve all agreements signed with international financial institutions.

CSOs' behavior in the elections themselves also reflected these views. In April 2006, the CMS spurned the PT's request for a direct endorsement of Lula's candidacy for re-election, even as the PT leadership stressed the need for social movements to support Lula in the streets if impeachment threats moved forward (Glass 2006). The organizations were divided internally between supporters of especially the PT and PSOL, and many of them do not take formal positions as organizations in any elections.[13] None of the organizations that have historically been most closely associated with the PT formally endorsed Lula's candidacy in the first round, although the CUT did in the second. Yet even in the first round—the CMS's major electoral event, meant to put forward a "Brazilian Project" of sovereignty, national development, democracy, and rights—included an insistence that Brazil should not return to the "*entreguista* [roughly, sell-out] neoliberal rightist" days of the PSDB-PFL alliance. There is no data on how members of these organizations actually voted as individuals, although it is likely that they are among the members of the electorate whose votes for other leftist parties in the first round prevented Lula's victory then—before a second-round vote for him over the PSDB.

The Future of the CSO-PT Relationship

This chapter has documented that ways the PT's first national administration strained and even broke many of the party's historic ties to civil society organizations. The roots of estrangement were substantive, in that CSOs did not manage to "make a real leftist out of Lula." CSOs' inability to use participatory opportunities to gain their desired policy outcomes—which they had thought they shared with Lula and the PT—left them disillusioned with consultative strategies. The corruption and scandals that permeated the administration knocked out the third leg of the PT's historic political project—its reputation for probity. In these ways, many CSOs lost their longstanding presumption that helping the PT reach ever-higher offices was a sound political strategy. This conclusion takes up the question of what these developments mean for Brazilian democracy as a whole.

In terms of partisanship and electoral behavior, there is now considerably more fluidity on the political Left. Where the PT had once monopolized the partisan commitments of many CSOs, there is now much more real competition for them. In both partisanship and voting, other leftist parties now represent the first choice of some of the PT's historic supporters. Lula's first-round shortfall in his bid for reelection is vivid evidence for this. This is likely to increase overall electoral volatility in Brazil, especially in the various electoral contests that follow proportional representation electoral rules. Yet there are limits to this fluidity. The new dissident parties picked up some votes in 2006, but neither surpassed the 5 percent threshold needed for full political rights in the legislature. In addition, even those most disappointed with the PT stand with it or at least do not join its opponents when political choices become polarized. Polarization has been clearest in presidential politics, where the PT and PSDB have fought for the heavyweight title in every election since 1994. The second round of the presidential election in 2006 is the latest example of this kind of face-off. Most CSOs' interpretation that impeachment of Lula would translate into a PSDB electoral victory helped to save his presidency. Thus in contests that can be cast in "mass versus elite" terms, CSOs and their sympathizers are likely to still swing to the PT.

This chapter has focused on *organized* civil society and its partisan relationships, but CSOs' relations with unorganized citizens are also highly relevant for assessing their impact on Brazilian democracy. The CSOs discussed here number in the tens of thousands and represent several million citizens fairly directly—still, only a fraction of Brazil's 190 million people. They are demanding, often radical, contentious, and sometimes use tactics that other Brazilians do not approve. The many poor Brazilians who apparently re-elected Lula on the strength of regular handouts like the Bolsa Família program (Hunter and Power 2007) appear indifferent to CSOs' critique of those kinds of programs as very weak alternatives to real substantive change. At the same time, those same poor Brazilians —as well as Brazilians of other classes—make regular use of many services CSOs provide, and some of them join their mobilizations. They count on the more active CSOs to speak for social interests in the councils and consultative processes that still flavor Brazilian politics.

CSOs' most important contribution to Brazilian democracy may lie in the role they play for the subset of Brazilians whose critique of representative democracy is very strong. They are deeply disappointed with the meager returns of an electoral win and with the party that carried their hopes of transformation for twenty years. Yet they are not promoting any of the undemocratic or violent options so often considered in Brazil historically. Whether plebiscites, recalls, and continued joint mobilizations can succeed in achieving the changes they want is unknown, but they want to try them. Borrowing from Reginaldo Moraes, who in turn borrows from the MST itself, "The Brazilian government should give thanks to God for the fact that this movement exists; if not, the wretches of the countryside (and the city) would have only the options of crime or suicidal political and social strategies" (Moraes 2005, 202). Given that many ordinary Brazilians no longer believe in meaningful change through elections, CSOs provide them an alternative route of representation, to at least express their preferences peacefully. The fact that Lula's first administration avoided any massacres of protesters or open confrontations with them, indeed welcomed them, is its half of the bargain.

PART II

The Institutional Debate in Brazil

4

Political Institutions and Governability from FHC to Lula

Fabiano Santos and Márcio Grijó Vilarouca

The predominant view about Brazilian political institutions until the 1990s, the decade in which Peter Kingstone, Timothy Power, and collaborators were preparing *Democratic Brazil*, was that it consisted of a dysfunctional political system. Institutional choices made during the National Constituent Assembly of 1988 were viewed as imposing serious constraints on governability. Authors focused on the combination of presidentialism with open-list proportional representation, which was thought to steer the system toward personalism, ad hoc coalitions and measures, clientelism, and pork-barrel politics (Power 2000). Taking an opposing tack—which subsequently stimulated a wealth of important studies on Brazilian congressional politics—Argelina Figueiredo and Fernando Limongi published a series of articles (1994, 1995a, 1995b, 1996) contending that presidents in Brazil negotiate with political parties, not with individual legislators. Moreover, they argued, behavior on the legislative floor is predictable and consistent, thus engendering governability. In this revisionist view, there is no institutional malaise inherent in Brazilian institutions.

We will review the literature on how the Brazilian political system has worked since the Constitution of 1988, then move beyond the period originally covered by *Democratic Brazil* in order to highlight the period represented by President Cardoso's second term (1999–2002) and the first term of Lula (2003–2006). In spite of rather common views that Brazil exhibits a difficult combination (Mainwaring 1993), signs of institutionalization can be found in the Brazilian political system. Though not without mixed tendencies, the political system displays a noticeable degree of stabilization and reasonable conditions for governability. The shortcomings of institutional design in Brazil do not justify the adoption of any radical reforms.

The Electoral and Party Systems

A number of criticisms have commonly been leveled against Brazil's electoral system. According to some analysts, the electoral system has had a direct role in bringing about a high level of inconsistency and fragmentation in the party system. Certain historical events have been important in the evolution of Brazil's party system, and the system has stabilized around five relevant parties in the several layers of electoral competition. Two of these, the PT (Partido dos Trabalhadores) and the PSDB (Partido da Social Democracia Brasileira), have played a leading role in recent presidential contests.

Electoral System and Inter-Party Alliances

Brazil has twenty-seven national electoral districts with legislative contingents of varying sizes, which coincide geographically with the states. However, the share of seats in the Chamber of Deputies allotted to the states does not reflect their share of the country's inhabitants, due to a constitutional clause that provides for the minimum magnitude of eight and the maximum magnitude of seventy seats for each state. A key feature of any electoral system is its district magnitude. The average magnitude of Brazilian districts is quite high (about nineteen seats).

Thus, the system does not restrict the formation of small parties, even when we consider the smallest districts. On the other hand, Nicolau (1996) has emphasized some properties of Brazil's electoral system that clearly favor the largest parties, counteracting party fragmentation. One of these properties is the d'Hondt formula of highest averages, the most disproportional proportional representation (PR) formula currently in use among the world's democracies. Also, votes cast for parties that do not reach the electoral quota are not included in the distribution of seats, which is another factor that acts in favor of large parties.

Yet, these mechanical effects of the system may be counteracted by rules that permit the formation of interparty alliances (known as *coligações*). The singularity of such alliances in Brazil lies in the fact that seats are not allocated according to the vote totals of each party within the alliance. Being an open-list system, there is no previous rank ordering of candidates by the parties, and it is the number of *personal* votes received by each candidate that determines the allocation of seats within lists. In addition, Brazilian voters can either choose a party or a candidate.[1] As a result, vote transfer across parties occurs when a candidate obtains a large number of personal votes but her party does not reach the electoral quota (the total attained by the alliance considered as a single party is what matters in this calculation). At the individual level, this means a voter could cast a ballot for candidate A but end up helping to elect candidate B, whom she dislikes. At the ideological level, votes in progressive parties might help elect conservative candidates and vice versa.[2]

It is then necessary to evaluate the consistency of *coligações* as a possible indicator of the party system's consistency as a whole. For the 1986–1994 period, Schmitt (2000) has found that around two-thirds of the alliances were forged entirely within the same ideological family. Machado (2005) has recently estimated the rates of ideological consistency. In 1994, consistent alliances were the plurality, 39.4 percent of the total; inconsistent ones were 27.1 percent; lastly, semiconsistent alliances were 19 percent.[3] Alliances between parties of the three ideological blocs added up to 14.5 percent (Machado 2005, 76).

If we add up consistent and semiconsistent *coligações*, we obtain the considerable rate of 58.4 percent, sufficient to say that ideology is not irrelevant in the Brazilian political landscape. According to Machado, the primary goal of party alliances is vote maximization; the secondary goal is to maintain associations within the same ideological bloc. Using a different approach, Krause (2005) compares electoral strategies in the elections for governor and president in the 1994–2002 period. According to her study, there is a very weak correlation between the sorts of alliances struck in these contests, which would imply a fragile process of nationalization of parties.

Two points are worth mentioning here. First, federal heterogeneity has to be taken into account, given the obstacles it imposes on coordination of party strategies across different sorts of contests—a point further highlighted by the relative weight of parties in different states. Secondly, as we saw, most alliances in the chamber elections are consistent, or more or less consistent, a fact that has direct consequences for the workings of national politics. This point must be stressed: there is a high level of consistency in the alliances, despite a large supply of parties for the competition.

In spite of the indicators discussed above, in 2002 the Supreme Electoral Court (TSE) restricted severely the autonomy of parties in entering into alliances. The so-called verticalization ruling, which was in force in the 2002 and 2006 national elections, mandated that parties allied behind a single presidential candidate must replicate such an alliance at the state level or else compete alone. For instance, if party A had launched a presidential candidate allied with party B, neither of them could ally at the subnational level with any gubernatorial candidate from party C, if party C had also happened to nominate a presidential contestant. In practice, however, parties who did not present or support a presidential candidate were free to make any kind of alliance, which induced some parties to skip the 2002 and 2006 presidential contests altogether.[4]

In reality, the TSE initiative failed to nationalize elections or to force the formation of consistent alliances, mainly because the decision to nominate a national candidate fell hostage to the strategies of the subnational (state-level) directorates of the political parties. Besides, parties learned to circumvent the law's effects in the states by giving "informal" support to candidates of other parties. Given the influence of federalism over the party system and the overall resistance of legislators to rules that restrain their electoral discretion, it is hardly surprising that in early 2006, Congress passed a constitutional amendment ending *verticalização*. The rule will no longer apply in 2010, when parties will have once again enjoyed complete autonomy to form incongruent national and subnational alliances.

Open-List Proportional Representation

The Brazilian variety of open-list proportional representation (OLPR) has always prompted an array of criticisms. In contrast to closed-list systems, in which the party determines the order of candidates on the list, voters have complete freedom of choice to pick their candidates in Brazil. In closed-list systems, there is a clear disciplinary mechanism guiding the behavior of both candidates and future legislators, which is absent in the open-list variety. Besides, competitors in Brazil are usually in charge of their own campaigns, gathering financial resources on an individualized basis. It is thus a fair assumption that they will invest solely in their own personal reputations.[5]

Brazilian OLPR should thus be expected to lead to weak parties and personalized politics. The process would be further reinforced by the way candidates are selected in the states, without interference from national leaders and with few incentives to publicize ideological appeals. This general pattern would have harmful effects on the executive-legislative relationship, expressed in such phenomena as weak party discipline, parochialism, and pork-barrel politics, and, finally, by a low governmental capacity of the executive (Mainwaring 2001; Ames 1995a, 1995b, 2001).

In this rather bleak view of the Brazilian political system, the key assumption is an immediate correlation between incentives coming from the electoral arena and congressional behavior in the legislative arena. We will deal with the errors of that approach in two ways. First, there are certain tools available to the president and party leaders that run counter to both party fragmentation and parochial incentives from the electoral arena. Institutions, we argue, provide several mechanisms that favor governability. Secondly, we present empirical data about the behavior of political parties in the Chamber of Deputies.

Evolution of the Party System

Brazil's party system has tended to stabilize around five main parties. Table 4.1 displays a classification based on the relative size of parties in the chamber and on their representation across the federal units.[6] This has shifted since the transition to democracy. The 1982 and 1986 elections were still fought under the cleavage created during the authoritarian regime, in which the ARENA/PDS (Aliança Renovadora Nacional/Partido Democrático Social) was the party in power and the PMDB (Partido do Movimento Democrático Brasileiro) the main opposition party. However, a group of congressional representatives left the main promilitary party in 1984 to form the PFL (Partido da Frente Liberal) with the explicit goal of supporting the presidential ticket (in an indirect election) formed by top PMDB leader Tancredo Neves and José Sarney, a key political boss in the PFL.

The popularity of the Cruzado economic plan in 1986, which temporarily succeeded in promoting economic stabilization, was crucial to the strong PMDB showing in the year's election (the PDS, on the other hand, opposed the plan).

	Party size				
Year	Large[c]	Intermediate[d]	Small[e]	Micro[f]	Effective no. of parties
1982	PDS (49.1%) PMDB (41.8%)		PDT (4.8%) PTB (2.7%) PT (1.7%)		2.4
1986	PMDB (53.4%) PFL (24.2%)	PDS (6.8%)	PDT (4.9%) PTB (3.5%) PT (3.3%)	Six parties (3.8%)	2.8
1990	PMDB (21.5%) PFL (16.5%)	PDT (9.1%) PDS (8.3%) PRN (8) PTB and PSDB (7.6%) PT (7%)	PDC (4.4%) PL (3.2%) PSB (2.2%)	Eight parties (4.8%)	8.7
1994	PMDB (20.9%) PFL (17.3%) PSDB (12.1%) PPR (10.1%)	PT (9.6%) PP (7%) PDT (6.6%) PTB (6%)	PSB (2.9%) PL (2.5%) PCdoB (1.9%)	Seven parties (3%)	8.1
1998	PFL (20.5%) PSDB (19.3%) PMDB (16.2%) PPB (11.7%) PT (11.3%)	PTB (6%) PDT (4.9%)	PSB (3.7%) PL (2.3%) PCdoB (1.4%)	Eight parties (2.8%)	7.1
2002[a]	PT (17.7%) PFL (16.4%) PMDB (14.4%) PSDB (13.8%) PPB (9.6%)	PL (5.1%) PTB (5.1%)	PSB (4.3%) PDT (4.1%) PPS (2.9%) PCdoB (2.3%)	Eight parties (4.4%)	8.4
2006[b]	PMDB (17.3%) PT (16.2%) PSDB (12.9%) PFL (12.7%) PP (8%)	PSB (5.3%)	PDT (4.7%) PL (4.5%) PTB (4.3%) PPS (4.3%) PV (2.5%) PCdoB (2.5%) PSC (1.8%)	Eight parties (3.1%)	9.3

Table 4.1. Party Size and Nationalization in the Chamber of Deputies, 1982–2006

Source: Adapted from Nicolau (1996), IUPERJ.
Note: Center parties: PSDB and PMDB.
Leftist parties: PT, PCdoB, PSB, PDT, and PPS.
Rightist parties: PDS (which supported the military regime), PFL, PPB, PL, PP, PDC, and PTB.
[a]In 2002, the PSB, PDT, PPS, and PCdoB elected deputies in nine, twelve, ten, and ten federal units, respectively.
[b]In 2006, the PDT, PL, and PTB elected deputies in thirteen federal units and the PPS in fourteen units.
[c]Represented in more than 2/3 of federal units and 10 percent or more of seats in the Chamber of Deputies.
[d]Represented in 1/3–2/3 of federal units and 5–10 percent of seats in the Chamber of Deputies.
[e]Represented in 20–33 percent of federal units and 1–5 percent of seats in the Chamber of Deputies.
[f]Represented in up to 20 percent of federal units and <1 percent of seats in the Chamber of Deputies.

According to Lima Jr., this election "can be seen as still a part of the two-party cycle—as a final act—once it is in it that the electoral transference of institutionalized power to the PMDB takes shape, with the defeat of ARENA-PDS" (1993, 55)

In 1988, another party split—the foundation of the PSDB (Partido da Social Democracia Brasileira)—helped reshape the party system (the party began its existence with 7.6 percent of the deputies). Among several causes, the split from the PMDB was caused by the group's stance on key constitutional issues, especially the length of President Sarney's term and the conflict over the system of government (and also by the ultimate failure of stabilization policies, which threatened the PMDB electorally). Thus, a significant share of the fragmentation in the late 1980s was caused mainly by intraelite disputes.

In February 1989, Fernando Collor, a politician with a strikingly antiparty profile, founded the PRN (Partido da Reconstrução Nacional) with the goal of running for president.[7] Congressional elections in the following year showed a steep increase in party fragmentation, with no fewer than nineteen parties winning seats in the Chamber of Deputies. From this point on, a significant proportion of the fragmentation derived from electoral competition itself. However, beginning in 1994, we can notice the relative consolidation of the party system around four strong parties—PMDB, PFL, PSDB, and PT—and, to a certain degree, the PPR/PPB/PP (Partido Progressista Reformador/Partido Progressista Brasileiro/ Partido Progressista, the direct descendant of the PDS). According to our classification, these parties have more than 10 percent of chamber seats and elected deputies in more than two-thirds of the states. Taken together, these five parties combined were jointly responsible for 73 percent of the seats between 1994 and 2002.

Data presented in table 4.2 help reinforce our argument. In Lula's first year in office, the five major parties controlled 84 percent of the senate seats, 77.8 percent of the mayoralties, 69.2 percent of the state capitals, and 63.1 percent of the seats in state legislatures. Two parties from this group, PMDB and PFL, began the democratic regime in 1985 with their national machines already fully structured. The 1994, 1998, 2002, and 2006 presidential elections were fought mostly between two later arrivals, the PT and PSDB (see Power, this volume).

Parties in the intermediate category are the hardest to predict in terms of evolution. Their viability and eventual growth will be very influenced in the short term by viable presidential bids and electorally successful alliances. Recently, the medium-sized and small parties were greatly assisted when the Supreme Court struck down an electoral threshold that had been scheduled to come into effect with the elections of 2006.

Table 4.2. Party Shares of Other Major Elective Offices, 1994–2006

	Year	*PMDB*	*PFL*	*PSDB*	*PT*	*PP*	*PDT*	*PTB*	*PSB*	*PL*	*PPS*	*Others*
President	1994	4.4		54.3	27	2.7	3.2					8.4
% votes	1998			53.1	31.7						11	4.2
	2002			23.2	46.4				17.9		12	0.5
	2006			41.6	48.6		2.6					7.2
Senate	1994	27.2	22.2	13.6	6.2	7.4	7.4	6.2	1.2	1.2	1.2	6.2
% seats	1998	33.3	19.8	24.7	8.6	6.2	2.5	0	3.7	0	1.2	0
	2002	25.9	23.5	14.8	16	2.5	4.9	2.5	4.9	2.5	1.2	1.2
	2006	16	24.7	16	14.8	1.2	6.2	6.2	4.9	3.7	2.5	3.8
Governors	1994	9	2	6	2	3	2	1	2	0	0	0
(N)	1998	6	6	7	3	2	1	0	2	0	0	0
	2002	5	4	7	3	0	1	0	4	0	2	1
	2006	7	1	6	5	1	2	0	3	0	2	0
Assemblies	1994	19.6	15.1	9.1	8.8	10.8	8.4	6.9	4.2	4.8	0.3	12
% seats	1998	16.6	16.2	14.5	8.6	10.1	6.2	7.5	4.4	4.7	2	9.2
	2002	12.5	11.5	13.1	13.9	8.8	5.9	5.9	5.6	5.8	3.9	13.1
	2006	15.6	11	14.6	11.8	5	6.4	4.6	5.7	3.2	4	18.1
Mayoralties	1996	1,295	934	921	110	625	436	382	150	222	33	895
(N)	2000	1,257	1,028	990	187	618	288	398	133	234	166	260
	2004	1,060	789	871	400	449	306	423	175	383	306	398
Mayoralties	1996	5	4	4	2	4	3	1	3	0	0	0
of state	2000	4	3	4	6	1	2	1	4	1	0	0
capitals (N)	2004	2	1	5	9	0	3	1	3	0	2	0

Source: Nicolau (1996), IUPERJ, and TSE.

Note: 2002 and 2006 presidential vote is for first round only.

The Electorate: Volatility and Party Identification

Examining several surveys conducted between 1989 and 2002, Carreirão and Kinzo (2004) found that on average, 46 percent of voters (ranging from 41 percent to 54 percent) identified with some party. The authors dispute the literature that suggests that such preferences are transitory and hostage to short-term electoral pressures. They observed a relatively small variation in party-identification rates in the period, with the exception of 1989 and 1990, in which the outsider Fernando Collor rose to prominence. Based on the surveys, the authors conclude, "Even if high rates of party identification are not to be found, there is a reasonable degree of stability of these preferences, with variations that are not abrupt" (Carreirão and Kinzo 2004, 13).[8]

Furthermore, Santos and Vilarouca (2004) have found in a survey that voters were able to discern differences between political parties on the issue of inequality. An average of 44 percent of voters could identify some informational content in the party labels. Responses formed a certain pattern around the images associated with specific parties (contrasting the PT to the PFL and center parties). Strikingly, this view was prevalent not only among in interviewees who identified with some party but also among those who express no party preference.

If these figures still fall short of showing a fully stable and structured party system, they are far from irrelevant. Key aspects of the institutional-legal framework of the Brazilian political system, such as a high number of parties and the intense formation of alliances between them—not to mention the behavior of the political elite itself, with feverish party-switching coupled with party mergers and splits—should logically hamper any exercise of political awareness with regard to party identification (Ames, Baker, and Rennó, this volume). And yet, this is not the case, according to the data shown above and the available evidence concerning electoral volatility.

It is frequently suggested that the party system is poorly institutionalized due to an unstable preference structure in the electorate. Peres (2002) has acknowledged that the rate of electoral volatility in Brazil is much higher than in Europe, but typical for Latin America. However, he claims that electoral instability is not high enough to "prove" the assertion that the party system does not shape electoral preferences. He argues that in the case of recent democracies, where electors and even leaders are still structuring and forming preferences, the rates of volatility should be used more cautiously. Besides, in the Brazilian case the large supply of party options is a fact that may intensify electoral competition. The author

Table 4.3. Ideological and Electoral Volatility in Chamber of Deputies Elections, 1982–2002

	1982–1986	*1986–1990*	*1990–1994*	*1994–1998*	*1998–2002*	*Average*
Party volatility	35.3	35.4	19.5	14.5	15.2	23.9
Ideological volatility	11.5	19.8	6.4	1.5	10.3	9.9

Source: Data kindly shared by Paulo Peres.

Note: The index of party volatility corresponds to the module of the difference between each two elections calculated for all parties, divided by 2. In the calculation of ideological volatility, we consider the parties that belong to the same ideology as a single party/ideological bloc, keeping the algebraic expression.

calls attention to such features as the huge territorial area, with considerable regional diversity and federalism. These features induce the existence of "distinct speeds of institutionalization of the party system" (2002, 28).

Both electoral and ideological volatility increased between 1982 and 1990, subsequently falling in the two elections won by Fernando Henrique Cardoso (PSDB). The formation of a heterogeneous alliance by Luiz Inácio Lula da Silva (PT), who invited several right-of-center parties into his fold, coincided with a renewed increase of ideological volatility in 2002. Thus alliances struck by the PT and the PSDB have brought together political forces from different ideological blocs, in a move that has been crucial to structuring the political system. To sum up, we can simplify the debate by asking whether the system is efficient in organizing different ideological alternatives. "In thc Brazilian case, a relatively high party electoral volatility coexists with a relatively low ideological electoral volatility, which means that the party system organizes preferences in ideological terms and that there is an intense competition between parties that belong to the same ideological bloc. Hence the system is competitive and the largest competition takes place among parties that share the same ideology" (Peres 2002, 42).[9]

Executive-Legislative Relations and (Un)Governability

Cabinet Formation under Coalitional Presidentialism

Several scholars have noted the negative effects of presidentialism combined with a multiparty system on governability. According to Mainwaring, "the combination of presidentialism, a fragmented multiparty system, [and] undisciplined parties" are not—under Brazil's system of "robust federalism"—compensated by the institutional powers granted to the president, should he endeavor to muster a stable base of support (1997, 56). Another prediction with wide currency in the literature is that parliamentary systems provide strong incentives to the formation of governing majority coalitions, coupled with the expectation that parties with cabinet portfolios will act cohesively on the floor. All this stands in marked contrast with the expected result for separation-of-powers regimes: unstable parliamentary bases of support for the executive, dependent on ad hoc coalitions.

Notwithstanding such expectations, it can be shown that Brazilian governments in the two democratic periods (1946–1964 and 1985–present) have striven to build cabinets that reflect the strength and relative weight of parties in Congress (Abranches 1988; Meneguello 1998; Amorim Neto 2000). Even though they lack the dissolution threat inherent in parliamentary systems, presidents can promote cabinet changes in order to build and rebuild their congressional support.

Basic data about all the governing coalitions formed between 1985 and 2006 are shown in table 4.4. Most administrations fashioned cabinets with enough parliamentary support for the passage of their agendas in the Chamber of Deputies.

Even though the Collor administration was not particularly fond of coalitional strategies in the beginning, the president surrendered to political forces in Congress afterward, which can be seen by his final attempt to create a more inclusive cabinet. Both the Cardoso and Lula governments strove to maximize the proportionality between the distribution of ministries and the parties' relative weight within governing coalitions, although the size of Cardoso's coalition was larger than Lula's.[10] Lula's coalition held 49.3 percent of the seats in the chamber at his inauguration in January 2003, but by the end of that year he was already negotiating the entry of the PMDB into the governing coalition. This inclusion of the PMDB brought the coalition up to the three-fifths majority necessary for passing constitutional amendments.

In the federal Senate, for instance, Cardoso's coalition could nearly always rely on a formal base of support above 70 percent of senators, with the exception of 1998. Nonetheless, President Lula's ranks were always insufficient to approve constitutional changes, which forced him to reiterated negotiations with the opposition. The key point to be emphasized here is that the veto ability of the opposition in the Senate (in practice a situation of divided government) did not imply a legislative deadlock—the dreadful state of affairs that is considered intrinsic to systems of separation of powers in the most pessimistic evaluations of Brazil's political system.

Table 4.4. Presidential Cabinet Formation from Sarney to Lula

Presidents and cabinets	*Duration*	*Parties with cabinet posts*	*Cabinet coalescence rate*	*Joint size of cabinet parties in the chamber (%)*	*Nonpartisan ministers (%)*
Sarney I	03/85–02/86	PMDB, PFL, PTB, PDS	0.66	93.5	18
Sarney II	02/86–01/89	PMDB, PFL	0.64	69.3	14
Sarney III	01/89–03/90	PMDB, PFL	0.41	53.3	35
Collor I	03/90–10/90	PMDB, PFL, PRN	0.40	50.3	60
Collor II	10/90–01/92	PFL, PDS, PRN	0.40	29.6	60
Collor III	01/92–04/92	PFL, PDS	0.30	26.2	60
Collor IV	04/92–10/92	PFL, PDS, PSDB, PTB, PL	0.46	43.7	45
Itamar I	10/92–01/93	PMDB, PFL, PSDB, PTB, PDT, PSB	0.62	61.6	20
Itamar II	01/93–05/93	PMDB, PFL, PSDB, PTB, PDT, PSB, PT	0.59	67.4	38
Itamar III	05/93–09/93	PMDB, PFL, PSDB, PTB–PSB	0.51	53.3	38
Itamar IV	09/93–01/94	PMDB, PFL, PSDB, PTB–PP	0.48	58.6	52
Itamar V	01/94–01/95	PMDB, PFL, PSDB–PP	0.22	55.3	76
Cardoso (1) I	01/95–04/96	PSDB, PMDB, PFL, PTB	0.57	56.3	32
Cardoso (1) II	04/96–12/98	PSDB, PMDB, PFL, PTB, PPB, PPS	0.60	76.6	32
Cardoso (2) I	01/99–03/99	PSDB, PMDB, PFL, PTB, PPB, PPS	0.70	74.3	23.8
Cardoso (2) II	03/99–10/01	PSDB, PMDB, PFL, PPB, PPS	0.59	68.2	37.5
Cardoso (2) III	10/01–03/02	PSDB, PMDB, PFL, PPB	0.68	62.0	31.6
Cardoso (2) IV	03/02–12/02	PSDB, PMDB, PPB	0.37	45.1	63.2
Lula I	01/03–12/03	PT, PSB, PDT, PPS, PCdoB, PV, PL, PTB	0.64	49.3	17.2
Lula II	01/04–07/05	PT, PSB, PPS, PCdoB, PV, PL, PTB, PMDB	0.51	62.0	14.3
Lula III	06/05–08/05	PT, PSB, PCdoB, PV, PTB, PMDB, PL	0.56	59.8	15.1
Lula IV	08/05–09/05	PT, PSB, PCdoB, PV, PTB, PMDB, PL	0.55	69.0	19.3
Lula V	09/05–04/06	PT, PSB, PCdoB, PV, PTB, PMDB, PP, PRB, PL	0.52	69.0	19.3
Lula VI	04/06–	PT, PSB, PCdoB, PV, PTB, PMDB, PP	0.52	58.4	22.5

Source: Data kindly shared by Octavio Amorim Neto.

Notes: Amorim Neto uses the indicator "cabinet coalescence rate" to show deviations of proportionality in the relation between party quotas in the cabinet and the size of party caucuses in the chamber. The index varies between 0, in which there is no correspondence linking the two variables, and 1, of perfect proportionality. The last column of the table indicates the percentage of ministers with no affiliation to any political party. The use of roman numerals refers to cabinets and arabic numerals refer to terms.

Besides satisfying party criteria, administrations have also tried to cope with federal diversity (Abranches 1988; Meneguello 1998). Academics and journalists alike have commonly made references to the influence of governors over the caucuses in the chamber. Thus, regional party subsystems are another relevant parameter in coalition building. The Southeast region has increasingly benefited from cabinet formation—in the Cardoso administration the region grabbed 67 percent of the ministries, with the Northeast a distant second (Meneguello 1998).

It is clear then that almost all Brazilian cabinets reflect a parliamentary majority. What can one say, however, about the discipline of propresidential coalitions in Congress? In the several governing coalitions analyzed by Amorim Neto (2000), party discipline is a function of the coalescence levels of each cabinet, the amount of time elapsed in the presidential term, and (depending on the party) ideological distance from the executive.[11] The outcome indicates that a greater coalescence rate has positive effects on the discipline of governing parties, but the same discipline decreases as the presidential term elapses. In addition to the distribution of ministries, as we will demonstrate below, the president and party leaders possess prerogatives that induce legislators to cooperate.

Presidential Agenda Powers

In the Republic of 1946, facing a legislative branch that possessed important decision-making discretion—and thus shared control of the legislative agenda with the executive (Santos 1997)—the most powerful asset available to the president was the use of patronage. Comparatively speaking, the 1988 constitution changed the balance of power drastically by awarding an array of agenda control tools to the executive branch. This dramatically increased the legislative approval rates of presidents. The administrations had lower rates of success (about 30 percent) in the pre-1964 period, while this relation becomes the reverse in the post-1988 period. Still more impressive is the great variation of these rates across governments in the first period (from 10 percent to 45 percent), while in the second period stability is the rule (from 65 percent to 72 percent). These findings suggest that recent institutional factors have played an important role, in spite of conjunctural factors and variations in the size of presidents' parties (Figueiredo 2000).

There is also greater discipline of governing parties in the post-1985 democracy. According to Santos (1997), part of the explanation lies in the origin of most of the legislative agenda, which is the executive, and in the speed of its consideration, typically through urgency provisions: in short, an imposed agenda.[12] The key difference between the two democratic periods then is that *patronage in tandem with agenda power* generates more solid congressional support in the current democratic era in comparison with the 1946 regime, in which presidents could resort only to the former resource.[13] The present pool of presidential agenda powers includes the right of exclusive introduction of bills in administrative and budgetary areas, the right to request urgency for bills, and especially the power to issue presidential decrees (provisional measures) with the force of law.[14]

Provisional Measures

Presidential decrees are the strongest form of agenda power. Theoretically, their use should be restricted to "urgent and relevant" matters, but they have come to be used even for routine problems of the administration. In accordance with the constitution of 1988, a *medida provisória* (MP) had immediate force of law and had to be passed in Congress within thirty days, or else lose effectiveness. In practice, however, the executive began to reissue expired decrees. The issuing and frequent reissuing of MPs permitted the executive to avoid the cost of forming majorities, transferring such collective-action costs instead back to the legislature.

Provisional measures strongly shape the pattern of executive-legislative relations. This pattern depends a great deal on the strategies chosen by the president, whether he chooses to form a coalition cabinet by handing out ministry posts to parties in proportion to their weight in parliament or to govern with weak linkages to congressional parties. In the former case, he will probably try to meet the interests of his supporting coalition and rule through ordinary legal means. Contrariwise, in the latter he is likely to nominate a noninclusive cabinet and issue original measures abusively (Amorim Neto 2000).

The Cardoso administration epitomizes the first case. Not only did the president form a cabinet with a reasonable degree of coalescence, but he permitted several reissued MPs to suffer piecemeal negotiated changes (Amorim Neto and Tafner 2002). President Collor, on the other hand, took the opposite direction right from the start. Congress reacted to his conduct by threatening to pass a bill that would restrict the scope of provisional measures, a move that softened the president's willingness to govern unilaterally (Power 1998b).

Additionally, provisional measures could protect legislators in the governing coalition from the effects of unpopular measures. According to Figueiredo (2000), with all the reissuing, party leaders would not take responsibility for the approval of decrees, though they partook in the changes made in their texts. For this reason, frequent reissuing should not be considered a congressional abdication of power. "Agenda power and control over the legislative process allow the governments to protect their supporting majority from unpopular decisions and to preserve policy agreements. In this sense, they foster concerted action between government and its supporting majority and consequently increased cooperation" (Figueiredo 2000, 12).

In 2001, the National Congress passed Constitutional Amendment 32, reformulating the use of MPs. Under the new arrangement, the measures are valid for a period of sixty days, at the end of which an extension of sixty days may be applied if the measure has not yet been passed in both houses. Crucially, if the MP is not passed within forty-five days after its publication, it goes to the top of the daily order of business of the house in which it is in, preventing evaluation of any other proposal until a vote is held. The aim of the amendment was to mitigate the effects of the executive's willingness to legislate unilaterally. Under this reasoning, the executive would send only relevant and urgent measures in order to avoid a legislative paralysis. But as is so common in matters related to political reform, the reality has come to be quite different. Instead of inhibiting the executive from issuing more MPs, the new rule produced a larger number of them by the end of the Cardoso administration, a pattern that continued under Lula (table 4.5).

At the same time, fourteen provisional measures were rejected in the previous administration, and ten under President Lula (another eight expired before voting due to a constitutional clause). Such rejections were rather rare under the old institutional arrangement, confirming the point about the political protection provided by the mechanism of reissuing, nonexistent in the current rule. Arguably, by eliminating reissuing and forcing a congressional decision on the measures, Amendment 32 brought about the possibility of an open and public conflict over them. Not surprisingly, Lula's reliance on decrees has stirred legislators to propose further constitutional checks on MPs.

Legislative Centralization

A further cause of centralization in the policy formulation process is the centralization within the legislature itself, as defined by the Chamber of Deputies' standing orders (*regimento interno*). In the chamber, the distribution of parliamentary rights is done via partisan criteria: the principle of party proportionality determines the make-up of the Directing Board and all committees. The stand-

Table 4.5. Original Provisional Measures (Presidential Decrees) by Administration

President	*Period*	N	*Monthly average*	*Total*	*Average for term*
Fernando Collor	Mar. – Dec. 1990	76	8		
	Jan. – Dec. 1991	9	0.75		
	Jan. – Oct. 1992	4	0.44	89	2.92
Itamar Franco	Oct. – Dec. 1992	4	1.33		
	Jan. – Dec. 1993	47	3.92		
	Jan. – Dec. 1994	91	7.58	142	5.26
Fernando H. Cardoso	Jan. – Dec. 1995	30	2.5		
	Jan. – Dec. 1996	41	3.42		
	Jan. – Dec. 1997	34	2.83		
	Jan. – Dec. 1998	55	4.58	160	3.33
FHC II, pre EC 32	Jan. – Dec. 1999	47	3.92		
	Jan. – Dec. 2000	23	1.92		
	Jan. – Sept. 2001	33	3.67	103	3.12
FHC II, after EC 32	Sept. 2001–Dec. 2002	102	6.8	102	6.8
Lula (entirely under EC 32)	Jan. – Dec. 2003	57	4.8		
	Jan. – Dec. 2004	73	6.1		
	Jan. – Dec. 2005	41	3.4		
	Jan. – Dec. 2006	69	5.8	240	5

Source: Presidency of the Republic.
Note: EC 32 refers to Constitutional Amendment 32, which altered presidential decree authority.

ing orders provide for a Council of Leaders, an organ of party leaders that has, along with the chamber president, control over the daily order of business.[15]

Through the use of urgency requests, party leaders direct the flow of legislative proceedings, bypassing committees and taking measures directly to the floor.[16] Unlike similar urgency requests used by the executive branch, these internal requests must be put to a vote and passed, though their deadlines are far shorter. Once approved, the request characteristically discharges a bill from the relevant committee or committees, bringing it to the floor for consideration.[17] In theory, this recourse can be initiated by a vote of at least one-third of the chamber's membership (or leaders representing this proportion), two-thirds of the members of any committee, or two-thirds of the Directing Board. In practice, this prerogative is nearly monopolized by party leaders, due to severe coordination problems plaguing backbenchers. The latter have, after all, only a minimal ability to shape the legislative agenda, since their leaders' signatures are representative enough to formally express party wishes (Figueiredo and Limongi 1999).

Furthermore, urgency requests severely restrict the right to propose amendments on the floor: amendments can only be considered if one-fifth of the deputies agree. Most of the urgency requests favor the executive; some 70 percent of them come from within Congress itself (Pereira and Mueller 2000). Interestingly, and confirming the key role exerted by party leaders in Cardoso's first term (1995–1998), the more extreme the median preference in the committee was in comparison with the median preference on the floor, the higher the probability of urgency requests being carried out (Pereira and Rennó 2001).

Committee assignments are handed down by the Directing Board in compliance with the written nominations of party leaders. According to Santos (2003), the selection of deputies is based mostly on their loyalty to the party on the floor. Both the committee and floor stages of legislative consideration are weakened as decision-making arenas, given that substantive issues are debated mostly within the Council of Leaders.[18] The participation of backbenchers is thus restricted to the final step of the legislative process, when the bill is put to the vote. The centralization favors the executive in reducing the uncertainties of the negotiation, for these would surely be heightened in a decentralized bargaining process (Figueiredo and Limongi 1999).

To highlight the scarcity of rights enjoyed by individual members, we draw attention to the speedy passage of issues on which there exists a prior agreement between party leaders and the administration—usually under urgency provisions. Moreover, bills introduced by the legislature itself (typically by individual legislators) take three times longer than executive bills to be passed. There are problems in the selection and deliberation due to congestion of measures and limited time. In sum, the highly centralized internal organization of the legislature is not optimized to deal with the demands of backbench legislators (Figueiredo and Limongi 1999).

The Electoral Connection: A Parochial Legislative Output?

Based on a certain kind of Mayhew-like "electoral connection" theory, an assessment with wide currency in the literature is that the predominant incentives in the Brazilian legislature favor the production of parochial policies (Ames 2001; Mainwaring 2001).[19] Nonetheless, recent empirical research on legislation produced in Congress does not confirm this expectation. Legislators do not focus on initiating bills with "particularized" benefits and "dispersed" costs. In truth, their effort is directed mainly toward bills of a national orientation (Lemos 2001; Ricci 2003).

In consonance with such analyses, Amorim Neto and Santos (2002) observed a large predominance of social issues of a national scope among the bills originated and passed in Congress. If we combine bills of national scope with bills of sectoral scope (regulating or benefiting professions and business sectors), this accounts for an impressive 85 percent of all bills. The authors emphasize, however, that the contents of these bills are restricted to small subjects, with little impact on the status quo: the concentration of powers in the executive branch implies that the president is the only relevant actor when it comes to innovating an agenda with a redistributive character.[20] We do not maintain, of course, that parochial incentives are nonexistent in the Chamber of Deputies (legislative decrees granting TV and radio concessions to municipalities are good examples of localism), but once again we note that the key aspect of legislative life is the centralization of the legislative process in the hands of party leaders and the president.[21]

Finally, one should ask whether the real focus of particularistic behavior might be the annual budget. The executive is the sole initiator of any budgetary bills and the recipient of most of the appropriations, which means that only a small slice of the budget is left over for congressional amendments. An array of rules protects the original proposal of the president; even the few expenditure authorizations that legislators obtain for themselves are dependent on the goodwill of ministries. In this regard, there has been a major controversy in the literature. Some scholars hold that authorizations buy support for the administration in key votes on the floor (Ames 2001; Pereira and Muller 2002), while others claim that the evidence is insufficient to support that assertion (Figueiredo and Limongi 2002).

In brief, the legislative arena is *not* institutionalized in a way that gives priority to the demands of individual members, either in terms of legislative production or agenda control. Rather, the system is structured so as to enhance governability, by centralizing the decision-making process.

Political Parties in the Chamber of Deputies

Empirical findings regarding party discipline allow us to expand the implications of our theoretical reasoning about executive-legislative relations in Brazil. We also examine two other issues: party switching and recommendations of party leaders in roll calls.

Positioning the Parties on the Legislative Floor

According to Figueiredo and Limongi (1999), it is possible to array political parties along an ideological continuum by analyzing the vote recommendations (*encaminhamentos*) of party leaders: that is, when leaders rise to instruct their members how to vote on the floor. They find that in the 1989–1998 period, the PPB, PFL, and PTB (Partido Trabalhista Brasileiro) are on the right; the PMDB and PSDB are center parties; lastly, the PDT (Partido Democrático Trabalhista) and PT are on the left. These parties account for almost 90 percent of the chamber seats in the decade analyzed. The assumption of this one-dimensional framework is that adjacent parties are more likely to give similar vote recommendations; conversely, the further apart the parties are on the continuum, the less likely is the occurrence of similar recommendations between them. By and large, this hypothesis is supported during the period analyzed by Figueiredo and Limongi, during which Brazil generally had center-right administrations opposed by a leftist bloc in Congress.

We have replicated Figueiredo and Limongi's procedure for Cardoso's second term and the Lula administration (to reflect recent partisan changes, we also added the PL [Partido Liberal] and PSB [Partido Socialista Brasileiro], whose joint share of seats increased to 10 percent under President Lula).[22] In the two terms of former president Cardoso, the pattern does not change significantly: vote recommendations clearly pit the center-right governing coalition against the Left. In table 4.6, we can confirm the hypothesis of ideological consistency in Cardoso's second term, but not for the early Lula period. The leader of the Partido Liberal joined the Left in most recommendations during the final four years of Cardoso's term (1999–2002), but the PL was then practically irrelevant, with only 2.4 percent of the chamber seats. This was in contrast to 2002, when the PL was the main electoral partner in Lula's alliance, supplying the vice-presidential nominee.

Ironically, this consistent pattern broke down with the ascension to the presidency of an ideological and highly structured party—the PT. Two right-wing parties, the PTB and PL, were brought into Lula's governing coalition. Even without controlling any ministries during Lula's first years in power, the PP (Partido Progressista), another rightist party, also supported the government on key votes.

Table 4.6. Similar Vote Recommendations from Party Leaders on the Floor (%)

	PFL	*PTB*	*PL*	*PSDB*	*PMDB*	*PDT*	*PSB*	*PT*
Cardoso administration II (1999–2002)								
PPB/PP	93	82	39	95	94	16	13	21
PFL		79	40	94	92	18	16	22
PTB			42	83	81	32	23	31
PL				39	41	69	69	65
PSDB					97	20	17	25
PMDB						21	17	26
PDT							82	82
PSB								85
Lula administration (2003–2004)								
PPB/PP	27	90	88	32	88	78	86	87
PFL		22	23	74	26	27	18	19
PTB			95	25	92	85	94	94
PL				27	92	87	92	93
PSDB					30	28	22	23
PMDB						82	89	90
PDT							87	88
PSB								98

Source: NECON database.

Part of the PMDB was induced (as usual) to follow the administration, but in 2004 the party joined formally the coalition. The two largest opposition parties, PSDB and PFL (which allied in the 1994, 1998, and 2006 presidential elections), displayed a rather weak level of coordination on the floor in 2003. Their leaders' recommendations coincided only 61 percent of the time in 2003, albeit increasing to 86 percent in the following year.

In fact, it is immediately apparent that an unprecedented phenomenon began to reveal itself under Lula. While all the previous governments of the current democratic regime—Sarney, Collor, Itamar, and Cardoso—exhibited clear ideological cleavages in the way party leaders recommended votes, this was no longer prevalent after the PT-led coalition took power in 2003. In the emerging pattern, party stances in Congress became less innately ideological and shifted instead toward a simple government-versus-opposition dynamic—reflecting the fact that the pro-Lula coalition brings together parties from across the ideological spectrum. Undoubtedly, this is a striking change in the workings of coalitional presidentialism in Brazil.

Party Switching

Party switching by federal legislators has been intense throughout the current democratic regime, regardless of the president in power. In the 1999–2002 period, 154 deputies (leaving out deputy substitutes) changed parties, which accounts for 30 percent of the chamber, a rate slightly higher than that of the previous legislative term (26.5 percent). The practice continued unabated during the Lula administration, with 158 deputies, about 31 percent of the total, changing parties. Some of them switched twice or more in a single legislative term, which was not unheard of in previous administrations.

Although the level of party switching is high, it is not as random as some might think. Congresspersons tend to switch to other parties *within the same ideological bloc* or, alternatively, into adjacent centrist parties.[23] The phenomenon occurs in a pattern that follows the electoral cycle. In the first year of the legislative term, for example, the switches are caused by postelectoral considerations such as presidential inducements (e.g., the composition of the cabinet) and parliamentary privileges (e.g., committee assignments). Municipal elections, which take place halfway through the quadrennial legislative term, also play a role in stimulating new formulas of political accommodation even in the first year. Party switching intensifies again in the third year of the legislative term, with the adjustments and deals aimed at winning reelection to the chamber in the following year (Melo 2000).

Undeniably, there is a strong tendency of migration toward the governing coalition. This point is crucial, since although the intensity of party switching may reduce the intelligibility of the party system and violate the will of the voters in certain respects, it has also greatly assisted each successive administration to increase the size of its support coalition in Congress. It is, in brief, another indicator of the centrality of the executive to the operation of the Brazilian political system.

Party Discipline

According to Ames (2001), Brazilian OLPR is prone to weak parties and personalized politics, resulting in overall indiscipline within the legislative arena. OLPR should prevent parties from controlling their candidates during cam-

Table 4.7. Party Discipline by Administration (%)

Party	*Sarney (1986–89)*	*Collor (1990–92)*	*Itamar (1993–94)*	*FHC I (1995–98)*	*FHC II (1999–2002)*	*Lula (2003–6)*
PT	98.8	96.7	97.8	97.1	98.9	94.4
PDT	93.5	92.9	91.0	91.5	94.3	90.5
PSDB	86.8	88.3	87.0	92.9	96.4	89.6
PFL	88.2	90.3	87.4	95.1	95.0	89.2
PPB/PP	85.2	90.9	87.4	84.3	91.2	84.1
PTB	79.5	84.6	83.9	89.7	87.0	86.8
PMDB	83.7	87.5	91.2	82.3	86.8	81.4
Mean score	88.0	90.2	89.4	90.4	92.8	88.0

Source: Figueiredo and Limongi (1999), as well as NECON database for FHC II and Lula.

Note: Party discipline is defined as the percentage of deputies who followed the recommendation of their floor leader in roll-call votes.

paigns and, later, their behavior as elected members of Congress, thus hampering any coherent aggregation of interests. An entirely different reasoning is developed by authors such as Figueiredo and Limongi (1999), who contest the notion that the inability to punish undisciplined members means that parties are irrelevant. As we have seen, the president and party leaders have several agenda control prerogatives that induce legislators to adopt cooperative behavior.

Table 4.7 displays the average percentage of deputies who followed the recommendations of their respective party leaders in roll-call voting. For the entire 1986–2004 period, the average discipline remained around 90 percent; this rate is significantly higher than what was observed in the 1945–1964 democratic regime (Santos 1997). Figueiredo and Limongi (1999) note that contemporary Brazilian rates of discipline are not far below what is found in other countries, even in Europe, where the most institutionalized party systems are to be found. According to the authors, one way of interpreting these data is to say that is that it is possible to predict the outcome of roll-call votes with 90 percent certainty simply by looking at party leaders' vote recommendations.

The two schools of thought discussed in this work have offered key contributions to the debate over the nature of party discipline. On the one hand, discipline rates based on roll calls might represent the final act of an intense bargaining process, as Ames (2001) has suggested. This fact is not in the least irrelevant, for the rates may not reveal transaction costs incurred by involved actors. On the other hand, it is also true that the discipline rates of the post-1985 period are consistently higher than the comparable figures for the earlier democratic regime (Santos 1997). We note that the first Brazilian democracy was presidential, federal, and used OLPR, just like the current one. However cogent Ames's argument may be, it does not address the puzzle arising from the variation between the two periods. But the research of Figueiredo and Limongi (1999) and Fabiano Santos (2003) offers an explanation for this puzzle. The explanation lies in the centralization of the decision-making process in the hands of the president and party leaders.

Implications for Political Reform

It is virtually impossible to summarize all the proposals for political reform and their proponents, ranging from academics and journalists to political actors themselves, many of whom have ready-made solutions to the country's institutional maladies.

In the National Congress, there is no shortage of political reform bills under discussion. Without going into every issue involved, we may point to four measures examined by a Senate special committee in 1999. They included the maintenance of the electoral threshold of 5 percent of the national vote (subsequently struck down by the Supreme Court in late 2006), the adoption of a mixed electoral system, the prohibition of alliances in proportional elections, and the removal of legislators from office if they leave their parties. On the other side of Congress, the Chamber of Deputies has been considering issues like the public financing of election campaigns, the adoption of a closed-list PR system (CLPR), the concept of "party federations" (that is, the idea that party alliances from a given election will be obliged to act as a single party for the following three years), and the requirement that candidates must be members of their parties for at least two years prior to the election.

Space considerations limit our ability to discuss each of these proposals, but nonetheless we wish to highlight two of them on account of their controversial, even radical, nature: the institution of a closed-list system and the recurrent idea of a mixed electoral system. In parallel fashion, we identify disagreements concerning both party alliances and the extent of restrictions on party switching.

The high uncertainty about electoral rules has generated a series of political expedients, usually with either short-term results or aims. One need only recall a few key examples. In 1997, Cardoso's governing coalition passed the right of re-election for the sake of its own continuation after the 1998 election. In 2002, the TSE ruled controversially in favor of the measure called *verticalização*, which Congress then overruled with a constitutional amendment in 2006. The "verticalization" of alliances will no longer be in force for the presidential election of 2010. The so-called electoral threshold, passed in 1995 and scheduled to take effect in 2006, was struck down only a month after the 2006 elections were held. As each term progresses, political rules are modified by temporary majorities (with the participation of the judicial system, through the Supreme Court and the Supreme Electoral Court). As Power (2000) noted in his contribution to *Democratic Brazil*, this is hardly the best way to institutionalize the political system, and similarly, the adoption of radical proposals may amount to no more than shots in the dark.

In our view, proposals for political reform should be carried out with prudence, preferably with surgical precision. First, the distortions coming from the electoral system should be addressed by setting an intra-alliance calculation to distribute seats in consonance with each party's contribution to the overall vote for the alliance. Second, stringent rules to punish party switching might be in order: for example, loss of public office for party switchers and a designated waiting period for affiliations to new parties.

In regard to the latter set of measures, the case of the Partido Liberal is instructive. The party was directly involved in the scandals that hit Lula's governing coalition in 2005 and had to face the negative spin of congressional committees of inquiry. Several party members left the PL to join a recently founded party. Contrary to the dominant view in the political media, these politicians seemed to understand that Brazilian voters *do* link parties with their legislators and candidates. If party labels are unimportant, as some claim, why take the trouble of changing one's skin? Strict rules to curtail party switching might thus stimulate a greater care in the selection of candidates and maximize concerns about the collective reputation of the party.

In conclusion, we should emphasize again that the Brazilian political system is far from chaotic in its workings. As we have shown here, the system presents important signs of institutionalization. Although we do acknowledge the existence of some distortions that hamper the system's intelligibility for voters, these shortcomings do not justify the adoption of any radical reforms.

5

Centering Democracy?

Ideological Cleavages and Convergence in the Brazilian Political Class

Timothy J. Power

In the presidential election of 1989, Luiz Inácio Lula da Silva was considered a leftist firebrand, propounding radical socialism at every turn. The campaign was laden with ideology, brinksmanship, and drama. "If I win, someone has to lose," Lula often remarked, in a thinly veiled warning to what he then referred to as the *burguesia*. The *burguesia* was grateful when Lula and the PT (Partido dos Trabalhadores) were defeated by Fernando Collor de Mello, a neoliberal populist whose economic proposals could not have been more different from Lula's. In 1994 and 1998, Lula was again defeated, both times by Fernando Henrique Cardoso (PSDB, Partido da Social Democracia Brasileira), whom Lula excoriated for having abandoned his once-progressive views and having allied with the political Right. Cardoso pursued a market-friendly reform agenda that was vehemently and unanimously opposed by the PT in almost every congressional vote. Polarization seemed to be the name of the game, one which the PT consistently lost.

However, in 2002, in his fourth run for the presidency, a newly moderate Lula—nicknamed *Lulinha Paz e Amor*—was finally victorious. Like Cardoso before him, Lula chose to ally with conservative parties in Congress and went on to implement an economic agenda so orthodox that his presidency was dubbed "Cardoso's third term." When Lula was challenged in 2006 by the PSDB's Geraldo Alckmin, foreign and domestic investors showed little interest in the campaign, perceiving that macroeconomic policy would remain largely the same regardless of the victor. Lula's victory margin of twenty million votes was so large and convincing that eleven political parties promised to support him in Congress in his second term. (Ironically, one of his more noteworthy supporters in the Senate—whose return to Brasília earned a favorable comment from the president—was none other than Fernando Collor de Mello.) In a speech shortly after winning re-election at age sixty-one, President Lula remarked,

> Today I am a friend of Delfim Netto [finance minister of the 1964–1985 military regime]. I spent twenty-odd years criticizing Delfim Netto, and now he is my friend, and I am his friend. Why am I saying this? Because I think this is the evolution of the human species. Those on the right are moving toward the center. Those on the left are becoming more social democratic, less leftist. These things blend together according to the amount of grey hair on your head, according to the responsibility that you have. There is no other way. . . . If you meet an elderly person who is leftist, it's because he's got problems. If you happen to meet a very young person who is right-wing, he's got problems too. When we hit 60 years of age, that's the point of equilibrium. Because we are neither one nor the other. We transform ourselves by taking the middle road. That's the road that must be followed by society. (Reuters, December 11, 2006)

The erstwhile ideologue of 1989, apparently, had now decreed the end of ideology in the Brazil of 2006. Whether sincere, or just a lighthearted mangling of Churchill, Lula's postelection remarks touched off a predictable firestorm of criticism from many graying *companheiros*.[1] But when interpreted against the backdrop of concrete political changes over the previous two decades, these presidential musings inspire some questions of empirical and theoretical import. How have ideological reputations and distances changed among Brazil's leading political actors? Have twenty years of democracy really attenuated any of the principal cleavages within the Brazilian political class, as Lula seems to suggest? If so, what accounts for these changes?

I explore these questions using data from five elite surveys conducted in Brasília between 1990 and 2005. Addressing these issues is not merely a retrospective exercise, because confirmation of ideological convergence in Brazil would have major implications for the country's future democratic development.

Why does convergence matter? First, at the most basic level of democratic legitimation, ideological convergence would suggest that the political class is unlikely to generate antisystem elements or a "disloyal opposition" (Linz 1978) that could threaten the survival of the regime. Second, although the configuration of the Brazilian political system features an excessive number of veto points and veto players (Ames 2001), attitudinal convergence makes it less likely that vetoes will actually be exercised on routine issues of policy. The sky may still have a lot of stars, but they prove easier to align. Third, ideological convergence lessens the danger of radical policy swings from one government to another, thus lowering the start-up costs for each new presidential administration and providing a relatively stable policy environment for economic and social actors. This is not to say that basic ideological disagreements can or should be eliminated, but if they can be *attenuated,* then the political capital that is saved thereby can be applied to pressing problems elsewhere in the polity and economy. As other chapters in this volume illustrate, Brazil has no shortage of policy challenges.

Using empirical tests of ideological convergence, I identify three principal cleavages that existed at the time of the transition of democracy in 1985 and trace their evolution over the next two decades. These include a traditional left-versus-right cleavage over the state's role in economic management), an authoritarian-democratic cleavage vis-à-vis the former military regime, and a political institutions cleavage over attitudes toward party building.

Background and Data Sources

I use elite surveys of the Brazilian national legislature to test for the presence of ideological convergence in the post-1985 democratic regime. I depart from the premise that the National Congress is an adequate proxy for the political class. This is intuitive. The national parliament of any modern democracy provides the central locus of action for its professional politicians: the only qualification to this would be if the assembly erected barriers to the entry of important factions and sectors. Brazil's legislature is highly inclusive; as Santos and Vilarouca (this volume) point out, the country uses a system of proportional representation with high district magnitudes, and there is no meaningful electoral threshold. It is true that less-developed states have enjoyed overrepresentation in Congress since the first transition to democracy in 1946, but this feature of the electoral system is by now largely inertial. The size and diversity of Congress—81 senators and 513 deputies drawn from twenty-seven states—allow an appropriate cross-section of the political class, and more importantly, Congress provides the roof under which national party politics is conducted.

It is also reasonable to assume that the fading relevance of the 1964–1985 military regime should facilitate greater consensus or convergence within the national political elite. The persistence of authoritarian-era cleavages colored Brazilian politics for at least the first decade after the transition to democracy (Hagopian 1996, Power 2000), but the Plano Real and the election of Cardoso in 1994 inaugurated a new phase of economic and political management. The Plano Real ended hyperinflation, the alliance between the PSDB and PFL (Partido do Frente Liberal) united forces that were on opposite sides of the coup of 1964, a broad reform agenda reshaped the overall development model in significant ways, and Cardoso's effective manipulation of "coalitional presidentialism" rewrote the playbook for the management of interparty alliances and power sharing. These changes had the effect of "rebooting" the democratic regime in the mid-1990s, sharply diminishing the relevance of the authoritarian-era cleavages that had shaped, for example, the writing of Brazil's new constitution in the late 1980s. This process has been reinforced by intergenerational population replacement within the political class: simply put, older politicians have died and younger ones have taken their place. The new recruits do not carry the baggage of 1964.

We should also recognize that Brazilian democracy since 1985 has had distinct phases of performance. Generalizing broadly, the first decade of democracy, but especially the period from 1987 to 1993, was characterized by poor macroeconomic performance and precarious governability. The period inaugurated with the Plano Real in 1994 was also characterized by formidable domestic and external pressures, including a major devaluation in 1999, but on the whole this second phase has objectively been more successful. Inflation has remained low, the party system has shown signs of consolidation, and there has been far greater stability in leadership. In the thirteen years from 1995 to 2008, Brazil has had only three finance ministers, compared to thirteen ministers in the shorter period from 1985 to 1994. Both Lula and Cardoso were elected and re-elected with solid majorities and worked together to engineer a successful transition between their administrations. Therefore, the more favorable socioeconomic conditions prevailing since the mid-1990s should facilitate greater convergence or consensus among political elites.

Table 5.1: Ratings of the Post-Transition Presidents as of Mid-2005 (Wave 5)

Question: I would like to know your general evaluation of various aspects of Brazilian democracy since 1985. Using a scale from 1 (most negative evaluation) to 10 (most positive evaluation), indicate your opinion of the following items. The administration of [president's name] . . . .

Presidency	*Mean score (1–10 scale)*
Sarney, 1985–1990	5.32
Collor, 1990–1992	3.35
Itamar, 1992–1994	5.99
Cardoso I, 1995–1998	6.53
Cardoso II, 1999–2002	5.80
Lula, 2003–mid-2005	5.84

Note: Maximum N = 124. About 80 percent of the survey responses were received prior to the eruption of a major corruption scandal affecting the Lula government beginning in June 2005.

The data employed here are drawn from survey instruments applied to all members of both houses of the Brazilian Congress in five waves, in each quadrennial session beginning with the Forty-eighth Legislature (1987–1991).[2] This was the first parliament elected under democracy, in 1986, and served simultaneously as the National Constituent Assembly in 1987–1988. In the Forty-eighth Legislature (survey applied in 1990), there were 249 respondents to the survey; in the Forty-ninth Legislature (1993), 185 respondents; in the Fiftieth (1997), 162; in the Fifty-first (2001), 139; and in the Fifty-second Legislature (2005), 124 respondents. Although the response rates have been declining over time (a problem increasingly facing all survey researchers in Congress), the samples are still very large, ranging from 21 percent to 43 percent of all federal legislators. Due to a minor but persistent problem of overresponse by the Left and underresponse by the Right, the results reported here have been reweighted slightly to reflect the actual partisan distribution of seats in Congress at the time of the surveys.

Table 5.1 illustrates that the respondents in wave 5 (2005) accept the idea that there have been peaks and valleys of performance in Brazilian democracy since 1985. Politicians rate the first two post-transition presidencies (Sarney and Collor) as significantly worse than the rest. The high rating given to Itamar Franco presumably reflects his strong finish rather than the whole period of his administration: in his final six months in 1994, he decreed the *Plano Real,* ended hyperinflation, and left office with stratospheric approval ratings. As of mid-2005,

Brazilian legislators rated the first administration of Cardoso (1995–1998) as the most successful phase of the current democracy.

Three Cleavages at the Time of the Democratic Transition

After twenty-one years of military dictatorship, Brazil became a democracy in 1985. The mid-1980s thus constitute a critical period in modern Brazilian history, reflecting the intersection of internal political change (liberalization and democratization), regional economic changes (the beginnings of structural adjustment in Latin America), and incipient, yet still uncertain, change in the international context (the final years of the Cold War). These years constituted the benchmark period for the current democracy, and not surprisingly, they ingrained several important cleavages into the Brazilian political class for years to come. In the analysis below, I privilege three such cleavages.[3]

The first is a conventional ideological cleavage, pitting Left versus Right and focusing mainly on the role of the state in economic management. At first glance there is nothing remarkable about such a cleavage—one which provided the central axis of politics almost everywhere in the twentieth century—but nonetheless, the democratic transition initially *sharpened* this division in Brazil. The transition to democracy coincided with the terminal crisis of the developmentalist state in Brazil, ending the long cycle of rapid growth in the 1950–1980 period; it occurred as Latin America was being pulverized by debt and recession and as neighboring countries were taking the first steps toward what would later become known as the neoliberal model; and it took place as a longstanding demand for the writing of a new constitution was about to be realized. Progressive parties and social forces, having been marginalized for two decades, seized the moment to advance a long list of "postponed" demands in economic management and social legislation. Conservative parties, rural oligarchies, and privileged business interests pushed back hard in the other direction (Dreifuss 1989; Nylen 1992; M. da Souza 1992). Fireworks ensued, but in the end the 1987–1988 National Constituent Assembly was largely viewed as a victory by the Left (Martínez-Lara 1996, 119). Subsequently, the center-right governing coalitions of the 1990s spent much of their political energies on reforming a constitution they criticized as anachronistically statist, and their counterattack ensured that the left-right cleavage of the 1980s was granted a long afterlife.

The second important cleavage of the mid-1980s was centered on the regime transition itself, particularly on nostalgia for and loyalties to the outgoing military regime. A large and growing sector of the political class embraced political democracy and sought the rapid elimination of what Fernando Henrique Cardoso termed the "authoritarian debris" (*entulhos autoritários*), by which he meant the policies, institutions, and legacies of military rule. Yet other sectors of the political elite adopted a resistant, foot-dragging approach to the legacy of dictatorship. While resigned to the fact of military withdrawal from executive power, these politicians remained unconvinced that democracy could provide either social order or economic development. Especially during the Sarney period, elements of the political Right sided with the armed forces in an attempt to maintain military prerogatives, including direct representation of the service branches in the cabinet and the right of the military to intervene to protect internal order (Stepan 1988). The effect of authoritarian nostalgia and impassioned defense of military prerogatives was nontrivial, given that both Sarney and the National Constituent Assembly did, in fact, rule in favor of the armed forces on several important issues, leaving the democratizing camp frustrated (Martínez-Lara 1996; Hunter 1997). Although this second cleavage (authoritarian nostalgia versus democratic renewal) overlaps with the first cleavage (statism versus economic liberalism) in important ways, the overlap is far from perfect, and the issues involved are analytically distinct.

The third and final cleavage to be examined here concerns the role of political institutions. Unlike the first two cleavages, this cleavage has never been salient electorally, but it has affected the conditions under which public policy could be shaped and implemented at the national level. At the time of the democratic transition, many observers commented on the challenges posed by the party and electoral systems in Brazil (e.g., Lamounier and Meneguello 1986; Reis 1988). Parties were held to be weak and the electoral system unrepresentative. Key decisions in institution building were made in 1985 and again during the Constituent Assembly of 1987–1988, and the debates surrounding those decisions revealed a divided political class. On the one hand, some political elites demanded reforms that would strengthen parties and improve accountability by limiting the freedom of action of individual politicians. On the other hand, many elites preferred a permissive set of representative institutions that would grant maximum latitude to politicians at the expense of parties—an orientation that Mainwaring (1999) termed "democratic libertarianism," or the idea that democracy meant freedom for free-floating politicians. Mainwaring noted that the first group of politicians was concentrated mostly on the left, while center and right factions favored catchall parties and a permissive electoral system.

This institution-building cleavage was seen as overlapping partially with ideology (Power 2000) but was also linked to the vote-getting patterns of individual politicians (Ames 2001). This cleavage was understandably salient during the constitutional convention—an eighteen-month laboratory of institutional design—and persisted throughout the first two decades of democracy, as continual crises led to recurrent calls for political reform.

This list of cleavages at the time of the transition to democracy is not exhaustive. Moreover, it obviously ignores historically or structurally given cleavages such as region and class. I do not intend to suggest that the three cleavages I examine here vacate the importance of older, embedded cleavages in Brazilian politics, nor do I intend to investigate the myriad ways in which these cleavages overlay one another. Rather, I wish to call attention to three cleavages in the mid-1980s that divided politicians as a class, were causally connected to the circumstances of the democratic transition itself, and posed major challenges to the sustainability of the post-1985 democracy for a number of years. The goal is to uncover evidence of change or convergence.

The Left-Right Cleavage

When one examines the evolution of the left-right cleavage over the first two decades of Brazilian democracy, there are several notable patterns. First, the Left has grown in electoral strength and in parliamentary representation. If we take the five most important left-wing parties (PT, PDT [Partido Democrático Trabalhista], PPS [Partido Popular Socialista], PSB [Partido Socialista Brasileiro], and PC do B [Partido Comunista do Brasil]) and look at the seats controlled by these parties in Congress, their joint representation increased from about 12 percent of Congress in 1990 to over 28 percent by 2005 (table 5.2). Second, even as the parliamentary Left has grown, there have been significant changes in the correlation of forces *within* the Left. It is easy to forget that in the 1987–1990 legislature that wrote the current constitution, Lula's PT was significantly smaller than Leonel Brizola's PDT.[4] Only in the 1994 election did the PT finally win more seats than the PDT for the Chamber of Deputies, and it is only from 1994 that we can say that the PT established itself as the hegemonic force on the Left (a fact later underscored when Brizola consented to serve as Lula's vice-presidential running mate in 1998). Third, despite the impressive growth of the Left in Congress, there has been relatively little change in the mean ideological self-placement of Brazilian legislators since 1990 (also shown in table 5.2). The

Table 5.2. Ideology and the Growth of the Parliamentary Left, 1990–2005

Survey Year	*1990 (N = 249)*	*1993 (N = 185)*	*1997 (N = 162)*	*2001 (N = 139)*	*2005 (N = 124)*
Mean self-placement, Congress	4.51	4.62	4.63	4.25	4.38
Size of left bloc (% seats in Congress)	11.9	16.4	18.4	20.9	28.3
PT seats as share of left bloc (%)	23.5	38.5	51.4	50.0	60.7

Note: Self-placement on a scale where 1 equals Left and 10 equals Right. Left parties are PT, PDT, PPS, PSB, and PCdoB.

Left has more than doubled in size, and the PT has assumed the vanguard, but neither of these trends seems to have shifted Congress sharply leftward nor changed its overall character. What is going on inside this black box?

Table 5.3, which presents the changing ideological reputations of four prominent parties, provides some clues. For reasons of space and simplicity, henceforth I will restrict myself to examining ideological change in the most influential left party (the PT), the two most important centrist parties (PMDB [Partido do Movimento Democrático Brasileiro] and PSDB), and the most prominent conservative party (the PFL).[5] These are also the four largest parties in Brazil and have jointly controlled about 60 percent of Congress in the years of Lula's presidency. Table 5.3, drawing on the five waves of survey research among federal legislators, presents the mean ideological placement of these four parties by respondents who are *not* members of the party being evaluated. This technique is used to neutralize the tendency of Brazilian politicians to locate their own party to the left of where everyone else locates it (Mainwaring et al. 2000). The placements, on a 1–10 scale where 1 is left and 10 is right, reflect the images of each party in the eyes of *other* elites, so the means can be interpreted as the "ideological reputations" of the parties within the Brazilian political class.

Table 5.3 presents a very rough map of the four main parties, but several features stand out. The PFL consistently anchors the right of the ideological spectrum, and its placements in wave 1 and wave 5 are virtually identical. The PSDB and PMDB, while sharing proximate positions in the center, nonetheless underwent an inversion of positions beginning with the legislature elected in 1994. When it was founded in 1988 by dissidents from the PMDB, the PSDB was considered a "social democratic" defection and acquired a center-left reputation for a short time, but this ended with the election of Cardoso (Power 2002). The

Table 5.3. Ideological Placement of Parties by Nonmembers, 1990–2005

Year	*PT*	*PSDB*	*PMDB*	*PFL*
1990	1.51	3.98	5.10	8.02
1993	2.02	4.39	5.17	7.73
1997	1.89	6.22	5.76	8.48
2001	2.27	6.30	6.19	8.59
2005	3.93	6.21	5.97	8.00

Note: Respondents were asked to locate all parties on a scale where 1 equals Left and 10 equals Right. The respondents' placements of their own parties were disregarded in the calculation of these means.

two biggest jumps in the table are the PSDB from 1993 to 1997 and then the PT from 2001 to 2005, and both are rightward. In both cases, the sharp revision to their reputations coincides with their *assumption of national power* (the PSDB with Cardoso in 1995, the PT with Lula in 2003). This is not surprising. To capture the presidency, both the PSDB and the PT abandoned earlier alliance strategies and accepted the support of right-of-center parties, thus muddying the ideological waters. Once in power, both parties used the presidency to implement pragmatic neoliberal policies that they had previously criticized. The effect on their ideological reputations was almost immediate: in making the transition to "governing parties," both the PSDB and the PT began to be seen as more conservative by their peers. Considerable distances have been traveled; as table 5.3 shows, the reputational space held by the PT in 2005 is essentially the same as that occupied by the PSDB fifteen years earlier.

This chapter is interested in convergence, so we need a measure of ideological distance between parties. Numerous distance measures are available, but one of the simplest to interpret is the one innovated by Giacomo Sani and Giovanni Sartori, who fortunately based their index on the same 1–10 scale used here. Their indicator aims to capture "the distance between any two groups of partisans, as measured by the (absolute) difference between their mean self-locations divided by the theoretical maximum, which, on the left-right scale in question, is 9" (Sani and Sartori 1983, 321). For example, the distance between two similar leftist parties at 2.00 and 3.00 on the scale, respectively, would be .11 (that is, the absolute distance of 1 divided by the theoretical maximum of 9), and the distance between a party at 2.00 and a right-wing party at 8.00 would be .67. In theory, the measure ranges from 0 to 1, but it is unusual to see Sani-Sartori distances

Table 5.4. Sani-Sartori Ideological Distances between Parties, 1990–2005

Dyad	*Context of dyad*	*1990*	*1993*	*1997*	*2001*	*2005*
PT-PFL	Main left and right poles of party system	.72	.63	.73	.70	.45
PSDB-PMDB	Main competitors for center, allied in 2002	.12	.09	.05	.01	.02
PFL-PMDB	Center and right, allied in democratic transition, 1980s	.32	.28	.30	.27	.23
PSDB-PFL	Center and right, allied in 1994, 1998, and 2006	.45	.37	.25	.25	.20
PT-PMDB	Left and center, core of Lula governing coalition	.40	.35	.43	.44	.23
PT-PSDB	Left and center, presidential rivals 1994–2006	.27	.26	.48	.45	.25

Note: Calculated from data in table 5.3. For construction of measure, see Sani and Sartori (1983).

above .70. As explained above, here I do not use self-locations, because they are suspect, but the indicator is easily adaptable to the reputational placements of Brazilian parties (as located by nonmembers).

Table 5.4 shows the changing Sani-Sartori distance scores for six dyads across the five waves of survey research. As expected, the distance between the polar parties, PT and PFL, is high for most of the time series, but diminishes considerably in 2005. A glance back at table 5.3 shows that this narrowing of distance has nothing to do with the PFL, but rather *is explained entirely by the perceived movement of the PT toward the political center.* The distance between the PFL and the PSDB has also changed: after the victory of Cardoso in 1994, the distance was cut almost in half, and the two parties governed in alliance from 1995 to 2002. Looking at the political center, the PSDB and PMDB began separated by a small distance, which has since vanished. But perhaps the most interesting relationship is that of the PT to the PSDB. Their distance was moderate in the early 1990s, but increased sharply during the Cardoso presidency, when the PSDB moved rightward and the PT assumed a position of uncompromising opposition. The gulf then narrowed again in the Lula years, with almost all of the change explained by the PT's centrist drift. From 1990 to 2005, the PSDB moved first to the center and the PT followed later, with the result that the perceived ideological distance returned to what it was fifteen years earlier.

Overall, table 5.4 shows evidence of ideological convergence: for all six dyads presented here, the Sani-Sartori distances are smaller than they were in 1990, in some cases considerably smaller. The earlier table 5.3 showed the directionality of change: it is to the right. Essentially, the PFL stood its ground, and the other three major parties drew closer to the PFL, albeit asynchronically.

One problem with ideological distance scores is that they are abstract; we cannot be sure that they are tapping into a cleavage regarding the state's role in economic management. To address this problem, I replicated a survey question written and asked of the Brazilian Congress in 1987 by Leôncio Martins Rodrigues. On the eve of the Constituent Assembly, Rodrigues asked federal deputies what economic system they preferred for Brazil, with the possible responses corresponding to, in his terms: a "pure" market economy, a "social democratic" economy with an equitable distribution of responsibilities between the state and the private sector, a "moderate socialist" system with the state predominant but some private enterprise maintained, or a "radical socialist" or command economy.[6] Table 5.5 shows that support for pure economic liberalism rose sharply from 1987 to 1997 but then returned more or less to the 1987 levels in the surveys conducted in 2001 and 2005. This curvilinear pattern of support for neoliberalism is intuitive. It reflects the fact that there was considerable elite support for the Cardoso reform agenda during the early years of the Plano Real (recall that politicians still rate this period as the best-performing phase of democracy), but that enthusiasm for the new development model diminished in Cardoso's second term. The financial crises of 1998–1999 and the energy crisis of 2001, both of which dampened GDP growth relative to the early Real period, are likely candidates for causal factors here, but the data may also reflect a cumulative learning process—in other words, elites discovered that neoliberalism was not a panacea. Despite this attitudinal correction in the later Cardoso years, we must recognize that the overall distribution of economic opinion (that is, "liberals" minus the two types of "socialists") was still more favorable to the market in 2005 than it was in 1987. If we take the ratio of free-marketers to socialists as a simple indicator of the correlation of forces, this figure increased from just under 2:1 in 1987 to well over 3:1 in 2005.

Drawing inferences about individual parties is difficult because the Ns are small, but nonetheless there are some interesting trends. In 1987, only 31 percent of the future PSDB supported the "pure market economy" option, but this jumped to 63 percent by 1997—the biggest change in any single party.[7] The PT

Table 5.5. Preference for Economic System, 1987–2005

Option	*1987*	*1997*	*2001*	*2005*
Pure market economy	40.0	57.1	41.2	42.0
Equal state and private sector	39.0	34.8	42.0	45.5
State dominant	15.0	7.5	16.0	12.5
Complete state control	6.0	0.6	0.8	0.0
Total	100.0	100.0	100.0	100.0

Note: The question was replicated with kind permission from Leôncio Martins Rodrigues; for wording, see text. The 1987 data (Rodrigues 1987) are for federal deputies only (N = 435).

has also clearly changed. Rodrigues surveyed all sixteen PT members in the 1987 Congress and found that ten supported radical socialism, six supported moderate socialism, and no *petista* chose either the social democratic or liberal options. In 2005, I surveyed twenty-one PT members (20.6 percent of the caucus) and found that none supported radical socialism, eleven favored moderate socialism, seven favored social democracy, and most notably, three responded that they supported a predominantly market economy with the least possible participation by the state. Such a distribution of PT responses would have been unthinkable a decade earlier.

Democratic Commitments and Authoritarian Nostalgia

We turn now to a second cleavage. How democratic are Brazilian political elites? One way to get at this issue is by assessing the intra-elite perceptions of the "democratic commitments" of political parties. In all five waves of survey research, federal legislators were asked, "How would you judge the capacity of the following political parties to act in accordance with the rules of the democratic game and thus contribute to democratic stability?" Respondents were presented with a list of parties and asked to rate them using a 1–10 scale in which 1 was "no capacity" and 10 was "maximum capacity." Again, respondents' placements of their own parties are disregarded. The partisan means should be interpreted as reputational, representing the intra-elite image of the democraticness of each party.

From 1990 to 2005, there was fairly little variation in the democratic reputations of three of the four parties examined here. The PMDB and PSDB, usually the highest-ranking parties, consistently received rankings of between 6.5 and

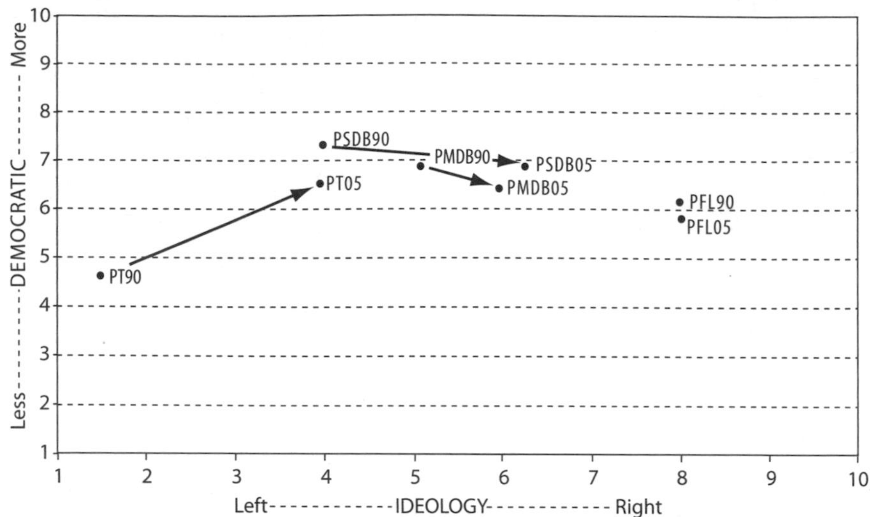

Figure 5.1. Perceived Party Shifts on Ideology and Democraticness, 1990–2005
Note: For ideology measure, see table 5.3; for perceived democratic commitments, see text.

7.5, while the PFL hovered at around 6.0 in all five surveys. The PT had a very different trajectory: its democratic image began at a low 4.60 in 1990 and rose in linear fashion, until reaching 6.54 in each of the last two surveys. The PFL actually outranked the PT in the first three surveys, but their positions inverted beginning in 2001. Clearly the PT was viewed as a somewhat suspect—perhaps antisystem—party in the early years of the democratic regime, but it gradually won the confidence of the rest of the political class. Figure 5.1, which combines both ideological and democratic reputations in a single graph, shows that the PT's growing reputation as a democratic party is clearly linked to its move toward the political center. Again, in 2005 the PT occupied a space similar to the one held by the PSDB in 1990, and overall the impression is that the main parties tend to cluster together in the center of the graph. On the democraticness dimension, the four main parties are now very close together, ranging from 6.07 to 6.93 in the 2005 survey.

It is clear that Brazilian politicians are "tough graders" when rating the democraticness of their peers: although the grading scale ranges up to 10, the actual distribution of scores suggests an implicit ceiling of about 7.5, and it is not clear why. Moreover, the question is abstract and does not disaggregate the concept

Table 5.6. Opinion on Civil-Military Relations and Authoritarian Legacies, 1990–2005

	Agreement (%)				
Survey statement	*1990*	*1993*	*1997*	*2001*	*2005*
Authoritarian regimes are better at stimulating economic growth than are democratic regimes.	15.4	18.7	15.0	11.5	6.8
In Latin America, it has been more difficult for democratic governments than for authoritarian governments to maintain social order.	49.1	49.9	36.4	28.9	28.0
The armed forces should have the constitutional right to intervene to maintain internal order.	56.3	57.4	44.7	41.8	50.9
Rather than having several military ministries, Brazil should have a single Ministry of Defense.	66.4	74.9	81.5	92.0	91.2
The Minister of Defense should be a civilian.	61.6	62.5	65.9	89.2	87.8

Note: Brazil created a Ministry of Defense in 1999, so the final two questions were reworded into the past tense in 2001 and 2005. Agreement combines the "agree strongly" and "agree somewhat" options.

of "democratic commitment" into discrete attitudes. One way to test for the presence of an authentically postauthoritarian cleavage in the political class is to ask a series of questions relating to specific legacies of the defunct military regime (and its counterparts elsewhere) and combine them into an index of authoritarian nostalgia. Three relevant questions in the surveys explored civil-military relations. Respondents were asked whether they supported the constitutional provision (Article 142 of the Constitution of 1988) that allows the military to intervene in order to preserve internal order, whether they supported the creation of a single Ministry of Defense (as opposed to the multiple military ministries that existed until 1999), and whether the Minister of Defense should be a civilian. Two additional questions explored perceived advantages of authoritarian rule: respondents were asked whether they thought that authoritarian regimes generally provide better economic growth than democratic regimes and whether they thought that social order was more difficult to preserve under democratic conditions. Table 5.6 presents overall legislative opinion on these issues and shows that for every survey statement, support for the prodemocratic or reformist position has improved since 1990—in some cases dramatically. I then recoded the responses so as to create an additive index of authoritarian nostalgia, where a score of 0 represents complete rejection of authoritarian legacies and a score of 5 represents complete endorsement of them. I computed mean scores for each of the four main parties studied here.

Figure 5.2 plots the mean "nostalgia" scores against perceived left-right placements. In the archetypal democratic transition in the Latin America of the 1980s, in which political systems were emerging from decades of domination by right-wing, anticommmunist military governments, we should expect a strong linear relationship between political ideology and authoritarian nostalgia: in the early years of democracy (the immediate post-transition phase), the Left should be hostile to the legacy of the past and the Right should be more supportive of it. This hypothesized relationship is represented by the diagonal line in figure 5.2, which in fact does a remarkably good job in predicting the locations of the parties in the first postauthoritarian legislature. The PT and PFL, for example, are in opposing quadrants of this two-dimensional space in 1990. But the figure also shows that after two decades of democracy, this elegant linear relationship falls apart in 2005. Except for a trivial exception on the part of the PT (which began from an extremely low baseline), the parties all decline on the nostalgia dimension. Most notable in figure 5.2 is the trajectory of the PFL, which is a direct descendant of the official party of the 1964–1985 military regime. Without any movement whatsoever on the left-right scale, the PFL travels due south on the nostalgia scale. Both in terms of the direction and of the attitudinal distance covered, this rather dramatic migration by the PFL is good news for democracy.

Figure 5.2 depicts a hypothesis that is confirmed in 1990 and falsified in 2005. Similarly to figure 5.1, the effect is one of a partial clustering of the parties. In the eyes of political elites, the four main Brazilian parties are seen as both having moved toward the political center and having stabilized their commitments to democracy.

Individualistic versus Party-Building Orientations

A third and final cleavage speaks to debates on institution development and political reform in post-1985 Brazil. The dominant view at the time of the democratic transition was that Brazilian representative institutions, especially parties, were weak and would have to be strengthened (e.g., Lamounier and Meneguello

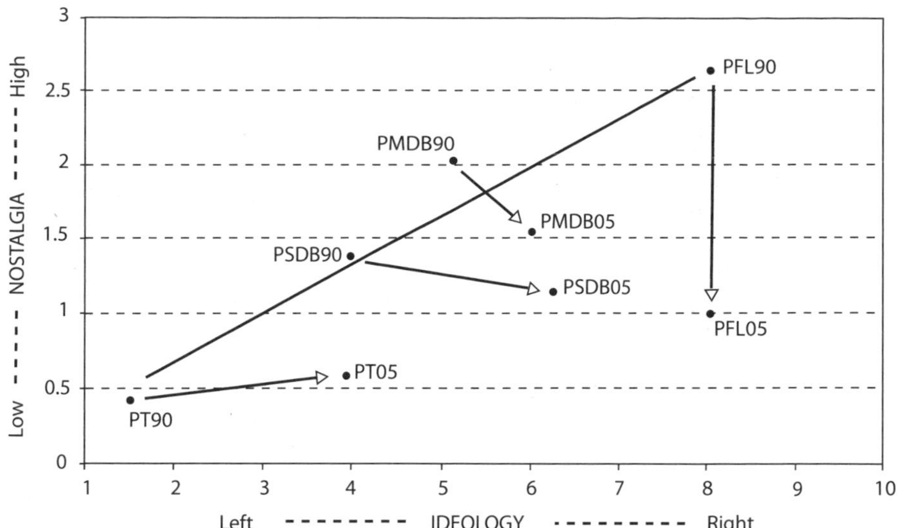

Figure 5.2. Perceived Party Shifts on Ideology and Authoritarian Nostalgia, 1990–2005

Note: Index of authoritarian nostalgia is constructed from the five questions presented in table 5.6 (see text). The dotted line represents the hypothesized relationship at the moment of the transition to democracy. For ideology measure, see table 5.3.

1986). Brazilian party weakness was often attributed to the electoral system of open-list proportional representation (OLPR), which privileges individual politicians at the expense of party organizations. A key argument here, developed at length in the influential works of Mainwaring (1999) and Ames (2001), was that weak parties and a permissive electoral system—an orientation of pronounced elite individualism, or in Mainwaring's term, "democratic libertarianism"—were authentic institutional *choices*, representing the preferences of rational politicians. Analysts often carved out an exception for the small ideological parties of the Left (such as the PT) but identified strong individualistic and antiparty orientations in the catchall parties of the Center and Right.

To what extent do Brazilian politicians favor personal autonomy over party-centered politics? One way to examine this is simply to examine preferences for electoral rules. Since 1990, my survey research has consistently shown strong support for a change to a mixed electoral system (on the order of 50–55 percent), followed by maintenance for a PR-only system (30–40 percent), with very weak support for switch to the U.S.-style single-member district plurality method

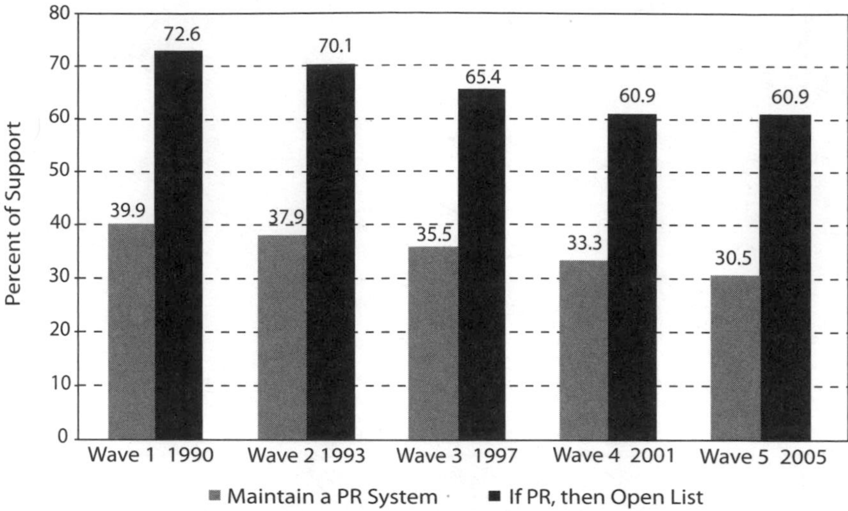

Figure 5.3. Preferences Regarding Open-List Proportional Representation, 1990–2005

Note: "Maintain a PR System" is one of three options for the respondent's preferred electoral system, the other two being pure single-member district plurality (SMDP) and a mixed system. The followup question asked: "If Brazil maintains a system of proportional representation, would you prefer that the order of the candidates on the list be determined by the party or would you prefer an open list (as exists now)?"

(10–15 percent). There is clearly overwhelming allegiance to the proportionality principle, though support for a PR-only system fell from 40 percent in 1990 to 31 percent in 2005 (figure 5.3). But the practical questions about proportionality are deeper, pertaining to (1) what *kind* of PR system should be used (that is, whether Brazil should continue with OLPR or opt for closed-list proportional representation [CLPR]), and (2) how this would be factored into the PR side of a mixed electoral system, which is the modal preference.[8] Therefore respondents were asked, "If Brazil maintains a system of proportional representation, would you prefer that the order of the candidates on the list be determined by the party or would you prefer an open list (as exists now)?" As figure 5.3 shows, support for OLPR has fallen over time, but in 2005 it still trumped the CLPR alternative by a margin of 61 percent to 39 percent. This suggests that although there has been some loss of enthusiasm for OLPR, Brazilian politicians are still extremely reluctant to move to a party-centered electoral system.

Any concept of elite autonomy vis-à-vis political institutions should not look only at electoral rules, but also at notions of representation and parliamentary behavior. For this reason, I created an additive index of political individualism based on three survey questions. The first question captures the electoral-system debate mentioned above: politicians supporting CLPR received a score of 0, while those supporting the current OLPR system received a score of 1. The second question taps into Burkean models of representation.[9] Respondents were asked, "Do you believe that in parliamentary life, a legislator should generally vote as the party indicates, or according to his/her beliefs?" Politicians opting for the party received a score of 0, and those stressing personal autonomy received a score of 1. The third question asked legislators whether they believed that their party should be able to close off debate on an issue (*fechar questão*) and impose party fidelity; those supporting discipline received the 1 value. Thus, the additive index of political individualism ranges from 0 (most proparty orientation) to 3 (most individualistic orientation).

The mean score for Congress as a whole fell from 1.66 in 1990 to 1.28 in 2005, suggesting a growing acceptance of the need for institutionally anchored politics. What is more interesting is the performance of the four main parties. Mainwaring (1999) argued that the ideological left parties such as the PT would rank low on individualism and the catchall parties such as the PMDB and PFL would rank high, and moreover that the early PSDB (a center-left party at its birth) would be in an intermediate position. This is exactly the pattern we see in the 1990 survey (figure 5.4). By 2005, however, all parties declined on individualism, with the minor exception of the PT, which slightly *increased* its score. This anomaly could be due to measurement error in 1990 (the PT amounted to a very small subsample, with the survey reaching seven of its sixteen federal legislators at the time); alternatively, it could also be due to broadening recruitment strategies by the party or the consequences of de-ideologization under Lula. In any case, change in the PT score is minimal and is far less than the change in other parties. But the general message of figure 5.4 is that the postauthoritarian relationships predicted by Mainwaring—in which ideology correlates with individualism—hold for 1990 but not for 2005. Similar to the findings on authoritarian nostalgia, the effect is one of clustering toward the center of the graph.

Note that in 2005 the PSDB has a very large vertical distance from the PMDB on the individualism dimension. This may be linked to the fact that the PMDB's status as a catchall party has been more consistent than the PSDB's. The PSDB grew larger and more unwieldy during the Cardoso years but became smaller and more clearly identified with the neoliberal Cardoso legacy when it retreated into opposition in 2003. Loss of national power refocused the

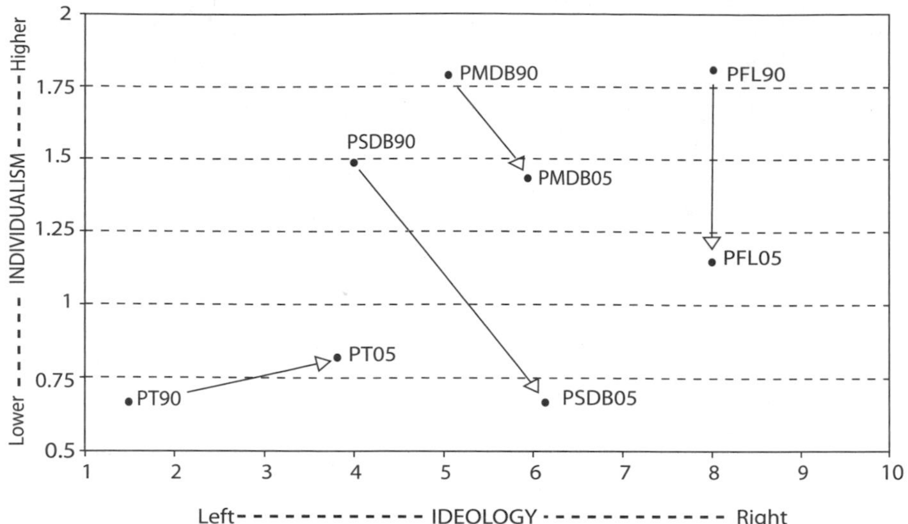

Figure 5.4. Party Shifts on Reported Individualism and Perceived Ideology, 1990–2005

Note: Index of individualism based on responses to questions on open-list proportional representation (OLPR), on party discipline, and on personal beliefs versus party wishes in legislative voting (see text). The index ranges from 0 (most proparty orientation) to 3 (most individualistic orientation). For ideology measure, see table 5.3.

party. Note also in figure 5.4 that the PFL declined dramatically on (professed) political individualism while holding its position on (perceived) conservatism. This may be explained in part by the PFL's historic shift into the opposition beginning in 2003: as the PFL became the most vociferous anti-PT, anti-Lula party, it is not surprising that its members would profess greater support for party-strengthening measures.

In the Brazilian context, political opposition can be seen as heightening the functional need for ideology and for party organization, whereas membership in the (typically broad) propresidential alliances tends to reduce the need for these political resources. Therefore, we should expect some oscillations in political individualism—and in support for political reform efforts—as parties move in and out of various alliance configurations. Role reversal might explain why, for example, in 2005 the PSDB actually ranked lower than the PT on individualism for the first time.

Overall, the evidence since 1990 suggests some *attitudinal* decline in "democratic libertarianism," but without concomitant *behavioral* manifestations that would lead to the wholesale redesign of political institutions. The weaker reform impulse here is not surprising, given that the political institution's cleavage is the one most directly connected to the political careers of elites: politicians are less likely to experiment with issues that affect their very survival.

Implications and Causal Assessment

The responses of Brazilian political elites to surveys—and again I should stress that the data are attitudinal, not behavioral—suggest that all three inherited cleavages have softened over the past two decades of democracy. The left-right cleavage in economic management is less severe, with the center having gained at the expense of left and right extremes. Nostalgia for the days of military rule has declined overall, and there is no longer much of a relationship between ideology and support for authoritarian values. Overall, the individualistic, antiparty orientations of the Brazilian political class seem to have moderated, and the relationship between party type (ideological versus catchall) and attitudes toward institutional strengthening is much looser than it once was.

Without overstating these findings, there is strong suggestive evidence of attitudinal convergence on a number of key dimensions. Two questions immediately spring to mind. First, survey research necessarily paints an incomplete picture, but does what we know about elite *behavior* seem to be more or less consistent with the attitudinal evidence reviewed here? Second, if the answer to the first question is affirmative, then *why* has there been convergence? I now take each of the cleavages in turn.

With regard to the first (ideological) cleavage, we have found that there has been aggregate ideological stability despite the growing incorporation of the Left into mainstream politics, that there have been sharp centrist or rightward turns by the PSDB and PT precisely at the moments at which they took the reins of government, and that distances of the major parties to the right pole (represented by the PFL) have diminished without the PFL seeming to move at all. Here the attitudinal clustering in the political center does, in fact, coincide with an obvious behavioral trend in Brazilian politics: the routinization of heterodox and noncontiguous interparty alliances since 1994. Parties that were once divided by ideology (such as the PSDB and PFL in 1994, or the PT and PL in 2002) have routinely cooperated in coalition politics at the national level (Power 2002; Machado 2005). Alliance politics is both a cause and a consequence of ideological convergence; without some minimal agreement, parties are unlikely to ally in the first place, but once they join forces in government around a mutually agreed-upon set of policies, then the ideological distances are likely to diminish further. If we accept this possibility, and we further accept that the creation of broad interparty alliances is a necessary feature of *presidencialismo de coalizão* in Brazil, we are on the verge of a counterintuitive proposition: that the dynamics of multiparty presidentialism may actually *reduce* ideological polarization. If confirmed, this, of course, would invert the classic hypotheses raised by Linz (1994) and Mainwaring (1993), but we cannot provide a direct test of these arguments here. The most that can be said is that political actors increasingly believe that they must ally with former enemies in order to achieve governability in the Brazilian journalistic sense: that is, in order to pass legislation of interest to the executive.

However, in explaining convergence, it is difficult to disentangle the alliance-based politics of *presidencialismo de coalizão* from a broader trend: the apparent reduction of policy space in Brazil over the past two decades. Here I refer to the challenges of macroeconomic management and state reform against a panorama of accelerating globalization. This is not the place to revisit these policy challenges (see Amaral et al., this volume), but suffice it to say that they have coincided with an increasing homogenization of policy proposals in Brazil. Lula's macroeconomic policies since 2003 are perhaps the best evidence of this. If these policies echo the Cardoso years, which in turn echoed the Collor years, it is because these three critical presidencies are part of a single historical process of structural adjustment since 1990. Rising to these challenges in 2002–2003 implied that the PT would abandon earlier dogmas, move to the center, ally with former enemies, and willingly shed its own left wing—exactly the process that the PSDB underwent in 1993–1994. It is not surprising, as table 5.3 and figure 5.1 show, that when the PSDB and PT entered government they began to be seen as more centrist by their peers. The narrowing of "inhabited" ideological space in figure 5.1 is clearly suggestive of diminished policy options over time. As Hunter (this volume) shows, the PT was aware that the ideological habitat for political parties was shrinking in the 1990s but concluded that the only way to capture the presidency was to remain inside the ever-contracting borders of *o sistema*. Considering the counterfactual alternative, under which the PT would have pushed for increased ideological polarization rather than aiming for the presidential palace, this pragmatic decision seems rather momentous in hindsight. Whether one approves of it or not, the PT's chosen path to power contributed to the routinization of democratic politics in Brazil.

With regard to the second cleavage—attitudes toward the legacy of 1964—we have found significant change. The perceived democratic credentials of the main political parties are now broadly similar. Support for military prerogatives has declined, assuaging some of the early concerns raised by Stepan (1988) about civil-military relations under democracy. There has been a lessening of authoritarian nostalgia across the board, but most notably on the political Right. These trends likely have multiple causes. First, in the period under review, the regional and global zeitgeist in support of democracy improved: the percentage of the world's countries classified as electorally democratic by Freedom House increased from about 45 percent to 65 percent (Freedom House 2008). Authoritarian orientations declined in legitimacy around the globe, and open expressions of antidemocratic sentiment virtually disappeared from mainstream Brazilian politics. Second, democracy in Brazil has not notably harmed the interests of the civilian political Right that once supported the authoritarian regime (Power 2000); whatever concerns remained in 1990 (shortly after the contentious Constituent Assembly) had mostly evaporated by 2005. Third, and less noted, there has been a major generational shift in the political class, with fewer and fewer elites having been socialized to politics under authoritarianism. In 1990, fully 76 percent of survey respondents reported a prior party affiliation to either ARENA (National Renewal Alliance Party) or MDB (Movimento Democrático Brasileiro), respectively the government and opposition parties during the imposed two-party system that existed between 1966 and 1979. By 2005, only 35 percent of respondents reported such an affiliation, suggesting that about two-thirds of Congress had been recruited to politics under competitive and pluralistic conditions. High-ranking partisans of military rule are now a small minority and should be expected to vanish altogether in the coming decade, but even their presence in the early years of democracy—mostly expressed via the PFL—did not prevent the formation of a consensus around democratic principles.

In Brazil, the democratic consensus appears far more secure at the elite level than at the mass level (see the introduction to this volume), and the objective successes of the regime in the absence of deep-rooted mass support suggests that the elite-centered democratization theories of the 1980s (O'Donnell, Schmitter, and Whitehead 1986; Burton and Higley 1987; Higley and Gunther 1992) were prescient. Moreover, the most recent survey in 2005 showed a strong degree of elite optimism about the regime's future. When presented with the survey statement that "in 2005, Brazilian democracy is consolidated," an astounding 90 percent of federal legislators agreed (strongly or somewhat) with this blunt verdict.

The third cleavage, pertaining to the building of representative institutions, is somewhat different from the first two. First, attitudinal change on this dimension, while detectable, has been less dramatic. Second and more importantly, attitudinal change on this cleavage is less obvious reflected in *behavioral* change than is the case with either left-right ideology or democratic values. Both of these observations require explanation. Support for electoral-system reform and party discipline seems to have earned some grudging support as the institutional debate has raged both in parliament and in the pages of political science journals over the past fifteen years (Santos and Vilarouca, this volume). Learning *has* occurred. But this debate departed from a very high baseline of individualistic orientations (73 percent support for the open-list principle in 1990), so change must be evaluated differently here. A linear projection of the trends in figure 5.3 would suggest that OLPR would only lose majority support around the year 2020—but it is not wise to make any linear projections at all, since there was no change in support for the open list from 2001 to 2005.[10]

It is also essential to note that the political institutions cleavage—unlike the first two—touches directly on the career strategies and political survival of politicians. Even if they recognize objective deficiencies in institutional design, political elites may be reluctant to alter the status quo, because, after all, it was *this* set of institutions (not an abstract or hypothetical one) that launched their careers and saw them through the last elections. This may explain the apparent contradiction between the degree of attitudinal change (moderate) and the degree of behavioral change (close to nonexistent) surrounding the key issues of political reform.[11] Again, there has been notable attitudinal convergence around the idea that free-floating politicians in Brazil—those who switch parties, defy their leaders, represent mainly themselves, and manage to get reelected (Ames 2001)—must somehow be constrained, but elites remain wary about the unpredictable (and possibly unintentional) effects of possible reforms.

Comparing all three cleavages as they appeared in the transition years and as they appear today, it is clear that elites have made attitudinal change on all three. Democracy, "world time," regime age, globalization, generational change, institutional incentives, and political learning have all played multifaceted roles in this complex process of evolution. There has been notable elite convergence on all three cleavages, but attitudinal change in the three dimensions has not occurred at the same speed, nor have the policy outputs in each dimension been of equal significance. Changes in elite ideology or authoritarian nostalgia can clearly be connected to patterns of behavior and policy, but this type of connection is harder to make in the case of democratic institutional design.

Lula's Middle Road

I conclude by returning full circle to Lula's remarks after his historic reelection in 2006: "We transform ourselves by taking the middle road. That's the road that must be followed by society." Is Brazil following Lula's advice? Have the cleavages inherited via democratic transition been softened over the past twenty years? Has Brazilian democracy been "centered" along the way?

The evidence presented in this chapter—which, again, is limited to the attitudes of elected politicians—suggest quite strongly that the answer is "yes." Surveyed across time, the Brazilian political class appears ideologically more homogeneous, and more secure in its own democratic self-image than was the case twenty years ago. For the most part, the survey responses seem remarkably consistent with what we see unfolding on the ground: solid behavioral compliance with democracy, the rollback of military influence, the institutionalization of interparty coalitions, and a fairly wide consensus about principles of macroeconomic management. Although there has been less consensus about how to redesign political institutions, the period since 1994 has seen the crystallization of strategies for coping with these institutions: that is, *presidencialismo de coalizão* with heterodox alliances. The last two presidents, Cardoso (PSDB) and Lula (PT), have epitomized these overlapping consensuses in various ways, all the while maintaining considerable popular and elite support. Note that in 2006, the PT and PSDB jointly received 90.3 percent of the vote in the first round of the presidential race—a bigger two-party share of the vote than the United States witnessed in the 1990s, and a rather decisive indication that the country does not object to the changes wrought by Cardoso and Lula since 1994. This degree of consensus is an impressive political achievement for democracy and would be barely imaginable in the Brazil of 1993.

Lula's pragmatic economic policies since 2003 are only one manifestation of a political system that has changed significantly since 1994. As suggested at the outset of this chapter, in retrospect it seems that 1994—the year of the Plano Real, stabilization, and surprising political alliances—was a major turning point.

But although this chapter has underscored convergence, it is well to recall that no trends in politics are irreversible. A man who died in the year of the Plano Real, Richard Nixon, was famous for saying in 1971 that "we are all Keynesians now," only to have his own party repudiate that statement a decade later. Only time will tell whether Lula's post-election remarks of 2006 will be recalled with a similar dose of irony.

6

The Quality of Elections in Brazil: Policy, Performance, Pageantry, or Pork?

Barry Ames, Andy Baker, and Lucio R. Rennó

POLITICAL SCIENTISTS RARELY SPEAK directly of the "quality" of voter choice and elections, but our work often betrays a vague sense that some determinants of voter choice are more likely than others to produce outcomes beneficial for the public good. Candidates' policy proposals, for example, are more important than their personal attributes. Success in guiding the national economy is more desirable than a history of providing clientelistic goods to particular groups. Policy-oriented ("issue") voting not only requires knowledge of candidates and issues; it also indicates the voter's commitment to a policy stance and to an overall perception of elections as a way of offering mandates that affect the way government shapes public welfare. And finally, evaluations of incumbent performance provide a tangible criterion that yields a reasonably accurate prediction of future governance and behavior. By contrast, a vote based on such personal traits as speaking ability, age, or appearance seems irrelevant to policy and governance and reveals a general lack of knowledge about issues. "Clientelistic" voters—

those voting for candidates who promise publicly funded private gains for their supporters—totally eschew any consideration of the public welfare.

The original *Democratic Brazil* comprehensively described various aspects of Brazil's political institutions and civil society, but it overlooked its elections, a defining element of Brazil's democracy. We remedy this omission by evaluating Brazil's election quality, that is, the degree to which election outcomes reflect knowledgeable, reasoned decisions by voters concerned with influencing governmental decisions about the collective good. We ask, moving from lower to higher quality, whether election outcomes in Brazil are mechanisms of pork-barrel distribution and patron-client exchange, "beauty pageants" that merely feature candidate traits, plebiscitary decisions over incumbent performance, or contestations over competing policy visions. We describe elections' "demand side"—what voters know and what criteria they use to decide—and their "supply side"—the context provided by elites and electoral institutions. Our analysis focuses on the three most visible and important levels of elections in Brazil: presidents, governors, and federal deputies. Brazilian voters, we conclude, are eclectic, and their abilities are usually underestimated by the scholarly community. All four criteria end up being important determinants of vote choice in Brazil. Most importantly, however, our findings contradict the conventional wisdom and instead indicate an impressive degree of issue voting for both executive *and* legislative posts.

We rely heavily on an extensive survey data set conducted during the 2002 elections in two mid-sized Brazilian cities: Caxias do Sul (Rio Grande do Sul) and Juiz de Fora (Minas Gerais). Most of our claims are based on a set of statistical models estimated using data gathered from thousands of interviews that were conducted in these two cities during the three weeks following the October 6 first-round election.[1] Although our discussion throughout is a nontechnical presentation of the models' substantive findings, the models assess the impact of each of the four factors on voting behavior, While our findings are mostly from these two cities, we improve our ability to generalize to all of Brazil by referring to findings and conducting analyses using data with a much broader geographical scope. In particular, we make occasional use of the 2002 Brazilian National Election Study (BNES), which was conducted on a nationwide sample.

The Supply Side: The Institutional and Informational Context of Voters and Elections

Institutional Arrangements

Brazil's electoral and party systems, and the perverse incentives they provide elites, have been widely criticized (Ames 2001; Mainwaring 1999; Power 2000). Less is known, however, about the impact of these institutions on citizens' abilities to make reasoned and knowledgeable voting decisions. It is crucial to account for this "supply side" before turning to citizen competence and voting behavior itself, because elite approaches to citizens and elite competition for citizens' votes structure the quality of citizen choice. Political parties, for example, facilitate voter decision making by providing consistent and persistent information shortcuts or cues (Lupia and McCubbins 1998; Popkin 1991; Rahn 1993; Sniderman et al. 1991). If parties in a given system agglomerate individuals with similar policy goals, then the party label itself conveys information to voters about the basic issue positions of candidates. Citizens can therefore make reasonably accurate inferences about the policies candidates would implement merely by learning their party affiliations.

When parties lack this sort of ideological coherence, however, partisan cues are limited or even inaccurate (Lupia and McCubbins 2000). Can the absence of ideological coherence affect citizen competence? "In politics, citizens characteristically are presented with an organized set, or menu, of choices. The choices they make are dependent on the organization of this menu. . . . The capacity of citizens to make consistent choices . . . is contingent on the organization of the menu of choices presented to them. . . . *Coherence at the level of individual citizens is conditional on coherence in the menu of choices presented to them to make as citizens*" (Sniderman and Bullock 2004; 338, 343, 346, emphasis added). If Sniderman and Bullock are correct, Brazilian voters should surely be among the world's most "incoherent."

Consider partisan cues. As a result of its high district magnitudes, its majority run off system for electing executives, and its strong federal structure, Brazil is a world leader in the sheer number of parties (Mainwaring 1999). The 2002 Chamber of Deputies had an effective number of parties of 8.5 (Laakso and Taagepera 1979); merely to know and remember so many partisan cues taxes citizens. At the legislative level, Brazil's open-list proportional representation electoral system also multiplies candidates. Though voters have the right to select either an individual candidate or a party, over 90 percent vote for individuals. Since each party may nominate a slate of candidates equal in number to 150 percent of the district magnitude (which varies from 8 to 70), voters must choose from an absurd number of candidates. In 2002, 4,297 candidates competed for federal deputy seats, an average of 159 per electoral district. Voters in São Paulo chose from a list of 700 candidates, and even the smallest states featured 50 or more candidates (Rennó 2006a).[2] An array of choices so large may overwhelm and confuse citizens.[3]

In addition, policy and ideology have not driven the formation of most Brazilian parties. Many parties, instead, are instruments of clientelistic exchange, with regional rather than ideological bases of support (Mainwaring 1999; Samuels 2000). Brazil is also a world leader in party switching by politicians (Desposato 2006; Marenco 2006; C. R. de Melo 2004). In recent legislative terms, one-fifth of incumbents have changed parties at least once, and 6 percent have changed twice. Some switched more than five times. Notable presidential candidates have also switched parties multiple times. Fernando Collor de Mello had been a member of five parties before his election as president in 1989. Presidential candidates Ciro Gomes (1998 and 2002) and Anthony Garotinho (2002) also switched parties after emerging on the national stage.

The Workers' Party (PT), more disciplined and ideologically coherent, is often mentioned as an exception in the panoply of Brazilian parties (Carreirão and Barbetta 2004; Carreirão and Kinzo 2004; Kinzo 2004, 2005; Samuels 1999, 2006; Singer 1999). But in recent years even the PT has shifted its ideological center. It has become more moderate, mainly to enhance its electoral appeal. As a governing party, the PT implemented liberal policies that it strictly opposed while in the opposition (Samuels 2004; Spanakos and Rennó 2006; Stokes 2001; also see Hunter in this volume).

Still, some order does exist in this apparent chaos. Scholars have found that the roll-call voting of parties in the Chamber of Deputies lines up roughly on a left-right spectrum, from statist to liberal (Figueiredo and Limongi 1999; Mainwaring, Meneguello, and Power 2000). So parties may not be as devoid of ideology as many claim. In addition, parties grew steadily more cohesive and coherent after 1994, Cardoso's first presidential term (Santos and Rennó 2004). Moreover, the large number of parties at the national level masks much simpler arrangements at the state (district) and even municipal level. Individual states, on average, have far fewer than the high effective number of parties found in the national Chamber of Deputies (Samuels 2000). Moreover, a very finite number of candidates tend to compete in each municipality, effectively winnowing the choice set for many voters quite dramatically: native sons and daughters tend to campaign almost exclusively in their cities of origin or residence (Ames 2002).

Elections for executive posts at both the presidential and gubernatorial levels are more orderly than those for federal deputy. In the presidential elections of 1989 and 2002, four candidates received more than 10 percent of the vote. While this number of viable candidates is quite high by international standards, it is certainly more digestible than the cacophony of the legislative level. Moreover, four of the five presidential elections occurring in the New Republic—those of 1994, 1998, 2002, and 2006—were effectively two-candidate races between Luiz Inácio Lula da Silva and an economic liberal from the centrist Party of Brazilian Social Democracy, the PSDB (Fernando Henrique Cardoso in 1994 and 1998, José Serra in 2002, and Geraldo Alckmin in 2006). Gubernatorial races almost always feature fewer than four, and typically just two, viable candidates. In sum, many of Brazil's institutional maladies may have their worst consequences for citizen competence and voter coherence in legislative, rather than executive, elections.

Overall, however, these elite-level partisan arrangements largely fail to establish deeply engrained "brand loyalties" among the masses. First, from 1989 to 2005 the percentage of Brazilians reporting a partisan sympathy ranged between 40 percent and 50 percent, placing Brazil below the international average (Samuels 2006). Second, only half of all partisans sympathized with one of Brazil's many nonleftist parties; half, and sometimes more, of all partisans were *petistas*. In other words, parties that held more than 80 percent of all elected positions forged partisan ties among just 20 percent to 25 percent of the electorate (Samuels 2006). Finally, while democratic party systems tend to lay down deeper societal roots as they age (Converse 1964), the number of partisans in Brazil has actually *declined* as the party system has aged. Between 1992 and 2005, the rate of partisanship in the electorate, and especially among the nonleftist parties, fell by about one percentage point per year, and even the number of *petistas* began to fall after 2005 in response to the party's corruption scandals (Samuels 2006).

Mediation Sources

How do citizens come to comprehend their many options and make voting decisions in lieu of partisan sympathies and cues? Rarely, of course, do voters actually meet the elites they select in elections. Instead, they learn about them through sources that mediate the flow of information from candidate to voter.

In Brazil, these sources are typical of any democratic society: campaign advertisements, mass media, interpersonal conversations, and so on. However, certain aspects of Brazil's mediation environment make the country unique, with notable consequences for how and what voters learn about elections.

Mediation sources providing political information between and especially during campaigns are potentially very important in Brazil because the nation's weak party system largely fails to instill durable political sympathies that might insulate voters from the impact of such mediation sources during campaigns (Samuels 2006; Campbell et al. 1960). In fact, a comparatively large percentage of Brazilians change their vote preferences during campaigns (Baker, Ames, and Rennó 2006). This is evident not only in the commonly observed shifts in aggregate vote preferences during campaigns—such as those experienced by Collor in 1989, Lula and Fernando Henrique Cardoso in 1994, and Ciro Gomes in 2002—but also in panel data from the two-city survey.[4] Over 30 percent of respondents switched from one candidate to another in the final six weeks of the campaign. Parallel figures from more established democracies are typically in the single digits (Blais 2004; Zaller 2004).

Which mediation sources make Brazil unique? First, Brazil is often referred to as the "Country of Television." TV viewership, in comparison to other mass-media sources, is high by international standards. Moreover, the viewing audience is heavily concentrated in a single network, TV Globo, whose programs often command 60–80 percent of viewers (including its prime-time news program, *Jornal Nacional*). TV Globo is notable in Brazil's political panorama not merely because of the audiences it commands but because historically its newscasts have championed conservative forces and candidates. Besides propagating news favoring Brazil's military dictatorship (1964–1985), TV Globo continued, in the first few presidential elections of the New Republic, its tendency to present conservative candidates in a more favorable light (Lima 1993; Miguel 1999). By 2002, however, strict new rules prohibited newscasts from injecting political biases into coverage, and the evidence indicates that such measures were largely effective (Porto 2007).

Second, Brazilian electoral rules stipulate that candidates have free access to television and radio programming in what is known as the Free Electoral Airtime (Horário Gratuito de Propaganda Eleitoral, HGPE). The HGPE campaign commercials monopolize television and radio coverage (major networks are required to carry the HGPE) for nearly two hours a day during the final seven weeks of the campaign. Because all parties are allocated time, this law democ-

Table 6.1. Most Important Political Information Source: Respondents' Self-Reports

Source	*Percent*
Television	53.0
Debates between candidates	28.7
Political advertising	16.8
News about candidates	7.5
Interpersonal discussion	21.5
Conversations with friends and family members	14.9
Conversations with work or school colleagues	6.6
Newspaper and radio	8.4
Churches, neighborhood associations	4.4
Other sources or no response	8.7

Source: 2002 Brazilian National Election Survey.

ratizes access to television and radio advertising (although parties receive blocks of time commensurate with their size). Parties are required to present candidates for all elected offices. As a result, even minor candidates for federal deputy receive their moment in the sun, although most enjoy only a few seconds of airtime per week and cannot disseminate any sort of substantive message. All told, the HGPE is in many ways a politico-cultural event in Brazil—its features become fodder for debate by citizens and other elements of the mass media.

Table 6.1 reports nationwide survey data indicating the importance of television as a source of political news. When asked in 2002 what was the "most important way" in which they decided to vote, 53 percent of voters mentioned a television source. In contrast, just 8.4 percent mentioned other media sources, such as newspapers and radio.

Third, despite the importance of media sources, informal discussion among citizens is a particularly important conduit of information exchange during election campaigns. Table 6.1 demonstrates that interpersonal discussion was the second-most frequently mentioned source of political information. Moreover, while discussion is certainly a significant element of political mediation in any society, Brazilians seem especially prone to engage in meaningful discussions with concrete political consequences: that is, the changing of votes. In fact, 42 percent of respondents in the two-city data mentioned at least one political "discussant" (a friend or relative with whom they discussed politics) who *dis-*

agreed with them, a number quite high by international standards (Baker, Ames, and Rennó 2006; Mutz 2006). In short, amiable and consequential conversations among disagreeing individuals are a common feature of Brazilians' mediation environments.

Finally, local-level officials invoke "reverse coattails" effects (Ames 1994; Samuels 2000). Governors, mayors, city council members, and even heads of neighborhood associations endorse candidates for higher office (Gay 1994). Because candidates compete for these endorsements, elites must perceive them to be important, and the evidence indicates that they are (Ames 1994).

The Demand Side: Voter Knowledge and Behavior

In many ways, findings about the Brazilian electorate's behavior in the New Republic parallel those from early studies of voting behavior in the United States. Information levels are reported to be quite low: few citizens can remember, just a few weeks after each election, which *deputado* they chose (Almeida 2006; Rennó 2006a). Scholars have claimed that Brazilian voters do not seem to hold opinions about major political issues, and many empirical tests of issue voting have failed (Kinzo 1992; Samuels 2006; Silveira 1998). Indeed, elites and masses alike often repeat the familiar mantra, "*o povo não sabe votar*," that is, "the people don't know how to vote." The high number of voters switching candidates during campaigns adds to the perception that citizens are subject to whimsical changes in preferences.

One study described the Brazilian electorate as "nonrational" (Silveira 1998). The nonrational voter is generally incoherent and inarticulate about political matters. Electoral choices are based on *personalismo*, including candidate characteristics such as honesty and decisiveness. Voters rarely link political and economic issue ideas with candidate choice, and they justify electoral decisions by saying, "I liked him," "he was the best candidate for the country," or even "he's good-looking" (Baquero 1994; Kinzo 1992; Von Mettenheim 1995). The amount of money spent on political marketing and the celebrity status of some political marketers also attest to the perceived importance of candidate imagery in voting decisions.

The prevalence of clientelistic relations in Brazilian state-society arrangements also underlies the perception that citizens do not politicize policy issues of national import (Hagopian 1996; Von Mettenheim 1995; Weyland 1996).

Clientelism, "the practice of favors in the political sphere and the institutionalization of exchanging votes for particularistic benefits granted by those with public power," is practiced mainly at the state and municipal level (Diniz 1982, 17). Clientelistic systems lack ideological conflict. Political conflict centers on competition over limited public resources and private benefits such as public sector jobs. Citizens develop attachments to their local political boss because they receive publicly funded resources (Auyero 2000a, 2000b). Therefore, although the clientelistic vote is a rational one (and an economically self-interested one), such voters lack an orientation towards the collective good.

Like the early work of some rational-choice theorists, a few scholars of Brazilian mass political behavior have attempted to "rescue" the Brazilian voter with a retrospective performance evaluation model (Fiorina 1981; Key 1966). Democracies work, they argue, by offering citizens the ability to dismiss an incumbent government based on whether life under its rule has been good or bad (Schumpeter 1942). The evidence for this type of voter is quite convincing for the Brazilian case. For example, the 1994 presidential election is clearly impossible to understand without a retrospective model. In this election, Cardoso benefited from retrospective judgments of his performance as finance minister. He played up his role as the father of the Plano Real, the currency and stabilization plan that had slashed inflation a few months before the election. During this same period, Cardoso's expected vote share grew from 19 percent (June) to 47 percent (September), and he won with 53 percent of the valid votes (Mendes and Venturi 1995). Several studies have demonstrated that the *Real* plan was decisive for Cardoso's victory (Almeida 1996; Meneguello 1995). Although the occurrence of retrospective behavior helps shore up ideas of democratic competence among Brazil's electorate, it remains quite distinct from issue voting—that is, voting based on candidates' competing programs to address societal problems.[5]

What is it that Brazilian voters know, and how do they decide? We consider four potential causes of voting behavior—pork and clientelism, candidate traits, performance evaluations, and policy debates or issue voting. To assess the independent impact of each potential cause, we estimated five different statistical (multinomial logic) models: presidential vote choice, gubernatorial vote choice in Caxias, gubernatorial vote choice in Juiz de Fora, federal deputy vote choice in Caxias, and federal deputy vote choice in Juiz de Fora.[6]

The independent variables or causal factors in each model include respondents' orientation toward pork-barrel politics (in the two legislative models), candidate trait assessments (only available in the presidential model), economic evaluations (in all models), issue positions (in all models), partisan identification (in all models), neighborhood effects (in all models), and demographics such as class, gender, and age (in all models).[7] The full results and technical details are not reported in this chapter.[8] Instead, we convey the models' claims about the causes of voting behavior by discussing each of the four factors' estimated *independent* impact (holding other observed variables constant) on the probability of voting for a particular candidate or party.[9]

What Voters Know

Before assessing the causes of vote choice, let us first establish some more fundamental facts about citizen knowledge. If citizens apply any criteria at all when making their vote choices, they must at least be aware of the alternatives from which they are choosing. How familiar with the candidate options are Brazilians? Figure 6.1 reports the number of candidates that respondents could spontaneously remember and report during the three weeks following the first-round elections of 2002. We asked respondents to name, in turn, as many candidates as they could remember from the presidential, gubernatorial, and federal deputy races. Because these responses were spontaneous—respondents are far better at recognizing politicians from pictures or lists than they are at spontaneously recalling them—they provide a minimum baseline of citizen knowledge about candidates.

The degree of recall of presidential and gubernatorial candidates is impressive. Almost 75 percent of respondents could name all four viable presidential candidates, and about 40 percent could name all of the top three gubernatorial candidates. Equally importantly, 89 percent of respondents could name at least two presidential candidates, and 71 percent could do so for the gubernatorial race, thus providing the basis to make choices between at least two options. On average, respondents named 3.4 presidential candidates and 2 gubernatorial ones. Finally, the percentage of citizens recalling zero candidates was low: 15 percent for gubernatorial candidates and just 9 percent for presidential ones. Perhaps most impressive about these results is that not a single incumbent, at either level, was among our respondents' candidate choice sets.

Recognition of federal deputy candidates is less common. On average, citizens named, from their hundreds of options, just one candidate. Over one-third, however, could recall none, and only 32 percent could recall two or more. National results from the BNES show similar patterns of confusion and forgetfulness regarding votes for federal deputy (Almeida 2006). Among those actually going to

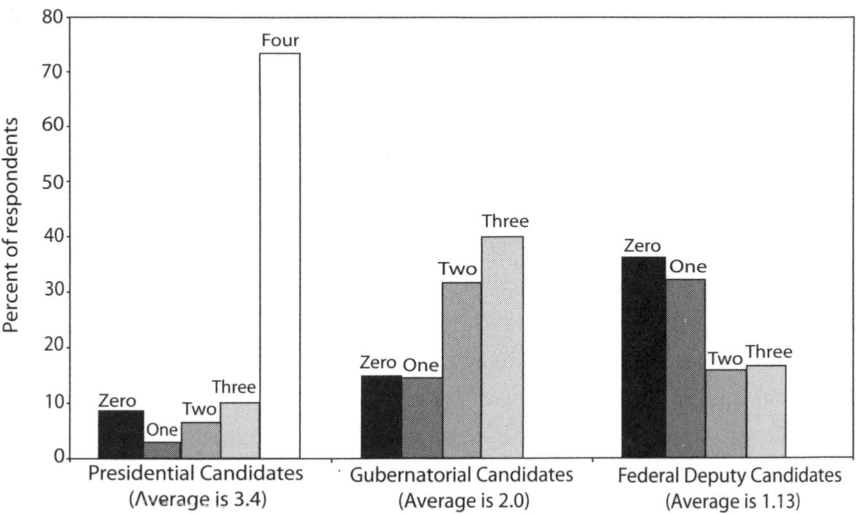

Figure 6.1. Spontaneous Recall of Presidential, Gubernatorial, and Federal Deputy Candidates

Source: Two-city data set, 2002.

the polls, 34 percent had forgotten their legislative choice only one month later, and another 15 percent gave an incorrect name. Only 21 percent could spontaneously and correctly name one of the many incumbent federal deputies in their state. By contrast, the number forgetting their gubernatorial vote one month later was only 3 percent, and the corresponding number for the presidential vote was 1 percent. Two-thirds of respondents could spontaneously name their state's incumbent governor. All told, Brazil's executive elections appear to be highly visible affairs, but legislative contests, to most citizens, are wholly forgettable.

How Voters Decide: Pork and Clientelism

Politicians' use of public funds to buy political support from voters receives various labels: clientelism, patronage, pork barrel. All these practices are distributive policies with diffuse costs and concentrated benefits, but there are important differences among them (Lowi 1964). We distinguish between the broad categories of *clientelism* and *pork barrel*. Clientelism implies an exchange of votes for private goods—that is, goods that benefit one or just a few individuals. Thus clientelism encompasses patronage (the offering of public-sector employment for political support) and the distribution of tangible goods or gifts (shoes, pressure cookers, T-shirts, even money) by candidates in the hopes of attracting votes.

A large literature characterizes Brazil's elections as ridden by such clientelistic tactics, much to the detriment of state finances and the overall collective good (Ames et al. 2004; Banck 1999; Diniz 1982; Fox 1974; Grindle 1977; Gay 1994). Such practices seem especially extensive in elections for legislative posts (at federal, state, and city levels) as well as those for mayoral positions. Moreover, they may meaningfully influence election outcomes at the presidential and gubernatorial levels through the "reverse coattails" effect, in which candidates for legislative or local office deliver votes to candidates for higher office in exchange for financial support for their own campaigns.

If self-reports by voters are credible, however, clientelism strictly defined directly affects only a small number of Brazilian voters. In the BNES national survey conducted soon after the 2002 elections, only 5 percent of respondents said they were offered some gift or item by any candidate in exchange for their vote. Similarly, in the two-city data, only 4 percent of respondents said they voted for their federal deputy candidate because the candidate had provided personal help to them.

In contrast, pork-barrel politics, a related but distinct phenomenon, seems far more extensive (Ames 1994). At the legislative level, pork-barrel politics refers to seeking votes for federal deputy candidates who have, in some capacity, garnered public funds for infrastructural investments to one's locality. In many instances, incumbent federal deputies obtain federal funds to construct such public goods as hospitals, schools, bridges, highways, and paved roads. These benefits are clearly distinct from the largely private goods offered in clientelistic exchanges, and such pork barreling is widespread in most democratic systems. As a result, the practice of casting votes for politicians who have delivered public works projects may be both rational and informed, especially in very unequal and less-developed countries where the need to improve basic infrastructure is high. When a main source of funds is the federal government, transfers intermediated by deputies play a significant role in improving the quality of life.

The main drawback of a pork-barrel vote, however, and the reason we classify it as low quality, is that it does not always have the collective, and especially national, good in mind. Excessive pork is bad for economic stability and fiscal discipline, especially when public works projects are constructed for the visibility they bring politicians rather than economic and efficiency benefits (Dornbusch and Edwards 1991). Projects distributed with a short-term political calculus squeeze out projects with greater long-term collective benefits. Pork also provides perverse incentives to federal deputies, who cast votes on national issues not on the merits of the issues themselves but on the executive's promises of pork projects (Ames 2002; Pereira and Rennó 2003). Finally, expenditures often leak into private bank accounts through schemes benefiting only a few corrupt individuals.

Citizens admit to casting pork-oriented votes. Almost two-thirds of the respondents in the two-city survey said they voted for their federal deputy candidates because they thought the candidate would help their city, while only one-third claimed their votes were motivated out of projects and issues of national interest. In other words, a majority of citizens select their deputy candidate with very local concerns in mind.

Still, a large minority orients itself nationally. In fact, the differences between these two groups—those preferring to elect deputies with an orientation towards national issues and those preferring deputies with a municipal orientation—have an important political relevance. Our statistical models explaining federal deputy vote choice revealed that voters reporting a more national orientation were 10 (Caxias) to 33 (Juiz de Fora) percentage points more likely to vote for a *petista* deputy candidate than voters reporting a preference for locally oriented federal deputies. In contrast, this latter group of voters was about 10 (Caxias) to 20 (Juiz de Fora) percentage points more likely to vote for candidates from conservative parties, such as the PSDB or PMDB (Party of the Brazilian Democratic Movement), than voters preferring candidates with a national orientation.

In sum, a desire for municipal-level public goods orients most, but not all, Brazilian voters when they consider their federal deputy choices. This orientation drives most voters to shun the PT and select a candidate from Brazil's wide array of more conservative options. At the same time, a sizable minority of voters does prefer nationally oriented candidates, and these individuals seem to form an important base for the PT in the Chamber of Deputies.

How Voters Decide: Candidate Attributes

The ranking of candidate traits as a criterion in our typology of election quality is probably the most debatable. Not all personal characteristics that voters deem important are superficial and politically irrelevant. Perceptions of honesty, administrative experience, ability to provide strong leadership—all are potentially valid indicators of the way a candidate will shape the collective good. Some political knowledge, moreover, is certainly a prerequisite for such impressions.

Consequently, our characterization of this criterion as mere beauty pageant surely exaggerates. Still, issue voting is certainly a higher-information affair than trait voting. Issue voting requires objective knowledge of candidates' positions and a stance of one's own. A vote according to candidate traits implies only some subjective impression of candidate attributes, an impression subject to flashy political marketing ploys devoid of substance (Silveira 1998).

To gauge the role of candidate traits, the two-city survey included a battery of questions asking how intelligent, decisive, honest, and compassionate were each of the four main presidential candidates—Lula of the PT, José Serra of the incumbent PSDB, populist Anthony Garotinho of the PSB (Brazilian Socialist Party), and Ciro Gomes of the PPS (Popular Socialist Party). We did not ask these questions about gubernatorial or federal deputy candidates, so this subsection focuses solely on the presidential election. The four questions produced a wealth of data, because the battery contained 16 questions: 4 candidates × 4 traits. Almost three-quarters of respondents provided a valid response to all 16 questions, with the average respondent answering 14.7 of them. At a minimum, then, almost all citizens do some thinking about candidates and their attributes.

Figure 6.2 portrays the independent impact each trait evaluation had on voters' presidential vote decisions. The figure reports the change in probability of voting for each candidate caused by a change from the most negative to the most positive evaluation of each trait.[10] For example, the leftmost bar (solid black, labeled "L" for Lula) signifies that changing a voter's evaluation of Lula's intelligence from very negative to very positive (while not changing that voter in any other way) would *increase* that voter's chances of voting for Lula by a probability of about 33 percent. By contrast, the leftmost white bar (fourth from the left, labeled "S" for Serra) signifies that this shift in evaluation of Lula's intelligence would *lower* the probability of voting for Serra by about 16 percent. Quite obviously, the larger the bars, the greater the impact of that trait on voting behavior.[11]

Clearly, candidate traits matter. Positive evaluations of Lula's intelligence, decisiveness, honesty, and compassion increased the probability of voting for him by 30 to 70 percentage points while decreasing the probability of voting for his main rival, José Serra, by 15 percent to 30 percent. Similarly, positive evaluations of Serra boosted the probability of casting a vote for him by 10 percent to 50 percent while decreasing the chances of voting for Lula by similarly large amounts. The magnitudes of the impact of trait evaluations were similarly large for Garotinho.

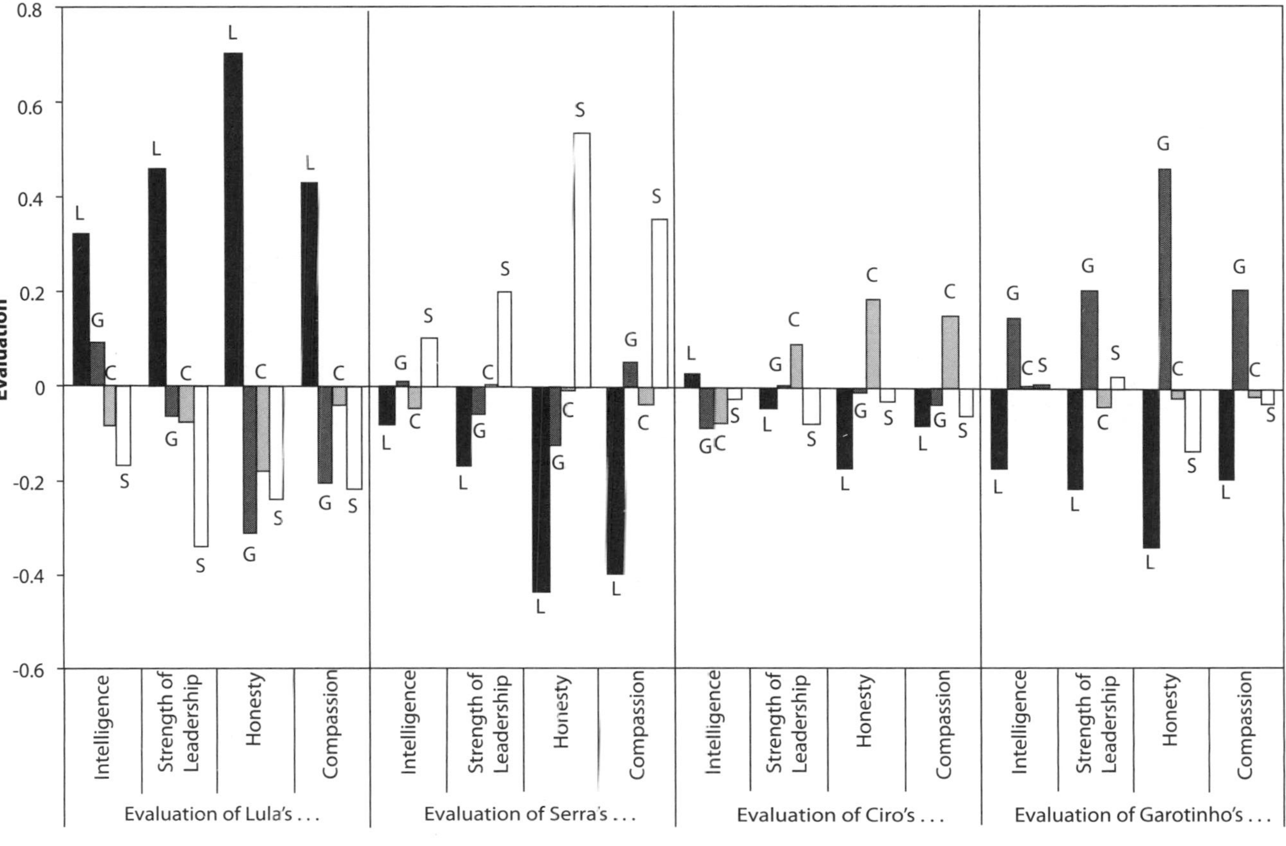

Figure 6.2. The Impact of Candidate Traits on Presidential Vote Choice

Source: Two-city data set, 2002.

All told, then, evaluations of candidate traits loomed large in Brazil's 2002 presidential election. Some important nuances and puzzles, however, are worth mentioning. First, candidate trait evaluations mattered more for Lula than for any other candidate. This may seem somewhat counterintuitive. As a *petista*, Lula had the largest base of stable partisan supporters who would have voted for any candidate the PT nominated. Because this base comprised *at most* 20 percent of the electorate, to win the election Lula had to appeal to many voters on other grounds. Part of this appeal was Lula's apparent integrity and leadership skills. By 2002, moreover, Lula was running for the presidency for the fourth time. Perceptions of his traits mattered because he was a well-known, polarizing figure about whom voters had strong opinions.

Evaluations of Ciro Gomes affected voting behavior very little. Ciro's voters, in other words, did not necessarily like his personal qualities more than those who chose one of his opponents. Ciro's support was not based on his star quality, a finding that is at once surprising yet expected. He was not from a widely supported party, nor did his campaign make fixed ideological appeals. His hot temper and other personal failings, however, became clear through a series of campaign gaffes, so it was difficult for him to appeal to voters via personal charm.

Finally, perceptions of honesty appear far more important than perceptions of other traits, with intelligence being the least important. The finding that honesty is the most important trait is also a puzzle in a country with a history of voting for successful candidates that "*rouba mas faz*"— that is, "steal but get things done." This is especially so given the reelection of Lula in 2006 after his party became embroiled in major corruption scandals. In sum, while candidates' traits clearly mattered in 2002, all of these puzzles suggest that there is more to Brazilian voting behavior and election campaigns than mere pageantry.

How Voters Decide: Performance Evaluations

Did evaluations of the economy influence voter choice in 2002? While such evaluations are potentially relevant, their ability to explain voter choice may be more limited in multiparty systems than in two-party systems like that of the United States. Citizens disapproving of incumbent performance may certainly decline to vote for that incumbent or the incumbent party candidate. Strictly speaking, however, the theory of retrospective voting cannot indicate which opposition candidates they will choose. This is especially the case in Brazil's legislative elections. Large district magnitudes, loose rules for candidate entry, and the pursuit of other offices by many federal deputies mean that incumbents seeking reelection are swamped by challengers (often by ratios of 10:1) (Samuels 2003a). Moreover, when incumbents themselves are barred from reelection or choose not to run, the linkage between retrospective evaluations and a candidate from the incumbent party may be weakened. The 2002 presidential elections and the gubernatorial elections in Minas Gerais and Rio Grande do Sul fit these scenarios: all featured at least three viable candidates and no incumbents. Thus the impact of performance evaluations could be weak in the contexts we consider.

Retrospective voting is nonetheless possible, even under these conditions, so we assess its impact on Brazilian voting behavior in our statistical models. We measured respondents' retrospective assessments of their family's and their own well-being, the country's economy, and their city's economy. We asked respondents if conditions had improved or worsened over the preceding twelve months. Conventional wisdom in studies of American politics holds that personal or "pocketbook" assessments are less important than sociotropic, or collective assessments, especially in presidential elections (Kinder and Kiewit 1981). Unfortunately, we do not have measures of state-level economic assessments to apply to the gubernatorial races.

Figure 6.3 reports the change in probability of voting for each candidate caused by a change from the most negative to the most positive economic assessment.[12] The probabilities associated with incumbents or candidates of incumbent parties are labeled in bold italic. If retrospective performance assessments work in the manner expected, then the bars for incumbents' parties should be positive—pointing upward—and those for challenger parties should be negative—pointing downward.[13]

For the presidential race, the sociotropic retrospective pattern is evident, statistically significant, but only mild in substantive impact. A switch from positive to negative assessments of the national economies decreased the probability of voting for Lula by a mere 3 percent, while it increased the probability of voting for Serra by just 7 percent.[14] Such assessments had virtually no impact on the probability of voting for Ciro or Garotinho, and pocketbook assessments had no effects on any candidacies. In short, differences in economic evaluations across voters did *not* lead to major differences in candidate preferences: Serra voters were only slightly more likely than Lula voters to think that collective economic trends had been negative in the preceding twelve months.

Results for the gubernatorial elections in Rio Grande do Sul are similarly weak. In that state, positive pocketbook assessments actually *increased* the prob-

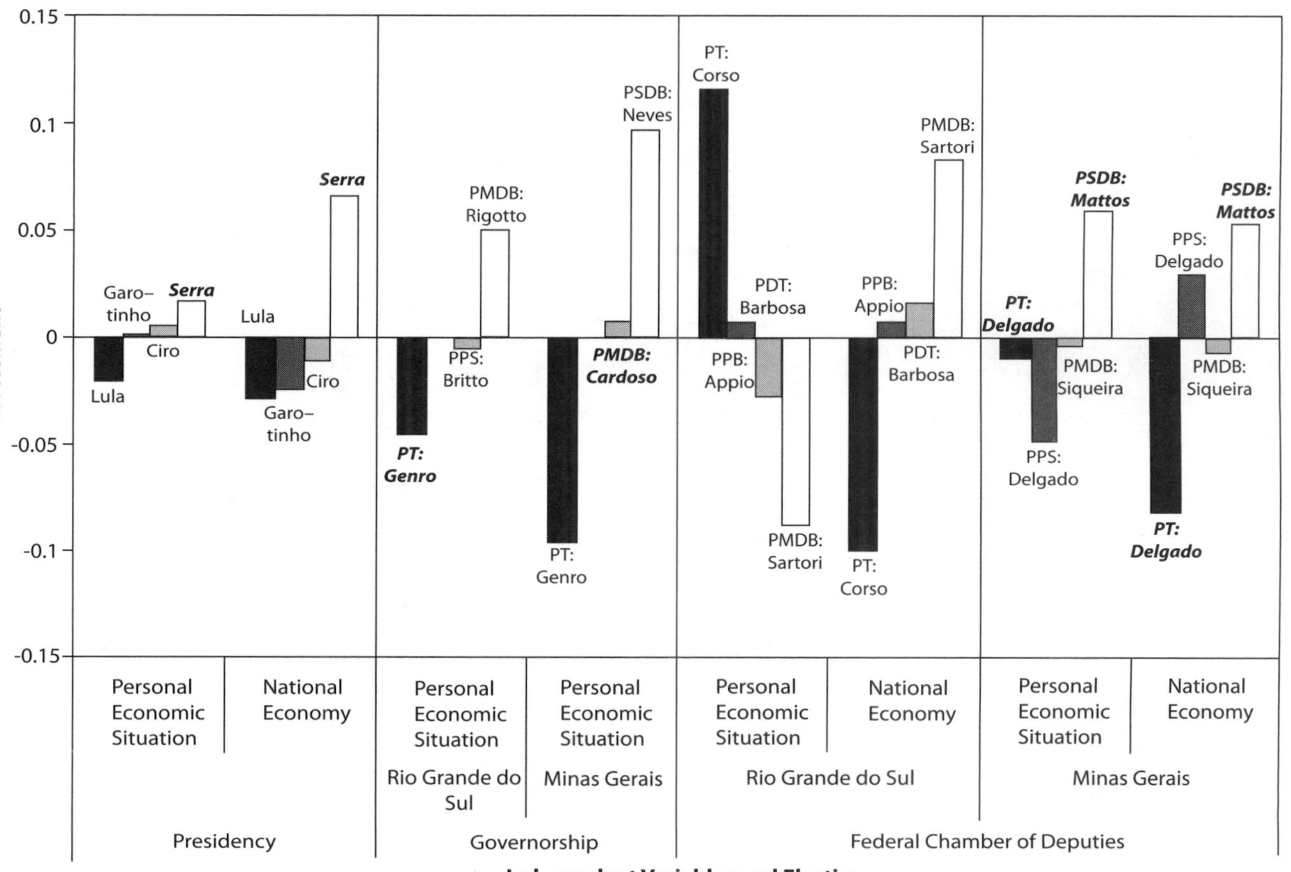

Figure 6.3. The Impact of Performance Evaluations on Presidential, Gubernatorial, and Federal Deputy Vote Choice

Note: Incumbents and candidates of incumbent parties are shown in bold and italic type.

Source: Two-city data set, 2002.

ability of voting for the incumbent party's candidate, *petista* Tarso Genro. The difference in probability, however, is not statistically significant. Voting patterns in the Minas Gerais gubernatorial election fit a much looser definition of retrospective voting. Performance evaluations did not affect the probability of voting for incumbent-party candidate Newton Cardoso (of the PMDB). Cardoso, however, garnered a mere 7 percent of the vote. The main contest involved two challengers, one from the PT (Nilmário Miranda) and eventual winner Aécio Neves of the PSDB. Interestingly, voters imposed a national lens on this race when translating economic assessments into vote choice. Although technically a challenger, Neves (of the incumbent president's party) was linked to the status quo such that he drew more heavily from citizens with positive assessments of economic trends than from those with negative assessments. In contrast, Miranda, of Lula's PT and the longstanding opposition, received a disproportionate amount of votes from those with more pessimistic economic outlooks. In particular, positive pocketbook evaluations increased the probability of voting for Neves by 10 percent, while decreasing the probability of voting for Miranda. In short, voters were retrospective in this gubernatorial race, yet they used the performance of the incumbent president and his administration, rather than that of the incumbent governor, to generate expectations about the future.

The role of collective economic evaluations played a similar role in the legislative elections. Interestingly, in Caxias *none* of the top four vote-getters, all native sons and daughters, were incumbents. This implies that most individuals with a positive view of economic trends chose not to reward any of their state's many incumbents, but rather cast their lot with a Caxias native. As in the Minas Gerais gubernatorial race, however, voters seemed to be aware of candidates' party affiliations with the government or the opposition at the national level, and they used this information in casting a retrospectively oriented vote. Performance evaluations influenced the relative probabilities of the top two vote-getters in each city. Positive assessments of the national economy boosted support for Caxias' leading conservative candidate—José Ivo Sartori of the PMDB—while diminishing that of *petista* Ana Corso, both by about 10 percent. A similar pattern held in Juiz de Fora, where *petista* Paulo Delgado, *despite his incumbent status*, experienced a decline in support from more positive sociotropic assessments, while Custódio Mattos (PSDB) enjoyed a boost in support.[15] In neither state, however, did pocketbook assessments matter for voter choice in the legislative contests.

Two main conclusions emerge from these findings on retrospective performance evaluations. First, evaluations of collective well-being had at best a mild impact on vote choice, while evaluations of personal welfare had virtually no impact. Second, such performance evaluations did not always encourage citizens to reward or punish strictly incumbent performance, but rather to reward or punish the national government and its numerous affiliates at all electoral levels. This suggests, of course, that some candidates' affiliations with the government or opposition are well known to voters. At the same time, these retrospective evaluations typically only distinguished between one *petista* candidate and one progovernment candidate. Still other factors are needed to understand voting in these multiparty elections.

How Voters Decide: Policy Debates

If issue voting is widespread in Brazil, voters with statist beliefs should vote for candidates holding statist issue positions. Likewise, voters with liberal beliefs should vote for candidates with liberal policy proposals. While seemingly straightforward, the cognitive demands of casting a vote based on policy or issues are relatively heavy (Downs 1957):

1. The citizen is cognizant of and holds an attitude on at least one issue debate.
2. The citizen knows the stance of at least two candidates on that issue.
3. The citizen favors the candidate whose issue position is most similar to his or her own.

To date, a few scholars have claimed that Brazilians do indeed vote on issues, but their viewpoint is a minority (Baker 2002; Singer 1999; L. E. Soares 2000). To assess the extent to which Brazilian voters fulfilled these three criteria in 2002, we examine two of the most visible and important, and therefore potentially polarizing, issues in Brazil's recent political economy: privatization and land reform. The privatization of state-owned enterprises created an important cleavage among elites since the initiation of economic liberalization programs during the Fernando Collor presidency (1990–1992) (Figueiredo and Limongi 2001; Mainwaring, Meneguello, and Power 2000). Likewise, the redistribution to landless peasants of rural farmland (mostly already owned by private landowners) has also been a divisive and sometimes bloody issue.

On the first requirement of issue voting, Brazilians score extremely well. An impressive 97 percent of respondents had an opinion about land reform, and 91 percent registered opinions about privatization. Whether these are nonattitudes —that is, meaningless doorstep opinions made up to satisfy prying interviewers—

remains to be seen (Converse 1964; Zaller 1992). Minimally, however, almost all respondents reported some evaluations of these two policies. Our sample also indicated that a vast majority of respondents had some perception of where candidates stood on these issues. A full 76 percent placed at least two presidential candidates on the privatization issue, with just 17 percent declining to place any of the four and 58 percent placing all four. The results for the land reform issue show an even greater willingness to place candidates: 81 percent placed at least two, 11 percent placed none, and 66 percent placed all four.

On average, Brazilians appeared to place the candidates near their objective stances towards these policies. Serra was considered the most proprivatization candidate; Lula the most antiprivatization. On a 1 to 5 scale, with 1 being the most antiprivatization and 5 being the most proprivatization, respondents gave Serra an average of 4 and Lula an average of 2. Ciro split the difference between the two with an average of 3; Garotinho scored 2.5. Even experts, of course, might quibble over the objective placements of the candidates and, in particular, the relative placements of Ciro and Garotinho. Still, the most important fact is that Serra and Lula were placed on opposite ends of the spectrum.

Were perceptions of land reform positions similarly accurate? Lula was seen as the most favorable towards land reform at 1.7 on a 1 (pro-) to 5 (anti-) scale, with Serra being placed at 3.25. The other two candidates, again, fell in between. In short, then, the first two elements of issue voting appear to be in place: most Brazilians report issue attitudes, and they know the objective stances of the candidates on these same issues.

Do these issue attitudes influence vote choice? Figure 6.4 indicates that, to a significant extent, they do. Figure 6.4 portrays the independent impact on vote choice of attitudes towards privatization and land reform. Like figure 6.3, figure 6.4 considers gubernatorial and legislative as well as presidential elections. The figure reports the change in probability of voting (generated from the statistical models) for each candidate caused by a change from the most statist to the most liberal stance on each issue. If issues mattered, then the black bars, which represent the resulting change in probabilities of voting for Lula and other *petistas*, should be negative (pointing downward) and the white bars, representing the change in probabilities of voting for Serra and other members of his conservative electoral coalition (PSDB and PMDB), should be positive (pointing upward).

In the presidential race, beliefs about privatization were particularly important. Switching from an avid antiprivatization belief to a proprivatization belief

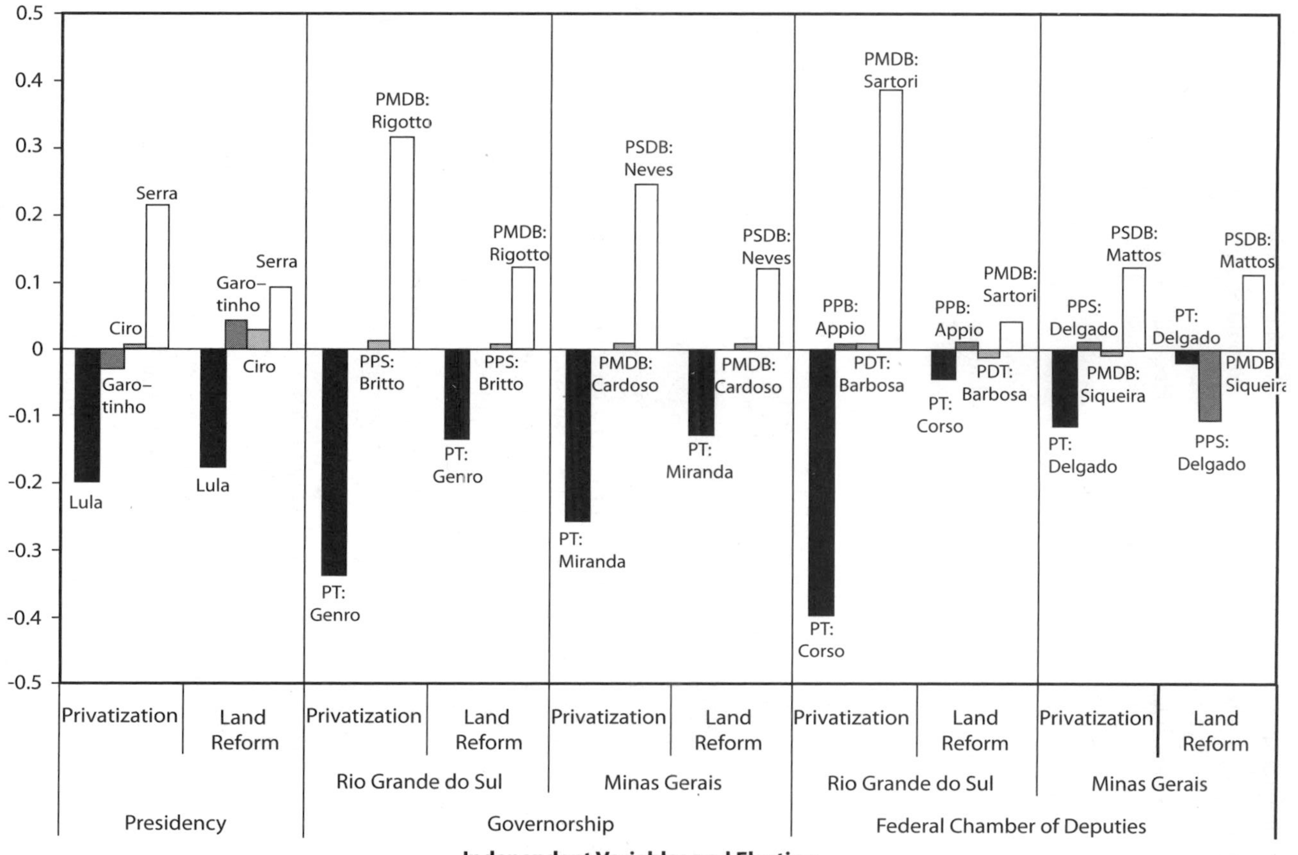

Figure 6.4. The Impact of Economic Issue Beliefs on Presidential, Gubernatorial, and Federal Deputy Vote Choice

Source: Two-city data set, 2002.

resulted in a 19 percent decrease in the probability of voting for Lula and a 21 percent increase in voting for Serra. Beliefs about land reform were slightly less influential, although they were important nonetheless: supporters of land redistribution were 16 percent more likely to vote for Lula than opponents, while opponents were 10 percent more likely than supporters to vote for Serra. The influence of these issue cleavages was far greater than the influence of economic performance assessments.

Nationwide data confirm the importance of issue voting in Brazil's presidential elections. According to statistical models we constructed using BNES data (not shown here but available from the authors upon request), supporters of land invasions were 11 percent more likely to vote for Lula than for his opponents. In contrast, strict opponents of land invasions were 9 percent more likely to vote for Serra. The impact of privatization was also statistically significant. Avid supporters of privatization were 18 percent less likely to have voted for Serra than for his opponents.[16] In short, Brazil's 2002 presidential election did reflect meaningful mass-level cleavages over crucial economic issues.

A look at gubernatorial elections and legislative elections confirms that issues mattered in these elections as well. In fact, privatization's role as a cleavage issue was *greater* in the gubernatorial elections than in the presidential election. A switch from opposition to support for privatization yielded a 25 percent and 30 percent boost in the probability of voting for Rigotto and Neves, respectively, two candidates with the endorsement of Serra and other conservative politicians and parties. In contrast, such a change resulted in an equivalent decline in the chances of voting for the PT's gubernatorial nominee in both states. Land reform had a slightly smaller but nonetheless important impact.

Finally, perhaps most surprising is the finding at the right-hand side of figure 6.4: Issue voting also existed for elections at the legislative level, although largely confined to the issue of privatization. In our Caxias sample, privatization beliefs sharply divided Sartori voters from Corso voters. A change from statist to liberal privatization beliefs increased the probability of voting for Sartori by a massive 40 points, while decreasing the odds of voting for Corso by the same amount. In Juiz de Fora, such a shift boosted support for Mattos of the PSDB by about 15 percent and lowered the probability of support for Delgado of the PT by 10 percent.[17] The fact that issue voting drove vote choice in Juiz de Fora, where politics is a more clientelistic and personalistic affair than in Caxias, is especially revealing of its importance. Do these findings about issue voting contradict our earlier claims about the extent of confusion and pork-barrel politics in election for the federal Chamber of Deputies? Not necessarily. In choosing among the top native sons and daughters, issues appear to play a role, but voters clearly prefer candidates who have a record of or show potential for delivering public goods to their municipalities.

How Voters Decide: Putting It All Together

Brazilian voters are eclectic in their approach to choosing from the menu of options elites offer. As earlier scholars have suggested, pork, pageantry, and performance *all* shape vote choices. Most novel, however, is our claim that issue voting is also widespread in Brazil. Issue voting, with its relatively high cognitive requirements, plays a role not only in executive elections but also in legislative ones.

Still, this summary papers over some important nuances. Brazil's oft-maligned institutional arrangements do hamper the ability of voters to make well-informed choices for legislative offices. The overwhelming number of federal deputy candidates and the personalistic nature of campaigns make it difficult for citizens to remember their choices or familiarize themselves with incumbents. Despite the fact that legislators are charged with voting on issues of mainly national import, most citizens prefer candidates preoccupied with local, not national, concerns

At the same time, our findings offer a basis for optimism about the quality of legislative elections. First, strictly clientelistic or private exchanges, reportedly prevalent in past elections (Diniz 1982; Gay 1994; Leal 1948), are no longer a widespread mechanism shaping voting behavior. Rather, pork-barrel projects, public goods that may actually help infrastructure development, fill the void. Second, while voters certainly prefer federal deputy candidates keen on delivering pork, they seem inclined to consider issues of national relevance when deciding which of their native sons and daughters to support. In other words, locally defined goals incline most voters to select a coresident of their city, but national policy concerns help dictate *which* native candidate they choose (Renno 2006b). Finally, a large minority of voters shunned pork-oriented legislative candidates, and such voters tended to choose the PT because of its more programmatic stance in the Congress.

Many of the institutional configurations making legislative elections so confusing and forgettable for voters do not apply in the executive sphere. Brazilian voters are very knowledgeable about candidates and issues surrounding presidential and gubernatorial elections, elections in which the pool of candidates is finite and offers distinct ideological options. In these contests, voters consider candidates' personal characteristics and their issue positions. Interestingly, however, we found evaluations of retrospective economic trends to have only a mild influence.

Our analysis is clearly not the last word in assessing Brazilian voting. First, Juiz de Fora and Caxias do Sul cannot be taken, singly or jointly, as perfect reflections of the Brazilian electorate. Neither sample contains rural residents, and both cities have above-average levels of wealth, education, and political consciousness. Still, over 80 percent of Brazil's population lives in urban areas with over 150,000 inhabitants. In this sense, the urban milieu of our respondents is typical, as are the ways in which voters tend to learn about politics. Second, in 2002 both cities featured a PT versus PSDB/PMDB ideological cleavage, a cleavage characterizing candidate competition in all five elections considered here. This cleavage was particularly strong in historically polarized Caxias.[18] Such a divide surely encourages an ideologically or policy-oriented vote at all levels. Indeed, our models tend to differentiate well between PT voters and PMDB/PSDB voters, but they do little to reveal why so many citizens prefer candidates from other, less ideologically oriented parties. Still, our own analyses of BNES data found evidence of issue voting, as have other nationwide studies of electoral behavior (Baker 2002; Singer 1999). Finally, the election of 2002 may have concluded an important era in Brazilian voting behavior. After the restoration of democracy in 1985, the PT ran as the ideological opposition, stressing its "good government" record. By 2006 the PT had moved to the center and had been tainted by several corruption scandals. Lula's relatively easy reelection victory may indicate that perceptions of candidate traits, especially honesty, have diminished in importance, while retrospective evaluations of personal well-being and government programs (especially antipoverty transfers) have grown more important (Hunter and Power 2007).

We conclude, then, that scholars have underestimated the Brazilian voter. Elections, especially for executive posts in Brazil, *do* reflect knowledgeable, reasoned decisions by voters concerned with influencing governmental decisions about the collective good. At least in part, Brazil's elections reflect contestation over differing visions of which policies and which candidates will be beneficial for the collective good. Clearly, our findings regarding knowledge about legislative contests reveal that part of the conventional wisdom is correct: the existence of multiple parties with weak ideological cues confuses voters. Moreover, corruption scandals and the decline in ideological cleavages may weaken issue voting in the future. In the end, nonetheless, we remain impressed with the Brazilian voter's abilities to make sense of the country's institutional morass but leery of elites' continuing capacity to undermine voters attempts to do so.

Appendix: Wording of Questions

Two-City Survey

Although this was a panel study with multiple waves, all results are from the third wave of the study. This was the "electoral wave," because it was conducted between the first and second rounds of the October 2002 elections.

Information

Presidency: "Many people don't know the names of the candidates for president. Do you know the names of any presidential candidates? (If yes) Which? Any more?"

Governorship: "Do you know the names of any gubernatorial candidates? (If yes) Which? Any more?"

Federal deputy: "Do you know the names of any federal deputy candidates? (If yes) Which? Any more?"

Clientelism and Pork

Federal deputy: "Did you vote for that candidate because you thought s/he would help your city, because you thought s/he would present proposals in the Congress of national interest, or because s/he once helped you with something you needed?"

Candidate Attributes

Do you think that Lula/Serra/Ciro/Garotinho is very intelligent, intelligent, a little intelligent, or not at all intelligent? (asked separately for each candidate.)

Do you think that Lula/Serra/Ciro/Garotinho is a very strong leader, a strong leader, not a very strong leader, or not at all a strong leader? (asked separately for each candidate.)

Do you think that Lula/Serra/Ciro/Garotinho is very honest, honest, a little bit honest, or not at all honest? (asked separately for each candidate.)

Do you think that Lula/Serra/Ciro/Garotinho is very compassionate, compassionate, a little compassionate, or not at all compassionate? (asked separately for each candidate.)

Performance Evaluations

Speaking of your personal economic situation, in the last twelve months, would you say that it has worsened a lot, worsened a little, stayed the same, improved a little, or improved a lot?

Speaking generally about the country in the last twelve months, would you say that its economic situation has worsened a lot, worsened a little, stayed the same, improved a little, or improved a lot?

And what about your city? Would you say that its economic situation has worsened a lot, worsened a little, stayed the same, improved a little, or improved a lot in the last twelve months?

Issue Voting

In the last ten years, state-owned businesses that were directed by the government were sold to private entrepreneurs in a process known as "privatization." With which of the following phrases about privatization do you agree more? Privatization is a good thing. Privatization is a bad thing

Another important issue in Brazil is land reform. With which of the following phrases do you agree more? The government should give land from large farms to landless workers. The government should not give land from large farms to landless workers.

Brazilian National Election Study

Information

For whom did you vote for federal deputy?

Can you mention the name of the governor of the state of [respondent's state]?

Can you mention the name of a federal deputy from [respondent's state]?

Clientelism and Pork

In this election, did the municipality or anyone else offer you something in exchange for your vote?

PART III

The Policy Challenges of an Unequal Society

7

The Limits of Economic Reform in Brazil

Aline Diniz Amaral,

Peter R. Kingstone, and

Jonathan Krieckhaus

THE ELECTION of the Workers' Party (PT) candidate Luiz Inácio "Lula" da Silva in 2002 was a watershed in Brazilian history. The very fact that Brazilians chose a former union leader whose socialist leanings had stirred talk of coups only thirteen years earlier says a great deal about the achievements of Brazil's young democracy. His reelection in 2006 was impressive as well. The scale of his achievement, however, has been marred by serious accusations of corruption, as well as by widespread disappointment among the PT faithful over his sharp turn to the right on economic policy. This shift was a betrayal of the most cherished principles of the Workers' Party and its traditional base in the organized working-class and progressive social movements. Lula campaigned in 2002 explicitly against the market-oriented neoliberal economic reforms embraced by his predecessor, Fernando Henrique Cardoso (PSDB, Partido da Social Democracia Brasileira). His opposition to these market-oriented reforms resonated among Brazilians, many of whom had become disenchanted with the course of economic policy under Cardoso. Why then would Lula betray his party, his loyal base, and his campaign promises in order to pursue economic policies that had been anathema to him over the entire course of his political career?

Various chapters in this volume deal with the causes and consequences of Lula's turn to the orthodox economic right. In particular, Wendy Hunter analyzes the internal party dynamics that allowed Lula to move the party to the right despite considerable internal opposition. Timothy Power demonstrates the extent of ideological and policy convergence towards the center within the Brazilian legislature. This chapter focuses particularly on the constraints on the government's room to promote progressive reforms.

We explore the issue by focusing on two test cases of Brazilian political economy: macroeconomic policy and the regulation of newly privatized, formerly state-owned enterprises. Macroeconomic policy is the area where foreign pressure is most likely to constrain leftist governments. Foreign financial markets pay close attention to macroeconomic indicators and signals of government intentions. Foreign financial actors can swiftly punish governments that deviate from their preferred policies by withdrawing investment or calling in loans. By contrast, regulation provides a different test of the extent to which constraints exist. The regulation of newly privatized firms does not draw intense foreign scrutiny, and the only truly interested foreign actors are investors or potential investors in the sector. These firms have much weaker mechanisms for influencing governments in developing countries: namely, withholding new investments. Thus, regulatory policy should be an area where left-wing, reform-oriented governments have considerable room for policy change.

Furthermore, both macroeconomic policy and regulatory policy provide good tests of the extent to which leftist governments, in particular, face constraints, because they are both areas where politicians face pronounced differences between the preferences of voters and those of financial markets. In macroeconomic policy, leftist governments may face a conflict between voters' desire for higher government spending and higher rates of growth on the one hand, and foreign financiers' preferences for macroeconomic stability on the other. In regulatory policy, leftist governments may find themselves torn between a desire to intervene actively in newly privatized sectors for a variety of reasons—ideological or political—and the need to encourage new private investment from foreign firms wary of government intervention. Thus, both these policy areas present a potentially difficult choice between hewing an orthodox course to please foreign financial actors or instigating reforms in order to address a disenchanted domestic audience. We argue that Lula found himself in precisely this situation in 2002, a circumstance that placed constraints on his policy choices.

The constraints arise from two sources. The first is the lack of a well-developed and clearly defined set of economic alternatives to neoliberal reforms in the wake of the collapse of communism (Castañeda 1994). Discontent with market-oriented reforms is not sufficient to promote growth; reformist governments need concrete solutions to promote competitiveness and productivity at the macro and micro level of the economy. To date, no real alternatives appear available. Yet, even if a technically sound policy were available, leftist presidents face a second and more critical constraint. In brief, dependence on foreign sources of finance means that governments in developing countries face potential limits to their policymaking autonomy. In particular, leftist governments may have very limited credibility in the eyes of foreign investors and creditors and therefore may feel significant pressure. Lula's conversion from one-time socialist to the steady guardian of orthodox economic policy praised by Wall Street may have multiple causes. We contend, however, that a central one is the way that international financial markets constrain policy reform and deviation from economic orthodoxy.[1]

A review of the economic strategy developed by the Cardoso administration will allow us to examine its successes and weaknesses. Brazil's debt and the need to finance it in international financial markets constrained Lula's choices about fiscal policies and spending priorities. Lula's professed desire to alter Brazil's privatization and regulation model gave way to the need to preserve investor-friendly economic policies, particularly in the absence of any clearly articulated alternative policy. The tension between satisfying the interests of foreign investors and addressing the concerns and preferences of Brazilian citizens has important implications for the types of policy choices that country leaders have in their arsenal.

Economic Development and the 2002 Elections

Lula's 2002 electoral campaign promised to foster social inclusion, increase investment in social programs and policy, champion social justice, promote national industry, and stop or even reverse the Cardoso administration's neoliberal economic policies. Lula's pledges were not particularly surprising. They were certainly consistent with the PT's positions over the course of the 1990s. But, they were also responsive to the country's widespread dissatisfaction with Cardoso's economic program. In fact, the Cardoso administration's economic policies were so unpopular that even José Serra, Cardoso's handpicked successor sought to distance himself from them.

To some extent, this widespread rejection of Cardoso's economic program was unfair and denied him credit for considerable economic achievements over the course of his administration. Cardoso had, in fact, made some important strides over the course of his time in office. Brazil's economic performance after the restoration of democracy was poor by just about any measure. The country registered little economic growth over the 1985–1994 period, while suffering from high and rising levels of domestic and foreign debt as well as seemingly intractable inflation. Economic policymaking under successive presidents, from Jose Sarney (1985–1990) to Fernando Collor (1990–1992) and Itamar Franco (1992–1994) shifted repeatedly as each successive president imposed his own programmatic preferences and introduced his own (woefully unsuccessful) attempts to contain inflation. Itamar Franco's appointment of Fernando Henrique Cardoso as finance minister in 1993 marked a genuine turning point in Brazilian political economy.

Cardoso inherited responsibility for an unstable economy that lacked a clear policy direction, although the country had the taken the first steps towards the set of market-oriented reforms commonly referred to as neoliberalism. Among the measures undertaken before Cardoso (especially by President Collor), the most notable included commercial liberalization, deregulation, the beginnings of financial liberalization, and the beginnings of privatization of state-owned enterprises. As finance minister, Cardoso successfully contained inflation, and subsequently as president, he pushed the country further in the direction of neoliberalism. By 2002, the Cardoso administration's reliable, steady, and coherent stewardship of the economy had translated into an enviable mix of reasonable economic growth, low inflation, and dramatic increases in foreign investment. In the early 1990s, the chaos of Brazilian political economy led Rudiger Dornbusch, a noted economist from the International Monetary Fund (IMF), to declare that Brazil was "drunk." By the end of the decade, Brazil was among the better performing economies of Latin America and one of the leading recipients of foreign investment in the entire developing world.

It is important to note, however, that Cardoso and his economic team were not committed neoliberal ideologues (in contrast to Chile, for example), and economic policy under his government remained quite heterodox and pragmatic. In fact, the Cardoso administration had two overarching economic goals that helped define their policy orientations. First and foremost, the Cardoso team was committed to currency stability: that is, maintaining low inflation. Cardoso indicated early in his term that low inflation was the linchpin of all progressive social policy. Furthermore, Brazilian voters had experienced inflation's destructive power and had become highly intolerant of it. Pedro Malan, Cardoso's finance minister and a noted orthodox monetarist economist, maintained strict control on all fiscal and monetary policy decisions to make sure that both government spending and the money supply served the larger goal of keeping inflation low. This was not an easy task; Brazil had (and still has as of 2008) several areas that were desperately in need of investment, including education, health, and infrastructure. But Cardoso also inherited a fiscal mess rooted in a perverse form of federalism compounded by high foreign and domestic debt and a severe financial shortfall in the country's public pension system. As a consequence, Cardoso had little choice but to pursue neoliberal orthodox spending and monetary policies to keep inflation under control, while attempting gradual reforms of the underlying structural problems.

While currency stability was the highest priority, promoting economic competitiveness was also an important goal of the Cardoso administration, and privatization/regulation was considered a vital means for improving the competitive infrastructure of the economy. Thus, utilities such as energy and telecommunications occupied a central place in the administration's privatization plans, insofar as they could either facilitate competitive improvements in the whole economy if they operate efficiently or drag the rest of the economy down if they don't. Privatization alone, however, is not sufficient to raise competitiveness and efficiency. Private firms are driven by profit, and it is the profit motive that theoretically pushes them to operate more efficiently and productively than state-owned firms. But, if private firms have monopoly or oligopoly positions (which is common with utilities) they can also exploit consumers and avoid improving efficiency and productivity. Alternatively, politicians pursuing their own political ends may undermine efficient private firms and ultimately hurt overall welfare, no matter how progressive those ends may appear. For example, politicians may try to lower utility rates to make service more affordable for lower-class or middle-class consumers. But forcing firms to lower rates below profit levels undermines their efficiency, discourages further investment, and ultimately results in a kind of de facto expropriation of assets (Levy and Spiller 1996).

The Cardoso administration addressed this dilemma by following the prevailing model in the developed world. The solution in developed economies is to design regulatory agencies that are independent both of the government and the firms they monitor and regulate. The intention behind this solution was to promote economic growth by encouraging efficient, competitive firms in key infrastructure sectors while at the same time promoting improved social welfare. Thus, like with macroeconomic policy, an ostensibly conservative orthodox policy also served a more progressive set of goals for the Cardoso administration as it simultaneously enhanced social welfare and economic growth. Nevertheless, critics charged that Cardoso had abandoned his own social-democratic roots.

The criticism was exacerbated over time as Cardoso's successes were offset by weaknesses that manifested more and more clearly towards the end of his administration. Brazilians, especially poor ones, benefited directly from the end to chronic, severe inflation in 1994–1995, and the boost in average Brazilians' purchasing power led to a short-term boom of consumption. But, ending inflation provided only a short-lived, one-time benefit. Real and continuous improvements in Brazil's notoriously high levels of poverty and inequality required regular improvements in education, wages, and employment opportunities. These, however, were not forthcoming for reasons directly connected to Cardoso's policies. In particular, Cardoso's government needed to limit spending and to maintain extraordinarily high real interest rates in order to preserve capital inflows and thereby secure the stability of the currency. The Cardoso administration had also introduced new taxes (in particular the tax on financial transactions) on top of an already onerous and inefficient tax system as a way to increase government revenues. The resulting low inflation and greatly improved government revenues came at the cost of increasing public-sector debt, discouraging formal-sector employment, and weakening domestic business investment.

In fact, between Cardoso's reelection in 1998 and Lula's election in 2002, economic performance declined on several key indicators every year but 2000.[2] In essence, deficit management and inflation fighting trumped all other considerations, as unemployment increased, consumption declined, the real devalued sharply (further hurting consumers' purchasing power), and growth progressed at an anemic average rate of 2.1 percent over the 1999–2002 period (only 1.3 percent if 2000 is excluded). This weak economic performance combined with fear in the cities of rising crime, disappointment in the rural sector over slow land reforms, anger over a series of corruption scandals, and the disastrous 2001 energy crisis (with its resultant energy rationing) to set the stage for a campaign in which both candidates worked to distance themselves from Cardoso and portray themselves as the real alternative.

Lula was particularly sharp in his criticism, referring to Cardoso's legacy of social and economic ills as an "accursed inheritance" (*herança maldita*) and vowing an "inversion of priorities." It is important to highlight that these criticisms were consistent with the PT's traditional views and those of its base. They also reflected real problems in the economy, and thus they constituted a serious (that is, not populist or demagogic) critique of failings of the orthodox, neoliberal economic program. Yet, with only a few months left before the presidential elections and the polls pointing clearly to a PT victory, Lula began to shift course with his "Carta ao Povo Brasileiro" ("Letter to the Brazilian People," discussed below).[3] By early in his term, critics were already referring to his presidency as the "third Cardoso term." This was not a painless shift, and in many areas the administration was divided internally over economic policy orientation. In the end, however, the administration's choices consistently reflected their perceived need to satisfy foreign investors and creditors. In the sections below, we explore in greater detail the breakdown of Lula's commitment to reform and frame it within a larger theoretical context.

International Constraints

Lula's decision to maintain Cardoso's policies was not inevitable. Cardoso's program was sufficiently unpopular that both Lula and José Serra ran against it. So why did Lula end up endorsing Cardoso's policies? To some extent, the PT had already moderated its approach well before the election, as discussed in other chapters of this book. For most observers, however, an equally salient factor was that international capital markets severely constrained Lula's options—a view that Lula himself articulated (Rennó and Spanakos 2006). Investors prefer fiscal discipline, so if Lula had not conformed to this preference, investors would have moved their money out of Brazil. Such capital flight would have generated substantial economic costs, which Lula rationally sought to avoid.

This argument, however, is incongruent with the larger political-economy literature on capital flows. The more general cross-national literature usually suggests that domestic policymakers are *not* seriously constrained by international investment. Mosley (2003), for instance, reviews a large body of literature on the OECD (Organisation for Economic Co-operation and Development) and concludes that "many of these studies imply that international economic constraints are relatively small, and domestic political pressures and institutions remain central to the selection and implementation of government strategies" (13).

Mosley (2000) argues that these constraints will be broader in developing countries, but here too the literature has not demonstrated strong effects. Maxfield

(1998), for instance, surveyed the empirical literature on the determinants of capital flows and concluded that foreign investors generally do not care much about a country's economic policies but are instead motivated by issues such as international liquidity and world interest rates. More recently, Wibbels and Arce (2003) find that capital markets do react to domestic politics and tax policy, but there is nonetheless little evidence that these capital markets *influence* domestic economic policy. "Consistent with research on global markets and national politics in OECD countries, many of the most notable components of globalization have no effect on tax burdens across countries and through time" (Wibbels and Arce 2003, 115).

How can we reconcile this conventional wisdom in the cross-national literature with the common understanding in Brazil (and in Latin America more generally) that Lula was constrained by international markets? Simply put, we argue that in comparative perspective, Brazil in 2002 was in an unusual situation, making it particularly susceptible to international pressures. Most importantly, the economy was on the brink of crisis, such that ignoring international sentiment would have pushed the economy over the edge, resulting in substantial economic costs. This pressure was then exacerbated by the discrepancy between international investors' preferences and Lula's preferences. Somewhat ironically, international investors sought greater fiscal discipline from Lula than they would have from a conservative policymaker, precisely because investors did not believe that Lula actually wanted to rein in public spending.

Economic Context

During 2002, Brazil was closer to an economic crisis than any other major country in Latin America: "Everybody knows that Brazil's solvency is on a knife edge" (*Financial Times*, Oct. 15, 2002). Moreover, when observers speculated as to whether Brazil would fall into severe crisis or instead manage to muddle through, it was clear that the major determinant of this outcome was going to be international investor sentiment.

The big risk on investors' minds was a default on the public debt. Default is a relatively rare event, but Argentina had defaulted just the year before, and investors saw Brazil as the most likely culprit for future defaults. Default risk rises when countries have difficulty financing their fiscal deficits or their current account deficits. In Brazil, both fiscal and external accounts had deteriorated substantially prior to 2002.

Net public-sector debt doubled in merely eight years, rising from 30 percent of GDP in 1994 to 59 percent in 2002 (Williamson 2002, 4). Moreover, most analysts argued that debt growth would continue into the indefinite future. The external debt was also rising precipitously, from around 12 percent of GDP in 1996 to 36 percent of GDP in 2002 (Banco Central do Brasil 2004). Indeed, Brazil's current-account deficit, at 4.6 percent, was greater than any other major country in Latin America and was more than twice the regional average (calculated from World Bank 2005).

It is difficult to prove that Brazil was close to a default in 2002, but there is little doubt that most investors *believed* that it was close to default. Williamson (2002) wrote a long analysis, for instance, evaluating whether Brazil would lapse into an Argentine-style crisis. Similarly, the financial press speculated about a possible Brazilian default, while investment banks downgraded Brazilian bonds into the "underweight category" due to default risk (e.g., *Financial Times*, Oct. 29, 2002). Brazil was, in short, on the brink of crisis.

International investor sentiment was the critical determinant of whether Brazil was going to fall into crisis or not. The recent economics literature on foreign-exchange crises emphasizes the importance of multiple equilibria, in which a country's economic fundamentals are consistent with both a stable outcome and a crisis outcome. Which of these two outcomes prevails is primarily dependent on expectations. If most investors believe a country cannot defend its currency, the resulting speculation will overwhelm the country's defenses. On the other hand, if most investors believe the country can successfully defend its currency, then there is less pressure on the currency, and a relatively stable outcome ensues.

Williamson (2002) argues at length that this is precisely the situation in which Brazil found itself prior to Lula's elections. Whether or not Brazil would be able to service its external debt, for instance, was primarily dependent upon international investors' sentiment: "If lenders were prepared to roll over their credits on terms broadly comparable to the existing ones, then Brazil would have no problem in financing itself over the coming year or two. . . . But . . . if the markets continue to be spooked by political fears, they will be able to look to short-term worsening of the debt indicators to rationalize a decision to refuse to roll over debts on reasonable terms. In that case Brazil's situation will become impossible even without capital flight, some of which also has to be expected under these circumstances" (Williamson 2002, 10).

Investor sentiment was equally decisive for Brazil's fiscal accounts. Fully 42 percent of Brazil's public debt was dollar denominated, such that speculation against the real could dramatically drive up the debt burden (Williamson 2002, 5). Moreover, negative investor sentiment increased domestic interest rates, since Brazilians needed to offer higher interest rates to compensate investors for their greater (perceived) risk. For a sense of how much investor sentiment can negatively influence fiscal accounts, consider the evolution of Brazilian economic variables during 2002. The real plummeted by over 50 percent during the first half of 2002, leading by definition to a 50 percent increase in the dollar-denominated debt (Martínez and Santiso 2003, 370). Interest rates were at usurious levels (over 20 percent), constituting a further crippling drag on debt service.

In short, if the capital markets had decided Brazil was insolvent, the resulting pressure on the real and domestic interest rates would guarantee that Brazil would, in fact, be insolvent. If capital markets had decided Brazil was solvent, Brazil would, in fact, have been solvent. The investor community was entirely aware of this role, noting that Lula needed to strongly signal a fiscally conservative orientation so that he could "win the game" of investor sentiment. Paulo Leme, speaking for Goldman Sachs, for instance, predicted economic crisis unless Lula strongly signaled neoliberalism, in which case a positive equilibrium was attainable. "This is a situation for which a viable solution is possible, provided that the new management is perceived as being strong, and brings a sound economic program. Therefore, we believe that a strong confidence shock (based on an orthodox economic policy and team) from whoever wins the elections could immediate shift the economy to a better equilibrium. . . . Otherwise, we believe that a tractable economic crisis could worsen" (Goldman Sachs 2002b, 4).

In short, not only was Brazil on the brink of crisis in 2002, but international investors were explicitly looking to Lula to tell them which of two equilibria they should expect—a positive equilibrium, in which improving sentiment would lead to a stronger real and lower interest rates, thus leading to a manageable debt, or a negative equilibrium, in which deteriorating investor sentiment would lead to devaluation and high interest rates, which in turn would lead to debt default and severe economic crisis.

The latter outcome would have been catastrophic. In Argentina, such a crisis substantially increased poverty, from 37 percent of the population in 2001 to fully 58 percent of the population in 2002 (World Bank 2003, i). An increase of this magnitude in Brazil would easily have dwarfed any positive contribution that Lula might have had made through heterodox policies. As such, when capital markets told Lula that he needed to strongly signal fiscal discipline or markets would enter the negative equilibrium, he was under enormous pressure to give those signals.

Political Context

We have seen that Brazil was in a vulnerable stage in 2002, such that investors might have unusually large sway over any given presidential candidate. We now argue that the leverage inherent in Brazilians knife-edge economic context was exacerbated by Lula's left politics. First, and most obviously, bond markets did not like Lula. Martínez and Santiso (2003) examine Lula's popularity in the run-up to the presidential election and take this value to be a proxy for the likelihood of Lula's governing. They compare this with the interest-rate premium on bonds. They demonstrate a correlation between these two variables, with higher probabilities of a Lula electoral victory leading to a higher interest-rate premium (a "risk premium") in the bond markets.

The implications of this point are perhaps somewhat obvious, but nonetheless important. Right-leaning policymakers do not face much pressure from capital markets, given that they adopt more or less the same policies that the market wants in any event. It is only the political Left that feels strong pressure from markets, given that the Left desires different policies than capital markets.

Moreover, ironically, when the Left does feel the need to signal its neoliberalism, it must signal this much more strongly than does the Right. Simply put, markets did not trust Lula, and he was going to have to act inordinately neoliberal in spirit if he was to gain this trust. Hence, the Left is not only constrained in the obvious sense that it has to change its policies further to the right, but it is further constrained by the need to shift policies even further to the right than the Right would itself, so as to convince investors of its credibility. It is the combination of Brazil's nascent economic crisis and Lula's left politics, therefore, which explains Lula's unwavering commitment to fiscal discipline.

Lula's Reaction to the Market

Lula clearly understood that Brazil was posed on the brink of crisis, and that this gave international investors considerable control over domestic economic policy: "We remain at the mercy of speculators, who many times barely know where the countries are on the map" (Goldman Sachs 2002a). Loose fiscal policies would not merely have reduced investment on the margin, but indeed would have risked the much more disastrous possibility that negative international sentiment would push the Brazilian economy into an Argentine-style crisis.

In June of 2002, Lula explicitly told the Brazilian people that foreigners were concerned about the Brazilian economy and that this would constrain Brazilian policy in the months to come.[4] He underlined that there was a "strong worry in financial markets about the poor performance of the economy and its current fragility" and, more especially, a foreign concern "about the capacity of the nation to service its internal and external debt."[5] More importantly, he explicitly noted that this external crisis was so severe that it gave Brazilian policymakers little room for autonomous policy choice: "What is important is that this crisis must be avoided, because it would cause irreparable suffering for the majority of the population. To avoid this crisis it is necessary to understand the margin for maneuver in the short run is small."

Consistent with his words, Lula's speeches and actions in the months leading up to the elections were designed to shift Brazil from a bad-equilibrium outcome to a good-equilibrium outcome, primarily by convincing international investors that he would strongly endorse their policy preferences. What were these policy preferences? Four goals come up again and again in market commentary on Lula (e.g., *The Financial Times*, Oct. 23, 2002). Concerning economic policy per se, there is no doubt that that single most important goal was for Lula to increase the primary surplus. More generally, there was strong interest in Lula appointing an economic team that investors liked. Perhaps less important, but also relevant, was the desire for greater central-bank independence and structural reforms.

Lula strongly signaled his desire to meet these goals. The best clue as to a candidate's future economic policies is his or her economic platform, and the pressure from international markets led to radical change in the year leading up to the election. As late as December 2001, the PT's program indicated suspicion of foreign capital and spoke of "breaking with the current economic model, which is based on opening the market and radical deregulation, and the consequent subordination of the dynamic of the national economy to the interests and whims of global financial capital." Moreover, this same platform promised to increase tariffs, regulate foreign capital, and renegotiate the international debt (Williamson 2002, 12).

In light of Brazil's knife-edge economic status, and the consequent increase in international pressure, the PT's rhetoric became substantially more market friendly. Just six months later (July 2002), the platform promised that Lula "would not break contracts or revoke established rules" and that the primary surplus would be maintained or even raised. Inflation targeting was also added, which usually entails contractionary policies that are antithetical to the Left. It is possible that these changes were aimed at a domestic audience, but the sorts of issues at stake (contract enforcement, fiscal discipline, and inflation targeting) do not seem to have a strong domestic constituency but are precisely those policies desired by foreign investors.

Concerning the cabinet, Lula again appears to have altered his preferences. Once elected, Lula appointed a "market friendly" economic team that was committed to fiscal and monetary stability (Martínez and Santiso 2003, 376). He also appointed Henrique Meirelles, a prominent market-oriented economist and a member of Cardoso's PSDB, as president of the Brazilian Central Bank. Concerning the third desire of international investors, Lula's cabinet floated the idea of making Brazil's Central Bank independent (although it is less clear that Lula himself supported this), in direct contradiction with the PT's earlier opposition to this move (Samuels 2006, 8). Finally, concerning structural reforms, probably the most important reform in investors' eyes was a reform of the public-sector pension system, in order to control spending. Here again, Lula backed pension reform, directly contradicting the PT's earlier position. In all four domains, then, Lula provided international investors with the policy outcomes they wanted.

The Lula experience provides an important lesson for the literature on globalization and its constraining effects. Despite widespread belief that the international arena constrains policy, the cross-national literature has generally not been able to show much effect. We argue that this literature would benefit from greater attention to context. Mosley (2000), for instance, provided an important step forward by arguing that capital flows constrain a *broader* range of policies in developing countries than in developed countries. We argue, analogously, that capital flows constitute *deeper* constraints when countries face economic crisis and elect left-leaning politicians.

Brazil's knife-edge economic status raised the salience of international investor sentiment by an order of magnitude, such that policymakers (rationally) decided that improving investor sentiment was the most important goal. Investors' distrust of the Left further constrained Brazil's options, forcing an even deeper policy adjustment than would have been required from the Right. In sum, in situations of near-crisis, when conjoined with a president from the Left, capital markets can wield striking power over domestic economic policy. By taking these contextual factors into account, scholars working within the statistical tradition might be able to better capture international markets' constraining effects.

The Limits of Regulatory Reform

Privatization and regulation illustrate another way that leftist governments face constraints on reform efforts. Foreign observers watch macroeconomic policy decisions and indicators very carefully but are not nearly as attentive to or concerned with regulatory policy (Santiso 2003). Early in the market-oriented reform process, international financial actors saw privatization as a key signal of credible commitment to policy reforms (Rodrik 1989). As a consequence, privatization was an important and highly visible policy. But, regulation is a more subtle, less salient area of policy, and ultimately the only foreign observers that pay careful attention are investors or potential investors in the privatized sector.

Regulation, however, is much more salient for leftist parties. Privatization has been highly unpopular in Brazil as well as in much of the rest of Latin America (Baker 2001; Lora and Panizza 2003) because voters associate it—rightly or wrongly—with a host of ills, including lay-offs, rising prices, poor service, and corruption, as well as a loss of national sovereignty. As a result, opposing privatization may make sense politically. But, leftist and nationalist parties in Latin America also have been particularly hostile to privatization because they saw state-owned enterprises as tools for promoting national development and social welfare. Thus, short of renationalization—an extreme step even for leftist presidents—the only real changes leftist presidents can effect are in the area of regulation. Governments can use regulations to actively influence newly privatized sectors on an array of issues like prices, access to and cost of services, and allocation of resources, as well as specific winners and losers among consumers and among investors. In short, governments can use regulatory agencies to promote social and development goals indirectly that they had previously promoted directly through state-owned enterprises. But, to do that would require changes to the regulatory model advocated by the World Bank and the IMF (and embraced by the Cardoso administration), as it was designed to protect exactly against this kind of government intervention.

The combination of low salience for foreign actors coupled with high salience for domestic voters and leftist politicians would suggest that there is greater room for policy reform vis-à-vis financial markets. But presidents, regardless of their ideological orientation, need to encourage continuing investments in vital areas of the infrastructure. As a result, would-be reformers are constrained by the concerns/demands of private investors. Ultimately, Lula was not forced to alter his program in as visible, rapid, and dramatic fashion as he was with macroeconomic policy. But, the need to encourage new investment forced Lula to retreat from a sharply articulated critique of the prevailing model of privatization and regulation in favor of the status quo. Moreover, he was further stymied by the absence of any clear alternative that would increase government control without discouraging the kinds of investment necessary for growth, that would lower prices for consumers, and that would expand access to service. As of 2008, the Lula administration has continued to articulate a preference for reform but has not been able to conceive of or advance one.

Privatization advanced in Brazil in the wake of the financial crisis that hit the country in the 1980s. The crisis led to a sharp reduction in the investment capacity of the state and a decline in the performance of state-owned enterprises, especially in vital areas like energy, transportation, and telecommunications. Concern about declining performance led to a favorable environment for adopting a series of structural reforms designed to promote renewed growth and a competitive integration with the international economy. Among those reforms, successive governments pursued a program of privatization that effectively broke the "statist" model of development that Brazil had followed continuously since the 1930s. In 1995, the Cardoso government deepened the program with a set of constitutional reforms that "flexibilized" state monopolies in vital sectors where the state was no longer capable of investing. The new challenge was to create a favorable environment for private investment in order to increase efficiency and expand services, especially in infrastructure, the modernization of which was crucial for encouraging new investments in productive sectors of the economy.

Privatization of infrastructure, however, raises significant challenges for governments, as it implies not only the sale of assets but also the concession of vital public services to private firms. It is one thing to sell off the phone company and all its network of lines; it is another thing to give up the power to subsidize prices for consumers or control who gets access to service. Public services have enormous direct effects on public welfare, and governments in developed and developing countries cannot simply allow private firms to make decisions without considering their effects on citizens. Therefore, privatizing governments need to devise a regulatory framework that defines the rules for operating these services for the new private providers. The state acts through regulatory agencies to balance the concerns of firms, on the one hand, and citizens on the other. Regulatory agencies act to assure stability and credibility of the rules to attract private investment while at the same time disciplining private firms to prevent market failures—that is, the failure to improve access to service at competitive prices. The idea behind regulatory agencies, then, is to simultaneously guarantee both socially and economically efficient outcomes.

The Cardoso government, benefiting from the macroeconomic stability that followed the Real Plan, carried out the largest number of privatizations and over its eight years created nine regulatory agencies in infrastructure and social services. [6] The regulatory agencies were first introduced into Brazil through the General Law of Telecommunications (LGT) of July 16, 1997, that established the new regulatory framework for the telecommunications sector and created the country's first fully developed regulatory agency, ANATEL.

Initially, political conflict exploded over privatization and regulation well before any tangible evidence of poor functioning emerged. In fact, the passage of the LGT in the Brazilian Congress revealed a great ideological gap between the PSDB (Cardoso) and the PT. The PSDB, under Cardoso, supported a more neoliberal orientation, while the PT (along with the Brazilian Communist Party, PCdoB) defended the most statist view (Amaral 2000). Opposition to privatization and the establishment of the regulatory system was intense and ideological. But the opposition, including the PT, had neither the votes in Congress nor concrete counterproposals to block the creation of the new regulatory agencies. Instead, the opposition launched a series of lawsuits designed to impede or delay their implementation.[7]

The intensity of the PT's opposition—within the Congress and through their grassroots mobilization, meant that there was good reason to suspect that a Lula victory would mean the end of the still-new and not fully consolidated regulatory model. When the polls indicated Lula as the favorite for the elections, Deputy Walter Pinheiro (PT), who had played a central role in opposition during the passage of the LGT, publicly called for the directors of all the regulatory agencies to resign upon the inauguration of the new government (*Folha de São Paulo*, Oct. 13, 2002). The statement was seen as a serious threat to the integrity of the regulatory model, as the agencies were supposed to be autonomous and independent of the government. To that end, they were administered by a Council of Directors, each of whom was nominated by the executive with approval of the Senate, and with fixed terms that did not coincide with the term of the president. The directors' mandate was guaranteed by Law 9,986 of 2000, which indicated that "councilors and directors will only lose their mandate through resignation, judicial condemnation, or administrative disciplinary action." In short, the law established a series of protections against exactly the kind of threat of overt political intervention implied by Pinheiro's demand.

Two months after this public call, the Lula government, elected but not yet inaugurated, made decreasing the agencies' powers its first objective. Armed with a number of complaints about the agencies' poor performance, Lula accused them of moving beyond their proper jurisdiction and meddling in issues that were legally in the province of the president and his cabinet. This included things such as the development of sectoral policies, which were part of national development policy and never meant to be part of the agencies' jurisdiction, as well as not maintaining neutral rules for investors (*Folha de São Paulo*, Sept. 9, 2002). In fact, many technical observers agreed with Lula's charge and argued that it reflected weaknesses in the regulatory framework established by Cardoso.

While the debate over jurisdiction was somewhat technical, investors' concerns about serious threats to the stability and the integrity of the regulatory model increased as Lula and the agencies entered into a much more visible fight over prices. Shortly after the installation of the new government, Lula expressed "surprise" at rate increases for fuel, telephone services, and energy—all privatized sectors and under the supervision of the regulatory agencies. He claimed to be particularly angry that he had only learned of the increases through the newspapers (28.75 percent for average telephone tariffs and almost 40 percent for electrical energy rates) (*Folha de São Paulo*, Feb. 20, 2003). He bitterly attacked the agencies, accusing them of "outsourcing" (*terceirização*) the state (*Folha de São Paulo*, Feb. 27, 2003).[8]

The question of how to adjust prices is actually one of the most important elements of the regulatory model and has the greatest potential for creating tension between investors and politicians. In general, when governments privatize state-owned utility companies, they need to establish a formula for how to readjust tariffs. Ideally, that formula is included in the contract signed with the new private firms. The formula needs to balance two almost inherently conflicting demands: consumers' demands for low prices (which politicians clearly want to support) and investors' demands for a reasonable rate of return on their investments in the sector (which is critical to encourage new investments). In the Brazilian case, the formula used a specific inflation index, the IGP (Índice Geral de Preços, General Price Index). It is interesting to note that this mechanism for adjusting tariffs passed through the Congress originally not only without sparking controversy but in fact virtually without notice from the opposition, which lacked the technical knowledge to understand the significance of the tariff adjustment process. Yet, the IGP soon proved politically unpalatable for the PT and thus became the fulcrum of the PT's attack against the regulatory agencies.[9]

The fight came to head in February 2003, when a sharp devaluation of the real affected the tariff-adjustment process and brought the issue to the forefront. In the case of telecommunications, for example, the IGP indicated a tariff adjustment of 25 percent, whereas the alternative IPCA (Índice Nacional de Preços ao Consumidor Amplo, Extended Consumer Price Index) indicated an increase of only around 14 percent—almost half the increase mandated by the IGP. ANATEL (the telecommunications regulatory agency), following the law, announced an average rate increase of telephone tariffs of 25 percent. The PT leadership was outraged, and in response, Miro Teixera, the minister of communications, actively encouraged private lawsuits against ANATEL and the announced rate increase (*Folha de São Paulo*, Sept. 24, 2006). Initially, the PT appeared to have won its fight with ANATEL when a lower court injunction was issued applying the IPCA 14 percent increase (*Folha de São Paulo*, July 16, 2003), but on July 1, 2004, the Supreme Court found in favor of the private firms—mostly foreign—and restored the rate increase in accordance with the IGP (*Folha de São Paulo*, July 1, 2004). The court's ruling in favor of ANATEL and the private firms highlighted the implications of the loss of control over vital public-welfare decisions and the need to advance reforms that restored the government's capacity to intervene in the sector.

It is important to note that Lula and the PT wanted to reestablish political control over the key utility sectors due to longstanding ideological concerns about privatization and regulation, but they also reflected broader societal debates as well. For example, some in the academic community supported the idea of restructuring the agencies because they perceived them as weak organizations, subject to capture by the very firms they were supposed to regulate in detriment to society (*Folha de São Paulo*, Feb. 22, 2003). Some sectors of the opposition, formerly in the government, supported reforms because they recognized that differences in the performance of the various agencies were a direct consequence of the specific model of privatization—successful in some cases and less so in others (interview with Arthur Virgílio, *Folha de São Paulo*, Mar. 2, 2003). Finally, consumers were also dissatisfied, indicating in a poll conducted by the Institute for the Defense of the Consumer that they did not believe that the agencies were fulfilling their role as a protector of consumer interests or acting in a transparent fashion.[10]

Thus, Lula's complaints about the regulatory agencies and his concerns about tariffs were taken as a credible and legitimate basis for promoting drastic reforms. In short, Lula had a strong domestic backing for reforming the prevailing model, regardless of the preferences of the private firms operating in the sector. The first year of the Lula government, in fact, did feature a number of specific attacks on the regulatory model and suggested that a profound restructuring of the agencies was coming. Among the elements that contributed to that belief, it is worth mentioning: the intense effort, especially through the sectoral ministries, to set rate adjustments below the levels established in the existing contracts; the creation of a commission in the office of the presidential chief of staff, under the coordination of José Dirceu, to study the regulatory agencies and to propose changes to the existing model and in the rules for their operation; the issuing of Decree 4,635 in March 2003 creating a Secretariat of Telecommunications within the Ministry of Communications to "guide, supervise, and monitor the activities of Anatel"; and the sharp restrictions on the agencies' budgets, undermining their financial autonomy.[11]

Yet, while the independence of the agencies was threatened early in the Lula administration, an ideological battle was emerging within the ranks of the executive. Early on, the two perspectives emerged between the finance minister, Antônio Palocci, defending the more neoliberal, proinvestor perspective, and Dilma Rousseff, the minister of mines and energy, under whose supervision were both the National Electrical Energy Agency and the National Petroleum Agency, who argued for their subordination to her ministry (*Folha de São Paulo*, Jan. 7, 2003).

Over time, the positions in the government hardened into two clear lines. The more interventionist line was supported by the presidential chief of staff, José Dirceu, while the minister of finance, Antônio Palocci, continued to defend the position preferred by private investors, who were concerned about threats of government intervention. The contradiction between the government's conservative macroeconomic policy and Lula's interventionist threats against the agencies led Gesner Oliveira, the former head of the Administrative Council for Economic Defense (Brazil's antitrust agency) to offer a stinging diagnosis: "The government's lack of credibility . . . contributes even more to the already high cost of capital, discouraging productive investment. In the microeconomic area, there are two governments. Two diametrically opposed visions are present within the same administration in the various sectoral ministries. The first defends a reform intended to perfect the policies already adopted by the previous government. The second, in frank opposition to the existing models, supports a high level of state intervention" (*Folha de São Paulo*, May 22, 2004). Oliveira's criticism pointed to the concern that unstable rules and fears of government intervention ("administrative expropriation") would drive away critically needed private foreign investment in vital sectors.

By the end of 2003, the government indicated that it recognized the need to encourage investment and the dangers of an interventionist stance. The shift was marked by a document prepared by the office of the presidential chief of staff—formerly the champion of the interventionist stance—entitled "Analysis and Evaluation of the Regulatory Agencies." The document removed any possibility of radical reform of the agencies and defended the importance of maintaining and respecting existing contracts. The only real change was a proposal to create instruments of increased social control. The text noted that "the presence of the agencies was indispensable for the success of private investment, which is central for overcoming the deficit in infrastructure investment in the country" (6). The document continued, "Among the consequences of strengthened regulatory agencies in the infrastructure sectors is their contribution to reducing the cost of capital in those sectors, with important effects on tariffs and the availability and access to these services" (6 and 7).

In sharp contrast to earlier threats against the agencies, the government's report now strongly defended the importance of the independence of the regulatory agencies and the need to insulate them both from political pressure and from capture by private actors. The actual bills presented to Congress in April 2004 reintroduced some reform elements, but they, too, revealed the retreat from the interventionist view and primarily reflected the perspective of finance minister Antônio Palocci. The government had abandoned their longstanding ideological and political opposition to the regulatory framework and instead offered only modest technical improvements on the model.

In brief, the government proposal preserved the general characteristics of the agencies but clarified their specific responsibilities. Under the proposal, the agencies would remain responsible for the supervision and regulation of the sectors, as well as the management of the contracts with the private firms, while the formulation of sectoral policies and the concession of contracts would fall under the jurisdiction of the ministries. In fact, the biggest surprise of the PT bills was that they avoided anything that would discourage foreign investors—a real risk during the seven months in which the issue was contemplated in the presidential palace. Some interventionist points did remain in the proposal: notably, the transfer of the power to concede contracts to the sectoral ministries and a variety of measures to increase oversight and accountability of the agencies. None of these changes, however, was inconsistent with the World Bank's approach to regulation. In general, what took place at the end of Lula's first year in government was a considerable repositioning in favor of private investment.

Ultimately, the Lula government reached the end of its first term without passing the regulatory reform bills. One critical reason for this failure was the conflict over the priorities established by the government and the historic, interventionist discourse of the PT. The Lula government found itself unable to promote a clearly neoliberal, proinvestor project, or a strongly investment-discouraging interventionist project. Ultimately, resolving the regulation issue was tabled when the corruption crisis involving the PT effectively paralyzed the legislative economic agenda, especially in the Chamber of Deputies, where the majority of priority bills were stuck. In the final analysis, the Lula administration accomplished little in a policy area that had been important for the party and that is vitally important for consumers and investors. Caught between the desire to reform the system in accordance with the PT's ideological preferences and the need to attract and maintain foreign investors, the Lula administration did nothing.

The Causes and Consequences of "Neoliberalism by Surprise"

Lula campaigned in 2002 on a platform of promises of reform: an "inversion of priorities" in favor of those on the bottom in Brazil's political economy. He claimed he would use government spending to promote social justice and denigrated Cardoso's commitment to monetary stability. However, as his victory appeared more probable he shifted his focus to reassuring financial markets and using his "Letter to the Brazilian People" to explain to his base that the previous government's errors left him no choice. Yet, his government ended up distinctly favoring financial stability over distributive or redistributive goals and thus continued Cardoso's practice of eschewing fiscal policy to promote growth, and social justice in favor of a strict, noninflationary monetary regime. Lula also campaigned against the regulatory agencies, drawing on broad hostility in Brazil to privatization and the agencies that regulated the new firms. He and his party argued that utilities, and the agencies that regulated them, needed to obey welfare concerns and political preferences on social objectives. In fact, Lula and his administration began openly attacking the agencies and intervening in the newly privatized sectors in favor of consumers and against the private firms. Yet, very quickly, his administration was forced to recognize the need to encourage new investments, and therefore it came to side with the needs of the market and the concerns of private investors.

Domestic political factors may have played a role in this conversion—and chapters by Hunter and Power in this volume highlight the PT's shift rightward. But neither the party's rightward movement nor Lula's "Carta" presaged the extent of the changes. Ultimately, the pressure to meet the expectations of foreign investors and creditors constituted a real limitation on Lula's policy choices. Foreign investors and creditors did not have to pressure the Lula administration actively or directly. Brazil, like all developing countries, simply needs access to investment from outside, and investors are loath to invest if conditions are not satisfactory to them. Ultimately, Lula's story illustrates the fundamental tension in developing countries between championing leftist, distributive/redistributive goals and depending on foreign sources of savings for investment and financial stability. However, voters' and foreign investors' preferences can be in agreement: for example, around a desire for low inflation or for increased investment in utilities (Rennó and Spanakos 2006). It is when they are not in line that the dilemma presents itself.

This dilemma suggests at least three unsettling conclusions. Susan Stokes observed, in *Mandates and Democracy*, that candidates who run on one platform and then govern on an entirely different one ("neoliberalism by surprise") weaken the meaning and quality of political representation. In theory, representative politics works because voters are offered meaningful choices of programs and policies in the political arena, and they vote for those candidates who most accurately reflect their preferences. But when candidates essentially "bait and switch," voters are duped into voting for somebody who may not, in fact, represent their preferences. One danger may be that voters become more suspicious of politicians and their own representative institutions—a trend that has been notable in Latin America over the past decade. It is not clear exactly what are the long-term effects of declining confidence in institutions, but it is certainly not an encouraging trend in young, still relatively fragile democracies.

Lula's "neoliberalism by surprise" also raises serious concerns about the capacity of the Left to offer an alternative to neoliberal policies. Lula is an important test case for asking about the capacity to develop a reformist agenda. As

Hunter and Hochstetler note in this volume, the PT was a coherent party with genuine roots in society and a well-articulated critique of neoliberal reforms. In many respects, Lula and the PT were widely seen as models for a reformist democratic Left in Latin America (Castañeda 1994). Furthermore, Brazil's great size and inherent attractiveness to foreign investors generally give policymakers greater flexibility in international financial markets than most other developing countries (Armijo 1999). Thus, Lula's inability to design and implement a genuinely leftist reform program is a discouraging statement about the extent to which dependence on foreign finance—whether it is loans, portfolio investment, or foreign direct investment—limits the possibilities of distributive/redistributive programs. As of 2008, the only alternative on the table is Hugo Chávez's oil-financed, populist cash handouts—but this is not a real option for Latin American nations without extensive oil exports, and the Venezuelan model is already showing dangerous signs of unsustainability in any event (Corrales 2006b). Unfortunately, neoliberal reforms have brought stability to Brazil and most of Latin America, but modest growth at best and little real reduction in the crippling poverty and inequality that assail the region.[12]

Which brings us to a final concern: Lula's need to hew a more orthodox economic policy line forced him to divorce his electoral strategy from the PT's traditional base. Instead, Lula's reelection in 2006 drew on votes from the country's poorest and least-educated voters and regions (Hunter and Power, 2007). As Almeida and Perlman note in this volume, these are often the citizens who focus least on honest governance and who often feel most excluded. Lula was able to buy these votes more cheaply on the backs of economic stability, a rising minimum wage, and the conditional cash transfers discussed by Melo in this volume. By contrast, the organized sectors of civil society that traditionally voted for the PT are among the citizens that care most about good government and have long defended the inclusive and participatory modes of decision making the PT called "*o modo petista de governar*" (the PT way of governing). Lula's betrayal of the policy goals and decision-making styles of this segment of the population runs the risk of entrenching "archaic" modes of politics. Thus, the limits of policy autonomy, especially for the Left, may have real consequences as well for the quality of democratic politics and the legitimacy of democratic institutions.

Ironically, Lula's betrayal of his promises has not cost in economic terms. Brazil's economy performed well during Lula's first term in office. In particular, Lula's commitment to financial stability helped the country take advantage of a confluence of very favorable factors, including a dramatic increase in global demand for Brazilian commodity exports (especially in China) and an accompanying appreciation of the real. The appreciation of the real, in turn, improved Brazilians' capacity to consume imported goods and to pay down the country's dollar-denominated debt at a time when the U.S. dollar was weakening sharply. We can add conditional cash transfers, an expansion of consumer credit, and Lula's reluctant agreement to increase the minimum wage to this benign set of conditions. All together, they have combined to give low-income Brazilians some of the best economic circumstances they have enjoyed since the 1970s. But, it is not clear that this is sustainable even in the medium term (Arestis et al. 2007). Unfortunately, Brazil also continues to face many of the same structural problems that Cardoso faced in less propitious economic circumstances, and at the outset of the second term there is little indication that Lula will be more successful in overcoming them.

8

Unexpected Successes, Unanticipated Failures: Social Policy from Cardoso to Lula

Marcus André Melo

THE EVALUATION OF PROGRESS made in the area of social policy under Cardoso and Lula requires a careful consideration of at least three puzzles. The first is that, notwithstanding severe fiscal constraints, Brazil has improved its social indicators significantly over the last decade, and several of its social programs—such as Fundef and Bolsa Família—have acquired international recognition. This success, in fact, was not anticipated by contributors to *Democratic Brazil*, who, writing in the late 1990s, shared a strong pessimism about Brazil's ability to overcome its social problems and institutional fragmentation (Kingstone and Power 2000). Admittedly, one of the contributors acknowledged that "successive presidents have defied scholarly expectations by passing a broad array of reforms" (Kingstone 2000, 186). Kingstone couched his argument in terms of gradualism, with each success establishing a base for the next round. But as argued in this chapter, the answer might be in the institutions themselves.

More generally, the literature on social policymaking in Latin America has also been pessimistic in the last decade because of the intrinsic difficulties of the so-called second-generation reforms. Thus, the arguments that make Brazil an unlikely case of policy success are of two sorts, the first stressing political fragmentation and the second pointing to inherent problems of reforms. They have in common the fact that both cannot account for the magnitude and scope of the positive policy outcomes found in the country.

Lula came to power in 2003, after a polarized and much-contested presidential race and after eight years of intense political competition between the PT (Partido dos Trabalhadores) and the PSDB (Partido da Social Democracia Brasileira). Lula personified the anti-Cardoso candidate par excellence because of the harsh criticisms addressed against the so-called neoliberal agenda of his opponent, which was based on privatization, monetary stabilization, and fiscal restraint. Yet—and here is the second puzzle—in the area of social policy, there is a remarkable degree of continuity between the two governments. Not only has the Bolsa Escola, which had been the flagship program of the Cardoso second term of office, survived a major shift in government, it has also become (under the new name of Bolsa Família) the flagship program of the Lula administration. Indeed, Lula's success in the 2006 presidential race has been attributed by the press and experts to the program.

Policy stability or continuity is also found elsewhere in other issue areas. Lula's government has maintained the stringent monetary stability and fiscal policies of Cardoso's second term of office. In fact, the fiscal management of the economy has become increasingly tougher and the targets for the primary surplus (budget surplus minus interest on the debt) have been raised. Equally significant is Lula's failure to implement his highly publicized Fome Zero (Zero Hunger) program. While monetary orthodoxy can be partly explained by the requirements of the international financial order and the penalties it imposes on governments that deviate from fiscal orthodoxy, the continuity in social policy is paradoxical and begs an explanation.

The third puzzle about social policy under Cardoso and Lula is provided by its increasingly universalistic character. By universalistic, I mean one that is non-particularistic—that is, whose policies and programs are addressed to broad constituencies and benefit large portions of Brazilian society.[1] These transfers are made with virtually no political intermediaries, be they politicians, states, or municipal governments. The states play virtually no role in the program, whereas municipalities are involved only in the registration of beneficiaries (under strict federal supervision). This is surprising, considering that current explanations of social policy in the Latin American case, and particularly in Brazil, have stressed the role of clientelism (especially at subnational levels of government) in social policy (Kauffman and Nelson 2004). The supposed effects of clientelism are twofold. By creating an incentive structure that favors narrow particularistic policies, clientelism would undermine efforts at implementing much-needed reforms associated with the provision of encompassing public goods (Samuels 2003). Patronage networks are viewed by many students of Brazilian politics as part and parcel of intergovernmental relations in the country. Thus universalistic reforms and programs would consequently be "undersupplied." Second, universalistic programs already in place, and made viable politically by "extraordinary politics" (including emergency situations and key "constitutional moments" [Nelson 2000]), would be corroded by clientelistic networks.

I offer an interpretation that is an alternative to rival explanations for these puzzles.

Social Policies from Cardoso to Lula

Brazil's record in the social arena during the administrations of Cardoso and Lula is indeed impressive. Recent innovations in social policy include highly acclaimed programs such as Bolsa Família; Fundef (Fundo de Manutenção e Desenvolvimento do Ensino Fundamental e Valorização do Magistério, Fund for Maintenance and Support of Basic Education) recently upgraded and renamed Fundeb; innovative preventative health care schemes (PSF, Programa de Saúde da Família, and PACS, Programa de Agentes Comunitários de Saúde); a fund for fighting poverty. The sheer figures involved speak for themselves. By 2002, Bolsa Escola cost some US$0.8 billion and benefited eleven million children (five million families). One out of every three children aged seven to fourteen in the country was a recipient of the stipend in that year. The funding came from a poverty fund created in 1999 that had accumulated, in 2002, to over R$2 billion (US$0.7 billion).

The Lula government has built on Bolsa Escola and fused it with three other smaller conditional cash-transfer programs (hereafter CCTs) in 2003 to create the Bolsa Família. The latter has been discussed as the largest CCT program internationally, both in terms of coverage and financing (Rawlings 2004). Rather than eliminating the program, the Lula government has expanded it and maintained its operational logic and overall philosophy. By September 2006, the program had reached 11.1 million families, benefiting some 55 million family members, two-thirds of whom were under the age of fifteen, and cost R$5.5 billion (US$2.2 billion) (*Folha de São Paulo*, Feb. 12, 2006; Daniela Ramos, Information Services Coordinator, Ministério do Desenvolvimento, interview).

The most innovative aspect of the program was how it was implemented in practice. Women—or men, in the case of families without a female adult—in each family are given a bank card from the state-owned National Savings Bank, which they could use to withdraw money at banks or other registered institutions (such as the post office). Payment was conditional on evidence that the qualifying children of the household were attending at least 85 percent of their classes. The age bracket was extended to children aged six to fifteen. In the Bolsa Escola scheme, families with qualifying children whose per capita income was less than 50 percent of the minimum salary would be entitled to R$15–45 per month, depending on the number of children. In the Bolsa Família, these values were kept and eligibility was extended to cover all children under the age of sixteen. In turn, the conditions were linked to both education and health measures.

The creation of Fundef, an incentive scheme to decentralize schools and improve teachers' salaries and school performance, led to impressive improvements in education indicators. The Lula government maintained the program and presented a proposal for a constitutional amendment (PEC 009) to upgrade it. The proposal calls for an increase in federal funding for basic education, which is predicted to reach R$4.5 billion (US$2.1 billion). Education expenditures considering all levels of government in Brazil increased in the 1995–2000 period, from 4.2 percent to 5.6 percent of GDP. The net enrollment rate at the primary level increased from 89 percent to 96 percent in the period from 1996 to 2001 (World Bank 2002). Municipal governments accounted for 34 percent of enrollment in public primary schools in 1996, but account for 54 percent of enrollment in 2001. At the same time, the weight of the different levels of government has changed, with municipal governments now accounting for nearly 38 percent of expenditures, compared to 27 percent of expenditures in 1995. Municipalities as a group spent nearly R$24 billion on education in 2000, nearly twice of what they were spending, in real terms, in 1995 (World Bank 2002).

The formation of Fundef created a powerful incentive structure for the decentralization of primary education. At the subnational level, 25 percent of government expenditures go towards education, and the program required that at least 60 percent of this amount was to be spent on salaries for teachers actively involved in classroom activities and or engaged in teacher training programs. It also mandated the establishment of standardized career trajectories for teachers marked by rules for promotion and uniform salary differentials. The resources required for salary increases and training funds were to come from a specific fund (or more appropriately funds because, in fact, each state had its own fund).[2] The latter would be the amount necessary to help those municipalities whose spending levels fell below the national minimum per capita spending, which was to set in the country's annual budget law. All transfers to and withdrawals from Fundef were automatic and based upon set formulas.

Fundef has indeed helped improving working conditions and salaries of teachers, particularly in the most remote areas (salaries increased, on average, 12 percent in one year; but in some cases salaries doubled or tripled) (Melo 2007b). Furthermore, there has been a reduction over time in dropout rates (from 35.9 to 27.7 percent between 1999 and 2002) and average class size (from 36.0 to 33.9 students during 1999–2003), as well as repetition rates and grade-age gaps (Mello and Hoppe 2006). Other factors may be contributing to these outcomes, but Fundef seems to be playing a role.

Fundef's most important innovation has to do with the mechanisms that govern the allocation of resources from the fund. Money is distributed according to the number of student enrollments at each level of government. This produced a revolution in the incentive structure of education. Mayors actively engaged in attracting pupils, because this would lead to more transfers from the fund. In addition, it encouraged decentralization from states to municipalities, because there would be negative transfers in some municipalities if the educational services were provided by the states. The new incentive structure produced two important results: it created strong incentives for municipal governments to expand coverage in their territories, and it encouraged municipalities to take over educational services provided by the states. [3]

The Evolution of CCT Programs: From Bolsa Escola to Bolsa Família

One of the key transformations in Brazilian social policy under Cardoso and Lula is the increasing centrality of CCTs within the social safety net. In fact, this importance extends beyond the narrow realm of public policy and involves the broader political discourse and political competition, which has come to be strongly marked by references to the *bolsas*. It should be noted that cash transfers to the elderly poor (subject to income requirements) have also expanded. However these programs preceded the Cardoso era—they were introduced by the constitution of 1988 and made operational by the subsequent enabling legislation (the LOAS [Lei Orgânica da Assistência Social] in 1993, the LOS [Lei Orgânica da Saúde] in 1990, and the LOPS [Lei Orgânica da Previdência Social] in 1992). The first unconditional cash transfer program to acquire visibility was the noncontributory rural pension scheme introduced by the constitution of 1988. The most generous of its kind in the developing world (pension eligibility is sixty for men and fifty-five for women, with no means test), this program has evolved to cover six million beneficiaries and costs 1 percent of GDP. The second-most-important cash transfer program is the Benefício de Prestação Continuada (BPC), a noncontributory program for the elderly poor (those with per capita family income equivalent to one quarter of the minimum salary) and the disabled. Under the name of RVM (Renda Mensal Vitalícia), the program was reformulated in 1996. The promulgation of the Statute of the Elderly in October 2003 lowered the eligibility age from sixty-seven to sixty-five, thereby extending coverage significantly.

The current CCTs were all introduced by the Cardoso and Lula governments and represent their major innovations (Draibe 2006). Their huge appeal is linked to the fact that they are universally targeted at the poor. Because poverty is widespread, this target makes them "universal" in practice: that is, they affect very large groups of the population and have clear and impartial rules for access. The evolution of the *bolsa* idea has involved a process of scaling up from the municipal experience, which was driven by political competition.

Cardoso created the Bolsa Escola program in 1997, but it was further modified significantly in 2001, and again by Lula in 2003 when the Bolsa Família was launched. As mentioned before, notwithstanding its status as one of the flagship programs of the Cardoso government, it evolved out of an intense process of policy competition and emulation between Cardoso and the PT. Paradoxically, the Bolsa Família has become a "flagship program of the [current Lula] government" (World Bank 2004, 15), and much of the current government's performance in the 2006 presidential election is discussed with reference to the program.

Behind the idea of the Bolsa Escola was a real policy innovator, Senator Eduardo Suplicy from the PT, and a number of innovative municipalities. Suplicy presented preliminary proposals for a universal basic income in the late 1980s when he was a federal deputy for the state of São Paulo. He was influenced by proposals that were being discussed in a number of countries and by a few isolated individuals in Brazil, including the negative income tax proposed by Milton Friedman. Particularly influential were his contacts with the European Basic Income Network. When Suplicy was elected senator he presented a bill

(PL 80) creating the Guaranteed Minimum Income Program. The bill stipulated that individuals whose earnings fell below forty-five thousand cruzeiros (then equivalent to 2.5 times the monthly minimum wage) would be entitled to a negative income tax. In the case of an employed person, this tax would equal 50 percent of the difference between that income threshold and his income. If the individual had no income, it would be equivalent to 30 percent of that difference.[4] The bill, however, was never put to a vote in Chamber of Deputies, because the government instructed the leaders not to do so.

Between 1991 and 1994, the issue of minimum income reached the press, and there were debates among economists about its desirability and effects. In 1991, in a meeting of PT economists, one of Brazil's leading poverty analysts, José Maria Camargo, suggested that the basic income had a purely short-term distributive effect but no impact on productivity or intergenerational poverty. He therefore suggested that it should be made conditional on school attendance. During the presidential campaign of 1994, Suplicy (who maintained close links to the circle of PT economists) managed to include the program in the Workers' Party Action Plan. In his view, "it did not receive the importance it deserved" (Suplicy, interview), but by 1998, the visibility of the issue was much higher, and it also was introduced in the party platform (Suplicy 2002, 130).[5] At the beginning of the decade, many political actors thought that Suplicy's crusade was an oddity. His charismatic style made it appear a utopian project without any chances of being actually implemented. After the link with education was established, however, policymakers and politicians turned their attention to the issue. The political dividends became too visible for it to be dismissed. During the debates of Suplicy's bill in the Chamber of Deputies, the rapporteur in agreement with him made a number of changes that were subsequently incorporated into the laws that established the program in 1997 and 2001. The first was the notion of multistage and gradual implementation, based on state- and municipal-level poverty criteria. Second was the link to school attendance, although in the proposal, the program would exclude poor families without children under the age of fourteen.

The first municipality to implement a basic income program was Campinas, São Paulo, in November 1994. This city became the laboratory of many experiments, which the Cardoso government subsequently extended to the federal level. Also, many of the bureaucrats working in Campinas were later appointed to key positions in the federal government and played key roles in the design of the Bolsa Escola and other programs such as Fundef. Its mayor, Magalhães

Teixeira (a.k.a. "Grama"), formerly a federal deputy and cofounder of PSDB with Cardoso, summoned his close aides to set up this program (Maria Helena Guimarães de Castro, interview with the author).

The mayor asked his team of advisers to prepare a bill stipulating that 1 percent of the municipality's revenue should be earmarked for a minimum income guarantee scheme.[6] The bill established that every family with an income falling below half the minimum wage and with children under the age of fourteen who were enrolled in school would have the right to a monthly income supplement equivalent to 50 percent of the minimum wage per capita. The bill also required prior residency in Campinas of two years (Maria Helena Guimarães de Castro, interview).[7]

At the same time that the program was being established in Campinas, the governor of Brasília, Cristovam Buarque (PT), created a similar scheme. The scheme was launched in January 1995 and acquired more visibility in political circles than did the one in Campinas, since it was implemented in the nation's capital by a governor who was a much more prominent political figure and intellectual. In Brasília, the residency requirement was five years and the age bracket covered was from seven to fourteen. The program reached fifty thousand children at its peak. Other mid-sized cities followed suit, as did large metropolises such as Belo Horizonte. At the end of the first Cardoso government (1998), sixty Brazilian municipalities and four states were already implementing minimum income programs conditioned on school attendance (World Bank 2001).[8] By 2000, 1,115 municipalities were participating in the program—a number well above the 187 municipalities that came to be controlled by the PT after the 2000 mayoral race. The federal government seemed to claim ownership for the program label.

In 1995 and 1996, six proposals for conditional income transfers linked to education were submitted to Congress: three in the Senate and three in the chamber. Cardoso was then convinced that the federal government had to respond, and his party leadership put an alternative bill to a vote, passing Law 9,533 in December 1997. The struggle for the authorship of an increasingly popular proposal reflected the intense political competition before the general elections—for president, governors, and the Congress—of November 1998. The bill authorized the federal government to transfer funds to the municipalities with both tax revenue and per capita family incomes below the average for the state in which they were located. The implementation would take five years to be fully effective.[9] The day after Cardoso sanctioned Law 9,533, Suplicy submitted a bill increasing the value of the benefit. The timing of his proposal and the subsequent development underscore the intense political competition around the issue. The government-dominated Senate approved the bill; however, before the chamber discussed it, Cardoso proposed a bill extending the benefits to all Brazilian municipalities. Furthermore, he christened Law 10219, of March 2001, as the "Magalhães Teixeira," in honor of the pioneering role played by the deceased Campinas mayor and prominent PSDB politician.

These developments are an illuminating example of policy competition driven by a combination of electoral incentives and genuine commitment to solve the issue. In fact, this occurred at various levels in Brazil, with governors and mayors claiming to be the first ones to introduce the scheme. The first state to introduce it was Rio de Janeiro, followed by Amapá, Goiás, and Ceará. There was competition also for having the highest benefit—particularly from municipalities and states governed by the opposition parties, the PDT (Partido Democrático Trabalhista), the PSB (Partido Socialista Brasileiro), and the PT. In 2002, 95 percent of the municipalities in Brazil were participating in the program. It benefited 4.5 million families—a population of almost 30 million people. By 2004, prior to the launch of a new program by the Lula administration, the program became virtually universal in its territorial coverage: 5,512 municipalities participated, and only 48 did not. By February 2006, there were only three municipalities not participating in the Bolsa Família (Daniela Ramos, Ministério do Desenvolvimento Social, interview 2006).

Because there are no intermediaries under Lula, the chances that the money actually reaches the families are very high. In the original Cardoso scheme introduced in 1997, the money was transferred directly to the municipalities. Because municipalities and the program's managers had different information about local conditions, the possibility that the fund was misappropriated or diverted to other uses was elevated. Indeed, local elites have favored social programs mostly because they could benefit directly from them corruptly. This innovation undercut their ability to do so, although the program has been vulnerable to local manipulation of the registration process.

The implementation of the federal Bolsa Escola by Cardoso's Ministry of Education prompted the establishment of similar programs in other sectors and other ministries. The most important of these was the Bolsa Alimentação that was managed by the Ministry of Health. Because the Bolsa Escola was restricted to the transfer of funds to families with children between the ages of seven and fourteen, the corresponding population with children under the age of seven was not covered. The Bolsa Alimentação—nutrition stipend—is designed to reduce nutritional deficiencies and infant mortality among the poorest households in the country Brazil. The program is a demand-side incentive, involving money transfers to very low income families with pregnant and nursing women, or infants and young children between the ages of six months and six years. To receive the cash transfer, women must commit to a "Charter of Responsibilities" that includes regular prenatal care, scheduled checkups, compliance with vaccination schedules, and health education. It was also expected that this would reinforce the bond between the local health services and marginalized families of limited resources.

The creation of the Bolsa Alimentação under Cardoso was marked by political competition between the heads of the two ministries: Paulo Renato of the Education Ministry, and José Serra of the Ministry of Health. Both were candidates in Cardoso's coalition in the upcoming presidential election of 2002 (since the Constitution did not allow Cardoso to run for a third term). In fact, key informants at the top level concurred that Serra's Bolsa Alimentação was his response to the potential threat posed by Renato's huge success with the Bolsa Escola (interviews with Sergio Tiezzi, Maria Helena Castro, and Gilda Portugal). According to Gild Gouvea, one of Renato's closest advisers, Serra's decision was primarily taken with the upcoming election in mind (Gouvea, interview with author).[10]

The Bolsa Escola survived the transition to the Lula government. The cash transfer programs were much debated during the presidential campaign in 2002. In fact, the centerpieces of Lula's discourse were his plan to eliminate hunger in the country and his pledge to maintain fiscal stability. His "Letter to the Brazilian People" was his response to the international credibility crisis Brazil faced following the first evidence of his upcoming victory in the race. Upon taking office, Lula announced the creation of new ad hoc Ministério Extraordinário para a Segurança Alimentar e Combate à Fome—MESA (Ad Hoc Ministry for Food Security). The showpiece of the new ministry was Fome Zero, or Zero Hunger, a program which would also operate on the basis of geographical targeting. Those municipalities with the lowest human development index would be selected as priorities for implementation over time, and households with per capita incomes of less than half the minimum wage would receive a food bonus of R$50. Equivalent to US$18, this bonus would be distributed via the Cartão Alimentação—a debit card that can be used in registered shops and vendors. Prepared by PT in 2001, one year before the electoral campaign, the program was launched as the cornerstone of the new PT administration. Lula demonstrated his commitment to eradicate extreme poverty in a series of well-publicized episodes, including the fact that the first ministerial meeting was held in a small town in one of Brazil's poorest areas.

Ten months after its announcement, the program was yet to be fully implemented. Mounting criticisms from several sectors, including policy experts and NGOs, about its *assistencialista* (paternalistic) nature and the technical flaws in the design of the bonus scheme prompted the government to phase it out. Under the scheme, a family would receive a stipend and must produce evidence that the resources were used to purchase food from registered local stores. This proved to be very difficult to implement. Critics from the opposition and from the government's policy circles argued that the program was modeled on failed food stamp schemes implemented by conservative governments in the United States. The Cartão Alimentação's alleged flaws were many and included the fact that it violated the poor's autonomy to use their judgment in how to use the money, deepened the poor's dependency on vendors who had the upper hand in transacting with them, was an attempt to regulate poor people's behavior, created the potential development of a black market for food cards, and was vulnerable to fraud.

Amidst intense criticism, the government dismissed Fome Zero mentor José Graziano and created a new "superministry" for the social sectors—the Ministério para o Desenvolvimento Social e Combate à Fome. At the same time, the government decided to introduce a single card—the Cartão Alimentação—which was to be used by the families to receive the food benefit plus three other CCT benefits. These programs are granted on the condition that the families engage in a number of activities, including vaccination and school attendance. In practice, the Lula government discontinued its initiatives and in fact started to unify the cash transfer programs created earlier under Cardoso. Figure 8.1 shows data on the gradual fusion of the four programs in the Bolsa Família scheme. The figures for the Bolsa Família represent both the incremental transfer of families for the new program and the incorporation of additional families to the program. Political ads associated with the 2006 electoral race prompted a surge in the number of families in the program, as some 1.5 million new families started receiving the Bolsa.

The four existing programs were highly fragmented: the Bolsa Escola fell under the rubric of the Ministry of Education, the Bolsa Alimentação was implemented by the Health Ministry, and the Auxílio Gás (cooking-gas benefit) was run by the Ministry of Energy. The idea of creating a single card or Bolsa

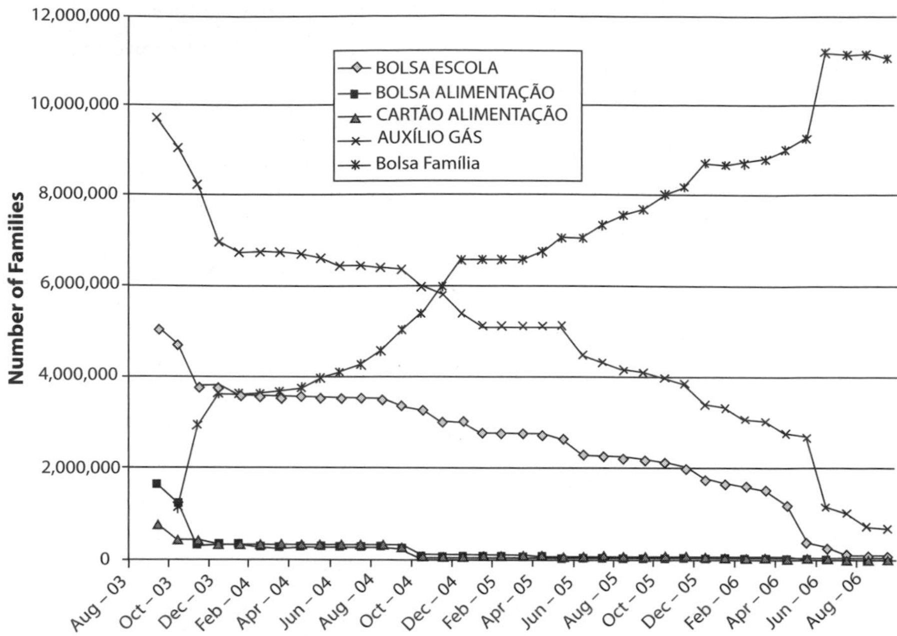

Figure 8.1. Evolution of Cash Transfer Programs under Lula

Source: Author's calculations on the basis on information provided by the Coordination of Information, Ministério do Desenvolvimento Social (MDS).

was not new and was already in course under the Cardoso government. It was developed much earlier in 2001, when the Caixa Econômica Federal (CEF, National Savings Bank)—the operational arm for cash transfers—started working on the Unified Registry of social programs (Cadastro Único) (FAO, World Bank, and IDB 2002).

The expansion of social transfers suggests a redefinition of the roles of the three tiers of government in the Brazilian federation. This phenomenon has crowded out investments in the improvement of basic services such as sanitation and health, which have stagnated (Afonso 2006). Spending in health as a percentage of total federal social spending declined from 12.5 percent to 11.7 percent between 2001 and 2005, whereas social transfers rose from 5.7 to 6.9 percent. The corresponding figures for sanitation for the same period are 1.3 percent and 0.6 percent (Giambiagi 2006, 50). Social transfers now represent 1 percent of GDP and are almost entirely funded by federal resources. They now occupy a key role in the public agenda and represent the entrance of the federal government in an area that traditionally has been the responsibility of municipalities and the states: antipoverty programs. The states play no role in these schemes, while municipalities work as information gatherers. The families withdraw their payments directly from the Federal Savings Bank using ATM cards. Thus, the municipalities' role is restricted to registering applicants and informing the CEF of their eligibility. The impact of the program is impressive—Barros (2006) credits the program with the drop in the Gini coefficient from 0.60 in 1998 to 0.57 in 2004—the first time there ever has been evidence of a sustained decline in this indicator of economic inequality (see also F. Soares et al. 2006).

Against the Odds

The achievements described in the previous section—in terms of innovative initiatives and of the coverage and the magnitude of resources channeled to social policy—would not have been predicted based on two arguments developed in the literature. The first argument is related to the intrinsic nature of the so-called second-generation reforms. Unlike first-generation reforms (which are based on expenditures, cuts, monetary reform, and privatization), second-generation reforms, to be effective, require significant institutional change and necessitate the cooperation of an array of actors situated at different levels of government. Furthermore, they impose concentrated costs to key constituencies of service providers and beneficiaries and generate diffuse benefits. Other factors that militate against this type of reform are the absence of clear models to follow and the low perceived costs of staying the course. Second-generation reforms are characterized by a syndrome of crucial needs and weak incentives: For example, the cost of the delay in expanding school enrollment is much lower than the corresponding cost of not taking action to curb hyperinflation.

The second argument asserts that political fragmentation produced by dysfunctional institutions make reform impossible in Brazil. Political fragmentation stems from an array of characteristics of the Brazilian institutional arrangement, including its electoral legislation (open-list proportional representation), multiparty presidentialism, predatory federalism, and the weak political parties. These features combine, the argument suggests, to produce decisional paralysis and policy inertia that undercuts the ability of the national executive to implement a reform agenda. Reforms are predicted to occur only after protracted negotiations involving presidents and Congress, and to come at a high social cost (Samuels 2003a; Ames 2001; Mainwaring 1999).

The recent revisionist literature has presented a more balanced view of Brazilian institutions. Two types of considerations have been made. First, some empirically oriented scholars argue that some institutional changes have taken place that have made the country more governable, such as, for example, the reconfiguration of intergovernmental relations. Others offer a conceptual argument based on belief that the received wisdom has overlooked the strong powers of presidents and the internal organization of Congress. These scholars have stressed that a number of prerogatives help presidents overcome party fragmentation and ensure that his or her agenda is implemented (Santos and Vilarouca, this volume). These prerogatives include, inter alia, the use of provisional measures; exclusive jurisdiction in tax, fiscal, and administrative legislation; the ability to command an immediate vote on designated bills; and line-item veto powers. All of this is in addition to the control of patronage positions in the vast federal administrative machine and the discretionary execution of legislators' budgetary amendments (Pereira and Mueller 2003). The internal organization of Congress also provides key instruments that help coalition management by the executive. It is structured along party lines and confers strong powers to the party leaders, which are used to guarantee support from individual legislators (Figueiredo and Limongi 1999). As Alston et al. (2006) argue, this does not mean that Congress is inert. In fact, presidents act as the managers of the coalition and trade pork in exchange for support for their agendas—a process that is mediated by party leaders.

The vision of a "predatory federalism" (Abrucio 1998)—a weak federal executive that is unable to overcome the pressures from the periphery of the political system—is at odds with the picture of federalism under Cardoso and Lula. As we anticipated at the beginning of the chapter, this argument is not consistent with the evidence on the recentralization of social policy in Brazil under Cardoso and Lula. Instead, we argue that an important transformation in the Brazilian federal structure took place essentially in reaction against the state of affairs—or more appropriately, the external shock produced by the Constitution of 1988.

The constitution of 1988 was written under unique circumstances, the most important of which was the fact that the federal executive played virtually no role in the process. Furthermore, the subnational actors, in particular governors, were the key actors in the constitution-making process. Because the first direct election during the political transition game was the gubernatorial elections, in 1982, governors acquired great legitimacy and became the guarantors of the new regime, actively negotiating the transition with the military regime. The fiscal implications of the constitution were felt in the early 1990s, and the subsequent evolution of intergovernmental relations under Cardoso reflects the federal government's reaction against that state of affairs.

As Alston et al. (2004) argue, Brazilian presidents have a strong incentive to stabilize the economy and to pursue sound fiscal policies due to two factors. The first is that the electorate became strongly inflation averse following the devastating effects of hyperinflation on everyday life in the 1980s and early 1990s. In addition, because of the failed heterodox experiments during the Sarney and Collor administrations—Plans Cruzado and Collor, respectively—citizens were not prepared to give electoral support to governments favoring unorthodox fiscal practices. But presidents had to reconcile their fiscal preferences with factors that would have impacts on their political survival, including the possibility of shouldering blame for policy failures. Presidents could be blamed not only for failure to rein in inflation, but for rising unemployment rates and poor performance of increasingly salient social indicators in health and education (a process discussed later in this chapter as the "federalization of credit claiming" for social citizenship improvements). Cardoso's and Lula's ability to reconcile these two imperatives explain part of his success.

The federal government's fiscal strategy under Cardoso also involved increasing taxation and retaining these new fiscal resources at the national level rather than distributing them among the states and municipalities, while constraining the subnational units' fiscal behavior. Between 1994 and 2002, the tax burden rose from 24 percent to 34 percent—an increase of 10 percent of GDP in a decade. This was accomplished mostly from *contribuições sociais*—a type of tax whose yields are not constitutionally shared with the states and municipalities. The *contribuições*' share in total revenue rose from 11 percent to 49 percent.[11] The federal government also managed to withhold part of the funds that were constitutionally mandated for distribution to the states and municipalities. To achieve this, it managed to approve a number of constitutional amendments calling for the lifting of tax earmarks. Prior to distribution, the resources would feed a fund controlled by the federal government (the FSE, Social Emergency Fund) for a specified period of time. This accounting strategy was renewed and renamed subsequently FEF (Fundo Estabilização Fiscal) and more recently DRU (Desvinculação das Receitas da União). The federal government was able to "flexibilize" the share of discretionary resources in the budget and at the same time circumscribe the fiscal autonomy of states and municipalities (See figure

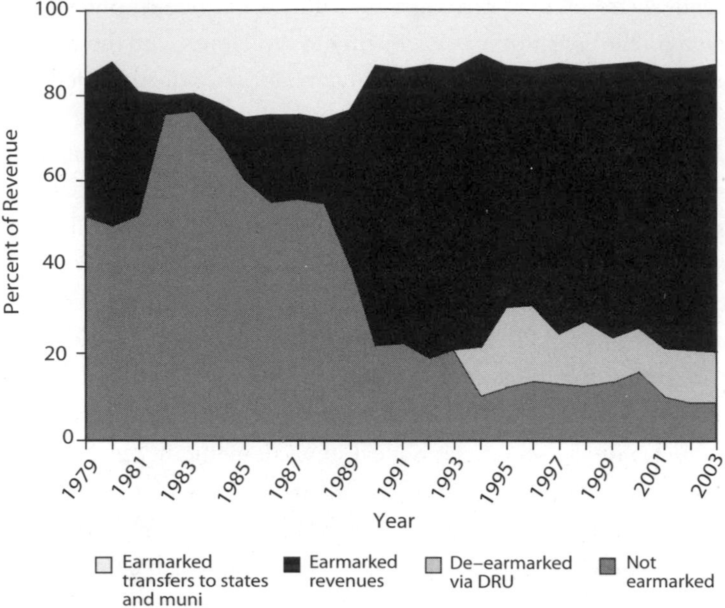

Figure 8.2. Share of DRU and Constitutional Transfers to Subnational Units, 1979–2003

Source: Secretaria do Orçamento Federal. This graph does not include revenues from government bonds or privatization.

8.2 for the process of lifting earmarks from the budget). The apex of this process was the approval of the Fiscal Responsibility Law in May 2000. As a result, the three tiers of government have been generating primary surpluses since 2001.

In sum, under Cardoso the federal government dealt fairly successfully with the fiscal constraints imposed by the country's high internal debt (Alston et al. 2004; Goldfajn and Guardia 2003). The government managed to control the chief cause of concern—subnational fiscal behavior—and at the same time strengthened its tax resources. It resorted to a two-pronged strategy. On the one hand, it curbed subnational spending and limited subnational fiscal autonomy. On the other hand, it enhanced the federal executive-branch fiscal space, by expanding the base of resources at its disposal and at the same time expanding its discretionary latitude. Expanded taxation helps explain how the government was able to increasingly channel resources to the social area, which has also become increasingly hardwired.

The reassertion of federal executive authority over subnational fiscal behavior was closely linked to increased *programmatic* control over public policy at the subnational level (Melo and Rodden 2007). This is exemplified in the education and health sectors with the Fundef, Bolsa Alimentação, and Bolsa Escola. These changes were made possible by an intense and successful process of constitutional change. As already mentioned, the Constitution of 1988 deepened the process of decentralization and extended social rights and social assistance entitlements. With 250 articles and seventy temporary provisions, the constitution was a very detailed document that engendered an intense constitutionalization of public policy.

Many subsequent reforms under Cardoso implied deconstitutionalizing issues: that is, deleting articles from the Constitution and subsequently (but not always) legislating about the issue via ordinary laws. The initial high level of constitutionalization produced great rigidity in public policy in general (Melo 2002). This did not prevent the Cardoso administrations, however, from passing their reform programs. The high degree of constitutionalization affects policymaking in the area of social policy in particular, because in a large and robust federation like Brazil, in which municipalities are strongly autonomous, any change in intergovernmental relations or taxation requires changing the Constitution. Most initiatives in the area of social policy and poverty alleviation were implemented via constitutional amendments and involved intense negotiations within the government coalition and also the opposition. These amendments were approved despite the important procedural hurdles involved, including supermajority requirements, two rounds of voting in the Senate and Chamber of Deputies, no procedural prerogatives for the executive, and so on.

The constitutional "big bang" started in 1995, when Cardoso proposed seventeen constitutional amendments to the Constitution. That year saw an enormous concentration of amendments: half of the total of amendments his government proposed and over a third (34 percent) of those submitted for the period 1988–2004. Social policy and federalism were the issue areas that attracted most attention. There were fifty-one constitutional amendments through January 2006, ten of which preceded the Cardoso era and six of which were promulgated during Lula's first two years in office (of these, two were proposed by the Cardoso government but promulgated subsequently). Nearly half (42 percent) of all the constitutional amendments passed refer directly to aspects of Brazilian federalism, a percentage that was even higher during the Cardoso years (48.5 percent). Of the total amendments pertaining to federalism, more than half (53 percent) are related to social policy or social rights.[12] Thus, Lula's government benefited from the labor of constitutional reform undertaken by Cardoso. It was in a position to consolidate the programs introduced by Cardoso. Lula's government prima facie lack of policy entrepreneurship or innovation can be partly explained by this, as we will discuss below (see also Melo 2007a).

Many of the predictions of the literature on second-generation reforms therefore seem to be not applicable or simply exaggerated. A strong executive has been able to overcome fiscal constraints. The emphasis on resistance proved to be exaggerated, because reform packaging was able to include not only costs but also benefits to those involved (teachers, in the case of Fundef). Finally, because coverage extension is still a big issue, the zero-sum games associated with the "politics of efficiency" was intermingled with the "politics of expansion" (Kauffman and Nelson 2004).[13]

Explaining Policy Continuity

A puzzling characteristic of social policy under Cardoso and Lula is the high degree of policy stability. This stability is also found in other issue areas, particularly monetary and fiscal policy. Possible explanations for the continuity in macroeconomic management include the pressures from international markets and globalization, as well as political explanations associated with fragmentation. There were virtually no changes in the rules of the political game in Brazil under Lula; thus, it could be argued that, given the changes introduced by Cardoso, the new government was consequently in an even better position to promote reforms and not to be stuck in some kind of policy quagmire. The fragmentation hypothesis seems thus to be even less successful in accounting for Lula's success than it was in accounting for Cardoso's success. This hypothesis is also inconsistent with the empirical evidence. Lula was able to approve two important reforms through constitutional amendments in the areas of taxation and social security. Both reforms show important degrees of continuity with the Cardoso agenda. The content of the proposals, in fact, aimed at important aspects that were not fully reformed during the Cardoso era, and they can be construed as the natural steps to take. The social security reform focused on civil servants' pensions, while Cardoso reformed INSS (Instituto Nacional do Seguro Social) pensions (the subsystem for private-sector employees). More significantly, despite the continuities, the issues involved were more politically costly, and their approval signals the new government's clout rather than its weakness. This reform had little impact on the social-assistance component of the social security system. The major social policy initiative of the Lula government was the Fome Zero program that was quickly dismantled, even though the elements initiated by Cardoso were maintained.

Policy continuity can be explained by three factors. The first is the increasing hardwiring of resources—the increasing earmarking of both revenue and expenditures for the social sectors. Hardwiring produces rigidity in the social area and as a consequence reduces policy innovation. The second factor involved is the intense mobilization around the poverty issue in the country. Alston et al. (2005) present a model of the Brazilian policymaking process, adapted from Spiller and Tomasi (2007), that explains policy stability and volatility across issue areas. The dynamics of the policymaking game yield policy outcomes that are classified into four broad categories: hardwired policies, stable but adaptable fiscal and monetary policies, pork projects, and residual policies. In this model, presidents' preferences are targeted at a strong economy and the satisfaction of the goals of economic growth, economic opportunity, and unemployment reduction. Presidents are punished for misbehavior in fiscal affairs by international markets and by inflation-averse citizens.

Members of Congress generally care more about redistributing gains to their constituents: that is, geographical redistribution. Given the differences in preferences and the relative powers of each, the legislative and executive branches can both benefit by exploiting the gains from trade. To achieve the goal of a strong economy, presidents focus first on fiscal and monetary stability: the Real Plan, pension reform, and tax reform. To achieve these ends, presidents have used pork, as well as other benefits, as the mediums of exchange to members of Congress in return for their votes on critical pieces of legislation. A key element in this exchange is the allocation of selected ministerial positions and appointments of managers of the state-owned enterprises and the bureaucracy. The executive might also exchange his or her policy agenda for other policies that legislators may care about in a typical logrolling exchange. The executive may, for instance, be interested in creating a new tax on financial transactions that would be important for the executive primary surplus. In order to get the legislators' compliance, the executive can exchange the allocation of a portion of the new tax for social policies such as health care. Given that a large proportion of the budget is hardwired in policy areas such as health and education, the pork traded for policy reform and fiscal policies comes only from the portion of the budget left over after hardwired spending. Once the exchanges of pork for policy have been consummated, the residual will be spent on infrastructure projects and more ideological policies such as land reform and the environment. The residual policies electorally impact the president and members of Congress differently, depending on the degree to which they achieve national goals—the president can claim more credit—or geographic goals—in which case the deputies and senators benefit relatively more electorally.

The "game" described in Alston et al. (2005) can be viewed as sequential, with veto players as well as external shocks constraining the president and Congress. The constraints from the other political actors and external shocks have budgetary implications, either positive or negative. The policymaking game is driven by the president's overriding incentive to keep the budget as a percentage of GDP within some target range, because greatly exceeding the budget-to-GDP ratio can have serious monetary and fiscal penalties imposed through international capital markets, which in turn will have economic impacts. In the Brazilian political system, it is the president, rather than members of Congress, who is held accountable for economic growth, low unemployment, and stable prices.

The second factor that explains policy continuity is the fact that once in place, the CCTs create their own constituencies. As suggested by Pierson (1994) and Grindle (2007), in contexts like these, beneficiaries of a program use their political influence to lock in place or deepen the policies that benefit them. In the competitive environment around Bolsa Escola, the direct beneficiaries primarily used the electoral process to exercise their influence. Part of the backlash against Fome Zero can be explained by the pressures from the beneficiaries and the policy elites and bureaucracies associated with the program. Beneficiaries were afraid that the CCTs could be converted into food-distribution programs. Schattschneider (1935, 288) argues that "new policies create a new politics," suggesting that a new policy creates or broadens the political support for the policy among the direct beneficiaries and the policy-specific suppliers, bureaucrats, and advocacy groups. Because people tend to be more motivated to defend the benefits they have than to seek the potential benefits of a different policy, the politics of new policies and the politics of retrenchment are asymmetrical. In Pierson's terms, public policy is path dependent: the current policies depend very much on the policies of the past. "That social programs provide concentrated and direct benefits while imposing diffuse and often indirect costs is an important source of their continuing political viability. Voters' tendency to react more strongly to losses than to equivalent gains also gives these programs strength" (Pierson 1994, 1)

In addition to beneficiaries, many militants and intellectuals associated with the PT, including members of the Catholic Church, also criticized the Fume

Zero program for its paternalism.[14] The PT itself in its party convention expressed concerned about the government's inability to show results and produce clear guidelines for the program.[15] The criticisms were also voiced by multilateral institutions, particularly the World Bank, and policy experts.[16] Within a few months, the backlash against Fome Zero reached great momentum, and the government abandoned it; both of its mentors left the government.[17] The Ministry for Food Security—then in charge of the Food Card—and the Ministry of Social Assistance were merged to form the Ministry of Social Development.

The federal government's direct involvement in poverty relief was a result not only of the identification of subnational initiatives with the two parties cited, but also represented the necessary end result of the strategic interaction of municipalities in the policy emulation game. This competition generated externalities because of the welfare "magnet effect" identified by Peterson and Rom (1990) for the U.S. case. A successful program attracted a lot of visibility and prompted the need to introduce barriers to entry, such as residency requirements, for potential beneficiaries. These, in turn, had both political and fiscal costs. Introducing restrictions ran counter to the inclusive philosophy of the programs. On the other hand, these welfare magnets faced tremendous fiscal problems. Because the scale of these problems surpassed the capability of the municipalities, the participation of the federal government was necessary in order to manage the fiscal problems of the municipalities.

The Paradox of Universalism: The Nationalization of Credit-Claiming for Social Programs

The third puzzle regarding social policies under Cardoso and Lula refers to the increasing universalism of social policies. Historically, education, health, and, most notably, social assistance have always been at the center of patronage games and clientelistic networks, typically involving local elites. A paradoxical development is that the CCTs in Brazil operate in a fairly transparent way, with minimal clientelistic mediation. Recent literature on the political economy of clientelism argues that public-good reforms require political competitors with an incentive to appeal to broad segments of the citizenry (Keefer 2006). Politicians who can make credible promises to only a few—clientelists, for example—do not have these incentives. In addition, in the case of programs involving service delivery, reform is most vulnerable to information asymmetries that dilute political incentives to give it priority. Policies targeted at improving quality in health and education, for example, face this problem of information asymmetry because they involve goods that are not very tangible and observable (quality) (Keefer 2006; Keefer and Vlaicu 2005). Citizens are not in a position to verify improvements in services. Neither can they verify whether or not politicians' promises have been materialized.

In Brazil, the lack of programmatic parties which could credibly claim to deliver public goods is, indeed, an obstacle to universalism. However, I claim that universalism as a policy outcome can be explained by the following factors. The first is the process of taking credit for social programs at the federal level. This reflects the process of centralization in the executive described below. The political logic underlying the expansion of cash-transfer programs is that it is not affected by the information-asymmetries problem. Cash transfers are tangible and highly targeted. Paradoxically, because of the positive externalities associated with them, and because of the scope of the program—which has reached about a third of the population—these transfers, which are private goods, produce collective benefits for society at large.[18]

Neri and Rios (2006) found strong evidence of a political cycle in income in democratic Brazil. In election years income levels rise, and in postelection years incomes shrink. The per capita income of individuals in households with minor children grows less in election years than that of households without children. In other words, pensions and unemployment benefits rise more than social transfers such as the Bolsas. We argue that a similar process is working in the case of the Bolsa Família. However, the clientele of the Bolsa Família is far larger than that of pension programs. There is a political logic governing the expansion of Bolsa Família.

In the past, before the introduction of the cash-transfer programs, the credit for social programs was mostly claimed by local political elites at the subnational level. Presidents have had a strong incentive for poverty reduction, because they have become accountable for social policy for the first time. Because the constituency of presidents is the whole country, they develop a strong interest in universal programs that are not geographically targeted or focused on narrow groups of the population. As Hunter and Power (2007) have argued, the evidence for the electoral appeal of the social programs is virtually ubiquitous when one looks at the 2006 presidential race. This sets in motion a dynamic that ultimately fosters a particular type of universalism.

As already indicated, the strong consensus on poverty relief in the 1990s set in motion a market for ideas for combating poverty, which came to be dominated by the innovative schemes put forward by the two modern forces in the political market: the PT and the PSDB, the two most programmatic political parties in the country. In this context, populist ideas or traditional clientelistic schemes lost appeal. An illustrative example of this is the episode involving the gubernatorial race in the impoverished state of Piauí; in this highly publicized episode, the PFL (Liberal Front Party) candidate registered in a public notary his pledge of maintaining the Bolsa Escola program that had been implemented by his opponent (*Folha de São Paulo*, Oct. 22, 1998). Another important evidence of the consensus around the issue was the number of editorials in the country's most important newspapers—even those that supported the government—condemning the newly elected governor of Brasília in 1999 for discontinuing the program in the nation's capital.

The intense process of policy competition led to the scaling up of the program and the adoption of a nationwide program with universal rules of eligibility. The stages that characterized the scaling up are very significant. First, the program was locally created and managed. It was then targeted at a specific type of municipality, to whom the federal monies would be transferred. Third, the municipalities were bypassed, and the money directly transferred to the beneficiary.

The second factor that helps explain universalism is that the very nature of cash transfers undermined the traditional mechanisms for clientelistic intermediation. The latter involve fraudulent public procurement, favoritism in the allocation of contracts, and so on. Modern technologies allowed the use of electronic cards, undercutting the ability of local elites to intermediate access to the program. The last bastion of local control has been the manipulation of the registration process. However, registration has increasingly been audited by federal control agencies and by the Caixa Econômica Federal—the public financial conglomerate that runs the program. Although fraud has been documented in the registration process, no case involving large-scale corruption has been detected. It is highly significant that the Controladoria Geral da União—the Federal Internal Audit Office—has changed its focus away from the federal administrative machinery and has focused instead on the misuse of federal transfers to municipalities in social programs and Fundef. In the case of Bolsa Família, it has focused on fraud in the local management of the registration process. In these cases, the political costs of fraud are borne by local officials and political benefits are reaped by the federal government.

In this chapter I have provided explanations for three puzzles about social policy under Cardoso and Lula: its relative success against the odds, the high degree of policy continuity between the two ideologically opposing presidents, and what I call the "universalism" that came to characterize social programs over the last decade or so. I have explained success by pointing to the Constitution of 1988 as an exogenous shock that was followed by the reassertion of federal authority and by transformations in Brazilian federalism. I argue that the first years of the so-called New Republic represented an interregnum following the enactment of the Constitution, which was drafted under exceptional circumstances: namely, the combination of strong governors and a weak president. Legitimized by their direct elections, these key figures of the transition managed to produce a constitutional charter that reflected primarily subnational interests. The political history of the 1990s is best described as the reassertion of presidential power and of recentralization.

I have argued that policy continuity is best explained by the "policies that create politics" argument and by the fact that hardwiring of social policy has produced rigidities. In this political logic, universalism is primarily the product of political survival and program scaling up. But it can be also explained by the gradual predominance of cash transfer and by the centralization of social policy in the federal government. Thus, universalism is paradoxically the end result of a process of federalization of credit claiming for social welfare outcomes made possible by the tangibility of the cash transfer, in contrast to improvements in education attainment and health care.

A key issue in discussing social policy in a context of political scarcity refers to how the federal government marshaled the resources to underwrite these universal programs. It should be noted that these programs are quite cheap in fiscal terms (which is why they are so appealing to international financial institutions). Indeed, as the analysis has suggested, the higher cost was a political one, borne by local and state elected officials. A key question in this regard is how the political cost was paid. The PT and PSDB were engaged in an intense competition that propelled policy innovation, and they are the two most programmatic parties. Once the programs were launched, they created their own constituencies. The incentives for the subnational actors to take on the federal party label is now stronger (although much reduced because of the *mensalão* scandal) and benefit from federal credit claiming. This is an optimistic view. One wonders why though it took nearly a decade and a half for the political logic governing the expansion of these programs to kick in. Perhaps this is how new democracies work.

9

Public Security, Private Interests, and Police Reform in Brazil

Anthony W. Pereira

"SECURITY YES, OMISSION NO!" "Fight violence with justice." "Security is the responsibility of the state." "Peace without voice is not peace—it's fear." "Down with impunity." "Our right is to live without fear." These were some of the slogans shouted and broadcast over loudspeakers in Recife, Brazil, on February 19, 2006. The occasion was a protest of some 250 people organized by the Antônio Carlos Escobar Institute (Instituto Antônio Carlos Escobar, IACE), founded in December of 2005 in the wake of the killing of a prominent psychiatrist. Lamenting the recent deaths of thousands of people in the state of Pernambuco and demanding better policing and social programs in order to stem the tide of violence, IACE protestors drove their cars through the city to the Governor's Palace. At the square in front of the palace, they placed three thousand black flags on iron railings, each flag representing a homicide victim.[1]

Perhaps more remarkable than the IACE protest itself—such demonstrations have become increasingly common in Brazil—was the official response to it. One hundred members of the military police guarded the Governor's Palace while the flags were put up, despite the small number and peaceful nature of the demonstrators. The governor did not address the protesters, nor did he subsequently issue a response to their demands to the press. Within three hours of the end of the demonstration, the black flags had been taken down. The government simply ignored the event. It seemed that no elected official was willing to draw yet more attention to the problem of public insecurity, especially in an election year.

Why, despite increasing public pressure for reform, has Brazil been unable to construct more-effective public security policies? Why, despite undeniable improvements in many other aspects of Brazil's democracy over the last twenty years, has fear of violence—including police violence—apparently increased?[2] Why is the public good of security so woefully underproduced, if rational politicians would be expected to provide it?

It is important to seek answers to these questions, because increasing insecurity reduces the quality of Brazil's democracy. Violence diminishes the full realization of civil rights, and the state's failure to adequately respond to it constitutes a breach of the rule of law (Mendez, O'Donnell, and Pinheiro 1999; O'Donnell, Cullel, and Iazzelta 2004; Pinheiro 2005; Ungar 2002). Public-opinion surveys indicate that public security is one of the most important issues to Brazilians, ranking alongside employment and health, and candidates in elections find it increasingly necessary to sound knowledgeable and to address voters' fears in this area.[3]

Brazil has followed a pattern of development in recent decades in which urbanization, economic liberalization, and slow growth have combined to generate an urban landscape of extreme deprivation and sharp inequalities. There are certain crucial institutional aspects of the problem, and a new agency at the federal level has made some progress in establishing, for the first time, a national public security policy with incentives to state governments to collect data and enact reforms. However, serious barriers to the success of reforms exist, including the interrelated problems of public-sector fragmentation, police politicization, and the privatization of security. A recent, violent attack by an organized criminal group in São Paulo illustrates the challenges facing public-security reformers in Brazil. The question remains as to how the reform measures are likely to play out, given these barriers to success.

Insecurity and Development

The global capitalist order is an increasingly unequal one. The ratio between the average income in the richest twenty countries and the average income in the poorest twenty went from thirty-five in 1950 to seventy-two in 2000 and (United

Nations Human Settlements Programme 2003, 36). At the same time, economic globalization has opened up growth opportunities for developing and transition countries, especially large ones such as Brazil, China, India, Indonesia, Mexico, Nigeria, Russia, and South Africa. However, for middle-income countries such as Brazil, competitive exports tend to be natural resources and agricultural commodities, on one hand, and capital-intensive and technologically advanced goods, on the other. So-called Fordist industries requiring large amounts of relatively low-skilled labor have declined in Brazil, as they have in many other middle- and high-income countries in the global capitalist economy. This reflects a pattern of development that is highly unequal and exclusionary (Harriss 2000, 331–38).

In addition to becoming more unequal, the world is also becoming more urban. The modernization of agriculture has reduced the demand for labor, and millions of the rural poor have streamed into cities, where their birth rate exceeds that of better-off and longer-established urban residents. In the last fifty years, the world's population increased by roughly 3.5 billion, most of it in cities in developing and transition countries. For the first time in history, more than half of the world population is now urban, and this proportion will increase in coming decades (United Nations Human Settlements Programme 2003, 25). Roughly 32 percent of the global urban population—almost 1 billion people—lives in slums, defined as densely populated urban areas in which residents live in poor-quality housing, have insecure property rights, and lack adequate access to safe water, sanitation, and other infrastructure. An estimated 128 million slum dwellers live in Latin America and the Caribbean (United Nations Human Settlements Programme 2003, xxv).[4] These residents work largely in the informal sector, have only precarious access to educational and health services, and experience the daily realities of a "citizenship gap" in which their civil and social rights are routinely violated (Cumper 2005, 113).

The expanding slums of cities in developing countries are spaces in which various forms of violence can flourish. Drug and arms traffickers, politically motivated terrorists, and private security organizations such as militias can all operate in slums. Organized criminal groups skim off profits from protection rackets, extortion, kidnapping, prostitution, money laundering, gambling, car and house theft, and other rackets. Murderers-for-hire can be contracted cheaply. Overburdened judicial systems and corrupt and overwhelmed police forces provide a sense of impunity to criminals. The end of the Cold War has witnessed the emergence of an "age of insecurity" in which "violence could arguably be considered the central—if not defining—problem" in the contemporary world (Davis 2006, 178; see also Mann 2002).

It would be simplistic to attempt to explain Brazil's urban violence exclusively with reference to global, structural factors. Local factors, especially institutional ones, are important in understanding the impact of global changes within a given national, regional, or urban territory. Nevertheless, recent transformations at the level of the world economy represent background conditions that help to explain striking similarities in patterns of crime and policing in large cities in the developing world. For example, in Mehta's (2004) vivid portrait of Bombay (Mumbai), India, all the elements familiar to analysts of public security in Brazil—organized crime, increasing violence, corrupt and brutal police, backlogged courts, and the growth of private security—are present (N. V. Oliveira 2002).

There is an extensive and growing literature on the causes of Brazil's increasing violence, typically measured by homicide rates. The country's homicide rate increased from 11.7 per 100,000 in 1980 to 28.5 in 2002, an average increase of 5.6 percent per year (Cerqueira 2005, 4). About forty-five thousand people are murdered each year in Brazil—a quantity that almost equals the number of U.S. troops lost during the entire Vietnam War—and most are killed by handguns. Brazil's arsenal of 15.3 million light arms has been estimated as the eighth-largest in the world.[5] Homicide is now the leading cause of death for youths between the ages of fifteen and twenty-four in Brazil's major cities (Cardia 2000, 7). Violence and crime are problems not just of security, but of public health, seeing as they lead to substantial state and private expenditure and a host of deleterious impacts on society (Mir 2004). One study estimated that the direct costs of violence—resources devoted to the police and public security, including the prison system, the cost of treatment of victims, the loss of human capital and goods, and private security and insurance—accounted for just over 5 percent of Brazil's gross domestic product in 2004.[6]

Causes of the rising violence are multiple, but various studies have identified some of the main factors. Misse (Misse and Kant de Lima 2006) argues against a tight correlation between violence and poverty in general. However, Cardia finds a correlation between fast urban population growth and rising homicide rates (Cardia 2000, 12). Rolnik (1999) argues that there is a link between homicide rates and the percentage of residents who live in slum housing. For Mir (2004, 908), the quintupling of the unemployment rate for São Paulo youths between the ages of fifteen and twenty-four between 1979 and 1998 helps explain the rise in the homicide rate in the same period from 8 to 66 per 100,000. According to Cerqueira (2005, 10), homicide rates in a given municipality are positively correlated with inequality of income, the proportion of youths in the population (individuals between the ages of fifteen and twenty-four), the degree of urbanization, and the extent of economic vulnerability, including lack of formal-sector employment, of the youth population.[7] He also argues that the immobility of the court system and widespread impunity reinforce the trend of rising homicide rates.

Other researchers point to Brazil's geographic vulnerability as a factor in the rising violence. Brazil has a very long coastline, much of it sparsely populated, and a 15,700 km land border shared with ten different countries (Magnoli 2005, 15), three of which are major producers of coca. The Federal Police are charged with patrolling these borders, but they count on only about thirteen thousand agents.[8] This is a relatively low figure, even though the Federal Police constitutes the best-paid and reputedly most efficient police force in Brazil.[9] The result is a country highly permeable to drug trafficking and other forms of organized crime. Criminal groups, in turn, can buy protection from political authorities, including the police and judiciary, which allow them to operate freely.

These and other studies suggest that the causes of increasing violence are at least partially spatial and socioeconomic. That being the case, the market's scant production of well-paid, stable jobs, and the Brazilian state's very limited ability to redistribute income and address poverty and inequality, are relevant in explaining this problem. Unlike many Latin American countries, the state in Brazil has a relatively high capacity to tax; Brazil has one of the highest tax burdens in the developing world, at 37 percent of GDP (M. A. Melo 2005a, 2). However, the relatively high tax rates stimulate tax avoidance and informal economic activity, reducing the absolute amount of revenue collection. The Brazilian state also relies heavily on regressive forms of indirect taxation, rather than direct taxation. Households in the top quintile of income earners pay an average of only 5 percent of their income in taxes—less than the rate paid by households in lower quintiles (Fitzgerald 2007, 19). Furthermore, on the spending side, almost 90 percent of the federal budget is tied up in constitutionally mandated or otherwise obligatory payments for interest on the public debt, social security, salaries, transfers to states and municipalities, and the like (*Veja*, Feb. 8, 2006, 57). The resources available to the Brazilian state for the purposes of poverty alleviation are thus miniscule in comparison to the extent of deprivation in society.[10]

Despite the fact that both patterns of socioeconomic change and the nature of state finances are unpropitious for the diminution of urban violence, Brazil's public insecurity is not inevitable. Other countries in Latin America, such as Chile, have experienced economic globalization, high income inequality, rural-urban migration, and fiscal austerity without experiencing the rates of violence that Brazil does. Part of Brazil's problem has to do with its public-security organizations—specifically, the way they relate to one another and are connected to private actors in ways that constrain their effectiveness in preventing and investigating violent crime.[11] The bulk of this chapter will concentrate on these political and organizational variables. The next section will discuss the creation of the National Secretariat for Public Security, a federal agency with a reform agenda. The subsequent sections will examine barriers to the achievement of that agenda.

Innovations in Public Security Policy at the Federal Level

In 1998, the government of then-president Fernando Henrique Cardoso created the National Secretariat for Public Security (Secretaria Nacional de Segurança Pública, or SENASP). This secretariat, housed within the Ministry of Justice, was founded to coordinate public-security policies among the states. This is no easy task, because the uniformed, patrolling military police and the investigative civil police are constitutionally under the command of twenty-six separate state governments and the federal district of Brasília. Consistent with the tendency to militarize public-security issues (Zaverucha 2005), the first head of SENASP was an army general. However, the agency, which does not have cabinet status, was largely invisible during the first two years of its existence.[12]

On June 12, 2000, a young black man with a gun hijacked a bus in the middle-class neighborhood of Jardim Botânico in Rio de Janeiro. Apparently high on drugs, Sandro do Nascimento held terrified passengers of Bus 174 hostage for four and half hours, as television cameras transmitted the event live to an audience estimated at sixty million people, or one out of every three Brazilians. The standoff ended with the killing of one hostage and the death of the hijacker after he was in police custody. Sandro, twenty-two, was later revealed to have been a survivor of the 1993 Candelária massacre of street children and a victim of violence in prison, a juvenile detention center, and at the hands of attackers who murdered his mother in his presence when he was six years old.[13] The hijacking, which in terms of media exposure was equivalent to the pursuit of O. J. Simpson on U.S. television in 1994, revealed seemingly intractable problems: poverty, racism, class inequality, drug addiction, police incompetence and violence, and the pervasiveness of fear in Brazilian cities. It shocked many viewers and led to demands for "something to be done."[14]

The Bus 174 incident, as it came to be known, triggered the passage of a bill in Congress to create a National Fund for Public Security (Fundo Nacional de Segurança Pública). This fund was intended to provide incentives to state governments to improve their public security systems. However, SENASP had eight directors from 1998 to 2002 (an average tenure of seven months for each) and thus lacked the continuity of leadership to have much of an impact on activities in the states. This situation changed with the election of Luiz Inácio Lula da Silva in 2002. President Lula's victory led to the arrival of a new team of administrators at SENASP that took charge in January 2003.

This team advocated a new style of policing in Brazil that reconciles efficient data management and the intelligent use of force with proximity to communities and respect for human rights (L. E. Soares 2000). It drew up a National Plan for Public Security and created a section within SENASP devoted exclusively to crime prevention.[15] The new cadre of SENASP managers also established a Unified System of Public Security (Sistema Único de Segurança Pública or SUSP) modeled on the unified public health system created in the 1990s. An important component of SUSP involved the attempt to collect crime data from the states, along the lines of the U.S. Federal Bureau of Investigation's Unified Crime Reporting system, and to use this data to assess results and refine policies.[16]

Under President Lula, there was greater continuity of leadership of SENASP than before. Although the president's first appointee as secretary of the agency left after only nine months, his successor remained throughout President Lula's first term in office and enjoyed the longest tenure of any director of SENASP. The agency embarked on an ambitious series of activities, distributing R$829 million (roughly US$463 million) from 2003 to 2005, mostly to state secretariats of public security but also to municipal governments for activities such as training.[17] This spending was doled out with the help of a statistical system, created in 2004, that gathers data on homicides and other crimes, police personnel, population, GDP per capita, the human development index, and other indicators from 224 *municípios* (counties) with populations over one hundred thousand people. SENASP administrators claim that the statistics enable them to distribute funds on the basis of need rather than political criteria.[18]

SENASP's official approach stands in contrast to traditional, repressive approaches to policing that emphasize vehicles, men with guns, and the heavy-handed use of force. SENASP puts forth the proposition that public security is not just a question for the police, but also for communities, as well as state agencies in the areas of health, education, employment, leisure, housing, and the arts. The secretariat therefore encourages municipal governments to engage in crime-prevention programs for at-risk youth, such as job training, sports, cultural, and educational programs. It runs a distance-learning course for public-security professionals and community members involved in violence prevention. The agency gives annual awards for community policing and has promoted the creation of community councils (*conselhos comunitários*) at both the local and state levels to institutionalize dialogue between leaders of police forces and civil-society organizations. SENASP brings law-enforcement officials together at national conferences and promotes integrated management (*gestão integrada*), the coordination of the military and civil police at the state government level.[19] It also offers training to modernize the civil police, for example in the area of crime-scene investigation.

SENASP is also a major sponsor of research, much of it carried out by university research centers with close ties to policymakers. By commissioning and promulgating dozens of different studies in the area of public security, SENASP has been able to highlight reforms that appear to be successful and promote the diffusion of best practices derived from such studies.[20] Examples of these successes include the city of Diadema in São Paulo, where the homicide rate was reduced by 67 percent between 2002 and 2006 thanks to programs in schools, the participation of community organizations, an increased role for the municipal guard (Guarda Municipal), and the early closing of bars.[21] Another example of successful reform is Belo Horizonte, where the use of an information system similar to one pioneered in New York City (Beato Filho, Alves, and Tavares 2005) and a central dispatch unit for the civil and military police have been credited with contributing to reductions in levels of violent crime.

SENASP has also promoted programs that seek to control Brazil's notoriously high levels of police violence (Amnesty International 2005; Cano 1999; Pereira and Ungar 2004; Pinheiro 2000). It has encouraged the creation of ombudsmen's offices (*ouvidorias*), state agencies that can register citizen complaints about the police and encourage their investigation.[22] The National Secretariat for Human Rights, with money from the European Union, works in tandem with SENASP to support the *ouvidorias*, organizing databases on complaints against the police, providing courses for ombudsmen and their staffs, training police personnel in human rights, launching a campaign against torture, and organizing public meetings on the role of the *ouvidoria*.[23]

In August 2007, the Lula government announced a National Program of Public Security and Citizenship (Programa Nacional de Segurança Públicans e Cidadania, Pronasci) that gave new resources and responsibilities to SENASP and other agencies inside and outside the Ministry of Justice. Pronasci is an ambitious package of programs, with a projected budget of R$6.7 billion (roughly US$3.7 billion) over five years, that targets eleven cities with the highest homicide rates in the country.[24] Programs include the augmentation of salaries and housing assistance for the lowest-paid police, the payment of allowances to mothers in violent neighborhoods and at-risk youth, and the construction of special prisons for young offenders. Based in part on the Lula government's Bolsa Família (Family Stipend) program, the architects of Pronasci envision the eventual creation of a network of 3.5 million beneficiaries with a vested interest in reducing violent crime (Carvalho 2006, 3).

While it is probably too early to gauge SENASP's overall impact on public-security policy, the secretariat has articulated a new vision of public security within the federal government. Its national plan offers guidelines for reform to state governments, guidelines that encourage more-efficient collection and dissemination of information, the cooperation of multiple agencies in programs of crime prevention and community policing, the training of police personnel, the encouragement of community participation, and the establishment of curbs on police violence and corruption. The secretariat's fund represents the power of the purse, a mechanism that can be used to pull state governments in this direction.

Barriers to Reform: Fragmentation, Politicization, and Privatization

Despite the creation of SENASP and the recent trend towards greater federal involvement in public security that the secretariat represents, serious barriers to reducing violence remain. These have to do with the political environment and the nature of the state's coercive institutions at the state level. These constraints are well known and frequently discussed in Brazil, but will remain formidable even as more resources are devoted to public security. Three of the biggest problems are fragmentation, politicization, and privatization.[25]

Fragmentation

The overall political environment that SENASP operates in, particularly the presidential-legislative and presidential-gubernatorial relations at the national level, is complex and factious. Brazil's federalist system, electoral rules, and party system combine to produce elected presidents who lack a majority in Congress.

The "golden rule" for Brazilian presidents is therefore to stitch together a multiparty coalition in Congress (Amorim Neto 2005, 3). This requires a delicate balancing act in which the president offers pork to congressional delegations, state governors, and big-city mayors in return for support on major legislative initiatives (Alston and Mueller 2005). Within this system, there are constraints on how far presidents can successfully push to make public-security reform one of those major initiatives. This is because public security is still firmly in the hands of state governors, who control the military and civil police. While the latter have lost power in recent years, they can still be counted on to resist federal encroachment on their prerogatives to appoint police chiefs, to control police forces, and to allocate resources as they see fit.

It is true that Pronasci represents a major federal initiative in which the Ministry of Justice appears to be disbursing aid conditionally, demanding certain kinds of changes in public-security policy in return for its resources. However, the question remains as to how far the federal government can really go in requiring change, when so much of the day-to-day responsibility for public security rests with state governments. Pronasci is, in some respects, an artful and ambiguous political pact between the federal government and the states: federal officials respond to public pressure by devoting resources to security, while state governors retain overall responsibility for the success of the initiative. Each can claim to be responding constructively to the problem, but each can also blame the other if adequate results are not obtained.

In the past, SENASP has been reluctant to use its limited power of the purse to induce states to reform. In the words of two specialists, the national fund "could be a more efficient instrument to obtain the state governments' adhesion to the measures and commitments initially proposed in the PNSP [National Plan for Public Security]" (Costa and Grossi 2005, 27). It appears that in many instances SENASP merely transferred resources to states that used the money to do what they otherwise would have done, rather than to induce and fund the creation of new programs and procedures. This is what critics fear will also occur under Pronasci.

As at the national level, close examination of the nature of public-security institutions at the state level reveals the problem of fragmentation. State police forces are divided between uniformed military police who patrol the streets and the plainclothes civil police responsible for criminal investigations. This division of labor leads to competition and duplication of effort, especially in large cities, and hinders the effectiveness of police responses to crime. In many states, civil and military police do not even share radio frequencies or basic information about their operations. Relations between the two forces are often strained. The civil police complain that the military police dominate the secretariats of public security and that they are deprived of adequate resources and lack incentives to conduct investigations. The military police are often deployed in a repressive fashion, applying force on the street but with inadequate training for more sophisticated policing functions. Integration of the two police forces occurs in a pro forma fashion at the state level, encouraged by SENASP, but this integration appears to be almost nonexistent at the local level.[26]

Police-prosecutor relations are another source of overlapping competencies, friction, and information hoarding within the public-security system. Civil police *delegados* (investigators), who are trained in the law, have responsibility for drawing up the initial investigative report (*inquérito*) that forms the basis of any criminal prosecution. However, these reports are often hoarded in police stations and not sent to the prosecutors' office (Ministério Público, Public Ministry) within the specified time period (ten days when a suspect has been detained, thirty days when suspects are at large). Whereas in the United States the police are required to turn over evidence within a short period of time to the prosecutors in the district attorney's office, who can conduct their own supplemental investigations, in Brazil the *delegado* often sits on cases for months and even years. Prosecutors are almost entirely reliant on the *inquérito* to prosecute cases, but *delegados* do not always have strong incentives to produce high quality *inquéritos* within a reasonable amount of time. No one in a position of superiority to the *delegado* in her or his organization reviews the *inquéritos*, establishes guidelines for their production, or rewards or punishes people on the basis of the quality of these documents.[27] The police blame the subsequent low rate of prosecution and conviction on prosecutors and the judiciary, while the prosecutors and judges blame poor police investigations and the specifications of the criminal code. The end result is that prosecutorial oversight of the police is virtually impossible, prosecutors and the police are competitors as much as they are collaborators, and the public is denied both transparency and accountability in the criminal-justice system.

Examples of fragmentation occur at the municipal level and not just the national and state levels. Most recent examples of successful curbs on violence, both in Brazil and other countries, have occurred at the municipal level. However, municipal security forces (Guardas Municipais) are weak, and city governments lack the policy and organizational tools to implement comprehensive public-security policies. The roughly five hundred *guardas* in Brazil are not police forces in a constitutional sense or formally part of the public-security system, and were originally created only to guard municipal property. However, in recent years and in part due to funding and training initiatives from SENASP, *guardas* have become larger and more active in public security, often functioning as a kind of frontline municipal police force, able to resolve low-level disputes but apt to defer to the military police when it comes to serious crime. Where mayors and state governors are from different political parties, however, cooperation between *guardas* and state secretariats of public security, as well as other police forces, can be lacking. Furthermore, public understanding of the difference between the *guardas* and the military police is often limited, leading to confusion, competition, and overlapping jurisdictions in practice.

Accountability mechanisms to control the state's public security institutions are abundant in Brazil, but also exhibit the problem of fragmentation. Police *ouvidorias* or ombudsmen (present in fourteen states) have been established to facilitate the investigation of cases of alleged police corruption, brutality, and other misconduct brought to its attention by members of the public. However, since the Public Ministry also has the constitutional responsibility of investigating police misconduct, it is unclear why the police ombudsmen were needed in the first place. In addition, the ombudsmen do not have the power to independently investigate the police. Instead, they turn their complaints over to *corregedorias*, police internal-affairs agencies, staffed by police officers themselves. The latter lack genuine independence and are subject to byzantine procedural rules, hampering their effectiveness. For this reason, the innovation represented by the police ombudsmen is more formal than real, and effectively prosecuting police who engage in illegal violence and other illicit acts is extremely difficult (especially in cases involving high-ranking military police officers).

Partly because of the ineffectiveness of accountability mechanisms, the predisposition of the Brazilian military police is often to apply coercion in the streets rather than to arrest. This kind of coercion creates no paper trail and is much less susceptible to oversight than arrests. In 2006, for example, the military police in Rio de Janeiro killed 1,063 people—more than three times the number of people killed by all the police forces in the United States in the same year.[28] In addition, because judges must give priority to cases in which the defendant is in prison, the tendency on the part of the police not to arrest means that many crimes are not investigated and do not result in punishment.

The results of the lack of coordination between the state's public-security organizations, with their separate forces for patrolling, investigating, prosecuting, and judging violent crime, can be seen in the low figures for the proportion of homicides that result in prosecutions and convictions. For example, a study of the 2,917 homicides in the northeastern city of Recife in 2000 showed that only 3 percent resulted in prosecutions, with only one case resulting in a judicial sentence (Zaverucha 2003, 89).[29] The clearance rate for homicides—the proportion that result in arrests—also appears to be low (Wellford and Cronin 2000). A 2005 analysis of murders in Recife by the newspaper *Jornal do Commercio* revealed that most murders were not investigated but merely resulted in (often incomplete) reports of the circumstances in which the victim's body was found. It is no wonder that anthropologist Roberto Kant de Lima argues that the real function of the Brazilian police is the registration of crimes, rather than their investigation.[30]

Even if the civil police could investigate more crime, their training is spotty and sometimes nonexistent. The initial training is apparently weak in the area of investigation, and opportunities for extra courses later on in one's career are rare. A former *delegado* recounted that he worked in the area of auto theft without ever having received any training in the investigation of that particular crime. He learned on the job. "The policeman is not a professional," he declared. "He's an amateur. . . . The police do not receive police education."[31]

The fragmentation of Brazilian police forces is also relevant to an understanding of how community policing works in the country. As we have seen, SENASP promotes community policing by organizing courses and providing technical and monetary resources and other incentives to state police forces. While the definition of the term is open to interpretation, in most versions of it, the police attempt to establish close relationships with people in the community by limiting their activities to small areas, patrolling on foot or bicycle instead of cars, participating in neighborhood meetings, and the like. In Brazil, despite the ubiquity of community policing as a slogan, the structure of the civil and military police militate against such policies. Both corporations are state-level entities in which personnel can be and are transferred to any district in the state. The military police are stationed in barracks that are separated from civilian populations and are subject to rigid command and control structures and divisions between officers and enlisted men; these inhibit their interaction with residents of the neighborhoods they patrol. The civil police, for their part, spend a considerable amount of their time in the station (*delegacia*) dealing with paperwork, rather than in the streets. The two forces do not usually operate within the same geographical districts and often do not share basic operational information with each other.

These organizational characteristics affect police-community relations, which, like police-police relations, can be mutually hostile. One area in which this can be seen is in police attitudes towards human rights organizations. The police complain that human rights NGOs are indifferent to the fate of police officers killed in the line of duty and are only interested in the rights of "bandits" rather than good citizens (*pessoas de bem*). The human rights organizations argue that many police officers do not accept that respecting the procedural rights of criminal suspects—even convicted "bandits"—is an integral part of the rule of law.

The Manichean discourse of bandits versus good citizens, favored by many police but also many citizens, was much in evidence during the debate over the gun-control referendum of October 23, 2005. This referendum was to decide the fate of a proposed prohibition on the sale of guns and ammunition in Brazil. One of the arguments against the proposal that resonated strongly was that the police simply could not be trusted to be the only bearers of arms in society. The proposal was rejected by a vote of 64 percent to 36 percent.[32]

In summary, the wide array of state organizations entrusted with public security are not effectively coordinated in Brazil. Competition, lack of trust, hoarding of information, and fragmentation between federal, state, and municipal levels characterize relations between police forces, between police and prosecutors, and between elected officials in different branches and levels of government. The result is an ineffective public-security and criminal-justice system that permits a high level of impunity for violent crime; impunity, in turn, acts as a stimulant to further violence.

Politicization

A second problem in Brazilian public security, closely related to the first, is the pattern of politicization of police forces and policy more generally. This can be seen at various levels of government. Nationally, the post-1985 era has seen the capture of parts of the federal bureaucracy by specific political parties.[33] This contributes to a lack of belief among political actors in the separation of politics from administration. In older democracies, such a belief is a fiction at best, but it can have real consequences if accepted by enough influential political figures. SENASP itself is not entirely free of this pattern of politicization. Almost all of its personnel are political appointees closely tied to the administration of President Lula. Were an opposition party such as the PSDB (Partido da Social Democracia Brasileira), to win the presidency in 2010, SENASP's staff would probably be swept out. The orientation of the secretariat would not necessarily change, but it could be; for example, there would be nothing to stop a new president radically downgrading it and discontinuing the Pronasci program.

In Brazil, the police and other public-security institutions are often seen as tools of the government in power. For example, the government of the state of São Paulo, in the hands of the opposition PSDB party, refused to participate in several SENASP-sponsored activities during Lula's first term, presumably because the federal government was controlled by the PT (Partido dos Trabalhadores or Workers' Party).[34] This partisan obstructionism seriously damaged SENASP's work, because it meant that the richest and most populous state, with the largest number of police, was effectively going it alone, impervious to the reform agenda being promoted at the federal level.

Like SENASP, state secretariats of public security are usually staffed by political appointees. While technical abilities are valued in such secretariats, considerations of political loyalty and sometimes patronage remain paramount. This is especially obvious when it comes to the release of information about crime, data that are often suppressed or massaged to make the government of the day look good. The political staffing of state secretariats of public security leads to abrupt discontinuities in policies, as new governments undo the work of their predecessors, manipulate information to maximize beneficial spin, and use the police to their own advantage. In the words of a high-level state prosecutor, "We don't have state policies for public security. We have policies of governments."[35]

This tendency is lamented by many officials within the police forces themselves and affects the police from top to bottom. For example, police officers complain that promotions are awarded more on the basis of political connections than on merit, and that everyone needs a political patron to get ahead. In the words of one military police lieutenant colonel, "The promotions that occur in the civil and military police are not based on leadership, but on political influence. So, if you are a politician and I am linked to you, have no doubt, I am in."[36] A former secretary of public security concurs, remarking, "In the police, everything is politics."[37]

The point here is not that the police are completely apolitical in other political systems, but rather that the degree of politicization in Brazil is higher than in many other places. In the United Kingdom, for example, multiparty police authorities insulate the police from the direct political pressure of governments and parties by choosing commissioners whose terms do not coincide with those of local county councils. It is also generally frowned upon for police officers to publicly voice partisan preferences.[38] In the United States, while elected mayors generally choose police chiefs, they usually refrain from interfering in day-to-day management and other internal decisions involving the police.

In Brazil, such separation of politics and policing is not taken for granted. Members of the police forces frequently run for city, state, and sometimes even federal offices, using police associations as vote banks. Both the civil and military police forces have also engaged in strikes in recent years, even though it is technically illegal for the military police to do so. These strikes can debilitate state governments and have become potent political weapons. But just as police power can be a political weapon, external political pressure is often brought to bear on day-to-day police activity. For example, because civil police *delegados* do not have the same job guarantees as judges and prosecutors, they can be transferred to different districts by the secretary of public security, an appointee of the governor. Elected politicians often use their influence with the governor to have troublesome *delegados*—especially ones investigating them or their political allies—transferred out of their constituencies.[39]

This type of politicization erodes the legitimacy of the police and adds to the perception that the police enforce a degraded rule of law that involves a separate set of rules for the powerful. The poor rightly complain that the system is biased against them and that they will be punished for transgressions that the better-off can commit with impunity. The murder of a high-profile citizen might get solved with alacrity, while homicides in poor neighborhoods are not even investigated, and this reinforces the widespread sense that the police are guardians of the state and its interests rather than the citizenry or the public order in a broader sense.

Privatization

The third problem, privatization, is related to the second and third. Privatization accompanies fragmentation because if a single public rationality cannot be imposed on the myriad agencies involved in public security, then it is easier for private logics to become prevalent within them. Similarly, if the police are seen to be politicized and acting in the interests of particular interests rather than the collective good, and those interests are not just partisan but also commercial and therefore private, then politicization and privatization can become two sides of the same coin.

The process of privatization is intertwined with the public-security system. Private security, as much as fragmentation and politicization, poses a challenge to SENASP's efforts to improve public-security policy. Because of their dismally low pay, the police are often in search of extra income. When this is not obtained through graft or extortion, a common option is to arrange a second job in the private sector. Even though it is technically illegal for the police to hold these second jobs—*bicos* or *virações*—the practice is widely tolerated by authorities. This means that many police officers give their best hours to private security firms. The then-head of the Rio de Janeiro civil police, Hélio Tavares Luz, said with a touch of exaggeration, "Police are like waiters. They have a signed workers' card and the minimum wage. The tips are their own" (*Veja*, Nov. 15, 1995, 10).

These "tips" increasingly come from private security, which is a booming sector in Brazil. An estimated R$11.8 billion (about US$6.6 billion) was spent on private security in Brazil in 2005.[40] Around five thousand private security companies are registered with the Federal Police. The number of registered private security guards is 1.4 million, more than two times the total number of civil and military police in the country. One estimate places the number of clandestine private security agents at around 2 million, although such estimates are rough guesses and vary widely (Mariz 2007; see also Mariz 2005). Although the Federal Police are supposed to regulate private security companies, it is unclear how much they can do in the face of the growing activity in this sector. Some aspiring private security contractors actually engage in crime, thus generating a demand for their services. In Rio de Janeiro, according to the sociologist Luiz Eduardo Soares, the police have perpetrated massacres in order to sell security to beleaguered communities.[41]

Private security, especially the high-tech variety, challenges the notion that security is, in fact, a public good. Public goods are nonrivalrous: once they have been created, everyone can enjoy them without taking away from anyone else's consumption of the good. They are also nonexcludable, in that it is difficult or impossible to prevent people from benefiting from the good (Cowen 2007). Luiz Eduardo Soares (2000, 45) assumes that security is a public good when he writes, "Fear, today, is a democratic sentiment. Under current conditions, security will either exist for all or for no one. There is no longer any space for exclusions [*exclusivismos*]."

However, one has to wonder if this is true, even in Rio de Janeiro, where the poor live on hillsides overlooking many of the better-off neighborhoods. (For the peculiarities of the situation in Rio, see Amar 2003; Arias 2003 and 2007; and Murilo de Carvalho 1997). In a very general sense, it seems accurate that even the very rich and protected cannot escape some risk from the increasing insecurity of public space. Nevertheless, the vitality of the private-security sector suggests that security, with the help of innovations in communication and transportation technology, architecture, and urban planning, can be refashioned into a private, or at least club, good.[42] To the extent that this occurs, the better-off will be as shielded from the ills of public security as they are from the problems of public health and education.

Like private education and private health services, therefore, private security feeds on the failures of the state. Sometimes the parasitic nature of this relationship becomes visible. In Recife, several luxury apartments were robbed on January 9, 2006, and the press prominently covered the robberies. The next day, a private security company specializing in reinforced, bullet-proof doors touted the benefits of its product with a reproduction of the previous day's headline in its advertisement.[43]

The problem of private security is not just that it deprives the state and its citizens of the best waking moments, the most acute energies, and often the most courageous acts of the police. The purchasers of private security are often buying state protection, because private security firms are staffed, managed, and sometimes owned by police officers. Many top public officials direct or profit from private security companies. Like the extra jobs of lower-level police personnel, such connections are illegal, but they can be disguised through the use of dummy boards of directors and similar ruses. This creates an insidious private-public nexus in which public resources are used to protect private interests and generate private profits, undermining efforts to improve the quality of the public good that police forces ostensibly produce.

Charles Dickens (1994 [1852–53], 503) wrote in *Bleak House*, "The one great principle of the English law is, to make business for itself. There is no other principle distinctly, certainly, and consistently maintained through all its narrow turnings. Viewed by this light it becomes a coherent scheme, and not the monstrous maze the laity are apt to think it. Let them but once perceive that its grand principle is to make business for itself at their expense, and surely they will cease to grumble." Substitute "English law" above with "Brazilian public security" and one gains an insight into a major problem with the security business in Brazil today. Many representatives of public order have a vested interest in selling private security services, which in turn thrive on the lack of existence of public security. This creates an enormous conflict of interest at the top of the public-security bureaucracy, where officials are part of an interlocking web of private and public agencies whose principle purpose is to make business for itself.

Private security is further stimulated by sensationalistic crime programs on television, such as *Cidade Alerta (City on Alert)*, *Brasil Urgente (Brazil Urgent)*, and *Bronca Pesada (Heavy Denunciation)* that focus attention on particularly heinous acts and convey the impression that protection for individuals or small groups is the only way to effectively respond to crime. The middle and upper classes withdraw from public space and retreat into fortified apartment buildings, bullet-proof cars, and private clubs, with increasing reliance on private security as an alternative to the public variant (Caldeira 2003). In poor neighborhoods, militias and vigilantism have become more common. Physical separation leads to social distance and mistrust, giving a free rein to heavy-handed policing outside of middle- and upper-class areas. Simplistic and voluntaristic calls to replace a "culture of violence" with a "culture of peace" do little to change this reality of segregation and fear.[44]

In summary, fragmentation, politicization, and privatization place high barriers to the realization of SENASP's vision of a gradual reduction in violence in Brazil. The scale of these barriers became apparent in 2006, when Brazil's deteriorating public-security situation gained international notoriety.

The PCC and the Politics of Fear

In May 2006 the First Command of the Capital (Primeiro Comando da Capital, or PCC), an organization of criminals that began in prisons in the early 1990s, staged a massive uprising in São Paulo. On May 12, 2006, the state of São Paulo's prison authorities transferred 765 prisoners believed to have been PCC members to a penitentiary in Presidente Venceslau, in the interior of the state. In reaction to this measure, the PCC organized rebellions in 83 of 105 São Paulo prisons and launched 274 attacks on police stations, schools, hospitals, the Public Ministry, individual police officers, and buses in the city of São Paulo. (Some 80 buses were attacked, many completely destroyed.) On Monday, May 15, the city of São Paulo was virtually paralyzed, as residents abandoned workplaces and schools to return home and the streets became clogged with traffic. In the first four days of the attacks, four civilians were killed, along with eight prison guards and thirty-one police officers and municipal guards (Cavallaro and Ferreira Dodge 2007, 53). The state's reaction was rapid and harsh, as suspected PCC members were gunned down in "confrontations" that in many cases appeared to be summary executions. A subsequent evaluation of the violence listed a total of 124 dead, including seventy-four suspected criminals and nine prisoners.[45]

The nature of the attacks belied political authorities' simplistic dichotomy between the state and organized crime, because it revealed the substantial interpenetration between both entities.[46] The attacks had been organized by prisoners using cell phones, ostensibly prohibited in prison but tolerated by guards colluding with the PCC. Some police officers had been attacked outside their homes, indicating that PCC members might have obtained addresses from suborned state agents. Furthermore, in order to quell the rebellion, São Paulo state authorities admitted that they had spoken with PCC leaders, showing the considerable de facto power that the criminal faction had obtained.[47]

In the wake of the PCC disaster, government authorities at the state and federal levels pointed fingers at each other. Critics of state policies observed that São Paulo's prison population had more than doubled between 1994 and 2006, without careful screening and segregation of prisoners as required by law (Athayde and Lirio 2006, 20–28).[48] The prisons were known for severe overcrowding and routinized torture. Another weak link in the criminal justice chain, the prisons, along with the police and courts, became the object of a frenzy of media analysis, with pundits and experts clamoring for everything from more super-max prisons to alternative sentencing. The loudest calls were to "get tough"—impose longer sentences for various crimes, restrict conditions in prisons (by, among other things, jamming cell phones), and reduce the age limit for criminal prosecution from eighteen to sixteen.

Few observers, however, seemed to believe that the cauldron of violence in the prisons would become tranquil any time soon. This sentiment was confirmed by continued PCC activity after the May revolt, most notably on August 12, 2006, when the crime group kidnapped a reporter and cameraman who worked for Brazil's most powerful television network, TV Globo. To win the freedom of its employees, Globo bowed to a demand to exhibit a four-minute PCC video (Athayde and Lirio 2006, esp. 20–21). The Globo journalists were released unharmed, but the incident further underlined the PCC's determination and impressive capacity for coordinated action, a capacity that stood in marked contrast to the fragmentation and demoralization of the forces of "law and order."[49]

The PCC attacks underlined the consequences of fragmentation, politicization, and privatization in Brazil's public-security system. Because it took place in Brazil's richest state, it also suggested that a lack of resources—frequently cited by specialists as a major problem for public insecurity—was not the only or even the principal factor behind the rising tide of violence.

There is no question that lack of resources is a serious problem. Low salaries contribute to police corruption and the siphoning of police personnel into private security. Small budgets also limit the effectiveness of police forces and the overall effort to make policing more effective and more humane. For example, SENASP funds represent a relatively small percentage—apparently around 1–5 percent—of the resources devoted to public security in the states.[50] In absolute terms, the funds SENASP disbursed between 2003 and 2005 add up to only about R$1.50 (or US$0.84 at current exchange rates) per capita per year. For a country in which the homicide rate has almost tripled in twenty-five years, this appears to be a very modest investment. To give a sense of proportion to these figures, in 2005 the Brazilian government payments towards interest on its public debt amounted to more than five hundred times the value of SENASP's annual budget (*Veja*, Feb. 8, 2006, 56).[51]

If the Pronasci funds are disbursed as projected over the 2007–2011 period — which is uncertain, considering that 2010 is a presidential election year—total SENASP funding per capita per year would be more than seven times higher, in that period, than they were in 2003–2005.[52] What difference could this make? It is worth noting that São Paulo's spending on public security was well above the national average, and the PCC attacks occurred there and not elsewhere in 2006. If resources are being poured into a system in which collusion between state agents and organized crime is common, in which corruption and illegal violence by state agents is widespread, in which basic sharing of information and cooperation between different agencies is often impossible, in which partisan political loyalties are more important than technical skill and diligence in police promotions and the implementation of state policy, and in which private security interests cream off public intelligence and personnel for profit—then much of these resources will be wasted.

The Future of Public Insecurity

"Security yes, omission no!" "Fight violence with justice." "Security is the responsibility of the state." "Peace without voice is not peace—it's fear." "Down with impunity." "We have the right to live without fear." The slogans of the Antônio Carlos Escobar Institute's protest of February 19, 2006, in Recife express the organization of a group of people anxious to participate in policymaking. The protesters were demanding an elemental, Hobbesian right—the right to security. Their cries are echoed by protestors reacting to different incidents of violence—but the same underlying problem—in cities, towns, and settlements all over Brazil.

A potential solution to the problem of violence lies in the program articulated by the federal public security agency SENASP—a program initiated by federal administrators, resources, and technical assistance, but depending crucially on civil society's participation and improvements in police-community relations. In the words of a civil police agent in Recife, "Hope lies in the organization of people. . . .The people have to participate, regardless of the ideology of the government."[53]

This vision of reform is promising, but it must overcome three formidable and interrelated obstacles: the fragmentation of state agencies responsible for preventing and responding to violent crime, the politicization of the police, and the increasing privatization of public security. Unless each of these problems can be addressed on some level, increases in funding for public security—which the federal government has committed to in the last years of President Lula's second term—are unlikely to lead to large-scale improvements to the problem of violence.

Looking to the medium to long term, three scenarios for Brazil suggest themselves. These are increasing privatization of the means of violence, increasing state capacity to repress crime, and, finally, reductions in violence based largely on redistribution and greater social consensus and not just repression. The first scenario has sometimes been referred to as the "Colombianization" of Brazil (which is somewhat misleading, given the latter's absence of guerrilla movements). In this vision, the role of public organizations in providing security will continue to decline, as the logic of privatization continues to undermine them. Drug traffickers and organized criminal groups of all kinds will continue to engage in an arms race with each other, in which the distinction between state and nonstate actors will become more and more meaningless. Militias will increasingly provide security in poor neighborhoods, and vigilante responses to crime will proliferate. For the upper and middle classes, private security companies will be in increasing demand, and these will grow parasitically on the back of ostensibly public police forces. The latter will be further penetrated by private interests, with police personnel increasingly willing to hire themselves out to the highest bidder. Brazil will come to represent the epitome of the "New Middle Ages" heralded by some social observers—the return of patterns of social organization familiar to students of early modern Europe, in which coercion is supplied by a bewildering array of small groups with various loyalties and motivations (Rapley 2006).

Such an unraveling of state control over the means of coercion is by no means inevitable, however. Another scenario might be the "Americanization" of Brazil.[54] In this scenario, fragmented public institutions overcome collective action problems to some extent and the beleaguered police, prosecutors, judges, and prison officials begin to more effectively investigate, prosecute, and punish crime. Increasing amounts of resources would be devoted to the criminal-justice system, rates of incarceration would continue their current upward trend, and Brazil's trajectory would resemble the movement towards the "prison" state that occurred in the United States after 1980. In the absence of broad redistribution of the benefits of economic growth, however, rates of violence would remain high. In the absence of the improvement of accountability mechanisms advocated by SENASP, levels of police violence might also remain high. In this scenario, the violent anarchy of "Colombianization" would be avoided, but the reassertion of state control over the means of coercion would lead to outcomes that are largely repressive.

A third possibility might be called the "social democratization" of Brazil. This would be the realization of SENASP's progressive vision. In this scenario, the broadening of economic opportunity and social programs integrate a generation of low-income urban youth into productive networks, such that crimes against life begin to decline. Community participation in public-security policy draws the police into closer contact with the most oppressed communities and pulls them into less violent and more consensus-driven forms of policing. Prevention leads the way—as violent crime rates drop, the burdens lessen on overstressed police, judicial, and prison authorities, leading to more effective investigation and prosecution of remaining crime and better treatment of prison populations. Economic growth and a shift in spending priorities further allow public agencies in the criminal-justice system more resources, and thus more capacity to solve problems. This third possibility lies closest to the ideal of peace with justice, or the dream articulated by some SENASP administrators of combining greater police efficiency with respect for human rights.

The three scenarios briefly spun out above give us some guidelines for imagining where Brazil's disastrous recent spiral of violence might lead. None is entirely implausible, and none is likely to prevail in its entirety. Because Brazil is a patchwork quilt, with different social conditions in various regions and wide latitude for policy experimentation at the state and, increasingly, municipal levels, the likelihood is that different places will approximate each of these different scenarios. The third scenario would be easier to fulfill in the relatively affluent south of the country, for example, while some observers might argue that the first scenario already is a reality for many Brazilian slum dwellers and residents of some remote northern states.

While the social democratic scenario is probably preferable to most Brazilians, it is not clear to what extent the public believes it to be attainable. In the absence of progress towards this hopeful vision, majorities might prefer the second scenario—increasing repression—out of fear of the first (increasingly violent anarchy). This would be especially likely if the politics of fear prevail—the manipulation of anxiety about public security by public officials for electoral and commercial gain.

The quality of Brazilian democracy is diminished by the politics of fear. Nevertheless, many Brazilians live with the perception that they are more unsafe than ever before. This is a worldwide phenomenon, but Brazil is paying a higher price than many other countries for its current inability to seriously address the problem of the violence in its midst.

10

Afro-Brazilian Politics: White Supremacy, Black Struggle, and Affirmative Action

Ollie A. Johnson III

> The history of Brazil is a history that has been written by whites, for whites, just as all of her economic, socio-cultural, military and political structures have been usurped by whites for whites.
>
> Abdias do Nascimento, *Brazil: Mixture or Massacre? Essays in the Genocide of a Black People*, 1989, 2–3.

AFRO-BRAZILIANS ARE increasingly rewriting the history of Brazil and working to change the structures that have exploited them. This process has been controversial, because activists and scholars are criticizing white privilege more directly than ever and highlighting the centrality of black life in the Brazilian experience. They are also advocating affirmative action, quotas, and other public policies to disrupt the monopoly whites have held and continue to hold on positions of power and influence. At the same time, some whites are joining blacks in recognizing the need for new thinking and action to challenge pervasive racial inequality and discrimination.

For most of the twentieth century, white political, economic, and social domination preempted and prevented a full national debate regarding race relations. Black activists have consistently resisted oppression and organized to protest and reverse this marginalization. However, rarely have their concerns been recognized as legitimate by the national elite and the public. Thus, when individual blacks criticized racial discrimination that they themselves and their people suffered, they were often accused of being racist. Similarly, when progressives and radicals demanded egalitarian reforms, they were often called godless communists. For more than one hundred years after the official abolition of slavery in 1888, there were few nationally known and influential black activists, scholars, politicians, and government officials.

Times are changing. Senator Paulo Paim, former Minister Matilde Ribeiro, Minister Gilberto Gil, former governor Benedita da Silva, Deputy Luiz Alberto, former senator Abdias do Nascimento, intellectual Maria Aparecida Silva Bento, professor Hélio Santos, activist Alzira Rufino, rapper MV Bill, professor Luiza Bairros, filmmaker Joel Zito Araujo, intellectual Diva Moreira, and activist Sueli Carneiro are some of the most visible Afro-Brazilians calling for an end to racial discrimination and poverty, respect for blacks in Brazilian society, and inclusive social policies. These leaders are working in their own communities, as well as with whites in government, the academy, social movements, religious institutions, and nongovernmental organizations to defeat racism, reduce racial inequality, and increase educational and employment opportunities for Afro-Brazilians.

In the 1980s and 1990s, for the first time in Brazilian history, black Brazilian leaders convinced key power brokers that historic and contemporary racism should be acknowledged and fought against. The confluence of several developments (transition to democracy, innovative black organizing and protest, and opposition electoral victories, among others) created an unprecedented situation in which white political leaders, government officials, and influential public figures began to acknowledge the legitimacy of black demands. As many white political and governmental leaders responded in a modest fashion, black activists embraced these responses and used them as the basis for more substantive proposals. In the last decade, black activists have insisted upon affirmative action and racial quotas as the best short-term procedures for integrating higher education and government employment.

Affirmative action has been one of the most significant developments in contemporary Brazilian politics. Governments, universities, and private institutions throughout the country have proposed, debated, and, in many cases, implemented policies to include members of the national population who had been excluded, underrepresented or simply absent. Women, Afro-descendants, public high school graduates, indigenous people, the poor, and the disabled have often been the target beneficiary groups (F. F. Santos 2004; Brandão 2007; S. Santos 2005). Despite the good intentions of its earliest sponsors, affirmative action has become an intensely polarizing public policy issue. Some of the country's best known intellectuals and most prominent politicians have denounced or defended affirmative action.[1] Opponents of affirmative action tend to reduce the variety of policies to racial quotas and narrow the potential beneficiaries to blacks (Fry et al. 2007).

The contemporary battle between white racial domination and black resistance has its origins in Portuguese colonialism and slavery. White racist rule was not defeated at independence, abolition, proclamation of the republic, and other key junctures in Brazilian history, and it has persisted to this day. This chapter argues that although white supremacy continues to be the dominant reality facing Afro-Brazilians, they are becoming increasingly successful in their struggle against it.[2] Black attempts to obtain formal education, decent jobs, adequate health care, safe housing, and to live free of racial discrimination represent the community's persistent commitment to the procedural and substantive dimensions of democracy. Afro-Brazilian politics are the efforts of blacks to gain and exercise full citizenship rights and to receive the respect and dignity they deserve.

Brazilian White Supremacy

Abdias do Nascimento, Afro-Brazilian activist, intellectual and politician, has made the most persuasive case that Brazil is a country whose key defining feature is white supremacy. In numerous books, essays, and speeches, Nascimento argues that 350 years of racial slavery, 100 years of racist legislation and public policy, and more than 60 years of the ideology of racial democracy have led to deep and systematic racial prejudice and discrimination against Afro-Brazilians, resulting in their subordinate and impoverished position in Brazilian society:

> Brazil as a nation proclaims herself the only racial democracy in the world, and much of the world views and accepts her as such. But an examination of the historical development of my country reveals the true nature of her social, cultural, political and economic anatomy: it is essentially racist and vitally threatening to Black people.

> Throughout the era of slavery from 1530 to 1888, Brazil carried out a policy of systematic liquidation of the African. From the legal abolition of slavery in 1888 to the present, this scheme has been continued by means of various well-defined mechanisms of oppression and extermination, leaving white supremacy unthreatened in Brazil (Nascimento 1989, 59).

Despite this overwhelming racist reality, the Brazilian ruling elite and their academic apologists have often described the country as a racial paradise where race relations are harmonious and any racial inequality and racist incidents are unfortunate legacies of slavery (Nascimento 1989, 59–90; 1982, 1985, 1993).[3]

According to Nascimento, a small, white elite has ruled the country for five centuries and successfully incorporated white immigrants into the system while relegating black and indigenous people to the margins. "Plantation owners, coffee, cotton, sugar and rubber barons, businessmen, industrialists, bankers, and the ruling military caste—all of Brazil's aristocracy and capitalists are Aryo-European, either of old colonial Portuguese stock or new immigrant tenor" (Nascimento 1989, 9). From Nascimento's perspective, Brazil's white supremacist system is comprehensive. All aspects of society have been contaminated by ideas of white superiority and black inferiority. Consequently, many African descendants have accepted the ideal of whitening and the myth of racial democracy, believing that a lighter complexion and more European facial features or hair textures are superior to dark skin and African features (Almeida, this volume). Correspondingly, the educational system has minimized the Afro-Brazilian contribution to Brazilian history, culture, and society through negation, distortion, and marginalization. Nascimento believes that school curricula and books have been instruments of white supremacy helping to brainwash Brazilians in general and Afro-Brazilians in particular (1989, 59–90; Filho 2003; Twine 1998; Daniel 2006).

During the twentieth century, three key aspects of historic white supremacy evolved in Brazil: the whitening of the population through European immigration, negative stereotypes and images of blacks, and exclusion of blacks from educational, employment, and other opportunities for upward mobility. These elements of white supremacy have strongly influenced Brazilian culture, society, and politics, while strongly discouraging manifestations of collective black group identity in religion, politics, activism, and social movements. Over the years, Afro-Brazilians have achieved a certain positive recognition as athletes and entertainers, especially as soccer players and singers. However, black activists, politicians, religious figures, scholars, and professionals have not received the same level of respect in the broader society.

Table 10.1. Brazilian Population by Color/Race (%)

Race	*1872*	*1890*	*1940*	*1950*	*1960*	*1980*	*1991*	*2000*
White	38.1	44.0	63.5	61.7	61.0	54.8	51.7	53.8
Pardos	42.2	41.4	19.4	26.5	29.5	38.4	42.6	39.2
Black	19.7	14.6	14.6	11.0	8.7	5.9	5.0	6.2

Source: Paixão 2003, 71.

To prevent the consolidation of an Afro-Brazilian majority after slavery, the Brazilian elite promoted the immigration of millions of Europeans. These Italian, German, Portuguese, and Spanish immigrants whitened the country and became a strong demographic force in the Southeast and South. From the 1880s to the 1920s, more than two million white immigrants arrived, worked the São Paulo coffee plantations, and became a visible presence in rural and urban settings. There was also Japanese immigration to São Paulo during this period. While the Brazilian government promoted and subsidized much of this immigration, it displaced and marginalized Afro-Brazilian workers. This displacement made it very difficult for blacks to survive (Andrews 1991, 54–89; Nobles 2000, 85–96).[4]

By the mid-twentieth century, the Brazilian white elite had achieved its goal of whitening the country. Table 10.1 shows that by 1940 whites had officially become more than 60 percent of the country's population. Blacks and *pardos,* who together constituted 60 percent of the population in 1890, saw their percentage decline to 35 percent within a 50-year period.

The white elite that stimulated European immigration held strong negative and racist views about blacks. In fact, fear of the deleterious impact that blacks would have on the country's progress contributed to the push for immigration. Attitudes out of the slave past and postemancipation white racist views contributed to widespread public and private, formal and informal images of blacks and blackness as ugly, deficient, suspicious, and less than human (Schwarcz 1999; Skidmore 1993).

Officially, the Brazilian government has consistently distinguished three main population groups based on color or race: whites, *pardos,* and blacks. Since the first census of 1872, these three groups have been the largest, representing more than 90 percent of the national population. A "yellow" category was later added to the census in recognition of the Japanese descendant population. As a result of the ideal of whitening and societal hostility towards blackness, many Brazilians were and still are reluctant or unwilling to claim and celebrate their African ancestry and heritage (Nascimento 2007; Souza 1983; Nobles 2000).

Racial identity in Brazil has been strongly influenced by the legacy of slavery and postabolition discrimination against blacks. This chapter follows the practice of numerous scholars in combining *pardos* and blacks (as Afro-Brazilians, African Brazilians, African descendants, blacks, and related terms) given their proximity in socioeconomic status. This approach does not deny that Brazilian racial identity is complex and that some *pardos, mestiços,* and *mulatos* do not classify themselves as African descendants. Black leaders know that Brazilians use many color terms and related descriptive labels to refer to themselves and others. However, these leaders generally characterize the division of *pardos* and blacks as a way to further divide and weaken the collective group identity of descendants of enslaved Africans (Da Silva et al. 1997; Nascimento 1978; Andrews 1991, 249–58; Sansone 2003, 21–58; Telles 2004, 78–106; Sheriff 2001).

Beginning in the 1930s and continuing throughout the twentieth century, Brazilian anthropologist and writer Gilberto Freyre popularized the alleged Brazilian tendencies of race mixture, cordiality, and nondiscrimination. Freyre rejected biological notions of race. However, he did not attack ongoing racial discrimination against blacks and the continuing legacy of the ideal of whitening. As a result, his celebration of Portuguese colonialism and racial democracy represented an unfortunate continuation of notions of white superiority rather than a complete rejection of the racist formulations of earlier Brazilian intellectuals such as Nina Rodrigues and Oliveira Vianna. Central to Freyre's Luso-Tropicalism perspective is the trivialization of the sexual violence against black women during and after slavery that resulted in the significant mixed population. As Elisa Larkin Nascimento (2007) notes,

> Freyre's theory allowed the Brazilian ruling class to celebrate and take pride in its penchant for miscegenation, which had earlier been a source of shame. This moral breakthrough soon intertwined with the ideological pretense of antiracism and welded into a denial of the existence of racial prejudice and discrimination in Brazilian society, forming the basis of the myth of racial democracy.
>
> Nevertheless, the notion of African inferiority remains the basis of the whitening ideal, which is the motor of miscegenation, and it has remained intact, if unexpressed, in the national consciousness. Also intact is the reality of de facto racial segregation and inequality. The ideology of white supremacy, silent in its operation, adaptable and flexible in its continuity, is always weaving new ways to perpetuate its domination. (53–54)

José Jorge de Carvalho argues that as Brazilian universities were growing in size and prestige, they became instruments of white supremacy because they excluded Afro-Brazilians and made no sincere or sustained efforts to diversify their faculty and student ranks. Blacks who had been in Brazil for centuries were denied opportunities for higher education, while the children and grandchildren of recent European immigrants were able to attend the new colleges and universities. Carvalho points to major universities like the Faculdade Nacional de Filosofia (later Universidade do Brasil) and the Universidade de São Paulo, founded at the same time that Freyre's views were gaining popularity in the 1930s, as institutions that were created by and for whites. This pattern of systematic and generalized exclusion of blacks is what Carvalho calls Brazilian academic racism (2006, 7–10, 20–24).

Carvalho insists that public universities in Brazil today remain essentially white. According to his research, the best schools, which tend to be federal and state universities, and their most prestigious departments and disciplines, have overwhelmingly white undergraduates, graduate students, professors, and researchers. He indicts the Brazilian higher education system for excluding blacks and Indians and not offering opportunities to outstanding and deserving black scholars such as Guerreiro Ramos, Edison Carneiro, and Clóvis Moura. He maintains that little was done during the twentieth century to diversify Brazilian public universities. Furthermore, Carvalho argues that Brazilian universities, especially the social sciences and humanities departments, perpetuated white supremacy through repeating and celebrating the Freyrean myths of racial democracy, racial mixing, and interracial cordiality (2006, 11–87).

Abundant evidence supports the view that white supremacy and racism remain alive and well in Brazil. Social scientists continue to document widespread racial inequality and an ingrained social hierarchy, with whites at the top and *mulatos* and blacks overrepresented at the bottom. Brazil has the unwelcome distinction of being one of the most unequal countries on earth. Whether focusing on income, wealth, housing, labor markets, education, access to health care, or other standard social indicators, there is a great gap between the rich and poor in Brazil (Henriques 2000; De Ferranti et al. 2004). Within this general context, race is a meaningful variable and racial inequality cannot be reduced to economic or social inequality. Specialists have noted that controlling for other variables shows that race influences the life chances of Brazilians. According to sociologist Edward Telles, "the Brazilian socioeconomic structure is largely divided along racial lines. On virtually all summary indicators of social conditions in Brazil, nonwhites score well below whites" (2004, 137).

Many scholars over the last twenty-five years have documented the fact that despite impressive economic growth during the twentieth century, Brazil remains a notorious case of racial inequality (Telles 2004; Hasenbalg 1979; Silva and Hasenbalg 1992; Hasenbalg et al. 1999; H. Santos 2001; Paixão 2003). These academics have shown that blacks remain concentrated at the bottom and on the margins of socioeconomic and political life in Brazil. Despite the reality that many whites are poor and that region, class, and gender are important variables for understanding poverty and inequality, black overrepresentation among the poor and underrepresentation among the rich are glaring. Afro-Brazilians are three times as likely to be poor as whites, who are five times as likely to be rich. Blacks are twice as likely to have no formal education as whites, who are four times as likely to have advanced degrees.

Given the legacy of slavery and the lack of government investment in public education, millions of illiterate Brazilians, including a large number of blacks, were prohibited from voting until the 1988 Constitution (Telles 2004, 122–31).

Racial discrimination against Afro-Brazilians is widespread and remains an important cause of racial inequality (Reichmann 1999; Bento 1998; Crook and Johnson 1999). Antonio Sérgio Alfredo Guimarães has analyzed hundreds of cases of racial discrimination that appeared in newspapers around the country (1989–1994) and others that were brought to the São Paulo racial crimes police station (Delegacia de Crimes Raciais de São Paulo, 1993–1997). He concluded that the antiracism law 7,716 and its interpretation by judges made it largely inapplicable to how racial discrimination is practiced in Brazil. He noted that law 7,716 punishes restricting or preventing someone access to a public or private institution based on racial or color prejudice. Proving this racist intent is often impossible, because the discrimination may be subtle and without racist commentary or the accused can usually invoke another reason for the discriminatory behavior such as inappropriate appearance, restricted access to members, and so on (Guimarães 2004, 36).

Where there is racial inequality, there is usually racial discrimination. Individual Brazilians in government, businesses, schools, social networks, hospitals, neighborhoods, and even families may discriminate against blacks by denying them the equal treatment, prestige, status, and opportunity granted to whites. The basis of discriminatory behavior is often anti-black attitudes and stereotypes (Telles 2004, 139–72; Almeida 2007, 215–72; Twine 1998; Hasenbalg 1979). National and subnational surveys show that a large majority of the adult Brazilian population (90 percent) believes that racism and prejudice exist. These surveys indicate that most Brazilians also believe that more racism and prejudice exist against blacks than other groups. At the same time, an even larger majority (96 percent) say that they are not prejudiced against blacks, whites, *pardos*, or indigenous groups. In sum, Brazilians recognize a generalized reality of racism and prejudice but deny that they specifically are racist and prejudiced (Santos and da Silva 2005; Venturi and Bokani 2004; Oliveira and Barreto 2003).

Black Struggle

Afro-Brazilians have consistently resisted their marginalization in the postslavery period. How they have individually and collectively fought against racial oppression has varied greatly, depending on their specific circumstances and understanding of their reality.

Black resistance to oppression often took the form of specific black advancement organizations and black participation in white-led organizations and movements. Nonetheless, black leaders have regularly urged blacks to draw on their own resources to improve their situation and to demand equal and fair treatment from public and private institutions. Black community life, political activities, social affairs, and cultural events were and still are chronicled in the black press (Gomes 2005; S. Santos 2007, 48–187; Nascimento and Nascimento 2000).

Three black organizations perhaps best captured the spirit of Afro-Brazilian activism during the twentieth century. The Brazilian Black Front (FNB), the Black Experimental Theater (TEN), and the Unified Black Movement (Movimento Negro Unificado, MNU) protested black subordination and successfully gained public space to encourage black participation in politics, public policies addressing the black condition, and full black inclusion in Brazilian society. These organizations challenged the notions that racial discrimination did not exist in Brazil, that blacks were less talented and capable than others, and that government should play no role in promoting racial equality. They all were successful in reaching Afro-Brazilians of various economic backgrounds, but incapable for various reasons of sustaining their most productive efforts (Pereira 1998; Butler 1998; Hanchard 1994; Nascimento 2007; Covin 2006; M. A. Cardoso 2002).

Founded in 1931 in the city of São Paulo, the Brazilian Black Front captured the imagination of blacks at a time of frustration and political change. The front encouraged blacks to unite following decades of massive European immigration, racial discrimination, and economic marginalization. A little more than four decades after slavery, blacks remained at the bottom of the social structure. The front created a meeting place for blacks who sought employment, education, health care, and other basic needs. The organization's newspaper, *A Voz da Raça*, expressed these concerns. As a result, the group's popularity grew rapidly. Within five years, the Brazilian Black Front had sixty thousand members in the major states of Brazil. Recognizing its political potential, the front reorganized itself as a political party in 1936. A year later, the Estado Novo dictatorship of President Getúlio Vargas banned all political parties. The Brazilian Black Front never recovered (Gomes 2005; S. Santos 2007, 74–86).

The Black Experimental Theater was born in 1944 in the city of Rio de Janeiro, the country's capital at the time. Founded by Abdias do Nascimento and others near the end of the Vargas dictatorship and World War II, TEN used drama, art, and culture to challenge racial discrimination, stereotyping, and lack of opportunities that blacks faced on a daily basis. TEN largely created black theater in Brazil by challenging the segregation and "whiteness" of traditional Brazilian theater, giving black writers and actors unprecedented opportunities, and protesting the unjust living conditions of the black majority. Recognizing that many Afro-Brazilians were illiterate, TEN offered literacy and education classes. Rejecting the inadequate treatment of blacks in Brazilian dramatic literature, Nascimento and others wrote plays affirming black humanity and exploring the conflicts and difficulties of black life. TEN's newspaper, *Quilombo*, was published from 1948 to 1950 and reported on TEN's activities and broader events of interest to blacks. Despite its limited financial resources, TEN criticized Brazilian racism directly and promoted black involvement in electoral politics, scholarship, and international affairs. TEN's leadership organized many of the key events of the black movement in the 1940s, 1950s, and 1960s. In 1964, when conservative politicians and military leaders overthrew the civilian government of President João Goulart, under the new military government, many progressives and radicals were exiled and banned from politics. To avoid possible imprisonment, Nascimento decided to go into exile in the United States in 1968. TEN effectively folded after his departure (Nascimento 2007, 164–226; S. Santos 2007, 87–103).

In the city of São Paulo in 1978, black activists created the Unified Black Movement to protest against the violence, discrimination, and disrespect faced by Afro-Brazilians on a daily basis. The MNU gathered thousands of members and effectively became a national organization during the 1980s and a national and international reference for black struggle against racism in Brazil. The MNU was the most prominent of many black organizations fighting against the military dictatorship and the myth of racial democracy. Public protests, marches, conferences, and gatherings, as well as private meetings, consciousness-raising sessions, and workshops were MNU activities intended to get blacks and the Brazilian population to consider problack alternatives. Zumbi dos Palmares was elevated to hero status for his leadership of the largest maroon community, the Quilombo dos Palmares, in the late 1600s. In this way, the MNU was rewriting Afro-Brazilian and Brazilian history from a black perspective and criticizing the traditional historical narrative that celebrated the abolition of May 13, 1888. In their newspapers, *Nego* and *MNU Jornal*, and other publications, the group challenged the romanticized image of Brazil as a racial paradise and informed readers of the brutal socioeconomic and political reality facing blacks (M. A. Cardoso 2002; Covin 2006).

During the 1970s and 1980s, a flourishing of black groups complemented the efforts of the MNU. Some of them were more political, others more cultural. Collectively, they represented an affirmation of black identity and a rejection of racial discrimination. Paulo Roberto dos Santos (1986, 7) classified them as religious, recreational, cultural, and political. He and Amauri Pereira, as black activists and intellectuals, also outlined some of the achievements, challenges, and failures of movement groups. Pereira, in particular, conveyed the excitement and difficulties of fighting against the military dictatorship and for recognition among the more prominent and established labor and leftist movements (1998, 24–51). Hundreds of black groups emerged in the 1980s and 1990s with distinct programs, agendas, and commitments. Despite disagreements and diverse organizing styles, these organizations concurred that black identity had to be emphasized to affirm black pride and challenge the myth of racial democracy (Barcelos 1999; P. Santos 1986; Fundação Cultural Palmares 2002; Lindsey 1999).

One of the most significant developments in Brazilian politics since 1980 has been the growing demand from a cross section of black leadership that blacks and their concerns be included in all aspects of politics and government. Consequently, blacks have been organizing in the labor, Catholic Church, democracy, amnesty, student, and neighborhood movements and in all areas of social life. This aspect of contemporary black struggle has involved black activists taking the agenda of the black movement into other groups and institutions. Black politicians have been most prominent in this regard. During the 1980s, black activists convinced the opposition political parties to address the specific concerns of Afro-Brazilians. For the first time in Brazilian history, political parties included clauses against racial discrimination and developed commitments to address the concerns of black leaders. This process occurred most clearly in the Democratic Labor Party (PDT), when black activists led by Abdias do Nascimento convinced the party to take bold, public stands against racism. Then the PDT, led by Leonel Brizola, embraced the fight against racism (Nascimento and Nascimento 1992, 64–79; Johnson 1998; G. Santos 1992).

The other major parties, especially the Party of the Brazilian Democratic Movement (PMDB), Workers' Party (PT), and Party of the Brazilian Social Democracy (PSDB), also developed black informal or formal caucuses and publicly criticized racism in Brazilian society. As the parties won elections at the municipal, state, and federal levels, their black members generally demanded their fair share of appointments, positions, and influence in the new administrations. In the parties and the new governments, there was resistance to these black demands. However, as women succeeded in gaining some high level appointments, the establishment of women's councils, and specific policies addressing the concerns of feminist activists, blacks also made incremental advances (I. Santos 2006; G. Santos 1992).

This process of black political progress was clear in the following problack government initiatives. In 1984, Governor Franco Montoro created the Council for the Participation and Development of the Black Community (Conselho de Participação e Desenvolvimento da Coumunidade Negra) in São Paulo, Brazil's largest state. In 1988, President José Sarney established the Palmares Cultural Foundation (Fundação Cultural Palmares) in Brasília, the nation's capital. In 1991, Rio de Janeiro Governor Leonel Brizola formed the Special Office for Defense and Promotion of Afro-Brazilian Populations (Secretaria Extraordinaria de Defesa e Promoção das Populações Negras, originally SEDEPRON and later changed to SEAFRO). On the three hundredth anniversary of the death of Zumbi dos Palmares, President Fernando Henrique Cardoso established the Interministerial Working Group for the Development of the Black Population (Grupo de Trabalho Interministerial para a Valorização da População Negra) on November 20, 1995. Most recently, President Luiz Inácio Lula da Silva created the Special Office for the Promotion of Racial Equality (Secretaria Especial de Politicas de Promoção da Igualdade Racial, SEPPIR) in 2003 (Johnson 2006; I. Santos 2006; H. Santos 1999).

These public agencies and policies were unprecedented in Brazilian history. They represented governmental responses to black demands for inclusion. Black activist-intellectuals with partisan loyalties were selected to lead these institutions. Since these appointments occurred in the largest states and in the federal government, they received media attention and public visibility. In each instance, black activist demands were at the root of these policy innovations. Invariably, however, black leaders soon complained they did not receive enough support or resources to do their jobs effectively. While unable to solve the major problems facing Afro-Brazilians, they nonetheless managed to direct attention to racial discrimination and inequality in education, employment, health care, the criminal justice system, and other aspects of society (Johnson 2006; I. Santos 2006; H. Santos 2000; Reichmann 1999). Their efforts helped create the political atmosphere for affirmative action.

Some scholars have criticized the new black political organizations, especially the Unified Black Movement, as small, ineffective, and elitist (Silva 1994; Burdick 1995; Hanchard 1994; Sheriff 2001). Anthropologist John Burdick has argued that black activists "adopt stances that marginalize and alienate many people in their targeted constituency who otherwise are sympathetic to their goals" (1998a, 5). In several works, Burdick has outlined how black activists unnecessarily pushed away potential members by emphasizing Afro-Brazilian religion (especially *candomblé*) while criticizing Christianity (especially Catholicism and Protestantism). He claims that black groups overemphasized black identity as a prerequisite for movement participation. He has also noted that activists tended to be better educated, lighter skinned, and more middle class than the black masses (1995; 1998a; 1998b; 2005). Burdick's recommendations are that the black activists be more flexible on questions of religion and racial identity and accentuate the movement's substantive concerns that connect most easily with black workers and the poor. While Burdick and other critics provide some insight into black activism, they tend to underestimate the pervasiveness of white supremacy and the effectiveness of black activists in challenging the racial status quo (Johnson 2006; S. Santos 2007; Cardoso 2002).

Scholars such as Alejandro de la Fuente (2001) and Livio Sansone (2003) suggest that black political activity centered on race is ineffective, simplistic, and imported from outside the region (Sansone 2003, 165–99). However, this type of activity should be examined as merely one of various modes of black political participation. Afro-Latin Americans and Afro-Brazilians have used diverse strategies and tactics to fight racism and improve their living conditions. De la Fuente (2001) and Sansone (2003) have also noted that in twentieth-century Latin America, there was rarely explicit and legal racial segregation. These scholars have emphasized that the large, publicly acknowledged, mixed population (*mulato* and *mestiço*) in Latin America has limited the effectiveness of using academic models and perspectives developed to understand race in the United States. However, they have not fully recognized that the myth of racial democracy facilitated and continues to contribute to the racial oppression of Afro-descendants by implicitly supporting the ideal of whitening and denying the legitimacy of black political organization (Johnson 2007; Dzidzienyo 2005; 1995; Nascimento 2007).

Affirmative Action

Black political struggle laid the foundation for the current debate over affirmative action, especially in the area of education. Since abolition, Afro-Brazilian leaders and organizations have advocated high-quality education for blacks and all Brazilians. Education has been recognized as the key to black individual and group advancement (S. Santos 2007). The same black activists, politicians, and intellectuals who created black organizations, demanded inclusion in political parties and achieved pro-black initiatives, also supported affirmative action. In fact, Abdias do Nascimento, the founder of TEN and editor of *Quilombo*, was one of the key black leaders demanding affirmative action policies in the 1940s, 1950s, and 1960s (Martins et al. 2004, 791–92; Nascimento and Nascimento 2000, 1992).

Nascimento spent most of the military dictatorship (1964–1985) in exile in the United States. Upon his return, he became one of the leaders of the PDT. Living in Rio de Janeiro, he represented his party for one term (1983–1987) in the Chamber of Deputies. There Nascimento renewed his commitment to affirmative action for Afro-Brazilians which he preferred to call compensatory action. For example, his bill 1,332/1983 sought to require, among other measures, all government bureaucracies in the country to target 20 percent of their jobs for black men and 20 percent for black women. Bill 3,196/1984 aimed to require the country's diplomatic training school, the Instituto Rio Branco, to reserve 40 percent of its seats for black men and women. Nascimento defended these pieces of affirmative action legislation by referring to the country's history of formal and informal discrimination against blacks (Nascimento 1985, 35–39; 1984, 91–92; Martins et al. 2004, 793–94).

Serving in the Federal Senate for brief periods beginning in 1991 and 1997, Nascimento again presented his affirmative action proposals. Although this legislation did not gain congressional approval, Nascimento was one of the earliest and most visible politicians to raise the question of affirmative action in Brazil. He not only presented legislative proposals, he defended them vigorously within the Congress and throughout the country. He traveled widely, lectured frequently, and wrote regularly, always encouraging blacks to study and work hard while articulating the government's responsibility to develop public policies to help improve the Afro-Brazilian socioeconomic situation (Nascimento and Nascimento 2001, 2000, 1992).

Nascimento was not the only black leader to support affirmation action. In the 1980s and 1990s, black elected officials such as Benedita da Silva, Paulo Paim, and Luiz Alberto worked in the Chamber of Deputies and the federal Senate to pass affirmative action laws. These black leaders also worked hard throughout the country to build public support for affirmative action (Martins et al. 2004, 791–99; Johnson 1998, 103–9; Johnson 2006). Friar David Raimundo Santos has emerged as one of the most important black grassroots activists defending affirmative action and racial quotas as necessary to break the structure of white privilege in Brazil. Friar David's organization, Educafro, has created community courses preparing poor and black students for the *vestibular*, the university entrance exam. Since 1993, Friar David has worked with the elite Catholic University in Rio de Janeiro (PUC-Rio) to secure scholarships and other support (transportation, housing, mentoring, and living expenses) for his students. Because of Friar David and Educafro, more than five hundred poor and Afro-Brazilian students have gained access to a prestigious university who probably would not have otherwise (F. Santos 2004; Sampaio 2004).

Friar David has noted that Brazil has had over the years various affirmative action programs to assist women, the disabled, and workers. These programs were successful in many ways and rarely caused a public outcry. He argues that affirmative action policies targeting Afro-Brazilians are polemical in part because they promote ethnic diversity in higher education and have the potential to threaten white middle- and upper-class privilege (F. Santos 2004). Friar David's experience highlights that key affirmative action initiatives in Brazil often involve black groups and private institutions in leadership roles. In São Paulo, Geledés–The Black Woman's Institute, began partnering with Fundação BankBoston, Colgate-Palmolive, Instituto Xerox, and the Palmares Cultural Foundation to create new opportunities for Afro-Brazilian youth, especially to prepare them for postsecondary education and employment. Since 1999, Geledés and its partners developed three projects: *Geração XXI*, *Proxima Parada: Universidade*, and *Afro-ascendentes*, and they have committed themselves to working closely with students, their families, schools, and communities to improve student skill levels, attitudes, and environments (Silva 2003a; Benedito 2005, 238–78).

Building on decades of advocacy by black groups, affirmative action became a national issue in the 1990s. In November 1995, black leaders organized the Zumbi March against Racism, for Citizenship and Life, in Brasília. Thousands of Brazilians from all parts of the country converged in the nation's capital to demand government efforts to promote racial equality. President Fernando Henrique Cardoso expressed sympathy with the cause and directed his administration to study the problem (Htun 2004; Martins et al. 2004). Black government appointees Hélio Santos and Ivair dos Santos led the administration's Interministerial Working Group for the Black Population (GTI). Through research, lobbying, and dialoguing with the public, this agency built support within the government and civil society for an intensive program of affirmative action (Johnson 2006).

The Cardoso administration's affirmative action efforts and black organizing for racial equality merged in preparation for the World Conference against Racism in Durban, South Africa, in September 2001. There were numerous public forums addressing the issue of racism and racial inequality that resulted in widespread media attention, Brazil's successful participation in the world conference, and pressure to implement a comprehensive affirmative action plan in Brazil. In 2001, the Rio de Janeiro state legislature approved an affirmative action policy requiring the two state universities to reserve 40 percent of their incoming class for blacks and browns (Martins et al. 2004; Htun 2004).

Since 2001, there has been an explosion of affirmative action policies in Brazil. Governments, public and private universities, businesses, and private institutions have debated and implemented measures in favor of racial equality. Rosana Heringer and other scholars have shown that these measures are occurring in all parts of the country and provoking lawsuits and heated debates (Heringer 2004, 2002). As Friar David has noted, the most controversial are the racial quotas for Afro-Brazilians. So far, the affirmative action advocates have defeated all major legal challenges. Over ninety years old, the venerable Abdias do Nascimento has witnessed the initial implementation of policies he first raised in the 1940s and later proposed in the 1980s and 1990s. In 2003, one of Nascimento's dreams came true when the federal government passed law 10,639 requiring the teaching of African and Afro-Brazilian history and culture in elementary and secondary schools (Martins et al. 2004, 805).

Within the universe of Brazilian affirmative action programs, university quotas for blacks and other groups have been widespread. In the last five years, more than thirty public universities have reserved a specific percentage or number of places in their entering undergraduate class for underrepresented groups. The exact percentage or number varies widely according to political negotiations, school decisions, and state demographics. When the reserved spots are not filled, other applicants gain those positions. Table 10.2 delineates the public universities that have implemented quota policies in admissions procedures.

Some of the most prestigious universities in Brazil, such as Universidade de São Paulo, the Universidade Federal de Rio de Janeiro, and the Universidade Federal de Minas Gerais, have rejected racial quotas as an affirmative action option. Nevertheless, the debate about affirmative action, racial quotas, racial inequality, and related issues has continued on university campuses, in the national Congress, and in the public.

To strengthen racial inclusion efforts, members of Congress have introduced affirmative action legislation to guarantee Afro-Brazilians places in federal universities and public employment. Two recent and controversial examples of affirmation action policies are pieces of legislation that had been debated and revised in the Congress over the last few years. The Lei de Cotas (Quotas Law) (PL 73/1999) proposes racial quotas for black and indigenous people in federal universities and civil-service positions, and gives benefits to private companies that practice affirmative action.

The second piece of legislation, the Estatuto da Igualdade Racial (Racial Equality Statute) (PL 3,198/2000) was introduced by former deputy and current senator Paulo Paim. This legislation requires the government to take specific steps to promote racial equality, diminish racial discrimination, and increase the education, employment, health care, and cultural opportunities of Afro-Brazilians. It also forces the government to collect comprehensive racial and color information on the Brazilian people so that it can have better and more accurate data and therefore implement new public policies more effectively. Paim's legislation strongly supports affirmative action, including quotas, and creates a National Council in Defense of Racial Equality and a Fund for the Promotion of Racial Equality that would be government funded and also able to receive funds from lotteries, private institutions, foreign governments, and fines paid by those guilty of violating the country's laws against racial discrimination. Moreover, the annual reports of cabinet ministers would be required to

Table 10.2. Public Universities with Quotas for Entering Students, 2002–2007
Quotas for black students
Universidade do Estado da Bahia (UNEB)
Universidade do Estado da Bahia (UNEB)
Universidade do Estado do Mato Grosso (UNEMAT)
Universidade Federal de Alagoas (UFAL)
Universidade Federal do Pará (UFPA)
Quotas for black and indigenous students
Universidade Estadual de Mato Grosso do Sul (UEMS)
Universidade de Brasília (UnB)
Universidade Federal de São Paulo (UNIFESP)
Quotas for indigenous students
Universidade Federal do Tocantins (UFT)
Quotas for indigenous and public school students
Universidade do Estado do Amazonas (UEA)
Quotas for public school students
Escola Superior de Ciências da Saúde do Distrito Federal (ESCS/DF)
Universidade do Estado de Pernambuco (UPE)
Universidade Estadual do Rio Grande do Sul (UERGS)
Universidade Estadual da Paraíba (UEPB)
Universidade Federal do Piauí (UFPI)
Universidade Federal Rural da Amazônia (UFRA)
Quotas for black and public school students
Universidade Estadual de Londrina (UEL)
Universidade Estadual de Ponta Grossa (UEPG)
Universidade Federal do ABC (UFABC)
Universidade Federal do Maranhão (UFMA)
Universidade Federal de São Carlos (UFSCar)
Quotas for black, indigenous, and public school students
Universidade Estadual de Feira de Santana (UEFS)
Universidade Estadual de Santa Cruz (UESC)
Universidade Federal da Bahia (UFBA)
Universidade Federal de Juiz de Fora (UFJF)
Universidade Federal do Recôncavo da Bahia (UFRB)
Universidade Federal do Espírito Santo (UFES)
Quotas for black, indigenous, public school, and disabled students
Universidade do Estado do Rio de Janeiro (UERJ)
Universidade do Estado de Minas Gerais (UEMG)
Universidade Estadual de Montes Claros (UNIMONTES)
Universidade Estadual do Norte Fluminense (UENF)
Centro Universitário Estadual da Zona Oeste (UEZO)
Universidade Estadual de Goiás (UEG)
Universidade Federal do Paraná (UFPR)

Sources: Santos 2007, 30–32; Ferreira and Andrade 2006; Carvalho 2006, 44–46.

have updates on their ministry's affirmative action policies, programs, and measures (Paim 2003).

In defending his bill, Paim describes Brazil as a country devastated by five hundred years of racial prejudice and discrimination against Afro-Brazilians. He argues that the racial hierarchy of the country includes a small dominant white elite and a mass of marginalized Brazilians, mostly blacks. "We propose a system of quotas to precisely minimize the negative effects of prejudice on the discriminated populations. We know that our universities and labor markets are occupied by an overwhelming majority of whites" (Paim 2003, 27). Paim goes on to note that there are quotas for women as candidates of the political parties. The Racial Equality Statute and Quotas Law became the subject of heated debate during the 2006 legislative and presidential elections in Brazil. Many observers thought that they would be approved. However, both were withdrawn for more debate when critics successfully argued that the bills were too controversial and unprecedented to be approved without additional debate and revision.

The controversy over these two bills produced a remarkable political development. Some of the country's most distinguished scholars of race, prominent activists and entertainment personalities supported open letters to members of Congress, one opposing and the other defending the legislation. These letters represented not only specific analyses of legislation, but also general statements of principle. They expressed an important division within the intellectual and political elite.[5] The first letter, "Todos têm direitos iguais na República Democrática," appeared on May 30, 2006, and criticized the two bills as having three fundamental problems. First, the bills would violate the principle of political and juridical equality. Second, the people's rights would be based on color or race. Third, the legislation would not eliminate racism and could worsen race relations. This letter, signed mostly by leading white professors at elite public and private universities, was a theoretical response to the proposed affirmative action legislation. The letter emphasized that universalist principles and rights would be violated and the intended goals would not be achieved. What was their solution? High-quality public services in education, health care, welfare, and job creation open and available to all Brazilians.

The second letter, "Manifesto em favor da Lei de Cotas e do Estatuto da Igualdade Racial," appeared on July 3, 2006, and utilized a more historical and pragmatic approach in analyzing the legislation. It also criticized the first letter. The manifesto argued that the historical roots of contemporary racial inequality and the extreme exclusion of blacks and indigenous groups as documented by the government's own statistics required public policies, including quotas, capable of interrupting the intergenerational reproduction of racial inequality and exclusion. The letter gave examples of popular demands for racial quotas and noted that affirmative action policies, including quotas, had already been implemented in more than thirty institutions of higher learning in the last four years. Finally, the second letter, signed by many more black academics and scholars, described the first letter as similar to past attempts to propose abstract, do-nothing solutions (e.g., the constitution of 1891) when specific positive solutions were called for.

The two open letters were illustrative of the new public discussion of issues related to race and politics. Both letters demonstrated an impressive intensity of opinion regarding the impact that the two bills could have on the future of the country. It is odd, therefore, that the first letter opposing affirmative action, racial quotas, and racial classification did not elaborate on the fact that these policies were already being implemented around the country. The national government has been classifying the population by color or race for decades (Nobles 2000). Presumably, the supporters of the first letter believed that the new bills would represent an "expansion" and "escalation" of the negative role race would play in the lives of Brazilians. The signatories of the second letter stated that race and racism had already played a monumentally exclusionary role against Afro-Brazilians and indigenous peoples and that now was the time for a formal policy reversal. The second letter implied that the government could successfully use race and affirmative action to create opportunities for those historically excluded and thereby promote a more egalitarian society.

Afro-Brazilians have struggled for centuries against white racial oppression in Brazil. That struggle did not end with the formal abolition of slavery. As is now clear, blacks lived for decades after 1888 in slavelike conditions throughout the country. As they organized to protest displacement, racism, and lack of opportunities, blacks were often called racists themselves, imitative of blacks in the United States, and troublemakers. Nonetheless, they persisted in their efforts because they knew that they didn't live in a racial democracy. However, as a result of the myth of racial democracy, the brutal reality of widespread prejudice and discrimination against Afro-Brazilians was often ignored by scholars.

Why, after decades of demands by Nascimento and other black activists, did affirmative action, especially racial quotas for blacks, become government and university policy in so many areas between 2001 and 2007? An unprecedented biracial coalition in favor of affirmative action emerged throughout the country.

Black activists and politicians played the leading role in placing the topic of affirmative action on the country's political agenda. Black university students protested for affirmative action within their universities and throughout the country. Black lawyers and judges defended the constitutionality and argued for the urgency of racial quotas and pro–racial equality measures to their colleagues. In sum, black advocates for affirmative action reached out to their white friends, comrades, and associates in political parties, legislative bodies, labor unions, religious congregations, universities, corporations, and other groups, and requested their support.

Major white political figures such as Brizola, Montoro, Sarney, Cardoso, and Lula responded positively to efforts by blacks to address problems of racial discrimination and racial inequality. Similarly, black-white alliances emerged within universities and other spaces to do something about racism. The transition to civilian democracy, years of exile and military repression, persistent black activism, and electoral victories by the opposition created a political and intellectual environment more open to black demands.[6] Opponents of affirmative action were outmaneuvered in this process. However, they have now begun to organize and mobilize their opposition forces more energetically to try to reverse the affirmative action programs that have already spread throughout the country.

Professors Peter Fry and Yvonne Maggie of the Universidade Federal do Rio de Janeiro are two of the leading academic critics of racial quotas. They have criticized quotas publicly and repeatedly as being counterproductive. These scholars have organized other intellectuals and lobbied politicians and elected officials against the Quotas Law and Racial Equality Statute (Fry et al. 2007; Steil 2006). According to Santos, many white experts on Brazilian race relations such as Fry and Maggie are against quotas because they tacitly support the educational and racial status quo. They fear the movement for affirmative action and racial quotas as a threat to their positions of authority (2007).

Alternatively, Professor José Jorge de Carvalho, a leading white scholar and supporter of affirmative action at the Universidade de Brasília, has argued that the country needs an emergency regime of racial quotas or preferences for black and indigenous people as undergraduates, graduate students, professors, and researchers at the fifty-three federal universities. He argues that the population of graduate students, faculty, and researchers is whiter than undergraduates and even more resistant to change. Carvalho believes that admitting graduate students, hiring new professors, and contracting researchers must be subject to affirmative action to truly diversify the Brazilian academy and defeat Brazilian academic racism. His reasoning is that if this change occurs at the most prestigious and well-funded class of Brazilian universities—that is, the federal universities—it will have a positive effect on the rest of Brazilian higher education (Carvalho 2006).

Afro-Brazilian senator Paulo Paim (1997) also asserts that undergraduate affirmative action is not enough. He has raised the question of reparations for descendants of slaves. Senator Paim's call indicts slavery as a crime against humanity and suggests that Afro-Brazilian politicians are going to continue to demand that their country confront the contemporary consequences of centuries of white domination. Black activists have consistently engaged in self-help efforts and demanded social democratic government policies. Because these efforts and demands have been sabotaged and rejected for so long, many black leaders are skeptical of "universalist" public policies that do not address the specificity of their community's situation.

Throughout the twentieth century, Afro-Brazilians have struggled to place the topics of racial inequality and racial discrimination on the country's political agenda. Affirmative action has been a longstanding demand of the black movement. Unacceptable black living conditions and historical white resistance to recognizing Brazilian racism have led many black leaders to support affirmative action in general and racial quotas in particular. The initial implementation of affirmative action policies represents a landmark victory for the black movement and those Brazilians supportive of social justice and a more egalitarian democracy. The controversy over racial quotas for blacks will likely inspire social scientists to probe more deeply into white supremacy, race and politics, and the role of Afro-Brazilians in the Brazilian political experience.

PART IV

Views of Democracy from Below

11

Core Values, Education, and Democracy: An Empirical Tour of DaMatta's Brazil

Alberto Carlos Almeida

IN CHAPTER 6, Barry Ames, Andy Baker, and Lucio Rennó analyzed the extent to which Brazilian voters are democratic. However, for 364 days out of the year, Brazilians are not voters. Therefore, in order to understand the broader socio-cultural conditions for democratic sustainability in Brazil, we also need to explore whether democratic values exist outside the political sphere as traditionally defined. To what extent do Brazilians exhibit values that are compatible with democratic practice at the micro level: that is, in their interpersonal relationships and day-to-day lives? How do they view the notions of equality, universalism, and the rule of law? Is there an emerging cultural basis for democracy in Brazil, and if so, what factors affect the expansion or erosion of this basis?

This chapter examines these questions by revisiting the depiction of Brazilian society advanced by Roberto DaMatta, Brazil's most influential anthropologist. DaMatta has long argued that Brazilian society is characterized by persistent hierarchy and particularism, which undermines the concepts of equality and the rule of law. Although DaMatta does not engage in macropolitical analysis himself, the implications of his argument are clear: the illiberal nature of Brazilian social interactions should be unfavorable to political democracy. I argue that DaMatta is largely correct, but I make an important qualification: the accuracy of his observations about values depends largely on the educational level of the Brazilians in question. As educational levels continue to rise in Brazil, archaic values are being gradually supplanted by modern ones, and this should be favorable to political democracy in the future. But, following DaMatta, there indeed is ample reason to be concerned about the present.

I will test some of DaMatta's central concepts using data from the Brazilian Social Survey (PESB), which allows me to analyze the role of educational attainment in shaping values.[1] I examine the impact of education on attitudes towards hierarchy, patrimonialism, sexuality, fatalism, and crime, and finally the challenge of persistent racism in Brazil.

Roberto DaMatta: The Brazilian Tocqueville

Roberto DaMatta is to Brazil what Alexis de Tocqueville is to the United States, except with the opposite sign. In the 1830s, Tocqueville, using an analytical model that was as simple as it was brilliant, illustrated the great differences that existed between U.S. society and that of his native France. For Tocqueville (1966 [1835]), his beloved France was characterized by social relations of an aristocratic nature. His compatriots were unequal, unalike. On the one hand, there was a certain style of behavior, of dress, of habits belonging to those at the top of the French social pyramid, and on the other hand, there was the behavior of those on the bottom. Frenchmen were differentiated by their appearance, by their speech patterns, and by various other elements of social mores. This was not the case in the America he observed.

A memorable part of Tocqueville's narrative is the passage in which he discusses forms of interpersonal address in the United States and England.[2] In Jacksonian America, just as today in the twenty-first century, everyone addressed one another as "you." Given that Americans saw each other largely as equals, there was no reason for the selective usage of different forms of address. This was not the case, Tocqueville observed, in countries characterized by aristocracy. He noted that in class-conscious societies, the informal second person (*tu*) was used in some situations and the formal "you" (*vous*, *Usted*) in others, depending on the interlocutor. Inequality in the United States was transitory and transactional, defined by contracts, like the ones between employers and workers. In Europe, inequality among men went far beyond contractual linkages, extending into all dimensions of social relations.

In his well-known analyses of Brazilian society, Roberto DaMatta finds inspiration in Tocqueville. In reality, DaMatta is the Brazilian Tocqueville, but with one critical difference. Tocqueville showed that the United States was a democratic society, by which he meant an equal society. DaMatta shows that Brazil is the opposite: a hierarchical society. It is no accident that the analytical "hook" used by DaMatta—equality versus hierarchy—is, in fact, founded on frequent empirical comparisons between Brazil and the United States.

In DaMatta's enormous body of work, there are two key monographs: *Carnaval, malandros e heróis* (1978, translated into English in 1991) and *A casa e a rua* (1984). In each book, the anthropologist lays out a very clear interpretation of social relationships in Brazil. He depicts a hierarchical nation in which social origin and social position are critical to determining what an individual can or cannot do, and to knowing whether a person is above the law or must obey it. In this way the heritage of slavery is clearly manifested in Brazil: people have a hard time dealing with equality.

DaMatta immortalized the phrase "do you know who you are talking to?" as emblematic of the hierarchical character of Brazilian society. According to DaMatta, the uttering of this expression is almost inevitable "in situations of intolerable equality" (yes, you read that correctly). It is through asking this question that one can park in an illegal space, cut in line in government offices, obtain some kind of special benefit from the law, or make oneself a special exception to a universalistic principle. Even I have made recourse to this device recently, in Rio de Janeiro in 2003, to avoid a regulation. I knew an important politician who had his office next to a parking lot. When the lot attendant tried to stop me from parking in a certain space, I found myself asking the question: "Do you know who you are talking to? I am a good friend of Joe Politician."

In Brazil, a hierarchical mentality predominates. In a more egalitarian society, according to DaMatta, a similar situation would be resolved with the opposite question: "Who do you think you are?"[3] As in: who do you think you are, to make you believe that you can get away with parking in this space? No one is more special than anyone else: the law is impersonal, applying equally to everyone. One of the most important consequences of the hierarchical mentality is that undermines respect for rules. Laws are ignored for various reasons. This could be because the person in question is important—a judge, a politician, an official—

or because he is close to someone important. It could also be because it is always possible, through a "good conversation," simply to *persuade* others that you deserve to be treated as an exception. Persuasion against equality: this is the *jeitinho brasileiro,* the Brazilian way of doing things.

In general, the technique of the *jeitinho*—the subject of an exhaustive doctoral dissertation by Lívia Barbosa (1992), directed by DaMatta—requires the person to *chorar miséria*. The literal translation of this is to "cry misery," but figuratively it involves resorting to a "sob story." In other words, to win an exception to a rule, one has to make a case, presenting all the facts of one's life that underscore just how difficult the present moment is. For example, in the photocopy shops that one finds in Brazilian public universities (in which it is accepted practice to make copies of entire books), those students who are able to implore (theatrically) that they are having a hard time or having a bad day can usually go right to the front of the line.

It is very hard to find a Brazilian who has not been on one or the other end of the *jeitinho,* either using it on his or her behalf or using it provide a benefit to someone else. Once again, the present author is no exception. In Rio recently, I was stopped by two motorcycle police officers while I was driving and talking on my cell phone at the same time (this is illegal in Brazil). I leaned forward on the steering wheel, lowered my head rather gravely, and intoned the following: "Given all of the problems I am facing right now, this fine is the least of them all. I know that I was wrong and now I have to pay. You can go ahead and fine me." The strategy worked. I drove away without a fine, thanks to the *jeitinho.*

It might be the *jeitinho brasileiro,* it might be "do you know who you are talking to?" but the end result is always the undermining of universalistic principles. The main casualty of the *jeitinho* is rule-compliant behavior. It is thus unsurprising that DaMatta compares Brazil to the United States. Is it possible to have a truly *liberal* society—in the classical sense of the term—where people conceive of one another as unequal? The law, the judicial system, and imported Anglo-Saxon ethics supposedly enshrine the rule of law, but the cultural socialization of Brazilians enshrines inequality and a whole slew of techniques to get around formal rules. The core values of Brazilians are incompatible with those that they profess in public. At the end of the day, there are very few of us who will admit to having used the *jeitinho* or the phrase "do you know who you are talking to?" According to DaMatta, this contradiction between actual values and professed values constitutes the great Brazilian "dilemma."

The Political Sociology of Brazilian Democracy

What are the implications of all this for democracy? Here I am not referring to democracy in the Tocquevillean sense, meaning conditions of equality, but rather the *political* democracy that has now completed twenty-three years of existence in Brazil. There is no doubt—as the title of the present volume suggests—that Brazil is a democratic country and that political competition is authentic. The question here is: does Brazilian democracy suffer in *quality* because of hierarchical social relationships?

The answer is undoubtedly "yes," an answer that anticipates one of the most important findings of the research I present below. But I will raise an important (and optimistic) caveat: Brazilian democracy will improve in quality as the overall level of education rises. This is entirely consistent with what decades of research—much of it inspired by Lipset (1959) and Dahl (1971)—have shown: that democracy is positively correlated with indicators of socioeconomic development. Not surprisingly, a more educated population results in more economic development and more political pluralism.[4] The process of development differentiates and multiplies the sources of power and the number of interest groups. It is more difficult to maintain an authoritarian regime in highly pluralized societies. Education has a strong impact on society, and this influences enormously the conduct of politics.

The rise in educational attainment is correlated with what Karl Mannheim called the "fundamental democratization of society" (1940). The perverse face of urbanization, which lures people out of their rural homelands, results in the gradual weakening of family and community ties. Religion becomes weaker, and higher authorities loosen their hold. On the other hand, people are exposed to new sources of information and become more skeptical.

Various studies, both classic and recent, reinforce the hypothesis that links educational levels with democracy. Robert Putnam (1993), in his seminal study of Italy, demonstrated essentially that there is "more democracy" in the north than in the south of that country. The regional governments of northern Italy are more responsive to the demands of society than those of the south. This has to do with civic culture and social capital, according to Putnam. But it is also no accident that the north has a higher aggregate level of education than the south. In their exhaustive analysis of the World Values Surveys, Inglehart and Welzel (2005) demonstrate that rising levels of wealth and education lead citizens to reject traditional forms of authority and to seek new forms of self-expression. People with higher levels of education tend to withdraw from authoritarian social institutions and to reject vertical social relationships in favor of more-horizontal arrangements.

All of these studies are to some degree indebted to Alexis de Tocqueville. Both Roberto DaMatta and Robert Putnam draw on Tocquevillean concepts to develop their own notions of the civic community. Inglehart and Welzel choose to emphasize changing worldviews, which—as Tocqueville might well have predicted—move in the direction from more hierarchical to more egalitarian. All of these authors are engaged in *political sociology:* they demonstrate that society, and its ways of dealing with interpersonal relationships, shape the political sphere.

Democracy, Core Values, and the Brazilian Context

Political institutions matter, and there is a massive literature demonstrating that this is true (e.g., Santos and Vilarouca, this volume). However, society is no less important. Within the sphere of society, the perceptions, beliefs, and attitudes of women and men—or to use a supposedly outdated term, their ideologies—help us to understand how democracy works in practice.

Thus, if it is true that from the purely *institutional* point of view, Brazilian democracy is now consolidated, it is also true that one can observe the beginnings of a *social* basis for the regime. There *is* a segment of the population with sufficiently high levels of educational attainment to defend so-called modern positions associated with political democracy. But there is also a large proportion of the population that continues to share a so-called archaic worldview. Given that educational levels are rising inexorably over time, one should expect that in the future the modern sector will become larger than the archaic sector. This is an irreversible process. As for my use of the controversial terms *modern* and *archaic*, I beg the reader's indulgence. They are used here only as descriptive shorthand for two ideal types, two contrasting ways of seeing the world. The results of the large-scale Brazilian Social Survey (Pesquisa Social Brasileira, or PESB) conducted in 2002 helps us to delineate these ideal types.[5]

The PESB zeroes in on what the literature calls core values. These values constitute the foundation on which other social beliefs are constructed. In every society, children tend to be socialized to the core values of that particular society.

Given the centrality of the socialization process, we should expect bedrock values to change only very slowly. This is, in fact, what happens in real life: core values change mainly via intergenerational population replacement: that is, as younger generations take the place of older ones. It will become evident below, for example, that the fundamental values of sexuality are closely correlated with age. Older individuals are far more conservative than young people when it comes to sex. It is well known in Brazil, for example, that virginity among young women was prized until approximately the 1970s. Today the opposite is often true: a teenage girl who remains a virgin may be stigmatized by her peers. A core value of Brazilian society changed relatively quickly, in the space of a generation. But in areas apart from sexual behavior, change is far slower, mainly because the engine of change is educational attainment—and this has been rising only at a modest pace.

The PESB measured the core values of Brazilians on a diverse number of topics, but it went beyond this by including a number of Brazil-specific constructs. The organizers of the PESB had no objection to the many global efforts to translate and apply, in a large number of countries, survey questionnaires first designed in societies such as the United States and Great Britain. But the PESB took the opposite tack. The researchers designed a survey instrument based largely on the insights of Roberto DaMatta and his associates. The result, not surprisingly, was a battery of questions flavored by the Brazilian sociocultural experience. How could you possibly translate the word *jeitinho* into English, for example? Would it be possible to ask German apartment dwellers to reflect upon their domestic servants using the *elevador de serviço* rather than the *elevador social*? Do such concepts really travel very well? Probably not. There are many reasons why the PESB questionnaire could not be exported to other countries, but that is the price to be paid for incorporating concepts and constructs based largely on the Brazilian experience. I repeat: this was the first time a truly indigenous, context-sensitive social survey was conducted in Brazil, and it would not have been possible without the contributions of Roberto DaMatta.

Core values, Roberto DaMatta, Alexis de Tocqueville, *jeitinho*, hierarchical society, Brazil according to Brazilians—I am pulling all of this together to make a very straightforward argument. Brazil is undergoing change, and this change depends largely on the evolution of the educational sphere. Educational expansion implies sociological, ideological, and macropolitical change. The plane has taken off, as it were, and is now at a cruising speed; this speed may increase, but the plane is not going to crash. Brazil is continuing on a trajectory that is increasing its aggregate level of formal education; and as I demonstrate below, Brazil is moving more and more—albeit very slowly—in the direction of a modern worldview. Score one point for democracy.

But the great challenge for Brazil today is that although the country is moving slowly but perceptibly towards a democratic outlook, the vast majority of less-educated citizens do not yet subscribe to the egalitarian, inclusive, and self-expressive values identified by Inglehart and Welzel (2005). The future is promising, yes, but the *present* still poses major challenges.

Education: The Wall Dividing Brazilians

Despite the presence of numerous social and economic cleavages, it is still possible to divide Brazilians into two groups: those with a diploma and those without. The PESB demonstrates beyond a shadow of a doubt that there are striking differences in mentality and behavior that separate Brazilian from Brazilian, based largely on whether the respondents have a university degree or less than a high school education. Their points of view on culture, justice, sex, and the role of the state, to name just a few, range from one extreme to another.[6] Table 11.1 reveals this massive distance. On one side there are those citizens who have completed a university education, and on the other side are those who have not finished high school. Clearly, they differ on everything.

All of this is merely probabilistic, of course. Take sexuality, for example. If we randomly select a Brazilian who has a college education, no matter who she or he is, it is very likely that the person will approve of diverse sexual practices such as oral sex, anal sex, sex between partners of the same gender, and other similar behaviors. On the other hand, it is also highly likely that if we randomly select a Brazilian who has not completed college, or who has an even lower level of education, he or she will oppose sexual practices that go anywhere beyond vaginal sex between a man and a woman.

Education is what shapes the worldviews of Brazilians. One group of citizens has an essentially modern outlook. These Brazilians are against the *jeitinho brasileiro*. They oppose extralegal punishments such as lynchings or the idea that convicted rapists should themselves be raped in prison. They possess higher levels of interpersonal trust. They reject the idea that one's destiny is entirely in the hands of God. These Brazilians are "modern" because they once sat in the halls of higher education and obtained a diploma.

Table 11.1. Contrasting Worldviews of Two Composite Citizens	
Completed university	*Did not finish secondary school*
College diploma, male, young, lives in a state capital in the Southeast or South	**No formal education, female, elderly, resident of the Northeast and of a town that is not a state capital**
Against *jeitinho brasileiro*	Supports *jeitinho brasileiro*
Against "do you know who you're talking to?"	Supports "do you know who you're talking to?"
Against treating public resources as something private, belonging to a person	Supports treating public resources as something private, belonging to a person
Nonfatalistic, does not believe in or care much about fate	Fatalistic, accords great importance to fate or destiny
Higher interpersonal trust	Lower interpersonal trust
Supports people collaborating with the government to care for public spaces	Against people collaborating with the government to care for public spaces
Against *lex talionis*, an eye for an eye, a tooth for a tooth	Supports *lex talionis*, an eye for an eye, a tooth for a tooth
Supports diverse sexual practices	Against diverse sexual practices
Against state intervention in the economy	Supports state intervention in the economy
Against censorship	Supports censorship

Source: Derived by author from responses to Pesquisa Social Brasileira (PESB) 2002.

But another, much larger group of citizens is characterized by an archaic worldview. These Brazilians are particularistic and familial. They approve of lynching and of the prison rape of sex offenders. They tend not to trust other Brazilians, and they believe that fate lies in the hands of God. These Brazilians are premodern, or "archaic," largely because they never had the chance to obtain a higher education.

What the PESB suggests is that *having or lacking a university education is the primary determinant of the social chasm dividing Brazilians*. Again, this is a probabilistic statement, but the PESB also tells us how we could make the social chasm separating two randomly selected Brazilians even larger. For this to happen, the person who has a higher education should be male, young, and residing in a state capital or in one of the states of the South and Southeast. The person without college education should also have failed to complete primary school,

Table 11.2. Education and Views on Sexuality

Question: I am going to read you several situations related to sex, and I would like you to tell me whether you are totally in favor, somewhat in favor, somewhat against, or totally against.

		Educational level					
Practice	*Opinion*	*Illiterate*	*Up to 4th grade*	*5th–8th grade*	*High school*	*Univ. or higher*	*All*
Use of pornographic magazines for sexual arousal	Against	81	76	72	57	47	
	Neither for nor against	2	2	2	4	3	
	Favor	17	22	26	39	49	33
Male masturbation	Against	82	76	61	42	26	
	Neither for nor against	2	3	3	4	4	
	Favor	17	22	36	53	71	54
Anal sex between a man and a woman	Against	92	87	81	63	52	
	Neither for nor against	1	2	4	4	5	
	Favor	7	11	16	32	43	36
Man performing oral sex on his female partner	Against	92	81	70	44	28	
	Neither for nor against	1	2	3	4	4	
	Favor	8	16	27	52	67	60
Male homosexuality	Against	97	94	92	86	75	
	Neither for nor against	1	2	2	3	5	
	Favor	2	4	6	11	20	18
Female masturbation	Against	85	81	62	43	23	
	Neither for nor against	2	3	3	5	3	
	Favor	13	16	35	51	74	60
Woman performing oral sex on her male partner	Against	86	83	69	42	26	
	Neither for nor against	2	3	3	4	4	
	Favor	12	14	27	54	70	58
Female homosexuality	Against	94	93	90	84	74	
	Neither for nor against	2	2	3	3	5	
	Favor	3	5	7	13	21	17
All types of consensual sexual relationships	Against	61	49	35	23	15	
	Neither for nor against	3	3	3	3	2	
	Favor	36	48	62	74	82	46

Source: Pesquisa Social Brasileira (PESB) 2002. N = 2,364.

Table 11.3. Education and Support for the *jeitinho brasileiro*

Question: In your opinion, do you think that using the *jeitinho* is something that is always right, usually right, usually wrong, or always wrong?

Opinion	*Illiterate*	*Up to 4th grade*	*5th–8th Grade*	*High school*	*Univ. or higher*
Right (%)	57	51	58	48	33
Wrong (%)	43	49	42	52	67

Source: Pesquisa Social Brasileira (PESB) 2002. N = 2,366.

and she should be a woman, older in age, resident in the Northeast, in a town that is not a state capital (table 11.1).

Many Brazilians with college degrees are horrified when accusations of political corruption—many of them known to be true—are "forgotten" by citizens who end up voting once again for indicted politicians. This is not just because of a lack of alternatives. The same Brazilians who support the rule-bending behavior known as the *jeitinho brasileiro* are more tolerant of political corruption than their compatriots who vehemently deplore the *jeitinho*. There are plenty of citizens who are not "forgetting" about corruption accusations: the accusations are simply unimportant to them.[7] These Brazilians tend to have low levels of formal education.

Again, the main difference between the archaic and modern groups is a college diploma. Many people with low education levels, who may or may not be religious, are scandalized when they see all the media coverage of the massive Parada Gay (gay pride march) in São Paulo. For them, such a public "disgrace" is incomprehensible: the situation calls for extreme measures. The world of porn films and sex shops tends to be very distant from Brazilians with low educational levels. This is not because they lack purchasing power, but because these types of behaviors and practices do not comport with the value systems of less educated citizens.

Brazilians with college diplomas are scandalized (or were scandalized) by the behavior of the formal federal deputy and president of the Chamber of Deputies in 2005, Severino Cavalcanti (Partido Progressista–Pernambuco).[8] Severino openly defended the idea that members of Congress and other public officials should hire their relatives to work in their offices. Severino did not have a college diploma. The public vilification of Severino by university-trained journalists and columnists was directed primarily at an audience that (like the journal-

Table 11.4. Education and Views on Hierarchical Values

Question: I am going to read you several situations, and then I would like you to tell me what the person should do.

		Educational level				
Situation	*The employee should...*	*Illiterate*	*Up to 4th grade*	*5th–8th Grade*	*High school*	*Univ. or higher*
Employer tells maid she can watch TV in the living room with her	Sit on couch with employer and watch TV	47	49	55	68	75
	Watch TV in living room but bring own chair OR watch it in her own room	53	51	45	32	25
Residents of apartment building say employees may use the "social elevator"	Use social elevator	24	33	38	50	72
	Use service elevator	76	67	62	50	28
Boss tells employee to address him as *você* (informal "you")	Use *você*	32	30	35	44	59
	Use *senhor* (formal "you")	68	70	65	56	41

Source: Pesquisa Social Brasileira (PESB) 2002. N = 2,360.

ists in question) had the benefit of a higher education. Severino's constituents, mostly less-educated Brazilians living in small towns in the interior of the Northeast, generally do not condemn the behavior of their congressman. In a literal sense, Severino truly *represents* this constituency. Once again, the main difference between Severino Cavalcanti and his constituents, on the one hand, and journalists and their readers, on the other, is a college diploma.

Those who work in financial markets in Brazil, many of whom have doctoral degrees, do not want to even hear the words *state* or *government*. According to liberal dogma, "small is beautiful." The less the state intervenes in the economy, the better. The PESB informs us that one does not have to work in the financial sector to think this way: one only needs to have access to higher education. When Brazilians experience university life, they tend to abandon a paternalistic worldview based on an overweening state in favor of one in which economic well-being is really an individual affair, and in which the state's main role is

Table 11.5. Education and Views on Patrimonialism

Question: I am going to read you several statements, and I would like you to tell me whether you agree strongly, agree somewhat, disagree somewhat, or strongly disagree.

		Educational level				
Situation	*Opinion*	*Illiterate*	*Up to 4th grade*	*5th–8th Grade*	*High school*	*Univ. or higher*
Everyone should take care only of what is theirs, and the government should care for what is public.	Disagree	20	15	20	31	47
	Agree	80	85	80	69	53
If someone is being bothered by his/her neighbor it is better not to complain about it.	Disagree	27	37	45	62	78
	Agree	73	63	55	38	22
If someone is elected to public office he/she should use the office as if it were his/her personal property, for his/her own benefit.	Disagree	60	69	83	95	97
	Agree	40	31	17	5	3
Given that the government doesn't take care of that which is public, no one should take care of public things.	Disagree	50	67	82	95	98
	Agree	50	33	18	5	2

Source: Pesquisa Social Brasileira (PESB) 2002. N = 2,362.

simply to guarantee the minimal conditions under which individuals can flourish. This is radically different from the worldview of less-educated Brazilians. The less educated tend to believe that their lives may improve as a function of government action—thus the necessity, in their view, of more state intervention in the economy.

The Two Brazils: Conflicting Values, Conflicted Society

Thanks to the empirical data and sound methodology of the PESB, the famous "two Brazils" of Jacques Lambert (1959) are portrayed here in a new way. These are two countries with very different mentalities. They are two separate nations: a veritable cultural apartheid, as it were. They are two nations engaged in a per-

Table 11.6. Education and Views on Fatalism

Question: I am going to read four statements, and I would like you to tell me which one you agree with most. People cannot change anything in their lives, their fate (*destino*) is decided by God. God decides fate, but people can change their fate a little bit. God decides fate, but people can change their fate a lot. There is no such thing as fate; people decide everything about their lives.

	Educational level				
Statement	*Illiterate*	*Up to 4th grade*	*5th–8th Grade*	*High school*	*Univ. or higher*
God determines fate.	51	47	36	23	9
God determines fate, but people can change it a bit.	24	29	32	32	17
God determines fate, but people can change it a lot.	18	15	18	30	47
There is no such thing as fate: people determine what happens in their lives.	7	9	13	16	27

Source: Pesquisa Social Brasileira (PESB) 2002. N = 2,355.

petual conflict, one in which the lower classes defends values that are (slowly) dying or fading away and in which the upper classes adhere to many of the same values that predominate in developed countries. There is no "right" or "wrong" side in this conflict. There is, however, a dominant side in gradual decline (that of the lower classes) and a less visible side that is strengthening as the aggregate level of education gradually rises in Brazil.

Generalizing broadly, to the extent that the vast majority of the Brazilian population has low levels of education, one can plausibly assert that Brazil is archaic, hierarchical, patrimonialistic, and fatalistic. One can claim that Brazil lacks a public spirit, that it endorses *lex talionis* ("an eye for an eye, a tooth for a tooth"), that it is against sexual freedom, that it demands more state intervention in the economy, and that it favors censorship.[9] However, supporters of such values have very little influence in the media outlets preferred by members of the upper classes. In contrast, defenders of traditional values are the main consumers of television programs like *Cidade Alerta.*[10] Brazil remains dominated by the archaic, but it is a divided nation, and the modern—although numerically a small minority—are increasingly likely to predominate in the future.

Table 11.7. Education, Vigilantism, and "An Eye for an Eye"

Question: I am going to read you several situations that take place in various parts of Brazil, and I would like you to tell me whether you think it is always right, usually right, usually wrong, or always wrong.

Situation	*Opinion*	*Educational level*				
		Illiterate	*Up to 4th grade*	*5th–8th Grade*	*High school*	*Univ. or higher*
A person convicted of rape is raped behind bars by other prisoners.	Right	29	40	45	41	26
	Wrong	71	60	55	59	74
The police kill muggers and thieves after arresting them.	Right	40	35	35	23	17
	Wrong	60	65	65	77	83
The police beat suspects so that they will confess to crimes.	Right	51	44	41	31	14
	Wrong	49	56	59	69	86
The people lynch suspects of very violent crimes.	Right	27	32	33	24	17
	Wrong	73	68	67	76	83

Source: Pesquisa Social Brasileira (PESB) 2002. N = 2,343.

Table 11.8. Education and Views on Censorship

Question: Please tell me whether you agree strongly, agree somewhat, disagree somewhat, or strongly disagree with the following statement: "A television program that criticizes the government should be prohibited."

Opinion	*Educational level*				
	Illiterate	*Up to 4th grade*	*5th–8th Grade*	*High school*	*Univ. or higher*
Strongly disagree	32	40	45	57	72
Somewhat disagree	11	13	23	22	19
Neither agree nor disagree	2	1	0	1	1
Somewhat agree	10	14	14	10	1
Strongly agree	46	31	19	9	7

Source: Pesquisa Social Brasileira (PESB) 2002. N = 2,357.

Table 11.9. Education and Views on State Control of Services

Question: I am going to cite several activities that in some countries are handled by the government and in other countries only by private firms (*empresas*). I would like you to tell me who you think should administer each one of these activities in Brazil.

	Educational level				
Service	*Illiterate*	*Up to 4th grade*	*5th–8th Grade*	*High school*	*Univ. or higher*
Education	74	74	72	67	57
Health care	76	78	72	67	63
Pensions and social security	81	81	72	68	60
Justice	80	82	77	78	89
Transportation	55	52	38	39	30
Roads and highways	71	78	71	63	51
Water supply	76	69	68	65	65
Sewer service	76	70	69	65	69
Garbage	78	73	66	57	57
Electricity	75	71	64	61	55
Landline telephone service	56	52	42	38	26
Cellular telephone service	54	41	28	21	15
Banks	77	67	54	40	23
Automobile manufacturing	36	33	21	16	7

Source: Pesquisa Social Brasileira (PESB) 2002. N = 2,360.

The result: it is impossible to privatize the Banco do Brasil or Petrobrás, because there is no critical mass of the population that would back such measures. At the same time, to the extent that the ranks of university-educated Brazilians are growing in proportional terms, it will be increasingly difficult to maintain these firms under state control. The transition from a state-owned Banco do Brasil to a private Banco do Brasil will be conflictual. This conflict is already in play: it is a conflict about values. Under such conditions, the policy option that will eventually stick—be it state ownership or privatization—is really a function of the power of public opinion or of the dominant values of society. Given that today the predominant values favor state ownership, it is not surprising that Brazil retains its state-owned bank and oil company.

But what can we say about the mini-conflicts that every Brazilian must live through on a daily basis, watching people cutting in line, using *jeitinhos*, resorting to the famous phrase "do you know who you are talking to?" The PESB results show that these are conflicts of values—opposing values whose main bearers are two different groups with contrasting levels of education. There are two sets of implications to be drawn from these data.

Education, Modernization, and DaMatta's Brazil

In Brazil, Roberto DaMatta is the most read and most cited scholar in university social science courses. His influence is enormous, and not by accident. DaMatta's interpretations of Brazil, invariably original, have helped Brazilians to understand themselves. As discussed above, his oeuvre is like a grand psychiatrist's couch for Brazilian society.

The PESB has shown that Roberto DaMatta is essentially correct. Brazil *is* hierarchical, familial, patrimonialistic, and strongly endorses the *jeitinho* and a range of similar behaviors. As show above, however, Brazil is not monolithic but rather sharply divided into an archaic segment of society that has low levels of education (the majority) and a modern segment that boasts university diplomas (a growing minority). Roberto DaMatta's Brazil corresponds to the first segment. However, when one identifies such a massive cultural distance between two different educational cohorts, it is fair to say that we are not dealing with a single culture, but rather two different and often contradictory ways of seeing the world.

Thus, it is possible to make an important qualification to DaMatta's contributions. Beyond an anthropological contribution to the understanding of Brazil, Roberto DaMatta has perhaps generated a sociological contribution to the understanding of less-developed societies wherever they may be. At stages in which the aggregate level of education of the population is very low, societies tend to legitimate the bending and breaking of rules and laws (the *jeitinho*), to believe that each person should respect his or her predefined social role (hierarchy), to hold that family ties are far more important than any other type of relationship, and so on. As societies become wealthier and more educated, these worldviews begin to fade away. This process, then, would not be exclusive to Brazil, but rather a generalized phenomenon, linked to a particular stage of development that each society must pass through. The modernizationists were right.[11]

Anthropologists may well contest this broad conclusion. Their argument would be simple enough. Brazilian culture *is* indeed different, and proof of this lies in the fact that a university-educated Brazilian is still more familial, hierarchical, etc., than a university-educated North American. To express this in more scientific language: even after controlling for educational levels, an anthropologist would still detect important differences between the two societies. The anthropologist would then depict these contrasts as enduring *cultural* differences. Culture exists and culture matters.

These two conclusions are not incompatible. Education matters and explains a great deal of the differences between social groups in a single country, and at the same time people from different countries with similar educational levels can hold very different worldviews. No matter how we look at it, Brazil will never be culturally identical to the United States, and vice versa. However, let's be provocative here: if we wanted some elements of North American culture to gain strength in Brazil with each passing year, the PESB data show us very clearly how to do this. The strategy would be via a massive and rapid expansion of higher education in Brazil. In doing this, Brazilians would become more similar to their rich neighbors to the north, although never exactly the same.

Just to be controversial, it is worth asking: will Brazilians never "be like them" because the two cultures are really different, or because North Americans will always hold an advantage with regard to educational levels? It is not inconceivable that on the day when the majority of Brazilians have college degrees, the majority of U.S. citizens will have masters degrees. And on that day, we will still not know *why* there are differences between the two countries: that is, whether they exist due to educational levels or due to culture. The overall cultural climate generated by a great mass of less-educated citizens is very different from that generated by a great mass of highly educated citizens.[12]

Revisiting an Old Controversy: Racism

As Ollie Johnson notes in this volume, in Brazil there persists the well-known myth of racial democracy. The origin of the racial-democracy concept is the work of Gilberto Freyre. In his comparison of Brazil with the United States, Freyre attempts to show that modern Brazil is a result of the blending of three races: white Europeans, African blacks, and the Amerindians who were present before the arrival of the Portuguese. According to Freyre, this mixture is not only accepted but also valued positively by Brazilians. In *Casa-grande e senzala* (1933, translated into English in 1946 as *The Masters and the Slaves*), Freyre argues that during the shaping of colonial, slaveholding Brazil, the social relations between whites and blacks were very different from those that characterized the equivalent period in North American history. Emblematic of these differences was widespread miscegenation in Brazil. The Brazilian path of race mixing, according to Freyre, created a "New World in the tropics" that was uniquely democratic in its race relations.

The racial-democracy thesis is today correctly dismissed as a myth, but it contains one kernel of truth that is relevant to politics: in contrast with the United States, modern Brazil has generally not been plagued by organized, militant racist groups. Still, despite its "debunking" (Owensby 2005) by modern social science research, echoes of the racial-democracy thesis persist in Brazil. A bestselling 2006 book by the journalist Ali Kamel, whose blunt title translates as *We Are Not Racists*, claims that the main problem in Brazil is not racial discrimination but rather discrimination based on social class (Kamel 2006). Is there or is there not racism in Brazil? That is the old controversy revisited by Kamel, but the overall debate is changing. Slowly but surely, Brazil is becoming aware of its racism and skin-color prejudices. But as the popularity of Kamel's book shows, there are contrarian voices—as in, contrary to the facts.

To address this controversy, we need convincing evidence that there really is racial prejudice. The 2002 PESB conducted a novel experiment. Respondents were shown a card containing eight photographs of individuals whose skin color ranged from *branco* (white) to *pardo* (mixed race) to *preto* (black). Of the eight photographs, six individuals—two whites, two *pardos*, and two blacks—were identified by the research team as having racial appearances that would be consensually recognized by respondents. Showing the photos, the interviewer then asked "I would like you to tell me which of these seems to be . . ." followed by either an attribute (either positive or negative) or a profession (of higher or lower social prestige). The question was repeated with seventeen different attributes or jobs. Interestingly, on average only about 6–8 percent of respondents replied spontaneously that it was not possible to determine these things on the basis of a photo. The results are reported in figures 11.1 through 11.3. In these bar graphs, the bars represent the percentage of respondents who picked one of the two whites, one of the two *pardos*, or one of the two blacks in the photographic display.

The data presented in these graphs strongly contradict the title of Kamel's recent book, *We Are Not Racists*. There *is* discrimination, and it is directed against

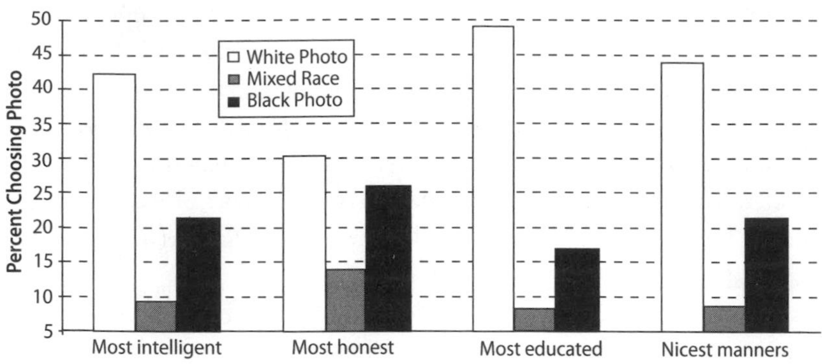

Figure 11.1. Perceived Attributes of Whites, *Pardos*, and Blacks
Source: Pesquisa Social Brasileira (PESB) 2002. N = 2,340.

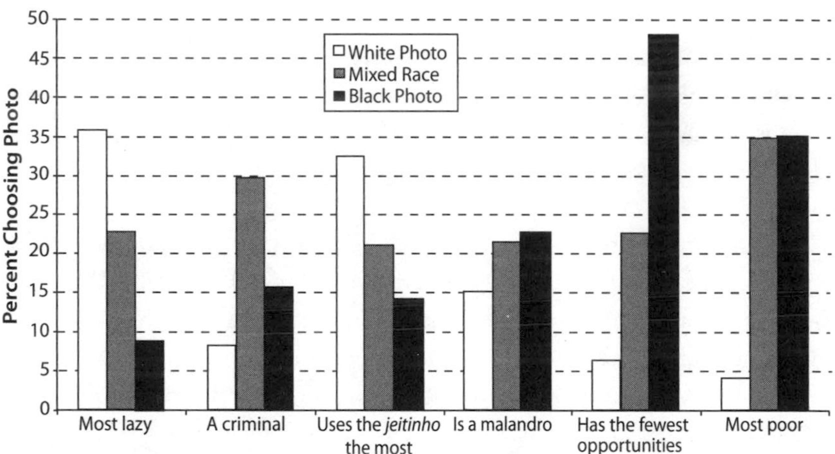

Figure 11.2. Perceived Attributes of Whites, *Pardos*, and Blacks (continued)
Source: Pesquisa Social Brasileira (PESB) 2002. N = 2,342.

blacks and those of mixed race. Their lives are much more difficult than those of whites. In some cases, *pardos* are more likely to be victims of prejudice than are blacks: *pardos,* for example, are seen as the most *malandros* (a word variously translated as rogue, hustler, or ne'er-do-well, with connotations of shiftiness and untrustworthiness). Under other conditions, blacks end up worse off than *pardos.* But the fact is there is no situation in which whites fare worse than *pardos* or blacks.

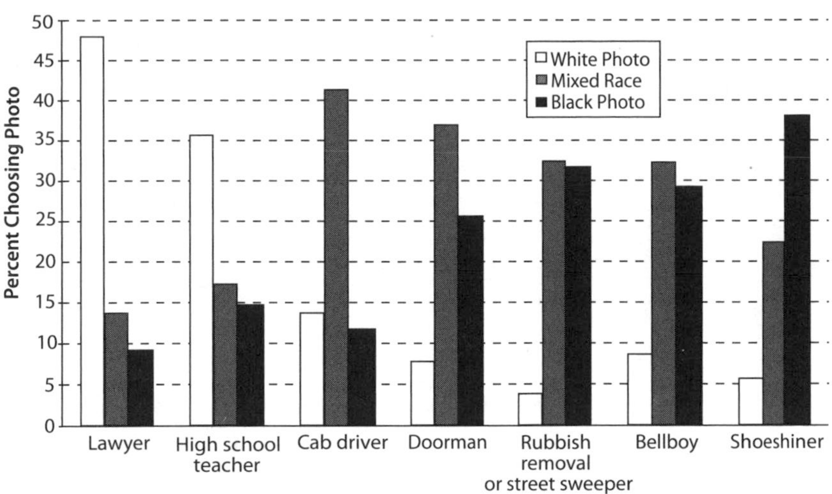

Figure 11.3. Perceived Typical Jobs of Whites, *Pardos*, and Blacks
Source: Pesquisa Social Brasileira (PESB) 2002. N = 2,341.

In another experiment designed to probe racial prejudices, respondents were given a different set of three cards containing passport-style photos of men. Card 1 showed a white auto mechanic, a *pardo* auto mechanic, and a black high school teacher, each wearing the clothing or uniforms associated with their jobs. The interviewers presented the men in the photos as "a mechanic," "a mechanic," and "a teacher," respectively, but did not mention their races. Card 2 showed a white Northeastern lawyer, a *pardo* high school teacher from the Northeast, and a black mechanic, and card 3 showed a white high school teacher, a *pardo* lawyer, and a black Northeastern lawyer. Again, the men in the photos were presented to the respondents purely in terms of their jobs and/or regional origin: for example, high school teacher or Northeastern lawyer. Respondents were asked, "Which one of these would you want your daughter to marry? If you don't have a daughter, imagine that you do, and in that case which one would you want her to marry?" For all three cards—regardless of occupation—the white face was the number one choice.

The white mechanic was the top choice on card 1, even though he had a lower occupational status than the black teacher. The white high school teacher was the preferred option on card 3, even though in occupational terms he would rank below the *pardo* lawyer and the black Northeastern lawyer. And on card 2,

Table 11.10. Who Would You Want Your Daughter to Marry? (overall)

Card	*White*	*Pardo*	*Black*
Card 1	39	14	25
Card 2	50	20	10
Card 3	47	20	13
Average	45	18	16

Source: Pesquisa Social Brasileira (PESB) 2002. N = 2,350.

Table 11.11. Card 1, Preferences for Marrying Daughter, by Race of Respondent

	Race of respondent		
Preference	*Black*	*Pardo*	*White*
White auto mechanic	22	36	53
Pardo mechanic	23	18	10
Black high school teacher	43	31	20
Doesn't matter, any one of them	12	15	16
None of them	0	0	1

Source: Pesquisa Social Brasileira (PESB) 2002. N = 2,347.

the one in which the white man has the highest social status among the three racial types, he was chosen at a much higher rate than when, as on card 3, the black and *pardo* men enjoyed more prestigious occupations. This methodology is a rather definitive response to those who, like Kamel (2006), claim that prejudice in Brazil is based on class rather than on skin color or race. The results here show that this is not true: prejudice is color driven, and social class plays a rather small role.

There is nothing better in Brazil than being a white male. This is something that many individuals know from experience. The fact is that now, with the release of the PESB data, Brazilian society has basically said as much. Those who continue to insist that there is no racism in Brazil, or if there is, that it is a "cordial" and "soft" racism, will have to face up to the data presented in this chapter. It is Brazilians themselves who have said they are racist, and not necessarily cordial.

Table 11.12. Card 3, Preferences for Marrying Daughter, by Race of Respondent			
	Race of respondent		
Preference	*Black*	*Pardo*	*White*
White high school teacher	35	47	57
Pardo lawyer	24	22	19
Black Northeastern lawyer	28	17	7
Doesn't matter, any one of them	12	13	16
None of them	1	0	0

Source: Pesquisa Social Brasileira (PESB) 2002. N = 2,355.

Table 11.13. Card 2, Preferences for Marrying Daughter, by Race of Respondent			
	Race of respondent		
Preference	*Black*	*Pardo*	*White*
White Northeastern lawyer	33	48	63
Pardo Northeastern high school teacher	29	26	16
Black auto mechanic	26	12	5
Doesn't matter, any one of them	11	15	16
None of them	1	0	0

Source: Pesquisa Social Brasileira (PESB) 2002. N = 2,351.

Roberto DaMatta Reconsidered

To be sure, there are scholars who are very critical of the work of Roberto DaMatta. The most aggressive is Jessé de Souza (1999), whose bark may be worse than his bite. But the results of the PESB allow us to advance a moderate critique—perhaps a friendly revision—of DaMatta's interpretations of Brazil. Like many critiques of anthropological approaches, part of the criticism rests on the concept of *change*.

If DaMatta is correct, then the country's Portuguese cultural heritage—with its weight of five hundred years—leads Brazil to be culturally very different from the United States, particularly when one compares relevant aspects of social life such as respect for the law. In this view, even if the educational levels of Brazilians were to rise dramatically, then change in culture, ideologies, and worldviews would be rather small in the face of the Iberian legacy. Brazil would still be very different from the United States or England. But if, alternatively, the PESB results are correct, then something very different would occur: a sharp increase in educational attainment would bring Brazil closer to the culture of other nations, including the Anglo-Saxon countries. To illustrate this idea with a non-Brazilian example, the population of today's South Korea—after decades of intense efforts in the area of education—is more culturally proximate to the United States than was the case fifty years ago. This is a generic criticism of anthropological approaches but also a specific criticism of DaMatta's work on Brazil.

But this is a generous and positive critique because, if correct, it puts DaMatta's work on another plane altogether: he would no longer be speaking specifically about Brazil, but rather about less-developed societies everywhere. The result would be a sort of anthropology of less-educated societies. This is what leads me to claim that the *jeitinho brasileiro* probably exists in some form (and with different names) in all societies that are less developed and that possess low levels of formal education. The opposite would be true in the advanced industrial societies of Europe and North America. In Spain, which has undergone a profound socioeconomic transformation in recent decades, has the use of practices similar to the *jeitinho* now fallen to the level found in the United States?

I am not denying national specificities. I am simply emphasizing that national cultures may be less important than the cultures of transnational social groups that are united by similar levels of formal education. The Iberian heritage will never be eliminated from the Brazil's cultural DNA, but it is possible to set Brazilians on the path of "rule compliance" by means of educational expansion. Portugal will always be the mother country, but to turn Brazil into a more *liberal* country it will be necessary to open the doors of colleges and universities to the masses. History and heritage will remain constants, but the expansion of higher education has transformative consequences for any society—one of them being, potentially, the consolidation of democracy.

12

Redemocratization Viewed from Below: Urban Poverty and Politics in Rio de Janeiro, 1968–2005

Janice E. Perlman

WHAT DOES BRAZILIAN DEMOCRACY look like from the viewpoint of the urban poor? Have the favela residents been included as full citizens since the return of democracy to Brazil?[1] How do the people who have been marginalized assess the changes in their lives since the end of the dictatorship? How have their political attitudes and behaviors changed over time from the height of the military dictatorship in 1968–1969 to the present? Are there systematic differences across generations in political saliency, knowledge, perceptions, and participation?

This chapter addresses these questions by looking at Brazil's democracy from the viewpoint of the underclass. The view from below (the *underview*) differs considerably from the view from above (the *overview*) as described in other chapters of this volume. This chapter demonstrates how these contrasting perspectives play out in the case of the urban poor in Rio de Janeiro. It is based on the findings of a longitudinal intergenerational study the author conducted in the favelas of Rio de Janeiro, first in 1968–1969, and then a follow-up with the same communities and people thirty years later (1999–2005). It covers four generations: the original study participants, their parents, their children, and their grandchildren.[2]

The results of the earlier study were published in 1976 as *The Myth of Marginality: Urban Poverty and Politics in Rio de Janeiro*, which was part of a larger paradigm shift from "blaming the victim" to "blaming the system" and from seeing squatter settlements as a "problem" to seeing them as a "solution," providing housing for millions of people priced out of the formal rental or ownership markets.

The core argument of that book is that the negative stereotypes of migrants and squatters (as rural rejects, vagabonds and criminals, parasites on the city's economy, and discontented/disconnected masses likely to foment revolt) were "empirically false, analytically misleading and insidious in their policy implications." The view that favelas were "cancerous sores on the beautiful body of Rio de Janeiro" and that those who lived in them were disposable waste akin to the discarded materials from which they built their dwellings, was used to justify massive favela eradication.

The same divide between myth and reality persists today: favela residents are not *marginal* to the system but rather *tightly integrated* into it, albeit in an extremely asymmetrical manner. Their labor supports the life of the rest of the city: they continue to work multiple jobs, performing tasks no one else would do, under exploitative and dangerous conditions for pay that no one else would accept. They contribute to the city's vibrancy through their culture, music, dance, humor, and language, but they are stigmatized and excluded from a closed class system. The political repression of the dictatorship years has been replaced by the immediate dangers of being trapped between the police and the drug dealers—aided by new forms of corruption and clientelism. In short, the favela population is not "passively marginal but actively marginalized" in service of preserving the vested interests of the status quo. [3]

During the Cold War era, when the original study was conducted, Brazil was at the height of the military dictatorship, and there was a pervasive fear that the newly arrived migrants and the squatters would become radicalized by seeing the wealth that surrounded them.[4] On the contrary, their reference group was not the rich urbanites, but rather the family and friends who had remained behind in the countryside—and were considerably more miserable. The squatters were happy with their move and expected that the future for their children would be better still. I remember a discussion I had in 1968 with Gilberto, a young man who had come to Rio by himself from the Northeast in 1961 and settled in Catacumba because he knew some people there from his hometown. When I asked him how he felt about looking across the Lagoa Rodrigo de Freitas every day at the luxury houses of the rich and seeing all the public services available in the upscale communities, while Catacumba did not even have running water or electricity, he replied, "It's not like that, not at all. We little people [*a gente humilde*] have a lot of patience. We do not compare ourselves to them. . . . Even as a *biscateiro* [odd jobber] I live much better than anyone in my family back home. We are not in a rush—after the government helps the rich and the less rich, then, later on, it will be our turn—our time will come."

Profound political changes occurred during the time span of this longitudinal study. The country went from the dictatorship through a period of gradual opening (*abertura*) to full transition to democracy in 1985 with a new constitution in 1988. The research period spanned the second mandate of Fernando Henrique Cardoso (from 1999 to 2002) and the rise of the Workers' Party, culminating in Lula's 2002 presidential victory.

Each of these transformations was the result of enormous struggle, conflict, and controversy among the major political forces vying for power. Yet, from the viewpoint of the favelados, none of these has made a great difference in daily life. The follow-up study in 1999–2005 revealed a deepened sense of exclusion, a keen awareness of the corruption of the political system, and an increasing belief in the *idea* of participatory democracy coupled with the *reality* of reduced civic and political participation. Paradoxically, the sense of disenfranchisement among those who lived through the dictatorship has become worse since redemocratization. In addition, as each generation becomes better educated and more knowledgeable about politics, they become increasingly cynical about the fairness of the political system and reluctant to participate in the political process. This disaffection of young people raises serious questions about the next generation's likelihood of fighting for fair, accountable, and transparent governance.

This chapter argues that from the perspective of the urban poor, Brazilian democracy has a long way to go in terms of consolidation, equality under the law, protection of its citizens from violence, and meeting the needs of the underclass. It draws upon the life histories, survey data, open-ended interviews, and participant observation that the author used to collect data between 2000 and 2005, comparing the findings with those from the original 1968–1969 study.[5]

To put this chapter in context, it must be remembered that Brazil is a country of cities and metropolitan regions, with 81.2 percent of the population living in urban areas (Instituto Brasileiro de Geografia e Estatística, 2000). The percentage of the population living in the informal housing sector or, to use the official

Table 12.1. Favelas in Brazil's Cities, 2000

City	*Favela pop.*	*Total pop.*	*%*	*Total dwellings*
Rio de Janeiro	1,092,476	5,857,904	18.7	308,581
São Paulo	909,628	10,434,252	8.7	229,441
Belém	448,723	1,280,614	35.0	100,069
Fortaleza	353,925	2,141,402	16.5	83,203
Belo Horizonte	268,847	2,238,526	12.0	67,441
Salvador	238,342	2,443,107	9.8	61,322
Curitiba	145,242	1,587,315	9.2	37,752
Porto Alegre	143,353	1,360,590	10.5	37,665
Recife	134,790	422,905	9.5	34,674

Source: Instituto Brasileiro de Geografia e Estatística (2000).

term of the Brazilian census, "subnormal agglomerations" ranges across cities but averages between 30 percent and 40 percent of the urban population. Rio de Janeiro has the largest favela population (5.8 million according to the 2000 census) and the greatest number of favelas (752), as shown in table 12.1.

Over time, Rio's favelas have grown up and over the hillsides, forming huge "complexes." The largest favelas, such as Rocinha, Jacarezinho, the Complexo do Alemão, and the Complexo of Maré are larger than many Brazilian cities (Instituto de Urbanismo Pereira Passos 2006). The favela population in Rio has grown faster than the city as a whole in every decade from 1950 to present, with the single exception of the 1970s, when 62 favelas were forcibly removed, displacing some 102,300 people in the first three years alone (Secretary of Planning, State of Guanabara, 1973).

The latest data from IBGE show an even greater differential in growth from 2000 to 2005. The population of Rio's favelas grew at a rate of 7.5 percent, while the nonfavela population grew at 2.7 percent. The figures from 2005 show almost four of every ten residents of the city of Rio (37 percent) live in informal housing: 19 percent in favelas, 12 percent in deteriorated public housing (*conjuntos habitacionais*), and 6 percent in clandestine subdivisions (*loteamentos clandestinos*).

Clearly, any democratic state that ignores the needs and perceptions of such a large segment of the population does so at its peril. The findings of this study suggest that government is very weak on the ground level and that the only representation of the state present in the poor communities are the police—weapons exposed and ready to "shoot first, ask later."

Looking at the narratives, life histories, and survey questionnaire results reveals deep disenchantment with democracy as it has evolved over the two decades since the end of the dictatorship. Four main themes emerged from the research:

1. *Disappointment with democracy:* The redemocratization after the end of the dictatorship did not empower the poor as hoped or bring benefits to their communities as expected.
2. *Corruption, clientelism, and cronyism:* Traditional misuse of privilege and power, somewhat curtailed under military rule, resurfaced with the return of the multiparty system and now permeate the polity at every level.
3. *Citizenship, rights and duties:* Over time and with each successive generation, more people can differentiate between citizens' rights and duties and *believe* in citizens' rights, in democratic participation, in trying to influence government decisions, and in the importance of taking an active role in politics.
4. *Belief-behavior disconnect:* Despite the belief in democracy as an ideal, political participation is low, and the younger, better-educated, most politically knowledgeable generation is also the most cynical about government and the least participatory.

This chapter explores each of these themes, working with three levels of comparison where appropriate: intragenerational comparisons—comparing the same individuals in 1969 and 2001; intergenerational—comparing the original interviewees, with their children and their grandchildren (in 2001); and community-level comparisons—comparing the responses of randomly selected residents of the same spatial/physical territories at two points in time, 1969 and 2003.[6]

Theme 1: Disappointment with Democracy

In a 2004 interview, Tio Souza, a seventy-four-year-old from Catacumba and founder of the girl's soccer club, who now lives in the housing project of Padre Miguel, said, "Politics is like this: at election time the candidates always appear, afterwards, they disappear. This has never changed and never will. It was always like this. . . . I vote because it's obligatory. [The candidates] make many promises and never do anything. At election time, they come to our community, hang up a huge banner across one of the buildings; once the election is over, and they disappear and never return."

With the return to democracy, the hope was that the accountability derived from direct vote for mayor, governor, and president (all of which had been effectively appointed positions during the dictatorship) would give the urban poor greater bargaining power and a stronger voice with which to negotiate for community improvements. However, the people we interviewed did not feel they had gained a voice in the political arena, only a *potential* voice. They did not perceive distinct change towards greater accountability or fair play among government officials. What they did see was the impunity of police and drug dealers, both of whom terrorized their communities. So, while the redemocratization may have granted the urban poor de jure citizenship, they do not feel as though they have de facto citizenship. They are pseudo-citizens.

The first point is how little impact the end of the dictatorship had on daily lives of the study participants in their own opinion. The most radical sea change in the political landscape in the past thirty years was redemocratization, yet the majority of our sample—79 percent of original interviewees—said the *end of the dictatorship had no significant impact* on their lives.[7] That in itself is a major statement about the difference between the view from below and above.

In response to the open-ended follow-up question which asked "in what way" did democracy make a difference, 32 percent said they felt there was the greater freedom (*liberdade*) and government transparency, while 23 percent said things had been better under the dictatorship (mentioning loss of work, security, tranquility, and political bargaining power). This response confirms a recent discourse about nostalgia in several Latin American countries for pragmatic authoritarianism, particularly for the rule of law and the safety of order during previous dictatorships (see especially UNDP 2004).

To further explore this, we asked all the respondents "How would you compare your life during the military dictatorship with what has happened since it ended?" in terms of a series of issues. The results showed agreement that certain things had indeed improved, such as access to (but not quality of) education (71 percent), access to public transportation (80 percent), and housing and sanitation (76 percent).

Assessments of the economic situation were more mixed, with 44 percent saying things were better, 32 percent saying they were worse, 14 percent saying it made no difference, and 9 percent saying they did not know. Likewise, the area of public health services generated conflicting opinions: 45 percent said it had improved, 44 percent said it had gotten worse, and 11 percent said it made no difference. And it came as no surprise that most said personal and family safety had gotten worse (68 percent).

The "disappointment with democracy" theme was revealed in the questions regarding political inclusion itself. This is where the concept of pseudo-citizenship came across. People we interviewed were much more aware of their rights and duties as citizens than they had been during the dictatorship (see below, as well as in discussion note in appendix), but when asked about how political reality had changed for them, the responses were counterintuitive and negative. Sixty-nine percent felt exclusion was the same or worse than it had been during the dictatorship; 69 percent felt that meaningful political participation had declined or stayed the same; and 81 percent said their bargaining power had diminished or stayed the same.

In fact, the faith in the good intentions of government was eroded, rather than strengthened, between 1969 and 2003. When asked "Do you think the government tries to understand and solve the problems of people like yourself?" 61 percent responded "yes" at the height of the dictatorship in 1969, but the percentage had dropped to 38 percent by 2003. This is diametrically opposed to expectations about democratization or the sense of citizenship in a polity.

Of course, government is not a single entity, and there are considerable differences between attitudes towards levels of government (local, state, and federal) and between the executive and legislative branches. We asked the question "In the past few years, have the authorities listed below helped or harmed people like yourself?" and then listed president of the republic, state governor, mayor, federal deputies, state deputies, city councilmen, and international agencies (such as the World Bank, the IMF, and the Inter-American Development Bank). The overall response of all three generations was that *government tended to harm more than help, but for the most part it did not matter at all.* Generally, respondents tended to give better ratings to lower levels of government. The children of the original interviewees were slightly less negative in their assessments, but even so, more rated the federal government and international institutions as harmful rather than helpful. They gave the city government the highest approval rating (35 percent), followed by the state government (29 percent)—nothing for the government to be proud of. The most prevalent answer in all generations was that government did not affect them either way, a profound problem for the democratic project.

Theme 2: Corruption, Clientelism, and Cronyism

Renewed party politics opened the way for a return to the pre-1964 system of patronage politics. The rising importance of party competition starting in 1979 led to the distribution of jobs and favors as the government party (ARENA, Aliança

Renovadora Nacional) was forced to compete for electoral support against the opposition (MDB, the Movimento Democratico Brasileiro). The inflated public sector and *empreguismo* (provision of state jobs as a form of patronage) became the norm under José Sarney who assumed the presidency after the untimely death of president-elect Tancredo Neves between his election and taking office.

While the market reforms of the 1990s involved some state layoffs, the political game of vote-buying and corruption continued unabated. As Mainwaring (1999, 209) so aptly put it, "Although the poor may receive a portion of politicians' patronage, this can hardly be qualified as a process of integrating the poor into the system; it is a mechanism to reinforce dependency, not to empower." I agree with his claim that "contemporary clientelism" is more detrimental today than in the past because it limits the legitimacy of the still-fragile democratic system, favors the elite minority over the poor majority, cripples the government's ability to work professionally, and weakens social programs by poor performance and diverted resources (Mainwaring 1999; see also Mainwaring 1995).

The old system of patronage politics—even at the height of the dictatorship—allowed some benefits to flow into favelas in exchange for votes, which were negotiated through the residents' associations. This channel of favors to the poor has been increasingly closed off since the mid-1980s, when drug lords began dominating residents' associations, robbing them of their independence and representative functions. As Desmond Arias shows in his recent work on criminal and community networks, the drug dealers who have taken over the residents' associations deal directly with the candidates and save the spoils for themselves (Arias 2006).

In general, the only presence of the state in the favelas is the police, who—when mandated to set up a police station within the communities—stay locked inside behind bars the entire day. When they do appear, it is in a surveillance helicopter or on a "blitz" of random shooting and looting. The photograph below shows how the police intimidate the youth and create what I call the "sphere of fear."[8] The film *City of God,* adapted from the book by Paulo Lins and now seen by people all over the world, depicts how the police collaborate with the drug dealers, confiscating arms and drugs in one place and selling them in another, meanwhile killing innocent residents with impunity.[9] There is no recourse in the judicial system or at higher levels of the political system, since the magnitude of drug money—and the willingness of the gangs to use deadly force—buys the complicity of the legal and political system all the way to the top.

Figure 12.1. Fear of Violence in Rio's Favelas

The degree of lethal violence is comparable to that experienced in modern civil wars. As shown below, one of every five persons interviewed had lost a family member to homicide, which the police have been unwilling or unable to control.

People report feeling trapped between the police and the dealers, both of whom commit acts of violence against them with impunity.[10] The popular idea that the drug dealers have created a benevolent "parallel state" that provides security, school fees, and access to medical services for the community residents is pure fantasy. There are isolated instances of patronage or service (a pregnant woman being driven to the hospital or a promising child getting a scholarship). But overall, both police and dealers are seen as harming more than helping the community, and the majority of people were afraid to even answer the question, as shown in figure 12.3.

The polity is clearly in deep trouble when people are no longer shocked by the impunity of gunmen who shoot innocent people on their way to or from work, or kill children playing in front of their own homes. When the police arrive for questioning, everyone disappears. They are too savvy to believe that jus-

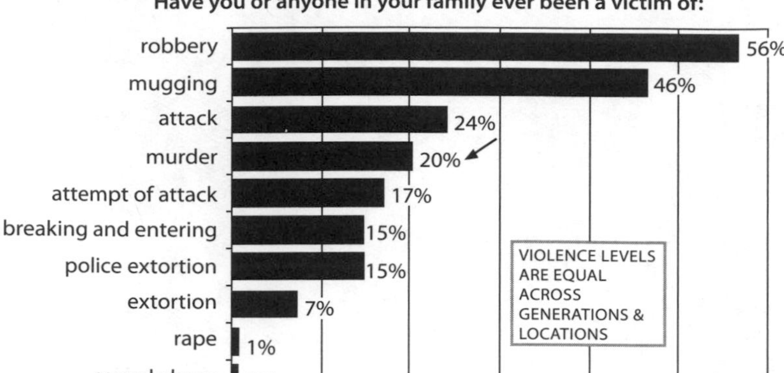

Figure 12.2. Experiences with Violence and Victimization, 2003

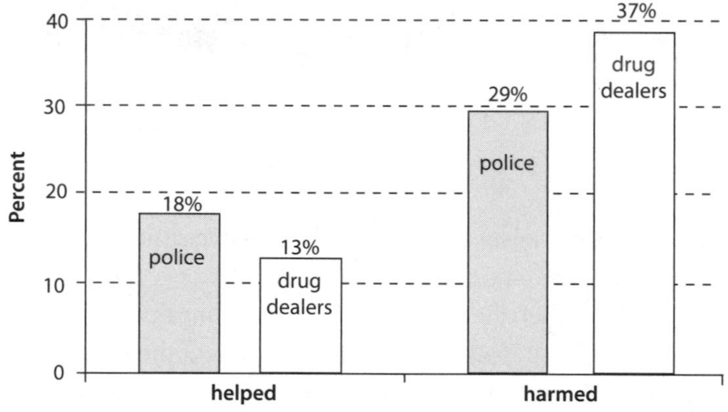

Figure 12.3. Do Police and Drug Dealers Help or Harm Favelas? (2003)

tice will be done and know that they risk their own and their families' lives by speaking out. When sensitive topics arise in discussion, people often say to me—while mimicking each phrase in body language—"we are like the three monkeys: we see nothing; we hear nothing; we say nothing. . . . That is how we survive." In 2003, when we asked the same question of the new random sample (1,224 men and women between the ages of sixteen and sixty-five) in the original study sites, their responses were similar, but even stronger: 88 percent reported acts of violence by the police, the drug traffickers, or both, or were afraid to answer the question.

Group	Percent
Police	22
Drug traffickers	11
Both	48
None	12
Don't know	7
Total	100

Table 12.2. Who Commits More Acts of Violence against the Community? (2003)

Source: New random sample from original communities.

The police are perceived as more violent (and less respectful of the local people) than the drug dealers, but just under half of the respondents say both commit random acts of violence against the community. The state seems to have lost control and can no longer guarantee the physical safety of its citizens. The residents' associations, formerly the official collective voice of the *favelados*, have almost all been taken over by drug dealers, with the former elected presidents run out of the communities (aided by police escorts) or killed.[11] The process of taking control of the residents' associations happened gradually and was completed only in the period from 2000–2005. The main exception is a West Zone favela, Rio das Pedras, which has neither drug dealing nor uncontrolled violence—it is run by militias, known as "death squads," composed of off-duty or former policemen who take justice into their own hands and kill dealers on sight. In any case, there is no doubt that violence and trafficking in arms and drugs are major obstacles to democratic consolidation in Rio de Janeiro, especially for the poor.

Theme 3: Citizenship, Rights, and Duties

In a 2003 interview, Maria Fernandes, a sixty-six-year-old from Catacumba, now living in the housing project of Quitungo, related her thoughts about the end of the military dictatorship: "The end of the dictatorship affected all of us. Before, if you came here with a tape recorder to interview me, I wouldn't have said anything, you know, right? Today it's not that way, a person can talk. It's freedom—we have the liberty to speak."

One important change revealed in the restudy is the growing understanding of citizens' rights under a democracy and the difference between rights and duties. When I was studying grassroots social movements in U.S. cities, I compared the task of poor people's movements to the struggle of the mythic Sisyphus, working mightily to roll the boulder up the mountain, only to find it slipping down again as soon as he came to a rest (Perlman 1983a).The status quo is like gravity; it does not need to make an effort to exert its ever-present force, and it is hardwired into society's institutions. Time after time I saw an entire community fight to preserve its integrity from a highway that would cut it in two, or a garbage dump in the middle of the neighborhood. Using Alinskian methods of community organizing, starting with small victories and working up to larger issues and more support, they often won their cause—at least temporarily (Alinsky 1969 [1946].

What eventually happened when the mobilization was over and no one was paying attention was that things just "rolled along," and in due time the highways or sewer treatment plants were built according to the original intent. The only thing that could not be eroded was the experience of victory by the powerless over the powerful. The pride of this experience was internalized in each person who participated, and nothing would change them back to believing they were without merit in their cause. I remember one elderly man I interviewed in San Francisco beaming with pride when describing a confrontational meeting at City Hall. His eyes lit up when he said, "They called me 'sir.'" That was the first time in his life that anyone in a position of power had ever addressed him with respect (Perlman 1983b).

What I saw in Rio reminded me of that moment—there was something in the transition back to democracy that couldn't be taken away, even by the most blatant corruption or inept governance—and that was a sense of entitlement to citizens' rights. One of the things I found most disheartening in 1969 was the inability of most people I lived with in the favelas to distinguish between duties (*deveres*) and rights (*direitos*). They generally said that their most important *duties* as citizens were "to obey the law, respect the authorities, and work hard," and that their most important rights were "to obey the law, respect the authorities, and work hard." In short, there was no distinction between the two.

In the 2001 interviews, virtually everyone in each of the three generations we interviewed was able to articulate what they thought were their most important rights and duties in response to the same open-ended question as had been asked during the dictatorship. The most frequently mentioned "right" was access to health care, followed by education and freedom of movement. The right to work and to unemployment insurance if they could not find work was next on the list, and finally the right to be treated with respect and dignity. There were slight variances by generation, with the older people placing more emphasis on unemployment insurance and health care; their children focusing on health and education, "freedom to come and go," and jobs; and their grandchildren prioritizing "freedom to come and go" as number one, followed by health care, then education.[12]

In terms of duties, all three generations put "obey the law" as first, and the original interviewees and children mentioned "the duty to work and meet their professional obligations" as second, while the grandchildren put "respecting their neighbors" as second. Third for grandchildren was the duty to work, while third for their parents was "following through with commitments" and third for the grandparents (the original sample) was "honesty and integrity."

The ability to distinguish rights from duties in 2001, as opposed to 1969, shows that structural change did indeed change people's cognitive maps. The very notions of *rights* and *citizenship* only entered common parlance as the dictatorship was winding down, during the democratic opening (*abertura*). There was a popular movement for "*diretas já*" (direct vote NOW) and "citizenship" (*cidadania*) as a set of entitlements and obligations entered the realm of popular discourse. However, the democratically elected political leaders did not go so far as redressing social and economic inequalities or ensuring all citizens the right to a decent quality of life, personal safety, and civil liberties.

Whether or not *favelados* are aware of their citizens' rights, they remain at the bottom of the totem pole in the political as well as in the social and economic arenas. They are vulnerable, and they are aware of their vulnerability. Some of the literature refers to the Brazilian's "high tolerance for inequality" as an explanation of how such deep societal divisions could persist. I think this interpretation is condescending and misleading. In my view, the persistence of inequality reflects Brazil's long history of exclusion and elitism. If the poor had ever experienced equality or even respect, I believe that they would protest if this were taken away. But as it has always been thus (even more so in the countryside where the migrants came from); they keep their heads down and go about their business of daily survival.

This is not to deny that the urban poor feel a profound sense of injustice. The only reason that their moral outrage does not translate into physical rage—or is not more manifest in the political sphere—is that the "view from below" lacks potency. Everyone knows how power is used and abused, and the poor are in no position to confront this self-perpetuating play of privilege. As one woman in the favela of Nova Brasília said to me, "Janice, what can we do? . . . Not only the policemen but the judges and the politicians 'way up there' are 'lining their pockets.'" This sense of impotence contributes to the gap between *favelados'* beliefs about rights and their actual behavior and was reinforced by the corruption scandals during the first Lula administration while we were in the field conducting interviews with the new random samples in the three study sites.

Theme 4: The Belief-Behavior Disconnect

Amazingly, despite the broken promise of citizenship and the poor assessment of government performance, the belief in the ideals of democracy took root among the urban poor—increasingly so with each generation. When asked whether "decisions should be left in the hands of the politicians or all Brazilians should participate," the percent favoring participation rose from 34 percent in 1969 to 90 percent among grandchildren in 2001, as shown in figure 12.4.

Comparing the random samples of the same communities in 1969 and 2003, the percentage saying all Brazilians should participate rose from 34 percent to 81 percent. The same pattern shows up in response to the question "Do you think that you can do something to influence government or do you think there is no possibility?" Paradoxically, the percentage of those believing they could influence government—despite widespread recognition that they had not had any success in so doing—rose dramatically, from under one-fifth to over one-half. Whereas only 19 percent of the original sample thought they could influence the government in 1969, almost twice as great a percentage (30 percent) of the same people thought so in 2001; as did 49 percent of their children and 51 percent of their grandchildren. Among the new random sample of 1,200 people across all generations in the same communities (conducted in 2003), 34 percent thought they could influence government, and 66 percent thought not.

The steady increase in each generation's reported perceptions of having political efficacy—while not accompanied by equally high levels of agency, action, or participation—shows the increasing penetration of the discourse on democracy and citizenship into the mindset of each generation. However, this upward trend must be interpreted in light of the fact that even in the cohort that boasted the highest percentage of those who felt that they could influence the govern-

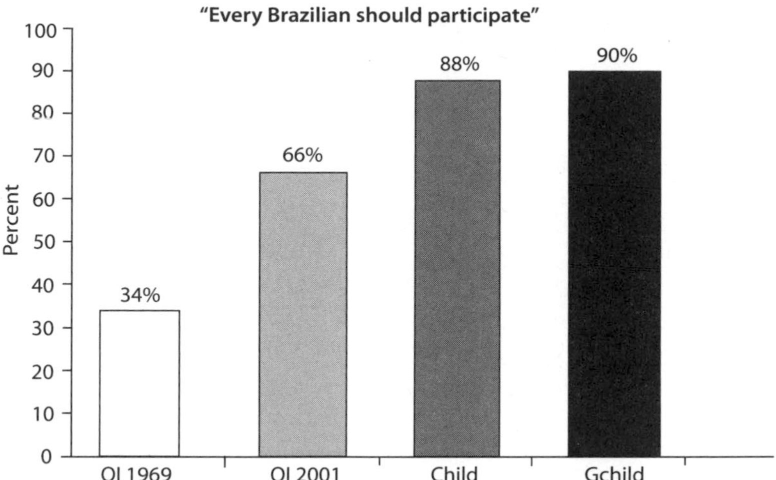

Figure 12.4. Belief in Democratic Ideals, 2004

Note: OI refers to original interviewees.

ment (the youngest generation), still only half of the respondents voiced this belief. This two-way pull arose in many conversations, with the appealing rhetoric of potency in producing change balanced against the grim reality of impotence and pseudo-citizenship.[13] In a 2004 interview, Alaerte Correia, a sixty-year-old from Nova Brasília, now living in Campo Grande, stated that, "I'm not going to vote, for sure. I don't like it. But I have voted in the past. I have been disappointed many times. I think they [politicians] are a band of scoundrels, of cowards. But it doesn't depend on me alone, so I can stay out of it. Just one person [not voting] is no problem."

It may seem paradoxical that while *belief* in political participation has increased over time, actual *participation* remains low. Yet is makes perfect sense, given the historic legacy of top-down politics. Table 12.3 shows levels of each type of participation for three points in time and for each of the three generations. Voting was the most frequent form of political participation for all except the grandchildren—for whom it was the least frequent. Neither is unexpected in Brazil, where voting is mandatory from the ages of eighteen through seventy and voluntary for sixteen- to eighteen-year-olds (as well as those over seventy). In addition, voting studies consistently show that younger cohorts of the electorate tend towards low voter turnout. Under half of any sample took part in any of the other forms of political participation, although in this case, it was the children's generation who had the highest rates of activism.

Table 12.3. Political Participation, 1969 and 2001 (%)

Activity	*1969*	*2001*		
		Original respondents	*Children*	*Grandchildren*
Vote[a]	40	72	39	7
Sign a petition	12	25	31	27
Attend a political meeting or rally	5	12	18	13
Work for a candidate	6	13	20	20
Participate in a demonstration	19	15	21	12

[a] In 1969 respondents were ask if they had ever voted in an election, and in 2001 they were asked if they had voted in the last presidential election. We judged the items sufficiently similar to be comparable in this table, but they are not part of the political participation index.

According to the Electoral Code (passed just after the new constitution in 1988) Brazilian citizens must show proof of having voted (*comprovante de votação*) to be hired for any public job (*cargo público*) or receive a diploma from any public institution. Failure to vote in three consecutive elections means annulling your voter registration card (*título de eleitor*) and causes problems with your identity card (CPF—*Cadastro de Pessoa Física*), which is, in turn, essential identification to maintain a bank account, get a telephone, or complete almost any fiscal transaction.

Within this context, it is surprising that a large percentage of people do not exercise their right (and civic duty) to vote, particularly because there is the option of protesting (or at least registering dissatisfaction) by going to the polls and voting a blank ballot (referred to as *votar em branco*). The sense of disenfranchisement among the urban poor must be extraordinarily high to risk exclusion from government jobs, schools, benefits, and so on.

In the 2001 study, less than half (47 percent) of those twenty-four or older reported having voted in the previous presidential election, and only one-tenth (11 percent) of those between the ages of sixteen and twenty-four said they had. Having listened to young people in the communities and talked with them at length leads me to believe that cynicism—not apathy—is what keeps them away. The youth are the best educated, best informed, and most politically savvy of all generations and have the greatest belief in the value of participation, yet they have quite low levels of political engagement. This is why I call it the "belief/behavior disconnect."

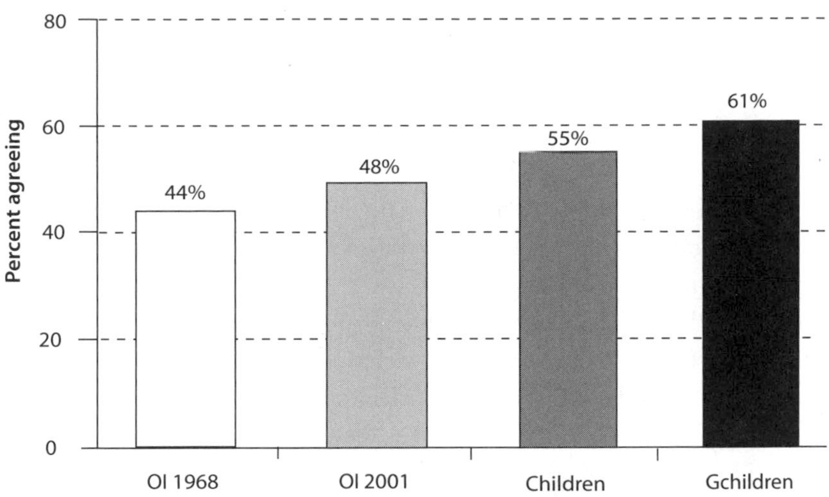

Figure 12.5. Brazilians Do Not Have the Capacity to Choose Among Candidates, 2004

Note: OI refers to original interviewees.

As with internalization of many forms of oppression, this alienation about the electoral process has also turned inward, as the urban poor increasingly blame themselves and the Brazilian electorate for their failure to elect candidates who will fight for their interests. For example, when asked whether "the Brazilian people have the capacity to make wise choices among candidates," an increasing number say they do not. As shown in figure 12.5, during the dictatorship, when voting was merely a memory, there was more faith in the capacity of the electorate than there is today. Recent experience with electoral democracy has perversely generated *less faith in the ability of citizens to vote wisely.*

In the long-recognized tendency towards "blaming the victim," the poor tend to blame themselves and the Brazilian electorate in general for their lack of capacity to select good candidates, rather than blaming the limitations on choice of candidates or the inability to hold them to their electoral promises. The roots of the problem and the conditions that lead Brazilians to doubt their capacity are systemwide. On the one hand, there is little or no accountability of elected officials to their constituents; on the other hand, there are no peoples' movements sufficiently powerful for the urban poor to make demands on the state. As the poor constitute one-third of the voters of the city, their mobilization around a policy platform or candidate could be the decisive force for electoral victory.

Who Are the Politically Participatory among the Poor?

The landscape of political participation from the grassroots is variegated, changes over time, and looks different to different individuals. To get an overall view of patterns within this panorama, we looked at voting separately and created an index of the other forms of political participation, combining signing a petition, attending a political meeting, working for a candidate, and participating in a demonstration.

Based on the literature in the field and the prevailing wisdom among Brazilian scholars, I expected to find certain factors associated with greater or lesser participation in the democratic project. The working hypothesis was that participation would be higher for males, whites, those who in 1969 owned or rented lots in subdivisions (as compared with favela residents), those who no longer lived in favelas or housing projects but in legitimate neighborhoods, those who had higher social capital and civic participation, and those who believed in agency over fatalism.

Three of these hypotheses were confirmed by the data: males did participate significantly more than females, although the gap tended to diminish with each generation; those who started out as legal renters or owners in the unserviced subdivisions in Caxias scored higher on participation that those who had been squatters. People with title to their land or inclusion in the formal housing market through renting tended to score significantly higher on indices of socioeconomic status (SES) and political participation; and a proactive (nonfatalistic) mindset—characterized by the belief in agency rather than fate or God's will—and optimism about the future were also positively correlated with political participation and SES.

Four of the expectations turned out to be irrelevant or related in the inverse direction from that predicted: race alone did not make any significant difference in overall participation; however, blacks were slightly more likely to have signed a petition (2001) or worked for a candidate (2003); living in a favela, housing project, illegal subdivision, or low-income legal neighborhood today made no significant difference in levels of political participation, political interest, or political knowledge; there was no clear pattern of correlation between membership in local associations and political participation (which varied by time period, by generation, by migrant versus Rio-born, and by whether religious organizations were included or not[14]); and social networks had opposite effects on participation depending on the type of network—individuals with greater "bridging networks" (external connections with people in diverse walks of life) had significantly higher levels of political participation (as well as higher SES and income) than average, while those with greater "bonding networks" (internal to the community) had lower indicators on all of these measures.[15]

Whereas race alone did not show a significant difference in levels of participation and gender did to some extent, combining the two was a powerful predictor of political engagement, a relationship that reversed its direction over time and generations. In 1969, white males had the highest participation scores and black females the lowest (with the highest white female scores still below the lowest black male scores). When these same communities were surveyed thirty-four years later, there was a total gender reversal. Females had higher participation scores then men (on the same index as in 1969), but the pattern within gender groups remained that the lighter the skin color, the greater the participation.

Three unanticipated factors were found to be strongly related to participation levels: proximity of original community to upscale residential areas and the city center, recognition of stigma in its multitude of forms, and personal or family exposure to violence. Unpacking each of these revealed the following:

Proximity: Being raised in favelas that were closer to the upscale neighborhoods of the "South Zone" (such as Ipanema, Leblon, Gávea, and Lagoa) was a strong determinant of greater political awareness and participation (and overall higher socioeconomic status), as opposed to being raised in working-class areas of the North Zone (such as Ramos or Bomsuccesso) or in the still more peripheral Fluminense Lowlands (Baixada Fluminense) in such municipalities as Duque de Caxias, Nova Iguaçu, São João de Meriti, or Nilópolis. Early contact with the middle and upper echelons of society, and with a broader mix of people through living in (or spending time) in the homes of the "madams" where their mothers were live-in maids during the week, created a worldview, a template of speech and behaviors for "presentation of self in everyday life," and a set of trusted contacts in the world of the elite that conferred lifelong advantages for those raised in South Zone favelas. This is not due to inherent differences in the favelas themselves, in their size, internal structure, or composition, or by their degree of independence from the drug traffic. By the end of the restudy in 2005, virtually all favelas were controlled by drug traffickers, except for those controlled by militias (death squads). It is due to the knowledge and networks that come with daily exposure (even immersion) in the life of the elites—whose homes they lived in during weekdays when their mothers were the maids, cooks, and nannies of the "madams." The children in the South Zone favelas played soccer and often went to public school with the children of the nearby affluent neighborhoods—and learned how about "presentation of self" accordingly. Among the 750 original interviewees, all but two had lived in the South Zone. Spatial location turned out to be critical.

Stigma: The greater the recognition of the many forms of stigma and discrimination in society, the higher the level of political participation. The question was "Do you perceive discrimination, and if so on what basis?" The answers in order of frequency were residing in a favela; skin color, overall appearance or "presentation of self" (*pinta*), place of origin, residence in the periphery (Baixada Fluminense) or in the North Zone, gender, and residence in a public-housing complex (*conjunto*). Figure 12.6 shows the findings for the original sample. The pattern for the descendents is similar, but the sense of discrimination was lower overall. Across the board, those with high scores on the index of perceived stigma were more likely to take political action: to vote, sign petitions, attend political meetings and demonstrations, and work for political candidates. They are also the ones most likely to believe that "all Brazilians should participate," rather than "leaving decisions in the hands of the politicians."[16] This might be due to the fact that the more experience each person has, the harder it is to ignore the multiple nuanced forms of exclusion and the more likely to act on his or her own behalf.

The new random sample of sixteen- to sixty-five-year-olds in the same communities perceived even more discrimination than the original interviewees, in contrast to the children and grandchildren of the original sample, who perceived less discrimination.[17] On average, 10 percent more of the 2003 sample said "yes" to each dimension of stigma than the original interviewees did in 2001 (as shown in the bar graph above). Prejudice against migrants (anyone not Rio-born) rose the most (17 percent), while the stigma of living in the Baixada declined. The order of perceived discrimination was similar, although the 2003 sample felt it had become relatively more detrimental to live in a housing project or in the North Zone and less prejudicial to live in the Baixada.[18]

Violence: The greater the direct experience of violence, the less likely a respondent was to vote or participate in community organizations but the more likely to take direct political action such as signing a petition, working for a candidate, attending political meetings or demonstrations, or affiliating with a political party.[19] This may reflect disenchantment with electoral democracy and willingness to take other actions for change, as those who scored high on violence were less satisfied with their lives and expressed a lack of unity in their communities.[20]

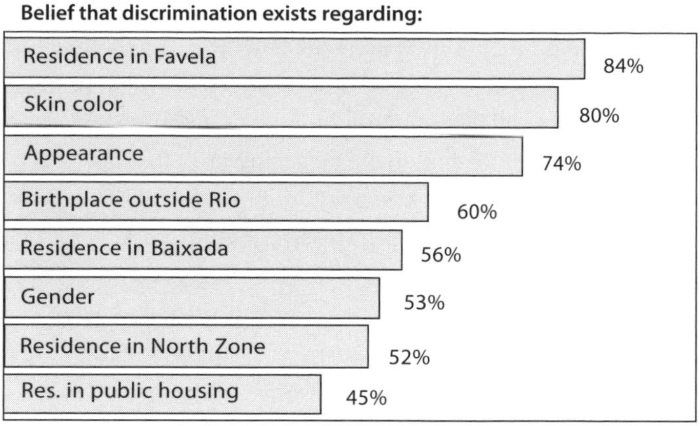

Belief that discrimination exists regarding:

Residence in Favela	84%
Skin color	80%
Appearance	74%
Birthplace outside Rio	60%
Residence in Baixada	56%
Gender	53%
Residence in North Zone	52%
Res. in public housing	45%

Figure 12.6. Belief in Stigma and Exclusion, 2003

Reflections

I see no quick fix for strengthening citizenship or building participatory democracy without deep-seated structural reforms towards a meaningful sharing of power. Even in the cities with successful experiences of participatory budgeting, such as Porto Alegre and Belo Horizonte, the poor are not full citizens as long as so many are unemployed and unprotected from police and drug violence in their communities. If the numbers of youth that die each day in the favelas of those cities were white and rich, the voices of their parents would be heard and heeded; instead, there is the sound of silence.

In my observation over the past five years, the plethora of NGO- and government-sponsored training courses for Rio's poor on *cidadania* (citizenship), "empowerment," and "capacity building" have met with varying degrees of success. However, they cannot provide reinforcement of the new leanings in a vacuum of real opportunity to exercise them. Giving the disenfranchised knowledge of the full extent of their citizen rights and how to demand them is necessary but not sufficient to give them power or opportunity.

The director of a municipal-empowerment training course for women in favelas confessed to being deeply conflicted about the work she was doing. "The women in the community are wonderful," she said, "but the program is a kind of tease—it raises expectations and increases frustration, given the lack of job opportunities or channels for exercising political power in real life. The reality they face after the diplomas are signed and handed out is a dead end." Her explanation fit with the analysis Jorge Casteñeda makes of "corporatist crony capitalism" characterized by "unemployment and a corrupt political system institutionalized to protect privilege by perpetuating inequality" (Strum 1995). This is what the newly trained community women are up against once they have been through the municipality's empowerment course.

Rio's favela dwellers illustrate the importance of Guillermo O'Donnell's (2004) effort to define democracy around citizenship, as discussed in the introduction of this volume. Several chapters in this volume reveal a democracy that functions reasonably if considered in terms of institutional and policymaking performance (particularly Santos and Vilarouca and Melo). Almeida, in this volume, points to important differences in attitudes between the "two Brazils," with one displaying modern, democratic attitudes and the poor and uneducated displaying archaic ones. But the differences lie in very tangible experiences of democracy as well. Inadequate employment, political access, and protection from violence mean that the poor and uneducated do not enjoy the full benefits of citizenship. Democracy cannot deepen without addressing the enormous inequality that undermines the quality of citizenship for the poor.[21] The words of Louis Brandeis regarding a critical juncture in the history of democracy in the United States are perfectly applicable to Brazil today. He said, "We can have democracy in this country, or we can have great wealth concentrated in the hands of the few, but we can't have both."

Appendix: Research Methodology

The restudy entailed two years of locating the surviving participants in the original research project, two years of interviewing these survivors and their children and grandchildren, two years of interviewing a random sample of residents and leaders in the same favela communities, and a year of in-depth interviews with the most and least successful survivors and with activist leaders, planners, policymakers, and academics as summarized in table 12.4.

The original 1968–1969 study was conducted in three communities at varying distances from the center of the city: Catacumba in the upscale South Zone; Nova Brasília in the industrial North Zone; and Duque de Caxias, a municipality in the Baixada Fluminense, where the sample was divided between favelas and unserviced subdivisions called *loteamentos*. In each community, two hundred people were selected at random (males and females sixteen to sixty-five

Table 12.4. Longitudinal Panel Study: Qualitative and Quantitative Methods

Phase	Activities
I	Exploratory research (1999) Feasibility study Ethnographic and contextual research
II	Multigenerational Restudy Questionnaire and life histories for original group, their children, and grandchildren (2000–2003)
III	Restudy of communities New random and leadership samples (2003–2004)

years old), and fifty leaders were selected by positional and reputational purposive sampling. The total number of interviewees was then 750.

In order to preserve anonymity during the dictatorship, only first names were recorded, along with descriptions of how to find the dwellings, given that most had no official address, lacking street name and numbers. These conditions, compounded by the strict control of entry into the favelas by drug gangs by the late 1990s, made locating the original sample members extremely difficult—especially as thirty years had passed since the original study. It was only due to the close ties of friendship and kinship maintained by these families that we were able to locate the original interviewees. The search for original study participants included the entire state of Rio and six other states.

Eventually we were able to locate 41 percent of the original study participants. In addition to interviewing these 308 original interviewees (using their closest living relative to complete their life histories if they had died), we interviewed a random sample of 367 of their children (who are at the same stage in their life cycle now as the original study participants had been in 1969) and a random sample of 208 of their children's children, their grandchildren. This gave us the chance to look at both intragenerational and intergenerational changes over four generations (as we had already collected data on the parents of the original sample). In the final phase, in order to see how the communities themselves had changed, we drew new random samples of four hundred men and women between the ages of sixteen and sixty-five from each of the original communities, and new leadership samples of twenty-five from each. The total sample size was 2,182. As the analysis yielded paradoxes and new puzzles, I conducted additional fieldwork in the summer of 2005.

Table 12.5. Where Are the Original Survey Respondents? (%)

Generation	*Favela*	*Public housing project*	*Legal neighborhood*
Random sample			
Original Interviewees	37	25	34
Children	36	16	44
Grandchildren	32	13	51
Leadership sample			
Original Interviewees	14	21	61
Children	24	17	56
Grandchildren	28	6	58

Over a third of the people from the random sample are still living in favelas, another 25 percent in *conjuntos* (public housing), and just over a third in legitimate neighborhoods, mostly on the urban periphery. A greater number of former community leaders managed to exit the favelas and establish homes in neighborhoods, but this advantage is diluted with each generation, as shown in table 12.5.

What about the communities? Catacumba had been removed in 1970 as part of a massive favela eradication program focused on the most desirable locations in the South Zone. Some of the residents had been sent to the now infamous City of God, but most went to newly constructed housing projects in the far North Zone, called Quitungo Guaporé.

In Nova Brasília the mud and wood shacks and single communal outdoor taps had been replaced by three-, four-, and five-story brick homes with electricity, running water, and (for the most part) indoor plumbing connected to a sewer system separate from drainage canals. The favela had become a commercial center in the area, grown up and over the hillside and joined with several favelas on the other side of the hill to become an enormous complex, called O Complexo do Alemao, widely known for its brutal violence and drug dealing.

In Caxias, the favelas showed the same signs of infrastructure upgrading and pervasive drug-related violence. One of the most famous drug lords, Fernando Beira-Mar, came from the favela by that name. The small lots had gradually become urbanized and integrated into the city and had lost the stigma of being informal settlements, with both owners and renters benefiting.

Notes

Chapter 2. The Partido dos Trabalhadores: Still a Party of the Left?

1. See Roma (2005) on rates of party cohesion.

2. See Mainwaring and Pérez-Liñan (1998) and Souza (2004) on rates of discipline and loyalty.

3. See also the analysis by Leal (2003).

4. The alliance issue has constituted one of the most ongoing sources of internal disagreement, with radical factions on the whole being less favorable than their more pragmatic counterparts to joining with nonleft parties. *Teoria & Debate*, the PT journal that publishes differing viewpoints on such debates, frequently features articles that speak to this issue.

5. In 1987, a time when few politicians reported an affiliation with economic liberalism, 62 percent of PFL deputies did so (Rodrigues 1987), a figure that rose to 70 percent in 1997 (Power 1998a, 58) and was estimated to be closer to 87 percent by a slightly different scheme (Rua 1995). The PFL's internal diversity should also be recognized. Its representations from the South tend towards liberalism more than those from the Northeast.

6. Hagopian (2005, 21) discusses some exceptions to this profile.

7. The PSDB's voting record in the Constituent Assembly debates would merit putting it somewhere between the PT and the PFL but arguably closer to the former in these years. The rise of economic liberals within the party and coalition-building efforts surrounding the 1994 presidential election contributed crucially to this reorientation.

8. The PSDB thus ranks among the highest of Brazil's parties in the studies of party cohesion (Hagopian 2005, 21; Roma 2005, 114–15).

9. See "Partidos começam a discutir alianças," *Jornal do Brasil*, September 13, 1999, A–2.

10. "PT reelege José Dirceu e abre para alianças," *Gazeta Mercantil*, September 1, 1997, A–8. This measure was criticized strongly by party radicals quick to draw a comparison with the PSDB-PFL alliance forged several years earlier, the "beginning of the end" of the once left-leaning PSDB, in their view.

11. "Impacto direto no PT," *Istoé*, June 4, 1997; "Bombas, denúncias e meias-verdades," *Folha Online*, June 22, 1997.

12. It is beyond the scope of this chapter to discuss why Lula and his close advisers chose this method of coping with the problem instead of others. For a fuller discussion that considers the alternatives, see Hunter (2007b).

Chapter 3. Organized Civil Society in Lula's Brazil

An earlier version of this paper appeared as "Civil Society in Lula's Brazil," Working Paper CBS-57-04 of the Centre for Brazilian Studies, University of Oxford, 2004. I would like to thank Jack Hammond and David Samuels for comments on the current version. I am, of course, responsible for any remaining errors.

1. Civil society is a heavily contested concept in social theory and a partial synonym of related concepts like social movements, popular organizations, the third sector, contentious politics, and nongovernmental organizations, among others. The debate is, in part, a definitional one, with different analysts including and excluding particular categories of actors. But it is also a normative one about the impact of these actors on key collective outcomes, such as democracy and social equity (Cohen and Arato 1992; Dagnino 2002). This chapter does not enter directly into the normative debates about civil society but simply uses the term descriptively to refer to actors who fit the classic definition of civil society as voluntary associative life between the levels of family and the state.

2. There were exceptions to this generalization as early as the 1980s. Many female participants in both movement activities and the PT exited the party in its first decade (Alvarez 1990, 239–40). Environmental organizations split, with some forming a Green Party in 1987, while others remained with the PT or preferred a cross-partisan strategy (Hochstetler and Keck 2007, 89–95).

3. Lula himself as president has regularly disavowed a characterization of himself as a leftist, and the PT as a whole has deemphasized its traditional discourse of wanting to achieve socialism over time (Samuels 2004).

4. Interview with Gilda Cabral, Technical Adviser of CFEMEA (Centro Feminista de Estudos e Assessoria), which is the Executive Secretariat of the FBO, Brasília, August 9, 2005.

5. It is worth pointing out that IBASE was also a founding member of the FBO. In addition, both the Ford Foundation and Action Aid Brazil were major funders of both the FBO and IBASE's Projeto Mapas, suggesting that a number of organizations were both skeptical *and* hopeful about the PT from the beginning.

6. http://www.presidencia.gov.br/cdes/informativos/Informativo_01.htm. Accessed July 5, 2005, hard copy in possession of author.

7. Online at http://www.socioambiental.org/website/noticias/noticia.asp?Fil...2003-10-20-13-07.htm, accessed October 23, 2003.

8. Interview with Marijane Lisboa, São Paulo, 12 August 2005. Lisboa was the secretary of environmental quality in the Ministry of the Environment in 2003–2004, when the GMO bill moved through the legislature.

9. The MST does not carry out all the land occupations recorded. Official figures tagged the MST for 63 percent (176 of 278) of the occupations from January 2003 to March 2004, with fifty other land-reform groups splitting the rest (*Folha de São Paulo,* April 18, 2004).

10. Interview with Gilda Cabral.

11. http://www.lainsignia.org/2005/junio/ibe_087.htm, accessed June 23, 2005.

12. Interview with Benedito (Dito) Barbosa, coordinator, Central dos Movimentos Populares and Movimento Nacional por la Reforma Urbana, São Paulo, June 29, 2006. Palocci continued as finance minister until another scandal months later forced his resignation.

13. Interview with Barbosa.

Chapter 4. Political Institutions and Governability from FHC to Lula

1. In other countries that employ the open list—Chile, Finland, and Poland (also Brazil during the 1946–64 democratic regime)—preference voting is required, and seats are distributed proportionate to the parties' contribution to the alliance (Nicolau 1999).

2. To fully grasp the importance of this phenomenon, one could take the 1994 elections as an example: seven out of eighteen parties with seats in the chamber did not meet the electoral quotient (Tafner 1997). This has varied and random effects on the political system, given the diversity of party systems in the subnational units. Parties that are large in some states might be small or medium-sized in others.

3. The classification is as follows: consistent alliances are left-left, right-right, or center-center; semiconsistent comprise alliances between either a leftist or rightist party with centrist ones; finally, inconsistent alliances include those that join leftist and rightist parties.

4. In 1998, without "verticalization," there were twelve candidates for president, but in 2002 this number dropped to six.

5. Notwithstanding all the incentives of the Brazilian system towards individualism, one should notice that there is one highly institutionalized party, with large percentages of party votes and a strategy clearly aimed at valuing the party's reputation: the Workers' Party (PT). The singularity of PT's behavior runs counter to conclusions that assume immediate automatic associations among OLPR, individualism, and antiparty behavior. Further examples converge on this point, such as the centralized party structures of Chile pre-1973, which checked individualism through resources access (Samuels 1997), and Finland, which had ideological and structured parties (Nicolau 1996). Samuels has pointed out that in "electoral systems centered on the candidate, the party structure affects the balance between collective and individual reputations, in spite of the electoral structure's influence" (1997, 500). For this reason, regardless of the individualistic incentives of the open-list system, the PT displays a party structure that inhibits that sort of behavior. This is done, by and large, through internal rules that favor discipline and a strict selection process pervaded by internal democracy. Together, these features fit well with the strategy of investing in the party's collective reputation (Leal 2003).

6. These criteria were set in Tafner's work (1997, 15). Some adjustments and changes in the classification were necessary here.

7. The 1989 presidential election was a stand-alone affair, unaccompanied by any other contest. From 1994 on, the electoral calendar provides for the concurrent election of the president, state governors, and federal and state deputies, all of them for four-year terms. Senate elections also occur on the same date every four years, but they rotate alternately between two-thirds and one-third of the seats. Senators have an eight-year term.

8. Nonetheless, the authors estimate a somewhat low influence of party identification on presidential contests. Taking into account voters who would vote for the candidate of their favorite party and those who would choose strategic voting within the same ideological bloc, the study estimates that party identification could have influenced the vote of only 30 percent of the electorate (compare Ames, Baker, and Rennó, this volume).

9. We should not ignore the fact that this interpretation is based on aggregate data.

10. A further and important dimension that we cannot address here is related to the political and budgetary powers of each ministry. Current measures do not capture this sort of variable and presuppose that all ministries have equal weight.

11. There are several underlying premises worth clarifying. The chief hypothesis—the

greater the coalescence rate, the more disciplined the behavior of governing parties—is linked to office-seeking goals. And yet political parties have other aims: vote maximization and the pursuit of their preferred policies. The former is accounted for by the second hypothesis: as the presidential term elapses, discipline falls due to future electoral considerations. The latter is accounted for by the third hypothesis: the more ideologically diverse the governing coalition is, the lower its discipline will be.

12. A good definition of agenda power is the following: "decision about the issues to be evaluated and determination of the steps and the sequence of procedures to be followed throughout the decision-making process" (Figueiredo and Limongi 1999, 69).

13. "It is fair to assume then that the dynamics underlying executive-legislative interaction will take on entirely different features in the absence of propresident agenda power. If the administration is unable to manipulate strategically the distribution of deputies' preferences and hold the agenda on the floor by stealing time from measures initiated within the legislature, one can imagine a scenario of extreme uncertainty for the president's intentions. Not only would deputies acquire greater legislative influence, their rate of cooperation with the president would tend to be systematically smaller" (Santos 1997, 477).

14. The president has also the power of vetoing bills, partly or totally, passed in Congress. These vetoes can be overridden by the absolute majority of both houses.

15. The Council of Leaders (Colégio de Líderes) is a decision-making body made up of party leaders and by the government whip leader (who has voice rights only). The council's decisions are expected to be reached by consensus; otherwise, the vote of each leader carries the weight of their respective parties on the floor in order to reach an absolute majority. Such a coalition can, therefore, determine the chamber's agenda (Pacheco and Mendes 1998). There is disagreement, however, about the real importance of the council: "As a forum for multiparty negotiations and bargaining, the *Colégio* was most active on unidimensional issues where lines of compromise were clear. On more complex, multidimensional issues, major actors must actively have sought compromise before the *Colégio* could play a role. Issues involving powerful states had to be resolved by the states and the executive before party leaders got involved" (Ames 2001, 242).

16. In accordance with the standing rules, leaders may speak during sessions for as long as the size of their party would allow. They can also participate without voting rights in all committees, recommend votes on the floor, register party candidates to the Directing Board, and nominate "vice leaders" for their respective caucuses (Pacheco and Mendes 1998).

17. This is a glaring contrast with the 1946 Constitution: "The lower chamber's standing orders did not allow legislative leaders to send bills to more than one standing committee. This implies that legislative leaders could not oppose the gate-keeping power of committees. Moreover, legislative leaders did not possess an institutional mechanism by which they could withdraw proposals from committees and send them to the floor" (Amorim Neto and Santos 2001).

18. The 1988 Constitution endowed committees with the power to pass bills without floor consideration under certain conditions, a prerogative called conclusive power. Notwithstanding its importance, data show that only 29 percent of all bills turned into law go through the ordinary process until reaching the floor, and only 16 percent are passed by the conclusive power. The majority, about 55 percent between 1988 and 1994, are evaluated and approved after urgency requests (Figueiredo and Limongi 1999).

19. The "electoral connection" theory holds that congressmen, as rational actors, have reelection as their primary goal. Therefore, they also have as a fundamental object to promote policies that benefit specific constituencies—typically their home district. As a result, representatives eventually develop a personalized relationship with their voters.

20. We do not deny that individualistic incentives do exist in the electoral arena. Instead, we suggest that one will hardly find in Brazil the legislative counterpart of the electoral connection model: a decentralized and highly structured committee system, as in the case of the U.S. Congress. American legislators can use the legislative structure more effectively to engage in particularistic policies, having more autonomy vis-à-vis their parties.

21. Legislators have few incentives in the legislative arena to introduce bills of a localized type. Their bills spend much more time in committee than executive proposals, increasing chances of rejection. They are frequently passed only in the legislative term following their introduction. Besides, institutional hurdles have to be overcome, such as party leaders or possibly unfavorable reports in committee (Ricci 2003).

22. Our sample includes votes in which there was some level of conflict, eliminating consensual votes. A consensual vote is defined as such if all leaders of the major parties —PT, PFL, PMDB, PSDB, PP, PTB, PL, PSB, and PDT—make the same recommendation, suffering the opposition of less than 10 percent of those voting on the floor. Thus we performed a slight change in the procedures suggested by Figueiredo and Limongi. Moreover, we used the same procedure in selecting controversial roll calls for the analysis of party discipline in the following section.

23. It has also been verified that rightist legislators switch parties more frequently than leftist ones.

Chapter 5. Centering Democracy? Ideological Cleavages and Convergence in the Brazilian Political Class

For support during the research phase of this chapter, I am grateful to the Helen Kellogg Institute for International Studies at the University of Notre Dame. I also thank Wendy Hunter and Peter R. Kingstone for helpful comments.

1. It is often claimed that Churchill declared "if you are not a socialist by the time you are twenty-five, you have no heart; if you are still a socialist by the time you are thirty-five, you have no head." There is no record that he ever said anything of the sort, but the phrase is most frequently linked to him (and similar versions to Disraeli, Bismarck, and George Bernard Shaw). In Brazil, the line is sometimes attributed to the polemicist and cultural critic Paulo Francis (1930–1997) or to economist and politician Roberto de Oliveira Campos (1917–2001), but most likely they were paraphrasing what they thought was a quote from Churchill.

2. For a description of the project and its methodology, including transcriptions of the survey questionnaires used in waves 1–3, see Power (2000), appendix C. The instruments used in wave 4 (2001) and wave 5 (2005) are largely replications of the earlier questionnaires.

3. My use of the term *cleavage* here differs from the dominant usage in the traditional literature on party systems. In this literature, heavily influenced by the historical experience of western Europe, cleavages are understood to express enduring societal divisions with regard to class, ethnicity, religion, urban versus rural areas, etc. (e.g., Lipset and

Rokkan 1967). The divisions among Brazilian politicians analyzed in this chapter do not necessarily rise to this standard—they do not mirror ingrained fault lines in society—but neither are they mere issue divides of the type that characterize day-to-day politics in competitive regimes. They were induced by a major macropolitical transformation, i.e., the transition from authoritarianism to democracy. To capture the gravity of this foundational process and its repercussions in Brazilian political life, I use the term *cleavages*.

4. Leonel Brizola (1922–2004), a populist and pretender to the Vargas legacy, was arguably Brazil's most important leftist politician from the late 1950s through the late 1980s. He was elected governor of Rio Grande do Sul in 1958 and was a leading adviser to his brother-in-law, João Goulart, the president ousted in the military coup of 1964. Brizola lived in exile until 1979, when he returned to Brazil to found the Democratic Labor Party (PDT). An early frontrunner for the 1989 presidential election, Brizola finished third, with 16.5 percent, behind Collor (30.5 percent) and Lula (17.2 percent), leading to an extended decline in his fortunes and those of his party.

5. The PFL was founded in 1984 in the final throes of the military regime, and its party statute always maintained that the party name was provisional. In March 2007, the PFL changed its name to simply Democratas (Democrats) and began to use the abbreviation DEM. For consistency, I refer to the party as the PFL throughout this chapter.

6. The question wording by Rodrigues in 1987 was, "In your opinion, what type of economic system would be best suited for Brazil? Choose only one option" (my translation). The possible responses were: "(1) a predominantly market economy with the least possible participation by the state; (2) an economic system in which there would be an equitable distribution of responsibilities between state enterprises and private firms; (3) an economy in which public enterprises and the State would constitute the main sector, but without eliminating the market economy; (4) an economy in which private capital would be completely excluded from the main economic sectors, with all large firms coming under state control." I replicated this question beginning in wave 3 of my survey research, so there are no data between 1987 and 1997.

7. The PSDB did not yet exist in 1987. I recoded as PSDB the responses of those legislators who joined the party when it was founded in June 1988, about eighteen months after Rodrigues conducted his survey.

8. A mixed electoral system would mean that half of the Chamber of Deputies would be elected in single-member districts (as in the United States) and other half would be chosen via some form of proportional representation. How the latter half would work is open to question. The PR half of the electoral system could use either a closed list (CLPR, strengthening party organizations) or could maintain the open-list rules (OLPR) that have existed in Brazil for decades. Preservation of OLPR rules, even if for only half of the legislative seats, would likely maintain many of the problems inherent in the current system (see Ames and Power 2007).

9. Edmund Burke identified two alternative models of representation: one in which representatives act autonomously with respect to constituent interests in favor of the common good, and one in which the representative is simply a delegate of the constituents and is not free to vote their conscience.

10. On June 29, 2007, a long-debated electoral-reform bill was finally voted upon by the Chamber of Deputies. The roll-call vote was 252 votes (58.2 percent) in favor of maintaining the open list and 181 votes in favor of the closed list. This result was remarkably close to what would have been predicted by the survey conducted in 2005 (see figure 5.3 for trends).

11. Tellingly, the major examples of political reforms in the current decade—such as regulation of interparty alliances, attempted implementation of an electoral threshold, and a partial ban on party switching—have emerged from court rulings by the Tribunal Superior Eleitoral (TSE) rather than from the actions of elected politicians. The increasing judicialization of the political reform debate is beyond the scope of this chapter.

Chapter 6. The Quality of Elections in Brazil: Policy, Performance, Pageantry, or Pork?

1. The two-city project as a whole encompasses a six-wave panel (repeated interviews with the same individuals) starting in March 2002 and ending in October 2006. We only use data from the 2002 "electoral" (third) wave in this chapter.

2. Data are available at http://www.ucam.edu.br/leex/Brasil/Compet/Federal.htm.

3. Scholars have long observed the weakness of partisan affiliations in Brazil. Reis and Machado (1992) surveyed residents of Belo Horizonte in 1982, during the dictatorship. They found that 67 percent of respondents earning less than twice the minimum salary—44.5 percent of the population—could spontaneously name no more than one political party. Among respondents earning two to four times the minimum salary—24 percent of the population—46 percent could name no more than one political party.

4. In 1994, Cardoso started the campaign nearly 40 points behind Lula, yet he eventually won the election by 27 percent in the first round. In 2002, Ciro Gomes began his campaign in fifth place with about 10 percent of the vote, surged to second place with nearly 35 percent of the vote, and finished a disgraced fourth with 12 percent on election day. Volatile campaigns are also commonplace in gubernatorial elections.

5. Note that we therefore refer to issue voting as positional issue voting, which is distinct from valence issues. Valence issues are issues about which all reasonable candidates and citizens would agree (lower crime, faster economic growth, more jobs) but which lead to elite contestation over who can best achieve such goals. Our treatment of performance evaluations falls under this category.

6. In the federal deputy models, we only consider voters of the leading four candidates in each of our municipalities. There are simply not enough voters for each of the other two to four hundred candidates to include all voters. However, our coverage is still good, because votes were concentrated enough in our two cities so that 66 percent of voters in Caxias and 58 percent in Juiz de Fora opted for one of the top four.

7. These are neighborhood "fixed effects," or a dummy variable for each neighborhood. In an ongoing project, we find neighborhood effects on vote choice to be vast (see Baker, Ames, and Rennó 2006). Dummy variable fixed effects control atheoretically for neighborhood influence, which is acceptable for present purposes, since we are not interested in neighborhood effects per se in this chapter.

8. All results and further details are available from the authors upon request.

9. The statistical significance of these impacts is typically reported in footnotes.

10. For example, the change in the intelligence-trait evaluation is from "not at all" intelligent to "very" intelligent.

11. Of course, there is possible endogeneity here. Voters might arrive at a voting decision because of issue positions, then decide they like the candidate. In other analyses that exploit the longitudinal nature of our data, we do find that candidate characteristics have a life of their own.

12. The most negative economic assessment is "worsened a lot" and the most positive is "improved a lot."

13. Readers should be careful about comparing impacts across figures, because the Y axes are scaled differently.

14. Although the substantive differences are moderate, they are statistically significant at the .01 level.

15. It is important to point out, however, that the statistical significance of these findings is marginal.

16. The BNES model controls for issue positions and (as a proxy for performance evaluations) presidential approval.

17. The Caxias findings are statistically significant at the .001 level, while those in Juiz de Fora are statistically significant at the .05 level.

18. Indeed, the PMDB we considered in Rio Grande do Sul is more ideologically consistent and conservative than the PMDB in the rest of the country, where it is largely a catchall party with many ideological and strategic divisions.

Chapter 7. The Limits of Economic Reform in Brazil

1. It is impossible to determine the balance between external constraints and genuine conversion. There are some indications that Lula's perspective, especially while in office (see Power, this volume), has become more pragmatic over time and less ideologically leftist. Yet, Lula's government has accepted policy positions on a number of crucial issues that were anathema to the party up until just prior to the election, and the switch provoked significant conflicts within the party. In all those cases, one can point to clear preferences of financial markets and investors. So, while it is impossible to know how much causal weight to assign to external versus internal factors, it is clear that external factors have nontrivial effects.

2. To be fair, Cardoso also suffered from particularly bad luck as Brazil, along with most of the rest of Latin America, suffered the consequences of repeated external financial shocks, beginning with a run on the Brazilian real in 1998, followed by the Russian ruble crisis in 1999, and the meltdown of the Argentine peso in 2001.

3. Some might point out, as Power and Hunter note in this volume, that the PT under Lula had already begun to shift rightward prior to the 2002 elections and therefore Lula's shift might be more cosmetic than real. It is certainly true that the party had been moving towards the center in the years before the election. Nevertheless, the party remained consistently critical of orthodox neoliberal orientations, especially of policies such as a macroeconomic policy centered on inflation targeting, privatization in general, which the party had resisted intensely under Cardoso, or pension reforms, which the party had steadfastly—and largely successfully—opposed as well. The fact that Lula either embraced or accepted all three upon his election constitutes a marked shift rightward, even taking into account the party's movement towards the center in the years preceding the election.

4. The document is entitled "Carta ao Povo Brasilerio" ("Letter to the Brazilian People"), and is available at http://www.democraciasur.com/documentos/BrasilLulaCartaPovoBrasil.htm.

5. The quotes in this paragraph and the next paragraph are our translations.

6. The country was the single major beneficiary of private investments in the 1990s,

with projects with private participation totaling US$125 billion, more than China, Indonesia, and the Philippines combined. Its privatization program was one of the world's largest, having involved the sales of assets in excess of US$80 billion. Privatization of Telebrás—the former state-owned telecommunications enterprise—yielded some US$29 billion (including debt transfers). Almost all Brazilian states privatized their electricity distributors between 1995 and 2000, with few exceptions. All the railway system was privatized, roughly 2,500 km of roads are conceded, and most port terminals have private operators (Correa, Pereira, and Muller. 2005, 5). The nine regulatory agencies and the date of their creation are Agência Nacional de Energia Elétrica—ANEEL (Dec. 1996), Agência Nacional de Telecomunicações—ANATEL (July 1997), Agência Nacional de Petróleo—ANP (Aug. 1997), Agência Nacional de Vigilância Sanitária—ANVISA (Jan. 1999), Agência Nacional de Saúde Suplementar—ANS (Jan. 2000), Agência Nacional de Águas—ANA (July 2000), Agência Nacional de Transportes Aquáticos—Antaq (Jun. 2001), Agência Nacional de Transportes Terrestres—ANTT (Jun. 2001), Agência Nacional do Cinema—ANCINE (Sept. 2001).

7. In September of 1997, the Workers' Party (PT) sought an injunction on grounds of unconstitutionality in the Supreme Court, claiming that the articles of the General Telecommunication Law would "directly harm the federal Constitution." In February of 1998, Deputy Walter Pinheiro (PT) sued the federal government (Ministry of Communication and ANATEL) in the Federal District Court, claiming that the General Plan of granting telecommunication services in the public domain was illegal, irresponsible, and harmful to the public interest. In April of 1998, Deputy Walter Pinheiro once again brought suit not only against the federal administration but also against the Ministry of Communication, Telebrás, Telebrasília, and ANATEL, claming that they neglected the public interest and the public patrimony in the process of privatization of Telebrás and Telebrasília. In July of 1999, the PT addressed a complaint to the public prosecutor of the Federal District against ANATEL for not taking care of society's interests, both on technical matters and on procedural aspects of the law. Other measures also included an unconstitutionality suit against the creation and functioning of the committee to deal with the country's energy crisis (Melo, Figueiredo, and Pereira 2005, 45, 46).

8. *Terceirização* is a particularly strong term in the Brazilian context and far more meaningful—and charged—politically than the English equivalent. The closest English word that might have the same powerful connotations might be "downsizing."

9. According to Luis Carlos Mendonça de Barros, minister of communications at the time of privatization (and one of its biggest protagonists), the government explicitly chose the IGP over the IPCA exactly because it favored investors over consumers. For the Cardoso administration, the critical need was to encourage investments in vital infrastructure projects (*Folha de São Paulo*, Mar. 21, 2003).

10. After receiving numerous consumer complaints about the agencies, IDEC conducted a study of consumer service. The study found that service was "bad" for seven regulatory and other public agencies. IDEC rated the seven on a scale of 0 to 10 and found the average score was 4.2. In addition, at the end of 2003, the Auditor General identified failures to achieve quality and universalization of access goals for fixed-line telephony in ninety-two out of one hundred municipalities surveyed in July and August 2003. Despite this, ANATEL had already certified compliance in 2002 for Telemar (the only Brazilian-owned private consortium in the fixed-telephony sector) and the Spanish Telefônica (*Folha de São Paulo*, Oct. 20, 2003).

11. In principle, the regulatory agencies are financially independent, as they are financed by user fees paid by the regulated firms. But, in practice, this money remains in the government's hands and can be withheld. The Cardoso government did routinely hold back some of the funds to contribute to efforts to maintain a general budget surplus. But, under Lula, the situation worsened dramatically, as the administration retained more than 50 percent of the funds in some cases, such as for ANEEL and ANP. For example, under Cardoso, less than 0.5 percent was withheld from ANEEL, whereas under Lula, the cut rose to 50.57 percent in 2003 and 56.56 percent in 2004 (*Folha de São Paulo*, Nov. 10, 2004). Although the administration backed off this indirect attack on the agencies and the percentage withheld fell through 2006, the agencies continue to face threats to their budgets and their autonomy (*Folha de São Paulo*, July 18, 2006).

12. Poverty rates have declined in some Latin American countries, including Brazil during the Lula administration. Poverty reduction, however, has had less to do with neoliberalism and more to do with favorable international circumstances that have eased debt and improved revenues from commodity exports.

Chapter 8. Unexpected Successes, Unanticipated Failures: Social Policy from Cardoso to Lula

I thank Timothy Power and Peter Kingstone for comments and editorial help, and Phillip Keefer, Sonia Draibe, Joan Nelson, Carlos Pereira, Lawrence Whitehead, Adailton Leite, and Bernardo Mueller for insightful comments and suggestions.

1. This usage is distinct from that in some social-policy literature, meaning programs that are unconditional and do not have eligibility requirements.

2. The fund's main sources of finance consisted of 15 percent of the FPM (Fundo de Participação dos Municípios, the intergovernmental transfers of states to the municipalities) and of the state's revenue from the ICMS (Impostos Sobre Circulação de Mercadorias e Prestação de Serviços, Taxes on Goods and Services); 15 percent of the state's VAT (ICMS); and the supplementary contribution from federal taxation. For a discussion of the politics of the Fundef, see M. A. Melo (2007b).

3. The municipalities in which primary education was provided mostly by the state governments were required to contribute a minimum of 25 percent of their revenue to Fundef but would not be able to draw any resources from it. This pattern prevailed in the large states of São Paulo and Paraná. Conversely, in the states where primary education was already decentralized to the municipal level—as was the case in most of the northeastern states, Rio de Janeiro, and Rio Grande do Sul—this would mean that there would be a redistribution of resources from the state to the municipalities, particularly to smaller and peripheral municipalities.

4. In the Senate Committee for Economic Affairs, the rapporteur suggested that that difference should be set at a minimum of 30 percent, reaching 50 percent in case the fiscal situation allowed it. He also suggested that the program should be implemented over a period of eight years. In the first year it would apply only to individuals over the age of sixty-four, and in the following year to those over fifty-five. In 2000, it would cover the entire population over twenty-five years of age. The committee approved the bill unanimously. It was not required that it should be voted upon the floor; however, a proposal calling for that was passed. The Senate floor, however, approved the bill by seventy-

seven "yeas," four abstentions, and no "nay" votes. During the discussions, all the party leaders praised the bill. Cardoso, as the leader of the PSDB, expressed skepticism; however, he ended up calling it a "realist utopia" and recommended the "yea" vote. Supposedly, Cardoso had stated to a fellow senator that he could not understand how such a bill could ever have passed in the chamber—to which his colleague replied that it was born in the Senate (Minutes of meetings, *Diario do Congresso Nacional*, http://www.senado.gov.br/eduardosuplicy/Rendaminima/conferencia/livroeduardosuplicy5.htm)

5. A radical wing within the party opposed the motion.

6. For Suplicy's account of these developments, see Suplicy (2002), 125–26.

7. This latter provision was introduced because the experts identified 3,700 families that would qualify, and the amount of resources needed far exceeded 1 percent of net municipal revenue.

8. The states were Amapá. Amazonas, Tocantins, and the Federal District.

9. In the first year, only the 20 percent of the municipalities with the worst indicators would be covered, in the next, an additional 20 percent would qualify, and so on until the whole group of municipalities was covered.

10. He personally insisted that the age bracket should be from birth to seven years, instead of from birth to four (Gilda Portugal, interview). Dr. Portugal was Renato's chief of staff and later became the second highest person in the ministry's hierarchy.

11. The increase of federal taxes was concentrated in the so-called social contributions for three reasons. Unlike the income tax or VAT, these do not require sharing with the states or municipalities. Moreover, the requirement that any new taxes would only acquire full legal effect in the following fiscal year did not apply to them; they can be collected three months after the bill is passed. More importantly, the key component of the fiscal debt was the social security debt of over 4 percent of GDP. This had two pillars: the actuarial disequilibrium of the civil servants' special pension system and the very large noncontributory regime for rural pensioners. While the former was essentially regressive in its effects on the population, the former was the most important mechanism for fighting poverty in the country. Cardoso, shortly after taking office, submitted a constitutional amendment for the reform of the social security system, with a focus on the civil service pensions, but kept the rural system intact.

12. The centrality of these issues within the process of constitutional change can be gauged by a comparison with other broad themes. Whereas federalism was the issue in about half of the amendments, the economy and institutional aspects unrelated to federalism were the target of 22 percent and 32 percent of all the amendments, respectively. These amendments were categorized as follows: issues dealing with economic sectors (telecommunications, public monopolies, etc.) were classified as economic; those pertaining to political institutions, decision rules, citizenship, etc., were classified as institutional; all amendments with the specific goal of controlling spending and fiscal discipline were classified as fiscal control issues.

13. The political process underlying "policies of expansion" are more likely to succeed than are policies aimed at changing the way a service is provided. This is because expansionary policies (e.g., those aimed at increasing the provision of education) may benefit some more than others but do at least bring some benefit to many different groups—they expand the social-welfare frontier. Policies aimed at improving efficiency and quality are quite distinct. They offer far less by way of immediate tangible benefits and generally concentrate heavy costs in a few particular groups (who, furthermore, are often the same

groups who benefited from earlier policies of expansion). The conflict takes the form of a zero-sum game.

14. These included D. Zilda Arns and Bishop Mauro Morelli, who were actively involved with the public debates in the social area and participated in several advisory councils for social policy.

15. "PT critica Fome Zero e pede governo 'eficaz,'" *Folha Online*, Mar. 17, 2003.

16. "Governo recebe novas críticas aos principais pontos do Fome Zero," *Folha Online*, Mar. 31, 2003.

17. These were José Graziano and Frei Betto.

18. In economic jargon, social transfers to families are not public goods, but rather private goods, because they do not meet the criteria of nonexcludability and nonrivality in consumption. Keefer's original argument focuses on the provision of public goods, but we extend his argument to social transfers because of the scale and social externalities involved.

Chapter 9. Public Security, Private Interests, and Police Reform in Brazil

Thanks to Arthur Costa, Marcus Melo, and Jorge Zaverucha for help in discussing some of the ideas contained in this paper, and to Peter Kingstone, Timothy Power, and Kenneth Serbin for comments on an earlier draft. I appreciate the comments of the anonymous reviewers for the University of Pittsburgh Press as well. As is usual, I free these individuals from all responsibility for the chapter's remaining errors.

1. Rita Pereira covered the demonstration on my behalf. For press coverage of the event, see "Carreata Lembra Vítimas de Crimes," *Jornal do Commercio* (Recife), Feb. 19, 2006, second edition, 18; and "Luto e Protesto," *Jornal do Commercio*, Mar. 1, 2006, 8.

2. While violence, crime, and insecurity are often bracketed together in Brazilian public debates, they are distinct phenomena. My focus on this chapter is on violence directed against people and crimes against life, including homicide. Crimes against property often involve threats of violence and actual violence against people, and to that extent are included in the scope of the chapter.

3. A Vox Populi poll of eight hundred people over the age of sixteen carried out in Pernambuco between November 19 and November 22, 2005, indicated that public security was the biggest concern of 20 percent of those interviewed, ranking third behind employment (36 percent) and health (27 percent). The margin of error of the survey was ±3.5 percent. In greater Recife, public security was the biggest concern for 26 percent of those polled, behind employment and health (both 29 percent) (Montenegro Filho 2005). A different, national survey of youths aged fifteen to twenty-four found that unemployment and the fear of premature, violent death were their chief concerns. The survey of 3,501 youths in 198 *municípios* in twenty-four states was carried out by the Citizenship Institute (Instituto de Cidadania) for the federal government at the end of 2003 ("Jovem teme desemprego e violência," *Jornal do Commercio*, Aug. 5, 2005, main section, 11).

4. Slum populations have increased both relatively and absolutely in many Brazilian cities. In Recife, for example, the 1913 census found that 44 percent of the city's residents (80,348 people) lived in slums, while in the 2000 census, the corresponding figures were 51 percent and 815,719 people (Alves 2006). See also Prefeitura do Recife/PNUD 2005.

5. The source of the figure on Brazil's light-arms arsenal is the 2007 Small Arms Survey, conducted annually by an organization based in Switzerland. From "Brasil Tem 80

Maior Arsenal do Mundo," *Diário do Nordeste* (Fortaleza), Aug. 29, 2007, 8. The figure of forty-five thousand homicides per year comes from the same source.

6. From "Violência Consome 5 por cento do PIB Nacional," *Jornal do Commercio*, June 26, 2007, 6. The study cited was carried out by researchers at two highly respected research organizations, the Instituto de Pesquisa Econômica Aplicada and the Escola Nacional de Ciência Estatística. However, estimates of the costs of violence in Brazil vary widely. A different study estimated the costs at 7–10 percent of the GDP (Montenegro Filho 2005, 11). The same article mentions a 2001 World Bank study that estimated the annual costs of violence in greater São Paulo to be R$14 billion, or almost four times the total amount the state of São Paulo spent on the police. For information on investments not made in Northeast Brazil due to investors' fear of insecurity, see Rosenthal (2006), 4.

7. Economic vulnerability in this study is measured by the percentage of houses without plumbing; the rate of formal-sector employment; the child poverty rate; the extent of overall poverty; the proportion of school-aged children who do not attend school; the illiteracy rate for school-aged children; and the proportion of teen mothers between the ages of fifteen and seventeen (Cerqueira 2005, 10).

8. In July 2007, the Ministry of Justice announced that it would increase the ranks of the Federal Police by another five thousand agents, bringing the total to eighteen thousand; "PF abrirá concurso para 5 mil policiais, diz Genro," *Jornal do Commercio* (Recife), July 4, 2007, 8.

9. For example, although the U.S. population is only about 60 percent larger than Brazil's (305 million compared to 190 million), the U.S. Federal Bureau of Investigation, Border Patrol, and Citizenship and Immigration Services have a combined number of employees that is more than 4.5 times greater than the number of employees of the Brazilian Federal Police (60,485 in the U.S. agencies as of December 2007 compared to 13,000 in the Federal Police); http://www.fbi.gov/aboutus/faqs/faqsome.htm, http://www.dhs/gov/xnews/releases, and http://www.uscis.gov/portal/site/uscis, accessed Dec. 2, 2007. The comparison is valid because the Brazilian Federal Police has responsibility for patrolling borders and controlling immigration; the difference is probably understated here, because other agencies within the U.S. Department of Homeland Security, such as the Coast Guard and Customs, are not being considered.

10. They are also dwarfed by the huge profits made by a relatively small number of creditors who loan money, on a short-term basis and at high interest rates, to the Brazilian government. In this sense, one of the main effects of the activities of the Brazilian state is to generate large profits for the already rich.

11. This is not to deny that the relationship between public-security agencies (especially the police) and violent crime is contested; see Eck and Maguire 2000. Nevertheless, this analysis accepts the premise, widespread in debates within Brazil, that the performance of public security agencies is a contributing causal factor in high rates of violent crime in the country.

12. Author's interview with Marcelo Ottoni Durante, head of research at SENASP, Brasília, Mar. 8, 2006. In this sense SENASP is different from the Special Secretariat for Human Rights, which has cabinet status.

13. The incident is analyzed in a riveting documentary film called *Ônibus 174* (2002), directed by José Padilha. Information about the film can be obtained at http://www.bus174.com, accessed Mar. 1, 2006.

14. For example, the journalist and television commentator Arnaldo Jabor wrote on the day of the hijacking, "All we have are ethical protests, expressions of horror and disgust before a maze of concrete things that, just like a slum made of nouns, spreads insolubly throughout the country. The 'violence' is insoluble. It could only be solved through a conjunction of social and political changes which no government has been capable of achieving." Two years later, when the *Bus 174* film was released, he urged, "Any state or federal government has to come up with a program to end this. And there's no more room for that 'budgetary priority' talk. . . . The bloody opera of poverty and crime has to be a national priority. . . . Try anything, any plan is fine, even if it goes wrong. We must try something. What happens before our very eyes shut with fear is too dirty. The federal government has to allocate resources for it right now"; http://www.bus174.com, accessed Mar. 1, 2006, translation from original.

15. From the author's interview with Cristina Gross Villanova, head of the preventive actions section of SENASP, Brasília, Mar. 14, 2006.

16. This is the Sistema Nacional de Estatísticas de Segurança Pública e Justiça Criminal; http://www.mj.gov.br/senasp.

17. At the time of writing, November 2007, the exchange rate was R$1.79 Brazilian per U.S. dollar. Other conversions from Brazilian reals to U.S. dollars in this chapter have used the same exchange rate. State secretariats have a variety of names in Brazil. For example, Bahia uses the traditional Secretariat for Public Security, while Pernambuco calls its the Secretariat for Social Defense. Ceará uses both locutions in its Secretariat for Public Security and Social Defense.

18. From the author's interview with Cristina Gross Villanova, head of the preventive actions section of SENASP, Brasília, Mar. 14, 2006. See also "Mecanismo de Distribuição de Recursos do Fundo Nacional de Segurança Pública" at the SENASP Web site, http://www.mj.gov.br/senasp.

19. This integration typically involves formally subordinating the top leadership of the military and civil police to a single cabinet-level secretary of social defense or public security. In this respect, it is not dissimilar to the creation of the Ministry of Defense at the federal level, carried out in 1999. For more on the latter, see Zaverucha 2005, 214–30.

20. From the author's interview with Marcelo Ottoni Durante, head of research at SENASP, Brasília, Mar. 8, 2006. See also SENASP's publications at http://www.mj.gov.br/senasp.

21. "Homicídios Caem 67 por cento em Diadema," *O Povo* (Fortaleza), July 17, 2007, 12.

22. There are currently fourteen *ouvidorias*. For an example of the activity of one *ouvidoria*, see Governo do Estado de Minas Gerais 2004.

23. Author's interview with Ana Paula Caldeira Souto Maior, then-director of the program for the support of *ouvidorias* and community policing, National Secretariat for Human Rights, Brasília, Mar. 14, 2006. The latter secretariat is not the only important partner for SENASP at the federal level. The Ministry of Health administers a national violence prevention network, which had a budget of R$5.5 million in 2005. From "Saúde Traça Ranking da Violência," *Jornal do Commercio*, Nov. 24, 2005, 8.

24. These cities are Belém, Salvador, Recife, Maceió, Vitória, Rio de Janeiro, Belo Horizonte, Porto Alegre, Curitiba, São Paulo, and Brasília (Carvalho 2007, 3).

25. The analysis in the third section is influenced by a number of important works about the police and public security in Brazil, including Ahnen 2007; Arias 2007; Brinks 2008; Cerqueira 2005; Costa and Grossi 2005; Hinton 2006; Macaulay 2007; Mesquita Neto 2006; Oliveira 2007; and Zaverucha 2003.

26. Apparently, cooperation is more common in small towns in the interior, but less so in large cities.

27. Interview with former civil police *delegado*, Madalena, Recife, Jan. 17, 2006.

28. "Polícia do Rio é mais letal que a de todos EUA," *Folha de São Paulo*, June 29, 2007, C2.

29. This study might have slightly overstated the extent of the problem because it limited its focus to a one-year period after the homicides; given the slow pace of criminal cases in Brazil, a few more cases might have subsequently been brought to trial.

30. Personal communication with Roberto Kant de Lima, Nov. 8, 2005.

31. Interview with former civil police *delegado*, Madalena, Recife, Jan. 17, 2006.

32. From "Referendo deu não," *Jornal do Commercio*, Oct. 24, 2005, special supplement, 1. A statistical analysis of the positions of voters in the referendum would provide an interesting cross-section of attitudes towards public security in Brazil.

33. João Paulo Peixoto, personal communication, Brasília, Mar. 14, 2006.

34. From author's interview with Cristina Gross Villanova, head of the preventive actions section of SENASP, Brasília, June 23, 2006. Ms. Gross Villanova's examples of the refusal of the São Paulo state government to cooperate with SENASP initiatives at that time include the following: the São Paulo integrated management council did not meet; the federal auxiliary police force, the Força Nacional, had no members from São Paulo; and the São Paulo secretariat of Public Security sent no representatives to SENASP conferences in November 2005 and June 2006, despite the existence of federal funds to pay for delegates to attend. Another SENASP official claimed that relations between the São Paulo secretariat of Public Security and SENASP improved after the arrival of a new secretary of Public Security in São Paulo in early 2007.

35. Interview with Francisco Sales de Albuquerque, then-attorney general of the state of Pernambuco and president, National Council of Attorneys-General, Recife, June 13, 2006.

36. Author's interview with military police lieutenant colonel, Recife, Apr. 26, 2006.

37. From Adriano Oliveira, 2007, "As promoções na policía civil," on the BLOG do Magno Martins, Dec. 3, 2007, received by email from adrianopolitica@uol.com.br.

38. Author's telephone interview with Bob Jones, West Midlands, U.K., police authority and county council member for the Labour Party, Mar. 15, 2007.

39. Oliveira 2007, for example describes how state legislators in Pernambuco use their influence to transfer "overzealous" civil police *delegados* out of the marijuana-producing region in the interior of the state.

40. The figure on private security spending comes from a presentation by economist Josué Mussalém (2005). It is a projection for the year 2005, made before the end of the year.

41. "Hípocrita criminalidade," *Jornal do Commercio*, Aug. 21, 2005, second edition, 2.

42. Club goods are rivalrous but nonexcludable: everyone within the club can enjoy the good, but outsiders can be excluded from it (Cowen 2007).

43. Valadares 2006, 1, and the advertisement for Home Safe doors, "Deixe a violência do lado de fora" *Jornal do Commercio*, Jan. 11, 2006, 9.

44. For an example of an appeal to a "culture of peace," see Pereira 2006, 6. In criticizing discourses about a "culture of peace," I am not denying the existence of cultural causes of the problem of violence but instead pointing to the emptiness of this kind of an appeal in the absence of other, more concrete changes.

45. "Polícia reage com caçada a bandidos," *Jornal de Commercio*, May 17, 2006, 6.

46. For an important analysis of the collusion between organized crime, the police, and elected officials in Rio de Janeiro's *favelas*, see Arias 2007.

47. "Governo nega acordo, mas admite 'conversa,'" *Jornal de Commercio*, May 17, 2006, 8.

48. São Paulo's prison population increased from 55,021 in December of 1994 to 143,384 in June of 2006, an increase of 261 percent (Athayde and Lirio 2006, 27).

49. For more on the PCC, see Caldeira 2006.

50. In 2005, SENASP funds represented 1 percent of a R$1 billion public-security budget in Pernambuco. "Verba Federal para segurança ainda não chegou ao Estado," *Jornal do Commercio*, Oct. 26, 2005. There were apparently some delays in the disbursement of these funds.

51. Veja reports that the interest on public debt consumed R$ 157.14 billion in 2005, or 8.1 percent of Brazil's GDP. SENASP's budget in the same year was around R$300 million.

52. This is a rough estimate, because it only includes the declared funds for Pronasci, not regular SENASP funds that will also be dispersed during the time period. It is also not completely clear to what extent Pronasci was a repackaging of already-committed resources and to what extent it represents a new infusion of Federal spending on public security.

53. Interview with civil police agent from Casa Amarela, Recife, Jan. 25, 2006.

54. As with the expression "Colombianization," "Americanization" is inexact in that homicide rates and levels of police violence are both higher in Brazil than in the United States. The metaphor is used here to refer to a movement towards a criminal-justice system that arrests, prosecutes, convicts, and incarcerates people at a higher level, along U.S. lines.

Chapter 10. Afro-Brazilian Politics: White Supremacy, Black Struggle, and Affirmative Action

I had the opportunity to discuss the topic of affirmative action in Brazil with many peple. I think Luiz Bairros, Vera Benedito, Cloves Oliveira, Sales Augusto dos Santos, Luiz Fernando Martins da Silva, Ivanir dos Santos, Luiz Claudio Barcelos, Rosana Heringer, and Marcelo Gentil for insight and guidance. Wayne State University provided important research support. The Department of Africana Studies and the Humanities Center, led by professors Melba Boyd and Walter Edwards, respectively, were great environments for research and writing. For generous feedback, I appreciate the specific comments of professors Melba Boyd, Kidada Williams, Lisa Ze Winters, David Goldberg, Gregory Portillo, Monica Evans, Todd Burroughs, Michael Mitchell and Lori Robinson.

1. See public debate in June and July 2006 during the electoral campaigns.

2. In this chapter, I use the concepts of white supremacy and white racism interchangeably. Fredrickson has defined white supremacy as "the attitudes, ideologies, and policies associated with the rise of blatant forms of white or European dominance over 'nonwhite' populations" (1981, xi). For Feagin and Sikes, racism refers "not only to the prejudices and discriminatory actions of white bigots but also to institutionalized discrimination and the recurring ways in which white people dominate black people in almost every major area of this society" (1994, 3).

3. For a structural approach to white supremacy and racism in the United States

which is relevant to Brazil and other Latin American countries, see the recent work by Eduardo Bonilla-Silva (2006; 2001).

4. The question of immigration is complex. For an analysis that highlights ethnicity and the remaking of multicultural Brazil, see Lesser 1999.

5. Both letters can be found on the Internet at http://www.observa.ifcs.ufrj.br/carta/index.htm. and http//www.observa.ifcs.ufrj.br/manifesto/index.htm, respectively.

6. A complete explanation of the emergence of affirmative action is beyond the scope of this chapter. Outstanding analyses can be found in the following sources: S. Santos 2007; Benedito 2005; Santos and Rocha 2007; Brandão 2007; and Santos 2005.

Chapter 11. Core Values, Education, and Democracy: An Empirical Tour of DaMatta's Brazil

1. In preparing the PESB, I was fortunate to benefit from the collaboration of my good friend Clifford Young. Many of the ideas expressed in this chapter grew out of discussions with him, and thus I owe him a debt of gratitude.

2. There are many editions of Tocqueville's *Democracy in America,* in dozens of languages. I am referring to volume 2, part 3, "The Influence of Democracy on Mores."

3. This aggressively egalitarian retort is what Guillermo O'Donnell suggests one would hear in a similar situation in Buenos Aires. It is profitable to read DaMatta's classic essay "Do You Know Who You Are Talking To?" (1978, reprinted in DaMatta 1991), followed by O'Donnell's *porteño* rejoinder "And Why Should I Give a Shit?" (1984, reprinted in O'Donnell 1999).

4. Verba, Schlozman, and Brady (1995) demonstrate that American democracy does not depend only on elections. The United States has the highest level of nonelectoral political participation among developed societies.

5. The PESB was based on a national probability sample and included 2,363 respondents from all twenty-seven states. Fieldwork was conducted between July 18 and October 5, 2002. The tables presented in this chapter focus heavily on educational attainment of the respondents. The educational profile of the sample was as follows: 208 respondents were classified as illiterate (9 percent), 599 had up to a fourth-grade education (25 percent), 536 had from a fifth- to an eighth-grade education (23 percent), 735 had a secondary education (31 percent), and 286 respondents had a university education (12 percent of the sample).

6. The literature on the relationship between education and values is vast and cannot be reviewed in this space. My point here is well established in many studies of socioeconomic modernization: the more educated a person is, the more modern his or her values tend to be.

7. Core values are one thing; elections and day-to-day politics are something else. Core values have nothing to do with a specific government—for example, they do not explain why President Lula was not impeached after the corruption scandals of 2005–2006. However, core values *do* explain why, on balance, there tends to be more corruption in any given Brazilian government (e.g., either Cardoso or Lula) than in other countries were the *jeitinho* is not valued.

8. Severino Cavalcanti is a traditional politician from the interior of Pernambuco, in Brazil's impoverished Northeast. There are many colorful stories from his political career,

all of which emphasize his clientelistic and patrimonialistic style. Severino openly argues in favor of nepotism and the spoils system. In the 1990s he became the unofficial spokesman for the *baixo clero*, the three hundred or so federal deputies who are backbenchers of no political importance in the Chamber of Deputies, and promised to increase their salaries and privileges. Because in 2005 the PT ran two candidates for the chamber presidency, thus splitting the vote, Severino was unexpectedly elected to this high office. He served for only seven months, resigning when it was shown that he was receiving kickbacks from the restaurant franchises in Congress.

9. My point here is to emphasize the extremes. In doing so, I note that according to data drawn from the Comparative Study of Electoral Systems (http://www.cses.org) and the International Social Survey Program (http://www.issp.org), in a sample of almost forty countries, Brazil has the worst recorded level of formal schooling apart from South Africa. Brazil really is a case of extreme situations.

10. *Cidade Alerta* (City on Alert) was an ultra-sensationalistic evening news program that ran on the Record television network from the mid-1990s until 2004. Like its predecessor *Aqui Agora* (which ran on the SBT network from 1991 to 1997), it was directed at less-educated viewers and featured reporters and cameramen literally running after violence, homicide, and sex crimes. The program relied on cinema verité camerawork that was later overdubbed with ominous theme music and hysterical narration. *Cidade Alerta* and similar programs were accused of exaggerating the crime problem, pronouncing suspects guilty on the air, encouraging vigilantism, and creating a climate favorable to police violence. Because they benefit from fear of crime but also aggravate the same fears, these programs are referred to in Brazil as *mundo cão* journalism (literally, a dog-eat-dog world), a concept similar to the "mean world syndrome" as used in U.S. media studies.

11. In Brazil, there is a correlation between religiosity and formal education. More-educated citizens tend to be Catholic, while the less educated are proportionally more affiliated with Pentecostal denominations. Additionally, church attendance and other indicators of religiosity are closely correlated with formal schooling. The more educated a given Brazilian, the less he or she is likely to practice religion.

12. The United States is by far the country with the highest level of formal schooling. According to the CSES database (http://www.cses.org), 62 percent of U.S. adults have university degrees completed or uncompleted. In France this percentage is 28 percent, in Germany it is 26 percent, in Italy it is 16 percent, and in United Kingdom it is 19 percent.

Chapter 12. Redemocratization Viewed from Below: Urban Poverty and Politics in Rio de Janeiro, 1968–2005

This chapter is part of a larger research project based on the original *Myth of Marginality*. For the full story of the research findings, individual narratives, and implications for theory and public policy see Perlman 2008. For a detailed description of the Research Methods, see Perlman 2003. For the story of social mobility and change, see Perlman 2007a. For the relationship between globalization and urban poverty in the favelas, see Perlman 2007b. For a discussion of the concept of marginality and how it has evolved over time, see Perlman 2005.

1. Favela is the Brazilian term for squatter settlement and is often applied to other informal-sector living arrangements, including deteriorated housing projects (*conjuntos*

habitacionais) and clandestine subdivisions (*loteamentos clandestinos*). The Brazilian census refers to these as "subnormal agglomerations."

2. I wish to thank Sarah Anthony for her excellent research assistance on this chapter. Help in the data analysis was provided by a Rio-based team under the supervision of Ignacio Cano, professor of Sociology at the State University of Rio de Janeiro.

3. "Eu Sou Favela," a popular samba by Noca de Porterla and Sergio Mosca, 1994, eloquently expresses this very point. See Perlman 2005.

4. The infamous Fifth Institutional Act, which tightened repression and forbade international scholars from taking data out of the country, was passed in 1968. The following year, the author was accused of being an "international agent of subversion" and forced to flee the country.

5. For the complete findings and methods, see Perlman (2008); for a brief description of the methods used for the restudy, see the appendix.

6. Comparisons between the political attitudes and behaviors reported by our sample and by samples of all favelas in Rio, of the city of Rio, and/or of Brazil as a whole are beyond the scope of this chapter.

7. The question was: "Did the end of the dictatorship and the return to democracy have any major impact on your life? " In a more detailed breakdown, of the entire group of original interviewees, 17 percent said they did not know and 66 percent said "no impact," leaving only 18 percent who said it made any difference in their lives.

8. Courtesy of O Gobo, Rio de Janeiro, archival images.

9. This is clearly shown in the documentary *Notícias de uma Guerra Particular*. See also Valladares (2003) and Leeds (1998).

10. For further detail see Perlman (2004) and Arias (2004).

11. The drug traffic started actively in the favela communities in the mid-1980s, coinciding with the end of the dictatorship and the decision of Governor Leonel Brizola to keep the police out of the favelas. It is not clear whether he intended to protect the favela residents from the police brutality that they suffered during the dictatorship or he yielded to the pressures to protect the rich and not squander security resources on the poor. Perhaps it was a *mistura fina* (fine mixture) of both.

12. This overwhelming priority in all three generations—good, accessible, and affordable heath care—shows how poor the Rio public hospital system has become ("people only go there to die") and directly disproves the myth of the drug lords as a "parallel power" providing needed public services such as health and education.

13. We do not have data on how this compares with the rest of the Carioca population, so we are limited to comparing across time, generations, and communities in our own sample. However, the literature on political efficacy supports our findings that there is often inconsistency between perceptions and behaviors.

14. The lack of relationship may be due to the exceedingly low levels of membership in local associations in the current configuration. For example, whereas in 1969 28 percent of interviewees belonged to their residents' association, in 2001 it was 3 percent (among their children who are approximately the same age as their parents during the first study). Membership in sports clubs, samba schools, and labor unions likewise fell dramatically. The only type of participation still robust is in religious associations, which fell only from 53 percent to 47 percent. For most generations, it appears that membership in religious associations (especially Pentecostal groups of various types) is negatively correlated with political participation and with income or SES.

15. This disputes the famous Robert Putnam thesis that the bonding networks are positively related to political and economic integration. We found clear differences by the community: People in Caxias (where the favelas, *loteamentos*, and the rest of the municipality are virtually continuous) and Catacumba (in the middle of the South Zone) had the highest levels of external networks; while Nova Brasília had the lowest (and the highest internal networks). The forced relocation of the favela of Catacumba to the Quitungo-Guaporé housing projects, which was absolutely devastating in 1970, has proven beneficial over time, as the residents of the *conjuntos* have many more ties to people and institutions outside the community. Favela communities that played a critical role in the integration of new migrants in the beginning eventually held some people back from moving out and up.

16. This is a good sign if it means that those who are most aware of the myriad forms of exclusion are the most willing to take action. The question was "Do you think discrimination exists regarding [a list of items drawn from the pretest]?" The order of the answers from the original interviewees was: living in a favela (84 percent), skin color (80 percent), appearance (74 percent), being a migrant (60 percent), and gender (53 percent). The answers of the children and grandchildren were almost identical. The index gave one point for each type of stigma recognized as each presents a barrier to participatory democracy.

17. Why would the children and grandchildren perceive less discrimination? Could it be that the youth had less experience of rejection or that they were able to "pass" more easily by their presentation of self in speech and dress? Testing the perceived stigma by level of education showed no significant relationship, which rejected the hypothesis that more schooling would reduce the sense of exclusion.

18. The following conditions were felt to be sources of stigma in the new 2003 sample: residing in a favela, 92 percent; skin color, 92 percent; appearance, 88 percent; birthplace outside of Rio, 71 percent, residence in the Baixada, 77 percent; gender, 62 percent; residence in the North Zone, 61 percent; and living in a public housing project, 65 percent.

19. We created a "violence index" from the question "Have you or anyone in your family been a victim of robbery, mugging, physical attack, homicide, breaking and entering, police extortion, other forms of extortion, and rape/ sexual abuse?"

20. Interestingly enough, there is no correlation between degree of violence suffered by the family and gender, race, age, original community, following news in the media, believing in political participation, saying Brazilians have the capacity to select good candidates, or seeing the class system as closed.

21. The conditional cash transfer programs (CCTs) discussed by Melo in this volume are clearly an effort to begin addressing the deep inequalities in Brazilian society, but at this point it is too early to comment on their effect. The CCTs, starting with the Bolsa Escola and leading up to Bolsa Família, were originally adapted from Mexico's Oportunidades program. They were distributed on the basis of a standard poverty measure and not adjusted for purchasing power parity. Therefore, the early recipients were almost entirely in the poorest regions of the country and in rural areas, where in some cases the majority of residents were in need of assistance for basic survival. The extension of the program into urban areas was gradual and also started in the poorest states and municipalities. At the time of this study, there was no evidence of CCTs in the favelas where I was working. Since then the program has grown, but further research would be needed to see how it has affected Rio's poor (not all of whom live in favelas) and favela residents (not all of whom are poor).

Bibliography

Abong. *Reforma política: Construindo a plataforma dos movimentos sociais para a reforma do sistema político no Brasil—Reflexões para o debate.* http://www.abong.org (accessed June 22, 2006).

Abranches, Sérgio. 1988. "Presidencialismo de coalizão: O dilema institucional brasileiro." *Dados* 31, no. 1: 5–33.

Abrucio, Fernando. 1998. *Os barões da Federação—Os governadores e a redemocratização brasileira.* São Paulo: Hucitec.

Abrucio, Fernando L., and Valeriano M. Ferreira Costa. 1998. *Reforma do estado e o contexto federativo brasileiro.* São Paulo: Fundação Konrad-Adenauer-Stiftung.

Afonso, José Roberto. 2006. "Novos desafios à descentralização fiscal no Brasil: As políticas sociais e as de transferências de renda." Paper presented at the XVIII Regional Seminar on Fiscal Policy, Santiago, January 23–26.

Ahnen, Ronald. 2003. "Democracy vs. Rights: The Politics of Police Violence and Public Safety Policy in Brazil." Book ms draft prospectus.

———. 2007. "The Politics of Police Violence in Democratic Brazil." *Latin American Politics and Society*, 49(1): 141–64.

Alinsky, Saul. 1969 [1946]. *Reveille for Radicals.* New York: Random House.

———. 1972. *Rules for Radicals: A Pragmatic Primer for Realistic Radicals.* New York: Random House.

Almeida, Alberto Carlos. 2006. "Amnêsia eleitoral: Em quem você votou para Deputado em 2002? E em 1998?" In Soares and Rennó, *Reforma política*.

———. 2007. *A cabeça do brasileiro.* Rio de Janeiro: Editora Record.

Almeida, Jorge. 1996. *Como vota o brasileiro.* São Paulo: Casa Amarela.

Alston, Lee, Marcus Melo, Carlos Pereira, and B. Mueller. 2006a. "Political Institutions, Policy-Making Processes and Policy Outcomes in Brazil." Research Network Working Paper no. 509, Inter-American Development Bank.

———. 2006b. "Who Decides on Public Expenditures: The Political Economy of the Budgetary Process in Brazil." Economic and Social Studies Series, RE1-05-006, Inter-American Development Bank.

Alston, Lee, and Bernardo Mueller. 2005. "Pork for Policy: Executive and Legislative Exchange in Brazil." Working Paper no. 11273, National Bureau of Economic Research.

Alvarez, Sonia E. 1990. *EnGendering Democracy in Brazil: Women's Movements in Transition Politics.* Princeton: Princeton University Press.

———. 1997. "Reweaving the Fabric of Collective Action: Social Movements and Challenges to 'Actually Existing Democracy' in Brazil." In *Between Resistance and Revolution: Cultural Politics and Social Protest*, ed. Richard G. Fox and Orin Starn. New Brunswick, NJ: Rutgers University Press.

Amar, Paul. 2003. "Reform in Rio: Reconsidering the Myths of Crime and Violence." *NACLA Report on the Americas* 37, no. 2: 37–44.

Amaral, Aline D. 2000. "O processo de formulação do novo arcabouço regulatório dos serviços de telecomunicações no Brasil." Master's thesis, Universidade de Brasília.

Amaral, Aline D., and Paulo du Pin Calmon. 2002. "A experiência regulatória brasileira: O caso das telecomunicações." Cadernos do Centro de Estudos Avançados Multidisciplinares no. 10, set/2002. Temas em Políticas Públicas. Universidade de Brasília.

Ames, Barry. 1973. *Rhetoric and Reality in a Militarized Regime: Brazil since 1964*. Sage Professional Papers in Comparative Politics. Beverly Hills: Sage.

———. 1994. "The Reverse Coattails Effect: Local Party Organization in the 1989 Brazilian Presidential Election." *American Political Science Review* 88, no. 1: 95–111.

———. 1995a. "Electoral Rules, Constituency Pressures, and Pork Barrel: Bases of Voting in the Brazilian Congress." *Journal of Politics* 57, no. 2: 324–43.

———. 1995b. "Electoral Strategy under Open-List Proportional Representation." *American Journal of Political Science* 39, no. 2: 406–33.

———. 2001. *The Deadlock of Democracy in Brazil: Interests, Identities, and Institutions in Comparative Perspective*. Ann Arbor: University of Michigan Press.

Ames, Barry, and Timothy J. Power. 2007. "Parties and Governability in Brazil." In *Political Parties in Transitional Democracies*, ed. Paul Webb and Stephen White, 179–212. Oxford: Oxford University Press.

Amnesty International. 2005. *"They Come in Shooting": Policing Socially Excluded Communities*. London: Amnesty International. http://web.amnesty.org/library (accessed December 12, 2005).

Amorim Neto, Octavio. 2000. "Gabinetes presidenciais, ciclos eleitorais e disciplina legislativa no Brasil." *Dados* 43, no. 3: 479–519.

———. 2002. "The Puzzle of Party Discipline in Brazil." *Latin American Politics and Society* 44, no. 1 (Spring): 127–44.

———. 2004. "O poder executivo, centro de gravidade do sistema político brasileiro." In *Sistema político brasileiro: Uma introdução*, ed. Lúcia Avelar and Antônio Cintra. São Paulo: Fundação Konrad-Adenauer and Fundação Editora da UNESP.

———. 2005. "A crise política de 2005: Causas e consequências político-institucionais." Paper presented at the Political Science Seminar, Center for Philosophy and Human Science, Federal University of Pernambuco, November 24.

———. 2006. "As conseqüências políticas de Lula: Novos padrões de recrutamento ministerial, controle de agenda e produção legislativa." Paper presented to the workshop Revisiting Governability in Brazil: Is Political Reform Necessary? Centre for Brazilian Studies, University of Oxford, May 26.

Amorim Neto, Octavio, Gary Cox, and Mathew McCubbins. 2003. "Agenda Power in Brazil's Câmara dos Deputados, 1989–98." *World Politics* 55, no. 4: 550–78.

Amorim Neto, Octavio, and Fabiano Santos. 2001. "The Executive Connection: Presidentially-Defined Factions and Party Discipline in Brazil." *Party Politics* 7, no. 2: 213–34.

———. 2002. "A produção legislativa do Congresso: entre a paróquia e a Nação." In *A Democracia e os Três Poderes no Brasil*, ed. Luiz Werneck Vianna. Belo Horizonte: Editora UFMG; Rio de Janeiro: IUPERJ/FAPERJ.

———. 2003. "The Inefficient Secret Revisited: The Legislative Input and Output of Brazilian." *Legislative Studies Quarterly* 28, no. 3: 449–79.

Amorim Neto, Octavio, and Paulo Tafner. 2002. "Governos de coalizão e mecanismos de alarme de incêndio no controle legislativo das medidas provisórias." *Dados* 45, no. 1: 5–37.

Andrews, George Reid. 1991. *Blacks and Whites in São Paulo, Brazil, 1888–1988*. Madison: University of Wisconsin Press.

———. 1992. "Racial Inequality in Brazil and the United States: A Statistical Comparison." *Journal of Social History* 26, no. 2: 229–64.

Alves, Cleide. 2006. "Recife impotente diante de favelas." *Jornal do Commercio*, February 19, 2006, 8.

Arias, Desmond. 2003. "The Infrastructure of Criminal Governance: Illegal Networks and Public Order in Rio de Janeiro." Paper presented at the meeting of the Latin American Studies Association, Dalas, March 27–29.

———. 2004. "Faith in Our Neighbors: Networks and Social Order in Three Brazilian Favelas." *Latin American Politics & Society* 46, no. 1: 1–38.

———. 2006. "The Dynamics of Criminal Governance: Networks and Social Order in Rio de Janeiro." *Journal of Latin American Studies* 38:293–325.

———. 2007. *Drugs and Democracy in Rio de Janeiro: Trafficking, Social Networks, and Public Security*. Chapel Hill: University of North Carolina Press.

Armijo, Leslie. 1999. *Financial Globalization and Democratization in Emerging Markets*. New York: St. Martin's Press.

Armijo, Leslie, and Philippe Faucher. 2002. "'We Have a Consensus': Explaining Political Support for Market Reforms in Latin America." *Latin American Politics and Society* 44, no. 2: 1–40.

Associação Brasileira de ONGs. 2005. *Nota Oficial* 2005. http://www.abong.org.br. (accessed July 28, 2005).

Athayde, Phydia de, and Sérgio Lírio. 2006. "O tiranossaulo." *Carta Capital*, August 23, 2006, 20–28.

Auyero, Javier. 2000a. "The Logic of Clientelism in Argentina: An Ethnographic Account." *Latin American Research Review* 35, no. 3: 55–81.

———. 2000b. *Poor People's Politics: Peronist Survival Networks and the Legacy of Evita*. Durham: Duke University Press.

Baiocchi, Gianpaolo. 2003a. "Radicals in Power." In *Radicals in Power: The Workers' Party (PT) and Experiments in Urban Democracy in Brazil*, ed. Gianpaolo Baiocchi. London: Zed Books.

———. 2003b. *Radicals in Power: The Worker's Party and Experiments in Urban Democracy in Brazil*. New York: Palgrave.

Baker, Andy. 2001 "The Art of Subtle Persuasion: Explaining Mass Responses to Market Reform in Brazil and Mexico." PhD diss., University of Wisconsin, Madison.

———. 2002. "Reformas liberalizantes e aprovação presidencial: A politização dos debates da política econômica no Brasil." *Dados* 45, no. 1: 77–98.

Baker, Andy, Barry Ames, and Lucio R. Rennó. 2006. "Social Context and Campaign Volatility in New Democracies: Networks and Neighborhoods in Brazil's 2002 Elections." *American Journal of Political Science* 50, no. 2: 379–96.

Banck, Geert A. 1999. "Clientelism and Brazilian Political Process: Production and Consumption of a Problematic Concept." In *Modernization, Leadership, and Participation: Theretical Issues in Development Sociology*, ed. Peter J. M. Naas and Patricio Silva. Leiden: Leiden University Press.

Banco Central do Brasil. 2004. "Dívida pública." http://www.bcb.gov.br/?DIVPUB. (accessed Jan. 1, 2007).
Baquero, Marcelo. 1994. "O desencanto com a democracia: Análise do comportamento dos gaúchos nas eleições de 1994." *Opinião Pública* 2, no. 2: 49–60.
Barbosa, Lívia. 1992. *O jeitinho brasileiro, ou a arte de ser mais igual que os outros*. Rio de Janeiro: Editora Campus.
Barcelos, Luiz Claudio. 1999. "Struggling in Paradise: Racial Mobilization and the Contemporary Black Movement in Brazil." In *From Indifference to Inequality: Race in Contemporary Brazil*, ed. Rebecca Reichmann. University Park: Pennsylvania State University Press.
Bartolini, Stefano, and Peter Mair. 2001. "Challenges to Contemporary Political Parties." In *Political Parties and Democracy*, ed. Larry Diamond and Richard Gunther. Baltimore: Johns Hopkins University Press.
Bayley, David H. 1985. *Patterns of Policing: A Comparative International Analysis*. New Brunswick, NJ: Rutgers University Press.
Beato Filho, Cláudio C., Bráulio Figueiredo Alves, and Ricardo Tavares. 2005. "Crime, Police and Urban Space." Working Paper Number CBS-65-05, Centre for Brazilian Studies, University of Oxford.
Benedito, Vera Lucia. 2005. "The Quest for Afro-Brazilians' Equal Opportunity: The Articulations of Affirmative Action Policies and Programs by Afro-Brazilian Advocacy Organizations and the State in Brazil, 1990–2004." PhD diss., Michigan State University.
Bento, Maria Aparecida Silva. 1998. *Cidadania em preto e branco: Discutindo as relações raciais*. São Paulo: Editora Ática.
Bernardino, Joaze, and Daniela Galdino, eds. 2004. *Levando a raca a sério: Ação afirmativa e universidade*. Rio de Janeiro: DP & A.
Blais, André. 2004. "How Many Voters Change Their Minds in the Month Preceding an Election?" *PS: Political Science and Politics* 37:801–3.
Bonilla-Silva, Eduardo. 2001. *White Supremacy and Racism in the Post-Civil Rights Era*. Boulder: Lynne Rienner.
———. 2006. *Racism without Racists: Color-Blind Racism and the Persistence of Racial Inequality in the United States*. Lanham, MD: Rowman & Littlefield.
Brandão, André Augusto, ed. 2007. *Cotas raciais no Brasil: A primeira avaliação*. Rio de Janeiro: DP & A.
Brazil. Câmara dos Deputados. Comissão Especial sobre Pobreza. 1999. *Relatório final*. Brasília.
Brazil. Câmara dos Deputados. 2000. *Regimento interno da Câmara dos Deputados*. Brasília: Centro de Documentação e Informação.
———. Casa Civil. 2003. "Análise e avaliação do papel das agências reguladoras no atual arranjo institucional brasileiro." Relatório do Grupo de Trabalho Interministerial.
Brazil. 1988. *Constituição da República Federativa do Brasil*. Brasilia: República Federativa do Brasil, 1988.
Brinks, Daniel. 2008. *The Judicial Response to Police Killings in Latin America*. New York: Cambridge University Press.
Brogden, Mike, and Preeti Nijhar. *Community Policing: National and International Models and Approaches*. Uffculme, UK: Willan, 2005.
Burdick, John. 1995. "Brazil's Black Consciousness Movement." In *Fighting for the Soul*

of Brazil, ed. Kevin Danaher and Michael Shellenberger. New York: Monthly Review Press.

———. 1998a. *Blessed Anastacia: Women, Race, and Popular Christianity in Brazil*. New York: Routledge.

———. 1998b. "The Lost Constituency of Brazil's Black Movements." *Latin American Perspectives* 25, no. 1: 136–55.

———. 2005. "Why Is the Black Evangelical Movement Growing in Brazil?" *Journal of Latin American Studies* 37:311–32.

Burton, Michael G., and John Higley. 1987. "Elite Settlements." *American Sociological Review* 52: 295–307.

Butler, Kim D. 1998. *Freedoms Given, Freedoms Won: Afro-Brazilians in Post-Abolition São Paulo and Salvador*. New Brunswick, NJ: Rutgers University Press.

Caldeira, Teresa Pires do Rio. 2003. *Cidade de muros: Crime, segregação e cidadania em São Paulo*. 2nd ed. São Paulo: Editora 3/Editora USP.

———. 2006. "'I Came to Sabotage Your Reasoning!': Violence and Resignifications of Justice in Brazil." In *Law and Disorder in the Postcolony*, ed. Jean Comaroff and John Comaroff, 102–49. Chicago: University of Chicago Press.

Campbell, Angus, Philip E. Converse, Warren E. Miller, and Donald Stokes. 1960. *The American Voter*. New York: Wiley Press.

Cano, Ignacio. 1999. *Letalidade da ação policial no Rio de Janeiro: A atuação da justiça militar*. Rio de Janeiro: ISER.

Cardia, Nancy. 2000. "Urban Violence in São Paulo." Working Paper no. 33, Woodrow Wilson International Center for Scholars.

Cardoso, Hamilton Bernardes. 1984. "Movimento negro: é preciso." In *Afrodiaspora*. 2, no. 3: (Oct. 1983–Jan. 1984): 43–58.

Cardoso, Marcos Antonio. 2002. *O movimento negro em Belo Horizonte: 1978–1998*. Belo Horizonte: Maza Edicões.

Carey, John, and Matthew Shugart. 1995. "Incentives to Cultivate a Personal Vote: A Rank Ordering of Electoral Formulas." *Electoral Studies* 14, no. 4: 417–39.

Carreirão, Yan de Souza, and Maria D'Alva G. Kinzo. 2004. "Partidos políticos, preferência partidária e decisão eleitoral no Brasil (1989/2002)." *Dados* 47, no. 1: 131–68.

Carreirão, Yan, and Pedro Alberto Barbetta. 2004. "A eleição presidencial de 2002: A decisão de voto na região da Grande São Paulo." *Revista Brasileira de Ciencias Sociais* 19, no. 56: 56–79.

Carvalho, Jailton de. 2007. "Contra a violência, mais Bolsas." *O Globo* (Rio de Janeiro), August 5, 2007, 3.

Carvalho, José Jorge de. 2007. *Inclusão étnica e racial no Brasil: A questão das cotas no ensino superior*. 2nd ed. São Paulo: Attar Editorial.

Casteñada, Jorge, 1994. "Latin America's Turn to the Left." *Foreign Affairs*, 35–38.

Castro Santos, Maria Helena de. 1997. "Governabilidade, governança e democracia: Criação de capacidade governativa e relações executivo-legislativo no Brasil pos-Constituinte." *Dados* 40, no. 3: 335–76.

Cavallaro, James, and Raquel Ferreira Dodge. 2007. "Understanding the São Paulo Attacks." *ReVista (Harvard Review of Latin America)* 6, no. 3 (Spring): 53–55.

Cavalleiro, Eliane, ed. 2001. *Racismo e anti-racismo na educação: Repensando nossa escola*. São Paulo: Summus.

Cerquira, Daniel. 2005. "O jogo dos sete mitos e a miséria da segurança pública no

Brasil." Paper presented at the I International Seminar on Public Security, Nucleus for the Study of Coercive Institutions, Federal University of Pernambuco, September 12.

Cerqueira, Daniel, and Waldir Lobão. 2003. "Planejamento Estratégico da Segurança Pública." *Conjuntura Econômica* 57, no. 3 (March): 54–57.

Cohen, Jean L., and Andrew Arato. 1992. *Civil Society and Political Theory*. Cambridge, MA: MIT Press.

Collucci, Cláudia, and Daniela Tófoli. 2006. "Votação do estatuto racial fica para 2007." *Folha Online*, July 7 (accessed on July 29, 2006).

Conlutas, N. D. *Conheça a conlutas*. http://www.conlutas.org.br/index.php?sc=21 (accessed November 4, 2006).

Converse, Philip E. 1964. "The Nature of Belief Systems in Mass Publics." In *Ideology and Discontent*, ed. David E. Apter. New York: Free Press.

Coordenação dos Movimento Sociais. 2004a. "Carta de São Paulo por um 2004 de Organização, mobilização e mudança." http://www.ivanvalente.com.br/CANAIS/noticias/2004/02_NOT/CMS_Coordenacao_Nacional_de_Movimentos_Sociais.htm (accessed Mar. 27, 2004).

———. 2004b. *Mobilização pelo Desenvolvimento Nacional com Soberania e Valorização do Trabalho* 2003. http://www.alainet.org (accessed Mar. 27, 2004).

Corrales, Javier. 2006. "The Many Lefts of Latin America." *Foreign Policy*, issue 157 (Nov./Dec.): 44–51.

———. "Hugo Boss." *Foreign Policy*, issue 152 (Jan./Feb.): 32–40.

Correa, Paulo, Carlos Pereira, and Bernardo Mueller. 2006. *Regulatory Governance in Infrastructure Industries. Assessment and Measurement of Brazilian Regulators*. Washington, DC: World Bank Publications.

Costa, Arthur Trindade Maranhão, and Bruno Grossi. 2005. "Relações intergovernmentais e segurança pública: Uma análise do Fundo Nacional de Segurança Pública." Unpublished paper.

Covin, David. 2006. *The Unified Black Movement in Brazil, 1978–2002*. Jefferson, NC: McFarland & Company.

Cowen, Tyler. 2007. "Public Goods and Externalities." In *The Concise Encyclopedia of Economics*. http://www.econlib.org/LIBRARY/Enc/PublicGoodsandExternalities.html (accessed Nov. 7, 2007).

Craveiro, Antônio C. de Norões. 1998. "O debate sobre o sistema eleitoral brasileiro: Alocação desproporcional, coligações e transferência de votos." Master's thesis, IUPERJ.

Crook, Larry, and Randal Johnson, eds. 1999. *Black Brazil: Culture, Identity, and Social Mobilization*. Los Angeles: UCLA Latin American Studies.

Cumper, Peter. 2005. Review of *People Out of Place: Globalization, Human Rights, and the Citizenship Gap*, ed. Alison Brysk and Gershon Shafir. *Human Rights Review* 6, no. 2 (Jan.–Mar.): 113–14.

Da Silva, Benedita, Medea Benjamin, and Maisa Mendonça. 1997. *Benedita da Silva: An Afro-Brazilian Woman's Story of Politics and Love*. Oakland, CA: Institute for Food and Development Policy.

Dagnino, Evelina, ed. 2002. *Sociedade civil e espaços públicos no Brasil*. São Paulo: Paz e Terra/Unicamp.

———. 2004. "¿Sociedade civil, participação e cidadania: De que estamos falando?" In *Políticas de ciudadanía y sociedad civil en tiempos de globalización*, ed. Daniel Mato. Caracas: FACES, Universidad Central de Venezuela.

Dahl, Robert. 1971. *Polyarchy: Participation and Opposition*. New Haven: Yale University Press.

Dalmoro, Jefferson, and David Fleischer. 2005. "Eleição proporcional: Os efeitos das coligações e o problema da proporcionalidade. Um estudo sobre as eleições de 1994, 1998 e 2002 para a Câmara dos Deputados." In Krause and Schmitt, *Partidos e coligações eleitorais no Brasil*.

DaMatta, Roberto. 1978. *Carnavais, malandros e heróis: Para uma sociologia do dilema brasileiro*. Rio de Janeiro: Zahar Editores.

———. 1984. *A casa e a rua: Espaço, cidadania, mulher e morte no Brasil*. São Paulo: Brasiliense.

———. 1991. *Carnival, Rogues, and Heroes: An Interpretation of the Brazilian Dilemma*. Notre Dame, IN: University of Notre Dame Press.

Daniel, G. Reginald. 2006. *Race and Multiraciality in Brazil and the United States: Converging Paths?* University Park: Pennsylvania State University Press.

Davis, Diane. 2006. "The Age of Insecurity." *Latin American Research Review* 41, no. 1: 178–97.

De Ferranti, David, Guillermo E. Perry, Francisco H. G. Ferreira, and Michael Walton. 2004. *Inequality in Latin America: Breaking with History?* Washington, DC: The World Bank.

De la Fuente, Alejandro. 2001. *A Nation for All: Race, Inequality, and Politics in Twentieth-Century Cuba*. Chapel Hill: University of North Carolina Press.

Desposato, Scott W. 2006. "Parties for Rent? Careerism, Ideology, and Party Switching in Brazil's Chamber of Deputies." *American Journal of Political Science* 50, no. 1: 62–80.

Dickens, Charles. 1994 [1852–53]. *Bleak House*. London: Penguin Books.

Diniz, Eli. 1982. *Voto e máquina política: Patronagem e clientelismo no Rio de Janeiro*. Rio de Janeiro: Paz e Terra.

Dornbusch, Rudiger, and Sebastian Edwards, eds. 1991. *The Macroeconomics of Populism in Latin America*. Chicago: University of Chicago Press.

Downs, Anthony. 1957. *An Economic Theory of Democracy*. New York: Harper and Row.

Draibe, Sônia Miriam. 2006. "Brasil: Bolsa-Escola y Bolsa-Familia." In *Transferencias con corresponsabilidad: Una mirada latinoamericana*, ed. Ernesto Cohen and Rolando Franco. Mexico City: FLACSO.

Dreifuss, René. 1989. *O jogo da Direita na Nova República*. Petrópolis: Vozes.

Dzidzienyo, Anani. 1995. "Conclusions." In *No Longer Invisible: Afro-Latin Americans Today*, ed. Anani Dzidzienyo and Suzanne Oboler, 137–55. London: Minority Rights Publications.

———. 2005. "The Changing World of Brazilian Race Relations?" In *Neither Enemies nor Friends: Latinos, Blacks, Afro-Latinos*, ed. Minority Rights Group, 345–58. New York: Palgrave Macmillan.

Eck, John, and Edward Maguire. 2000. "Have Changes in Policing Reduced Violent Crime? An Assessment of the Evidence." In *The Crime Drop in America*, ed. Alfred Blumstein and Joel Wallman. New York: Cambridge University Press: 207-65.

FAO, World Bank, and IDB. 2002. "Projeto Fome Zero: Report of the Joint FAO/IDB/WB/Transition Team Working Group." Manuscript.

Feagin, Joe R., and Melvin P. Sikes. 1994. *Living with Racism: The Black Middle-Class Experience*. Boston: Beacon Press.

Fernandes, Florestan. 1971. *The Negro in Brazilian Society*. New York: Atheneum.

Fernandes, Rubem César. 1994. *Privado porém público: O terceiro setor na América Latina*. Rio de Janeiro: Relume Dumará and Civicus.

Ferreira, Renato, and Allyne Andrade. 2006. "Mapa das ações afirmativas no ensino superior." Série Dados & Debates, no. 4, Programa Políticas da Cor na Educação Brasileira, Laboratório de Políticas Públicas, Universidade do Estado do Rio de Janeiro.

Ferreira, Yedo, and Amauri Mendes Pereira. 1983. *O movimento negro e as eleições*. Rio de Janeiro: Edição SINBA.

Figueiredo, Argelina. 2000. "Government Performance in Multiparty Presidential Systems: The Experiences of Brazil." Paper presented at the XVIII World Congress of Political Science, International Political Science Association, Québec City, August 1–5.

Figueiredo, Argelina, and Fernando Limongi. 1994. "O processo legislative e a produção legal no Congresso pós-constituinte." *Novos Estudos Cebrap* 38:24–37.

———. 1995a. "Mudança constitucional, desempenho do legislative e consolidação institucional." *Revista Brasileira de Ciências Sociais* 10 (29): 175–200.

———. 1995b. "Os partidos na Câmera dos Deputados." *Revista Dados* 38(3): 497–526.

———. 1996. "Apoio partidário no presidencialismo." *Monitor Público* (8).

———. 1999. *Executivo e Legislativo na nova ordem constitucional*. Rio de Janeiro: Editora da FGV/Fapesp.

———. 2001a. "Em busca do orçamento perdido: Primeiros rugidos." *Insight Inteligência* 14:64–73.

———. 2001b. "Em busca do orçamento perdido: O fisiologismo, se subiu, ninguém sabe, ninguém viu" *Insight Inteligência* 15:58–73.

———. 2002. "Incentivos eleitorais, partidos e política orçamentária." *Dados* 45, no. 2: 303–44.

Filho, Mario. 2003. *O negro no futebol brasileiro*. Rio de Janeiro: Mauad.

Fiorina, Morris. 1981. *Retrospective Voting in American National Elections*. New Haven, CT: Yale University Press.

Fishman, Robert. 2004. *Democracy's Voices: Social Ties and the Quality of Public Life in Spain*. Ithaca: Cornell University Press.

Fitzgerald, Valpy. 2007. "Fiscal Strategy and the Social Contract in Latin America." Paper presented at "Social and Political Exclusion: The Challenge of Inequality in Latin America," Chatham House, London, November 5.

Flynn, Peter. 2005. "Brazil and Lula, 2005: Crisis, Corruption and Change in Political Perspective." *Third World Quarterly* 26 (December): 1221–67.

Fontaine, Pierre Michel, ed. 1985. *Race, Class, and Power in Brazil*. Los Angeles: Center for Afro-American Studies, University of California.

Fórum Brasileiro do Orçamento. 2004. *Superávit primário: Cadernos para discussão*. Brasilía: Fórum Brasileiro do Orçamento.

Fredrickson, George M. 1981. *White Supremacy: A Comparative Study in American and South African History*. Oxford: Oxford University Press.

Freedom House. 2008. "Freedom in the World." http://www.freedomhouse.org (accessed June 30, 2008).

Freston, Paul. 2001. *Evangelicals and Politics in Asia, Africa, and Latin America*. Cambridge: Cambridge University Press.

Freyre, Gilberto. 1933. *Casa-grande e senzala*. Rio de Janeiro: José Olympio Editora.

———. 1946. *The Masters and the Slaves: A Study in the Development of Brazilian Civilization*.Translated by Samuel Putnam. New York: Alfred A. Knopf.

Friedman, Elisabeth Jay, and Kathryn Hochstetler. 2002. "Assessing the 'Third Transition' in Latin American Democratization: Civil Society in Brazil and Argentina." *Comparative Politics* 35 (October): 21–42.

Fry, Peter, Yvonne Maggie, Marcos Chor Maio, Simone Monteiro, and Ricardo Ventura Santos, eds. 2007. *Divisões perigosas: Políticas raciais no Brasil contemporâneo*. Rio de Janeiro: Civilização Brasileira.

Fuchs, Dieter, and Hans-Dieter Klingemann. 1995. "Citizens and the State: A Relationship Transformed." In *Citizens and the State*, ed. Hans-Dieter Klingemann and Dieter Fuchs. Oxford: Oxford University Press.

Fundação Cultural Palmares. 2002. *Catálogo Palmares: Entidades do movimento negro e instituições de origem africana*. Brasília: Fundação Cultural Palmares.

Fundação Perseu Abramo, ed. 1997. *Desafios do governo local: O modo petista de governar*. São Paulo: Editora Fundação Perseu Abramo.

Furtado, Celso. 1971. "Political Obstacles to Economic Growth in Brazil." In *Obstacles to Change in Latin America*, ed. C. Veliz. Oxford: Oxford University Press.

Garrett, G. 1998. "Global Markets and National Politics: Collision Course or Virtuous Circle?" *International Organization* 52, no. 4: 787.

Gay, Robert. 1994. *Popular Organization and Democracy in Rio de Janeiro: A Tale of Two Favelas*. Philadelphia: Temple University Press.

Gebrim, Ricardo. 2005–2006. "O papel das eleições na luta social." *Jornal dos Trabalhadores Rurais Sem Terra* 24 (Dec.–Jan.).

Gerring, John, Philip Bond, William T. Barndt, and Carola Moreno. 2005. "Democracy and Economic Growth: A Historical Perspective." *World Politics*: 57(4): 323–64.

Giambiagi, Fábio. 2006. "A política fiscal do governo Lula em perspectiva histórica: Qual é o limite para o aumento do gasto público?" *IPEA Texto para Discussão* 1169: pp–pp.

Glass, Verena. 2006. "PT pede apoio dos movimentos, mas opção é para autonomia com 'Lado.'" *Carta Maior*. http://www.cartamaior.com.br (accessed June 22, 2006).

Goldfajn, Ilan and Eduardo R. Guardia. 2003. "Fiscl Rules and Debt Sustainability in Brazil." *Banco Central do Brasl Technical Notes* 39.

Goldman Sachs. 2002a. *Emerging Market Daily Economic Commentary*, December 3. New York: Goldman Sachs.

Goldman Sachs. 2002b. *Latin American Economic Analyst*, October 17, 2002.

Gomes, Flavio. 2005. *Negros e politica (1888–1937)*. Rio de Janeiro: Jorge Zahar Ed.

Governo do Estado de Minas Gerais. 2004. *A ouvidoria de polícia de Minas Gerais mostra o que faz*. Belo Horizonte: Artes Gráficas Formato.

Graham, Carol, and Moisés Naím. 1999. "The Political Economy of Institutional Reform." In *Beyond Trade Offs: Market Reforms and Equitable Growth*, ed. Nancy Birdsall, Carol Graham, and Richard Sabot. Washington, DC: Brookings Institution/ Inter-American Development Bank.

Grindle, Merilee. 1977. "Patrons and Clients in the Bureaucracy: Career Networks in Mexico." *Latin American Research Review* 12(1): 37–66.

———. 2000. "The Social Agenda and the Politics of Reform in Latin America." In *Social Development in Latin America*, ed. Joseph Tulchin, Joseph and Allyson Garland. London and Boulder: Lynne Rienner.

———. 2004. *Despite the Odds: The Contentious Politics of Educational Reform*. Princeton: Princeton University Press.

———. 2007. "When Good Policies Go Bad, Then What?" In *Statecraft in the South: Understanding Policy Success in Developing Countries*, ed. Tony Bennington and William McCourt. London: Palgrave.

Grito dos Excluídos. 2005. "Manifiesto do Grito dos Exlcuídos/as 2005." http://gritodosexcluidos.com.br/documentos/07_manifesto_2005_port.pdf (accessed April 11, 2008).

Grupo de Trabalho Interministerial para a Valorização da População Negra. 1996. *GTI/População Negra*. Brasília: Fundação Cultural Palmares.

Guimarães, Antonio Sérgio Alfredo. 2003. "The Race Issue in Brazilian Politics (the Last Fifteen Years)." In *Brazil since 1985: Politics, Economy and Society*, ed. Maria D'Alva Kinzo and James Dunkerley. London: Institute of Latin American Studies.

———. 2004. *Preconceito e discriminação*. São Paulo: Fundação de Apoio à Universidade de São Paulo/Ed. 34.

Guimarães, Antonio Sergio Alfredo, and Lynn Huntley, eds. 2000. *Tirando a máscara: Ensaios sobre o racismo no Brasil*. São Paulo: Paz e Terra.

Hagopian, Frances. 2005. "Economic Liberalization, Party Competition, and Political Representation: Brazil in Comparative (Latin American) Perspective." Manuscript.

———. 1996. *Traditional Politics and Regime Change in Brazil*. New York: Cambridge University Press.

Hall, Anthony. 2006. "From *Fome Zero* to *Bolsa Família:* Social Policies and Poverty Alleviation under Lula." *Journal of Latin American Studies* 38 (November): 689–709.

Hamilton, Charles V. 2001. *Beyond Racism: Race and Inequality in Brazil, South Africa, and the United States*. Boulder: Lynne Rienner.

Hanchard, Michael George. 1994. *Orpheus and Power: The Movimento Negro of Rio de Janeiro and São Paulo, Brazil, 1945–1988*. Princeton: Princeton University Press.

Harriss, John. 2000. "The Second 'Great Transformation'? Capitalism at the End of the Twentieth Century." In *Poverty and Development into the 21st Century*, ed. Tim Allen and Alan Thomas, 325–42. Oxford: Oxford University Press.

Hasenbalg, Carlos. 1979. *Discriminação e desigualdades raciais no Brasil*. Rio de Janeiro: Edições Graal.

Hasenbalg, Carlos, Nelson do Valle Silva, and Marcia Lima. 1999. *Cor e estratificação social*. Rio de Janeiro: Contra Capa Livraria.

Henriques, Ricardo, ed. 2000. *Desigualdade e pobreza no Brasil*. Brasília: IPEA.

Heringer, Rosana. 2002. "Ação afirmativa, estratégias pós-Durban." In *Observatório da Cidadania*. Rio de Janeiro: Ibase.

———. 2004. "Ação afirmativa e promoção da igualdade racial no Brasil: O desafio da prática." In Paiva, *Ação afirmativa na universidade*, 55–86.

Higley, John, and Richard Gunther, eds. 1992. *Elites and Democratic Consolidation in Latin America and Southern Europe*. New York: Cambridge University Press.

Hinton, Mercedes. 2006. *The State on the Streets: Police and Politics in Argentina and Brazil*. Boulder: Lynne Rienner.

Hippolito, Lúcia. 2005. *Por dentro do governo Lula: Anotações num diário de bordo*. São Paulo: Editora Futura.

Hochstetler, Kathryn. 2000. "Democratizing Pressures from Below? Social Movements in New Brazilian Democracy." In Kingstone and Power, *Democratic Brazil*, 167–82. Pittsburgh: University of Pittsburgh Press.

———. 2006. "Rethinking Presidentialism: Challengers and Presidential Falls in South America." *Comparative Politics* 38 (July): 401–18.

Hochstetler, Kathryn, and Margaret E. Keck. 2007. *Greening Brazil: Environmental Activism in State and Society*. Durham: Duke University Press

Htun, Mala. 2004. "From 'Racial Democracy' to Affirmative Action: Changing State Policy on Race in Brazil." *Latin American Research Review*. 39, no. 1: 60–89.

Hunter, Wendy. 1997. *Eroding Military Influence in Brazil: Politicians against Soldiers*. Chapel Hill: University of North Carolina Press.

———. 2006. "Growth and Transformation of the Workers' Party in Brazil, 1989–2002." Working Paper 326 (August), Kellogg Institute.

———. 2007a. "Corrupção no Partido dos Trabalhadores: O dilema do 'sistema.'" In *Instituições representativas no Brasil: Balanço e reforma*, ed. Jairo Nicolau and Timothy J. Power. Belo Horizonte: Editora UFMG.

———. 2007b. "The Normalization of an Anomaly: The Workers' Party in Brazil." *World Politics* 59 (April 2007): 440–75.

Hunter, Wendy, and Timothy J. Power. 2005. "Lula's Brazil at Midterm." *Journal of Democracy* 16, no. 3 (July): 127–39.

———. 2007. "Rewarding Lula: Executive Power, Social Policy, and the Brazilian Elections of 2006." *Latin American Politics and Society* 49, no. 1 (Spring): 1–30.

Inglehart, Ronald, and Christian Welzel. 2005. *Modernization, Cultural Change, and Democracy: The Human Development Sequence*. New York: Cambridge University Press.

Instituto Brasileiro de Geografia e Estatística. 2000. *Censo Demografico*. http://www.ibge.gov.br/populacão_residente (accessed March 1, 2006).

Instituto Municipal de Urbanismo Pereira Passos. 2006. "Dados e mapas." http://www.rio.rj.gov.rb/IPP.

Inter-Redes. 2005. *Comunicado Inter-redes e ABONG* 2004. http://www.forumfbo.org.br (accessed March 9, 2005).

Jaccoud, Luciana, and Nathalie Beghin. 2002. *Desigualdades raciais no Brasil: Um balanço da intervenção governmental*. Brasilia: IPEA.

Jensen, N. M., and S. Schmitt. 2005. "Market Responses to Politics—The Rise of Lula and the Decline of the Brazilian Stock Market." *Comparative Political Studies* 38, no. 10: 1245–70.

Johnson III, Ollie A. 1998. "Racial Representation and Brazilian Politics: Black Members of the National Congress, 1983–1999." *Journal of Interamerican Studies and World Affairs* 40, no. 4: 97–118.

———. 2006. "Locating Blacks in Brazilian Politics: Afro-Brazilian Activism, New Political Parties, and Pro-Black Public Policies." *International Journal of Africana Studies* 12, no. 2: 170–93.

———. 2007. "Black Politics in Latin America: An Analysis of National and Transnational Politics." In *African American Perspectives on Political Science*, ed. Wilbur Rich. Philadelphia: Temple University Press.

Kamel, Ali. 2006. *Não somos racistas: Uma reação aos que querem nos transformar numa nação bicolor*. Rio de Janeiro: Editora Nova Fronteira.

Kaufman, Robert, and Joan Nelson, eds. 2004. *Crucial Needs, Weak Incentives: Social Sector Reform, Democratization and Globalization in Latin America*. Baltimore: Johns Hopkins University Press.

Keefer, Phillip. 2006. "Unbelievable Autocrats, Incredible Democrats and the Struggle to Improve Service Delivery." Paper presented at "The Politics of Service Delivery in Democracies Better Access for the Poor," Stockholm, April 27–28.

Keefer, Phillip, and Razvan Vlaicu. 2005. "Democracy, Credibility and Clientelism." Policy Research Working Paper 3472, The World Bank.

Key, V. O. 1966. *The Responsible Electorate: Rationality and Presidential Elections, 1936–1960*. Cambridge, MA: Harvard University Press.

Kinder, Donald R., and D. Roderick Kiewiet. 1981. "Sociotropic Politics: The American Case." *British Journal of Political Science* 11:129–45.

Kingstone, Peter. 2000. "Muddling through Gridlock: Economic Policy Performance, Business Responses, and Democratic Sustainability." In Kingstone and Power, *Democratic Brazil*.

———. 2003. "Democratic Governance and the Dilemma of Social Security Reform in Brazil." In *Latin American Democracies in the New Global Economy*, ed. Ana Margheritis. Miami: North-South Center Press.

Kingstone, Peter, and Timothy J. Power. 2000. *Democratic Brazil: Actors, Institutions and Processes*. Pittsburgh: University of Pittsburgh Press.

Kinzo, Maria D'Alva. 1992. "A eleição presidencial de 1989: O comportamento eleitoral em uma cidade brasileira." *Dados* 35, no. 1: 49–66.

———. 2004. "Partidos, eleições e democrâcia no Brasil pos-1985." *Revista Brasileira de Ciências Sociais* 19, no. 54: 23–40.

———. 2005. "Os partidos no eleitorado: Percepções públicas e laços partidários no Brasil." *Revista Brasileira de Ciências Sociais* 20, no. 57: 65–81.

Kinzo, Maria D'Alva, and James Dunkerley, eds. 2003. *Brazil since 1985: Politics, Economy and Society*. London: Institute of Latin American Studies.

Kitschelt, Herbert. 2003. "Landscapes of Political Interest Intermediation: Social Movements, Interest Groups, and Parties in the Early Twenty-First Century." In *Social Movements and Democracy*, ed. Pedro Ibarra. Basingstroke, UK: Palgrave MacMillan.

Kitschelt, Herbert. 1989. *The Logics of Party Formation: Ecological Politics in Belgium and West Germany*. Ithaca: Cornell University Press.

Krause, Silvana. 2005. "Uma análise comparativa das estratégias eleitorais nas eleições majoritárias (1994–1998–2002): Coligações eleitorais e nacionalização dos partidos e do sistema partidário." In Krause and Schmitt, *Partidos e coligações eleitorais no Brasil*.

Krause, Silvana, and Rogério Schmitt, 2005. *Partidos e coligações eleitorais no Brasil*. São Paulo: Fundação Konrad Adenauer and Fundação Editora da UNESP.

Laakso, Markku, and Rein Taagepera. 1979. "'Effective' Number of Parties: A Measure with Application to West Europe." *Comparative Political Studies* 12:3–27.

Lambert, Jacques. 1959. *Os dois Brasis*. Rio de Janeiro: Centro Brasileiro de Pesquisas Educacionais.

Lamounier, Bolivar, and Rachel Meneguello. 1986. *Partidos políticos e consolidação democrática*. São Paulo: Brasiliense.

Lavareda, Antônio. 1991. *A democracia nas urnas—O processo partidário eleitoral brasileiro*. Rio de Janeiro: IUPERJ/Rio Fundo Editora.

Lawson, Kay, and Peter H. Merkl, eds. 1988. *When Parties Fail: Emerging Alternative Organizations*. Princeton: Princeton University Press.

Leal, Paulo Roberto Figueira. 2003. "A unidade na diversidade: Concepções sobre representação política e práticas organizativas dos mandatos dos Deputados Federais do PT (Legislatura 1999–2003)." PhD diss., IUPERJ.

Leal, Victor Nunes. 1948. *Coronelismo, enxada e voto*. Rio de Janeiro: Forense.

Leeds, Elizabeth. 1998. *Cocaína e poderes paralelos na periferia urbana brasileira: ameacas á democratização em nível local.* In *Um seculo do favela*, ed. Alba Zaluar and Marcos Alvito. Rio de Janeiro: FGV Editora.

Lemos, Leany. 2001. "O Congresso brasileiro e a distribuição de benefícios sociais no período 1988–1994: Uma análise distributivista." *Dados* 44, no. 3: 561–605.

Lessa, Renato. 1992. "Presidencialismo de representação proporcional ou de como evitar a escolha trágica entre governabilidade e representação." *Agenda de Políticas Públicas* 2:25–44.

Lesser, Jeffrey. 1999. *Negotiating National Identity: Immigrants, Minorities, and the Struggle for Ethnicity in Brazil.* Durham: Duke University Press.

Levy, Brian, and Pablo Spiller, eds. 1996. *Regulations, Institutions, and Commitment: Comparative Studies of Telecommunications.* Cambridge: Cambridge University Press.

Lima Jr., Olavo B. 1983. *Partidos políticos brasileiros—1945/1964.* Rio de Janeiro: Ed. Graal.

———. 1992. "Reforma institucional: O aperfeiçoamento dos sistemas eleitoral e partidário." *Agenda de Políticas Públicas* 2:1–8.

———. 1993. *Democracia e instituições políticas no Brasil nos anos 80.* São Paulo: Edições Loyola.

Lima Jr., Olavo B., and Fabiano Santos. 1991. "O sistema proporcional brasileiro: Lições de vida." In *Sistema eleitoral brasileiro: Teoria e prática*, ed. Olavo Lima Jr. Rio de Janeiro: IUPERJ/Rio Fundo Editora.

Lima, Venício A. de. 1993. "Brazilian Television in the 1989 Presidential Election: Constructing a President." In *Television, Politics and the Transition to Democracy in Latin America*, ed. Thomas Skidmore. Baltimore: Johns Hopkins University Press.

Lindsey, Shawn. 1999. *The Afro-Brazilian Organization Directory: A Reference Guide to Black Organizations in Brazil.* Parkland, FL: Universal Publishers.

Linz, Juan J. 1978. *The Breakdown of Democratic Regimes: Crisis, Breakdown, and Reequilibration.* Baltimore: Johns Hopkins University Press.

———. 1994. "Presidential or Parliamentary Democracy: Does It Make a Difference?" In *The Failure of Presidential Democracy: The Case of Latin America*, ed. Juan J. Linz and Arturo Valenzuela. Baltimore: Johns Hopkins University Press.

Lipset, Seymour Martin. 1959. "Some Social Requisites of Democracy: Economic Development and Political Legitimacy." *American Political Science Review* 53, no. 1 (March): 69–105.

Lipset, Seymour M., and Rokkan, Stein. 1967. "Cleavage Structures, Party Systems, and Voter Alignments: An Introduction." In *Party Systems and Voter Alignments: Cross-National Perspectives*, ed. Seymour M. Lipset and Stein Rokkan. New York: The Free Press.

Lora, Eduardo, and Ugo Panizza. 2003. "The Future of Structural Reform." *Journal of Democracy* 14, no. 2: 123–37.

Lowi, Theodore. 1963. "American Business, Public Policy, Case Studies and Political Theory." *World Politics* 16, no. 4: 677–715.

Lupia, Arthur, and Mathew D. McCubbins. 1998. *The Democratic Dilemma: Can Citizens Learn What They Need to Know?* New York: Cambridge University Press.

———. 2000. "The Institutional Foundations of Political Competence: How Citizens Learn What They Need to Know." In *Elements of Reason: Cognition, Choice, and the Bounds of Rationality*, ed. Arthur Lupia, Mathew McCubbins, and Samuel Popkin. Cambridge: Cambridge University Press.

Macaulay, Fiona. 2007. "Knowledge Production, Framing and Criminal Justice Reform in Latin America." *Journal of Latin American Studies* 39, no. 3 (August): 627–51.

Machado, Aline. 2005. "A Lógica das coligações no Brasil." In Krause and Schmitt, *Partidos e coligações eleitorais no Brasil*, pp–pp.

Magnoli, Demétrio. 2005. "Uma ilha chamada Brasil." *Nossa História* 3, no. 25 (November): 14–19.

Mainwaring, Scott. 1990. "Brazilian Party Underdevelopment in Comparative Perspective," *Political Science Quarterly* 107 no. 4 (Winter): 677–707.

———. 1993. "Presidentialism, Multipartism, and Democracy: The Difficult Combination." *Comparative Political Studies* 26:198–228.

———. 1995. "Brazil: Weak Parties, Feckless Democracy." In *Building Democratic Institutions: Party Systems in Latin America*, ed. Scott Mainwaring and Timothy R. Scully, 354–98. Palo Alto: Stanford University Press.

———. 1997. "Multipartism, Robust Federalism, and Presidentialism in Brazil." In *Presidentialism and Democracy in Latin America*, ed. Scott Mainwaring and Matthew Shugart. Cambridge: Cambridge University Press.

——— 1999. *Rethinking Party Systems in the Third Wave of Democratization: The Case of Brazil*. Palo Alto: Stanford University Press.

———. 2001. *Sistemas partidários em novas democracias: O caso do Brasil*. Rio de Janeiro: FGV Editora.

Mainwaring, Scott and Aníbel Pérez-Liñan. 1998. "Party Discipline in the Brazilian Constitutional Congress," *Legislative Studies Quarterly* 22, no. 4 (November): 453–83.

Mainwaring, Scott, Rachel Meneguello, and Timothy J. Power. 2000. "Conservative Parties, Economic Reform, and Democracy in Brazil." In *Conservative Parties and Democracy in Latin America*, ed. Kevin Middlebrook. Baltimore: Johns Hopkins University Press, 2000.

———. 2000. *Partidos conservadores no Brasil contemporâneo: Quais são, o que defendem, quais são suas bases*. São Paulo: Paz e Terra.

Mann, Michael. 2002. "Globalization after September 11." *New Left Review* 15, November/December, 75–92.

Mannheim, Karl. 1936. *Ideology and Utopia*. New York: Harcourt, Brace, and World.

———. 1940. *Man and Society in an Age of Reconstruction*. Translated by Edward Shils. New York: Harcourt Brace,

Marenco, Andre. 2006. "Regras eleitorais, deputados e fidelidade partidária." In *Reforma política: Lições da história recente*, ed. Gláucio Ary Dillon Soares and Lucio R. Rennó. Rio de Janeiro: Editora FGV.

Mariz, Everaldo. 2005. *Segurança privada em Pernambuco*. Paper presented at the I International Seminar on Public Security, Nucleus for the Study of Coercive Institutions, Federal University of Pernambuco, September 13.

———. 2007. "País vive fenômeno perigoso das milícias." *Diário de Pernambuco* (Recife), July 1, 2007, A10.

Martinez, J., and J. Santiso. 2003. "Financial Markets and Politics: The Confidence Game in Latin American Emerging Economies." *International Political Science Review* 24, no. 3: 363–95.

Martínez-Lara, Javier. 1996. *Building Democracy in Brazil: The Politics of Constitutional Change, 1985–1995*. New York: St. Martin's Press.

Martins, Sergio da Silva, Carlos Alberto Medeiros, and Elisa Larkin Nascimento. 2004.

"Paving Paradise: The Road from 'Racial Democracy' to Affirmative Action in Brazil." *Journal of Black Studies* 34, no. 6: 787–816.

Matais, Andreza. 2006. "Deputado apresenta projeto em protesto a cotas para negros." *Folha Online*, June 30 (accessed July 1, 2006).

Matais, Andreza, and Felipe Recondo. 2006. "Grupo protesta no Congresso contra cotas para negros." *Folha Online*, June 29, 2006 (accessed on July 1, 2006).

Maxfield, S. 1998. "Understanding the Political Implication of Financial Internationalization in Emerging Market Countries." *World Development* 26, no. 7: 1201–19.

McAdam, Doug, Sidney Tarrow, and Charles Tilly. 1997. "Toward an Integrated Perspective on Social Movements and Revolution." In *Comparative Politics: Rationality, Culture, and Structure*, ed. Mark I. Lichbach and Alan S. Zuckerman. Cambridge, UK: Cambridge University Press.

McGoldrick, Stacy, and Paul Simpson. 2006. "Police, Riots, and New Orleans Political Culture, 1854–1874." Unpublished manuscript.

Medeiros, Carlos Alberto. 2004. *Na Lei e na raça: Legislação e relações raciais, Brasil–Estados Unidos*. Rio de Janeiro: DP & A.

Mehta, Suketu. 2004. *Maximum City: Bombay Lost and Found*. New York: Alfred A. Knopf.

Mello, Luis de, and Hope, M. 2006. "Educational Attainment in Brazil: The Experience of *Fundef*." Economics Department Working Paper 424, OECD.

Melo, Carlos Ranulfo de. 2000. "Partidos e migração partidária na Câmara dos Deputados." *Dados* 43, no. 2: 207–40.

———. 2004. *Retirando as cadeiras do lugar: Migração partidária na Câmara dos Deputados (1985/2002)*. Belo Horizonte: Editora UFMG.

Melo, Marcus Andre. 2002. *Reformas constitucionais no Brasil: Instituiçoes políticas e processo decisório no Brasil*. Rio de Janeiro: Editora Revan.

———. 2005a. "Institutions and the Politics of Taxation in Brazil and Argentina." Recife: Unpublished paper.

———. 2005b. "Positive Theories of Accountability and Normative Political Theory: Are There Universal Rules of Institutional Design?" Unpublished manuscript.

———. 2006. "The Politics of Service Delivery Reform: The Case of the FUNDEF in Brazil." Paper presented at workshop "The Politics of Service Delivery in Democracies: Better Access for the Poor." Stockholm, April 22–24, 2006.

———. 2007a. "Hiperconstitucionalização e qualidade da democracia: mitos e realidade." In *A democracia Brasileira: Balanço e perspectivas para o século 21*, ed. Carlos Ranulfo Melo e Saez and Manuel Alcântara, 237–66. Humanitas/Editora IFMG.

———. 2007b. "The Politics of Service Delivery Reform: Improving Basic Education in Brazil." In *The Politics of Service Delivery in Democracies. Better Access for the Poor*, ed. Shanta Devarajan and Ingrid Widlund. Stockholm: EGDI/Ministry for Foreign Affairs.

Melo, Marcus André, Carlos Mauricio Figueiredo, and Carlos Pereira. 2005. "Political and Electoral Uncertainty Enhances Accountability: A Comparative Analysis of the Independent Courts of Accounts in Brazil." Paper presented at the 9th Annual Conference of the International Society for New Institutional Economics, Barcelona, September 22–24.

Melo, Marcus André, Francisco Gaetani, and Carlos Pereira. 2005. "State Capacity and Institutional Change: Case Studies of Regulation and Agro-business in Brasil." Final report, Project State Reform and Governance in the Globalization Context. ORT/Universidad de la Republica/Inter-American Development Bank.

Melo, Marcus André, and Jonathan Rodden. 2007. "Decentralization in Brazil." Report submitted to the Independent Evaluation Group, The World Bank Task: Evaluation of World Bank Support for Decentralization, The World Bank.

Méndes, Antonio Manuel Teixeira, and Gustavo Venturi. 1994. "Eleição presidencial: O Plano Real na sucessão de Itamar Franco." *Opinião Pública* 2:39–48.

Mendez, Juan, Guillermo O'Donnell, and Paulo Sérgio Pinheiro, eds. 1999. *The (Un)Rule of Law and the Underprivileged in Latin America*. Notre Dame, IN: Notre Dame University Press.

Meneguello, Rachel. 1996. "Electoral Behavior in Brazil: The 1994 Presidential Elections." *International Social Science Journal* 146:627–41.

———. 1998. *Partidos e governos no Brasil contemporâneo (1985–1997)*. São Paulo: Paz e Terra.

Mesquita Neto, Paulo de. 2002. *Segundo relatório nacional sobre os direitos humanos no Brasil*. Brasília: Ministério da Justiça/Secretaria de Estado de Direitos Humanos.

———. 2006. "Public-Private Partnership for Police Reform in Brazil." In *Public Security and Police Reform in the Americas*, ed. John Bailey and Lucía Dammert, 44–57. Pittsburgh: University of Pittsburgh Press.

Mesquita Neto, Paulo, and B. S. A. Affonso. 2007. *Terceiro relatório nacional sobre os direitos humanos no Brasil*. Sao Paulo: Núcleo de Estudos da Violência da Universidade de Sã Paulo (NEV-USP)/Comissão Teotônio Vilela do Direitos Humanos (CTV).

Miguel, Luis Felipe. 1999. "Mídia e eleições: A campanha de 1998 na Rede Globo." *Dados* 42, no. 2: 253–76.

Miller, M., K. Thampanishvong et al. (2005). "Learning to Trust Lula: Contagion and Political Risk in Brazil." In *Inflation Targeting, Debt, and the Brazilian Experience, 1999 to 2003*, ed. F. Giavazzi, l. Goldfajn, and S. Herrera. Cambridge, MA: MIT Press.

Ministéria do Desenvolvimento Social. 2006. *Programa Bolsa Família, Guia do gestor*. Brasília: Ministério do Desenvolvimento Social.

Minority Rights Group, ed. 1995. *No Longer Invisible: Afro-Latin Americans Today*. London: Minority Rights Publications.

Mir, Luís. 2004. *Guerra Civil: Estado e trauma*. São Paulo: Geração Editorial.

Misse, Michel, and Roberto Kant de Lima, eds. 2006. *Crime e violência no Brasil contemporâneo*. Rio de Janeiro: Lumen Juris.

Montenegro Filho, Sérgio. 2005. "Desemprego é o grande vilão." *Journal do Commercio* 11 (Dec.): 6.

Moraes, Reginaldo. 2005. "Notas sobre o imbróglio do governo Lula, 2005." *Lua Nova* (May/Aug.): 179–202.

Mosley, Layna. 2003. *Global Capital and National Govnerments*. Cambridge: Cambridge University Press.

Movimento Negro Unificado. 1988. *1978–1988: 10 anos de luta contra o racismo*. São Paulo: Confraria do Livro.

Murilo de Carvalho, José. 1997. *Lei, justiça e cidadania: Direitos, vitimização e cultura política na região metropolitana do Rio de Janeiro*. Rio de Janeiro: ISER.

Mutz, Diana C. 2006. *Hearing the Other Side: Deliberative versus Participatory Democracy*. New York: Cambridge University Press.

Nascimento, Abdias do, ed. 1978. *O genocidio do negro brasileiro: Processo de um racismo mascarado*. São Paulo: Paz e Terra.

———, ed. 1982. *O negro revoltado*. Rio de Janeiro: Nova Fronteira.

———, ed. 1984. *Combate ao racismo: Discursos e projetos*. Vol. 3. Brasilia: Câmara dos Deputados.

———, ed. 1985. *Combate ao racismo: Discursos e projetos*. Vol. 5. Brasilia: Câmara dos Deputados.

———, ed. 1985. *Povo negro: A sucessao e a "Nova Republica."* Rio de Janciro: IPEAFRO.

———. 1989 [1979]. *Brazil, Mixture or Massacre? Essays*. Dover, MA: The Majority Press.

———. 1993. "*Quilombismo*: The African Brazilian Road to Socialism." In *African Culture: The Rhythms of Unity*, ed. Molefi Kete Asante and Kariamu Welsh Asante. Trenton, NJ: Africa World Press.

———. 2003. *Quilombo*. Fascimile edition. São Paulo: Editora 34.

Nascimento, Abdias do, and Elisa Larkin Nascimento. 1994. *Africans in Brazil*. Trenton, NJ: Africa World Press.

———. 2000. "Reflexoes sobre o movimento negro no Brasil, 1938–1997." In Guimarães and Huntley, *Tirando a mascara*.

———. 2001. "Dance of Deception: A Reading of Race Relations in Brazil." In *Beyond Racism: Race and Inequality in Brazil, South Africa, and the United States*, ed. Charles V. Hamilton, Lynn Huntley, Neville Alexander, Antonio Sérgio Alfredo Guimarães, and Wilmot James. Boulder: Lynne Rienner Publishers.

———. 2007. *The Sorcery of Color: Identity, Race, and Gender in Brazil*. Philadelphia: Temple University Press.

Navia, Patricio, and Velasco, Andres. 2003. "The Politics of Second-Generation Reforms." In *After the Washington Consensus: Restarting Growth and Reform in Latin America*, ed. Pedro-Pablo Kuczynski and John Williamson.Washington, DC: The Institute of International Economics.

Nelson, Joan. 2000. "Reforming Social Sector Governance: A Political Perspective." In *Social Development in Latin America*, ed. Joseph Tulchin and Allyson Garland. Boulder: Lynne Rienner.

———. 2005. "Unpacking the Concept of Social Service 'Reforms.'" Paper presented at the conference Democratic Governability in Latin America, Kellogg Institute, University of Notre Dame, October 7–8.

Neri, Marcelo, and Francisco Rios. 2006. "Ciclos eleitorais e indicadores sociais baseados em renda." Centro de Política Social working paper, Fundação Getúlio Vargas.

Nicolau, Jairo. 1996. *Multipartidarismo e democracia*. Rio de Janeiro: Fundação Getúlio Vargas Editora.

———. 1997. "As distorções na representação dos Estados na Câmara dos Deputados brasileira." *Dados* 40, no. 3: 441–64.

———. 1999. *Sistemas eleitorais*. Rio de Janeiro: Fundação Getúlio Vargas Editora.

———. 2002. *Dados eleitorais (1982–2002)*. http://jaironicolau.iuperj.br.

———. 2003. "A reforma da representação proporcional no Brasil." In *Reforma política e cidadania*, ed. Maria Victoria Benevides, Paulo Vannuchi, and Fábio Kerche. São Paulo: Instituto de Cidadania, Fundação Perseu Abramo.

Nobles, Melissa. 2000. *Shades of Citizenship: Race and the Census in Modern Politics*. Stanford: Stanford University Press.

Nylen, William R. 1992. "'Liberalismo para todo mundo, menos eu': Brazil and the Neoliberal 'Solution.'" In *The Right and Democracy in Latin America*, ed. Douglas Chalmers, Maria do Carmo Campello e Souza, and Atilio Borón, 259–76. New York: Praeger.

———. 2000. "The Making of a Loyal Opposition: The Workers' Party (PT) and the Consolidation of Democracy in Brazil." In Kingstone and Power, *Democratic Brazil.*

———. 2003. *Participatory Democracy vs. Elitist Democracy: Lessons from Brazil.* New York: Palgrave.

O'Donnell, Guillermo. 1996. "Illusions about Consolidation." *Journal of Democracy* 7, no. 2 (April): 34–51.

———. 1999. *Counterpoints: Selected Essays on Authoritarianism and Democratization.* Notre Dame: University of Notre Dame Press.

———. 2001. "Democracy, Law, and Comparative Politics." *Studies in Comparative International Development* 36, no. 1 (Spring): 5–36.

———. 2004. "Human Development, Human Rights, and Democracy." In O'Donnell, Cullell, and Iazzetta, *The Quality of Democracy*, 9–92.

O'Donnell, Guillermo, Jorge Vargas Cullel, and Osvaldo Miguelm Iazzelta. 2004. *Quality of Democracy: Theory and Applications.* New York: United Nations Development Programme.

O'Donnell, Guillermo, Philippe C. Schmitter, and Laurence Whitehead, eds. 1986. *Transitions from Authoritarian Rule: Prospects for Democracy.* 4 vols. Baltimore: Johns Hopkins University Press.

Oliveira, Adriano. 2007. *Tráfico de drogas e crime organizado.* Curitiba: Jurua Editora.

Oliveira, Cloves Luiz Pereira, and Paula Cristina da Silva Barreto. 2003. "Percepção do racismo no Rio de Janeiro." *Estudos Afro-Asiáticos* 25, no. 2: 183–214.

Oliveira, Nilson Vieira, ed. 2002. *Insegurança pública: Reflexões sobre a criminalidade e a violência urbana.* São Paulo: Instituto Braudel/Editora Nova Alexandria.

Ondetti, Gabriel. 2006. "Lula and Land Reform: How Much Progress?" Paper presented at the meeting of the Latin American Studies Association, San Juan, Puerto Rico. March 15–18.

Owensby, Brian. 2005. "Towards a History of Brazil's 'Cordial Racism': Race beyond Liberalism." *Comparative Studies in Society and History* 47, no. 2: 318–47.

Pacheco, Luciana, and Paula R. Mendes. 1998. *Questões sobre o processo legislativo e regimento interno.* Brasilia: Centro de Documentação e Informação, Câmara dos Deputados.

Paim, Paulo. 1997. *Em defesa da cidadania dos afro-brasileiros.* Brasilia: Centro de Documentação e Informação, Coordenação de Publicações, Câmara dos Deputados.

———. 2003. *Estatuto da Igualdade Racial.* Brasilia: Senado Federal.

Paiva, Angela Randolpho, ed. 2004. *Ação afirmativa na universidade: reflexão sobre experiências concretas Brasil-Estados Unidos.* Rio de Janeiro: Ed. PUC-Rio/Desiderata.

Paixão, Marcelo J. P. 2003. *Desenvolvimento humano e relações raciais.* Rio de Janeiro: DP & A.

Panizza, Francisco. 2000. "Is Brazil Becoming a 'Boring' Country?" *Bulletin of Latin American Research* 19:501–25.

Pereira, Amauri Mendes. 1998. *Tres impulsos para um salto: Trajetória e perspectivas do movimento negro brasileiro.* Rio de Janeiro: Universidade Cândido Mendes/Centro de Estudos Afro-Asiáticos.

Pereira, Anthony. 2006. "Democracy, Citizenship, and Police Procedure in New Orleans: The Importance of the Local Context for Defining Rights." In *Uniform Behavior: Police Localism and National Politics*, ed. Andrea McArdle and Stacey McGoldrick. New York: Palgrave Macmillan.

Pereira, Anthony, and Mark Ungar. 2004. "The Persistence of the 'Mano Dura': Authoritarian Legacies and Policing in Brazil and the Southern Cone." In *Authoritarian Legacies in Southern Europe and Latin America*, ed. Paola Cesarini and Katherine Hite. South Bend, IN.: University of Notre Dame Press: 263–304.

Pereira, Carlos, and Bernardo Mueller. 2000. "Uma teoria da preponderância do Poder Executivo: O sistema de comissões no Legislativo brasileiro." *Revista Brasileira de Ciências Sociais* 15, no. 43: 45–67.

———. 2002. "Comportamento estratégico em presidencialismo de coalizão: As relações entre Executivo e Legislativo na elaboração do orçamento brasileiro." *Dados* 45, no. 2: 265–301.

Pereira, Carlos, and Lúcio Rennó. 2001. "O que é que o reeleito tem? Dinâmicas político-institucionais locais e nacionais nas eleições de 1998 para a Câmara dos Deputados." *Dados* 44, no. 2: 133–72.

Peres, Paulo Sérgio. 2002. "Sistema partidário e inestabilidade eleitoral no Brasil." In *Partidos no Cone Sul: Novos ângulos de pesquisa*, ed. André Marenco dos Santos and Céli Regina Pinto. Konrad Adenauer/UFRGS.

Perlman, Janice. 1976. *The Myth of Marginality*. Berkeley: University of California Press.

———. 1977. *O Mito da Marginalidade*, Sao Paulo: Editora Paz e Terra,.

———. 1983a. "New York from the Bottom Up." *Urban Affairs* (May): 27–34.

———. 1983b. "Voices from the Street." *Development: Journal of the Society for International Development* 2, 47—52.

———. 2003. "Longitudinal Panel Studies in Squatter Communities: Lessons from a Re-Study of Rio's Favelas 1969—2003." Development Planning Unit, University College, London.

———. 2004. "Marginality: From Myth to Reality in the Favelas in Rio de Janeiro 1969–2002." In *Urban Informality in an Era of Liberalization: A Transnational Perspective*, ed. Ananya Roy and Nezar AlSayyad, 105–146. Lanham: Lexington Books.

———. 2005. "The Myth of Marginality Revisited: The Case of Favelas in Rio de Janeiro, 1969–2003." In *Becoming Global and the New Poverty of Cities*, ed. Lisa Hanley et al., 9–55. Washington, DC: Woodrow Wilson International Center for Scholars.

———. 2007a. "Elusive Pathways out of Poverty: Intra- and Intergenerational Mobility in the Favelas of Rio de Janeiro." In *Moving Out of Poverty: Cross-Disciplinary Perspectives*, ed. D. Narayan and P. Petesch. Washington, DC: World Bank; and Basingstoke, UK: Palgrave Macmillan

———. 2007b. "Globalization and the Urban Poor." WIDER Research Paper no. 2007/76, November.

———. 2008. *Favela*. New York: Oxford University Press.

Pessanha, Charles. 1999. "Medida (usurpação) por medida (provisória)." *Insight Inteligência* 5 (Nov./Dec./Jan.): 39–47.

Peterson, Paul E., and Mark C. Rom. 1990. *Welfare Magnets: A New Case for a National Standard*. Washington, DC: The Brookings Institute.

Pierson, Paul. 1994. *Dismantling the Welfare State: Reagan, Thatcher and the Politics of Retrenchment*. New York: Cambridge University Press.

Pinheiro, Paulo Sérgio. 2000. "Navigating in Uncharted Waters: Human Rights Advocacy in Brazil's 'New Democracy.'" *NACLA Report on the Americas* 34, no. 1 (July/August): 47–51.

———. 2005. "Démocratie et État de non-droit au Brésil." Unpublished paper.

Popkin, Samuel. 1991. *The Reasoning Voter: Communication and Persuasion in Presidential Campaigns*. Chicago: University of Chicago Press.

Porto, Mauro. 2007. "Framing Controversies: Television and the 2002 Presidential Election in Brazil." *Political Communication*. Forthcoming.

Power, Timothy J. 1998a. "Brazilian Politicians and Neoliberalism: Mapping Support for the Cardoso Reforms, 1995–1997." *Journal of Inter-American Studies and World Affairs* 40, no. 4 (Winter): 51–72.

———. 1998b. "The Pen Is Mightier than the Congress: Presidential Decree Power in Brazil." In *Executive Decree Authority*, ed. John Carey and Matthew Shugart. New York: Cambridge University Press.

———. 2000a. "Political Institutions in Democratic Brazil: Politics as a Permanent Constitutional Convention." In Kingstone and Power, *Democratic Brazil.*

———. 2000b. "Politicized Democracy: Competition, Institutions, and 'Civic Fatigue' in Brazil." *Journal of Inter-American Studies and World Affairs*, Vol. 33, no. 3, (Autumn): 75–112.

———. 2000c. *The Political Right in Post-Authoritarian Brazil*. University Park: Pennsylvania State University Press.

———. 2002. "Blairism Brazilian Style? Cardoso and the 'Third Way' in Brazil." *Political Science Quarterly* 116, no. 4 (Winter): 611–36.

Prefeitura do Recife, PNUD. 2005. *Desenvolvimento humano no Recife: Atlas municipal, 2005*. CD-ROM. Recife: Prefeitura do Recife.

Projeto Mapas. 2005. *A experiência do Projeto Mapas de monitoramento político de iniciativas de participação do Governo Lula*. Rio de Janeiro: IBASE.

Przeworski, Adam, with Carolina Curvale. 2005. "Does Politics Explain the Economic Gap Between the United States and Latin America?" Unpublished manuscript.

Putnam, Robert. 1993. *Making Democracy Work: Civic Traditions in Modern Italy*. Princeton: Princeton University Press.

Rahn, Wendy. 1993. "The Role of Partisan Stereotypes in Information Processing about Political Candidates." *American Journal of Political Science* 37:472–96.

Rapley, John. 2006. "The New Middle Ages." *Foreign Affairs* 85, no. 3 (May/June): 95–103.

Rawlings, Laura. 2004. "A New Approach to Social Assistance: Latin America's Experience with Conditional Cash Transfer Programs." Social Protection Discussion Paper Series 0416, The World Bank.

Reames, Benjamin. 2005. "Democratizing the Police of Brazil: The Strategies of a Professionalized Civil Society." Paper presented at the annual meeting of the Southern Political Science Association, New Orleans, January 6–8.

Reichmann, Rebecca, ed. 1999. *Race in Contemporary Brazil: From Indifference to Inequality*. University Park: Pennsylvania State University Press.

Reis, Fábio Wanderley. 1988. "Partidos, ideologia e consolidação democrática." In *A democracia no Brasil: Dilemas e perspectivas*, ed. Fábio Wanderly Reis and Guillermo O'Donnell, 296–326. São Paulo: Vértice.

Reis, Fábio W., and Mónica Mata Machado de Castro. 1991. "Regiões, classe e ideologia no processo eleitoral brasileiro." *Lua Nova: Revista de Cultura e Política* 26: 81–131.

Rennó, Lucio R. 2006a. "O dilema do rico: Número de candidatos, identificação partidária e accountability nas eleições de 2002 para a Câmara dos Deputados." In *Reforma Política: Lições da História Recente*, ed. Gláucio Ary Dillon Soares and Lucio R. Rennó. Rio de Janeiro: Editora FGV.

———. 2006b. "Informational Shortcuts in Complex Electoral Environments: The 2002 Brazilian Legislative Elections." Paper presented at the the annual meeting of the Brazilian National Social Science Association, Caxambu, Brazil, October 24–28.

Ricci, Paolo. 2003. "O conteúdo da produção legislativa brasileira: Leis nacionais ou políticas paroquiais?" *Dados* 46, no. 4: 699–733.

Rodrigues, Leôncio Martins. 1987. *Quem é quem na Constituinte: Uma anâlise sócio-política dos partidos e deputados.* São Paulo: OESP-Maltese.

Rolnik, Raquel. 1999. "Territorial Exclusion and Violence: The Case of São Paulo, Brazil." Working Paper Number 26, Woodrow Wilson International Center for Scholars.

Roma, Celso. 2005. *Atores, Preferencias e Instituição na Camara dos Deputados.* Doctoral Thesis, University of São Paulo. Department of Political Science.

Rosas, Guillermo, and Elizabeth Zechmeister 2000. "Ideological Dimensions and Left-Right Semantics in Latin America." Paper presented at the meeting of the Latin American Studies Association, Miami, FL, March 16–18.

Samuels, David. 1997. "Determinantes do voto partidário em sistemas eleitorais centrados no candidato: Evidências sobre o Brasil." *Dados* 40, no. 3: 493–536.

———. 1999. "Incentives to Cultivate a Party Vote in Candidate-Centric Electoral Systems: Evidence from Brazil." *Comparative Political Studies* 32:487–518.

———. 2000. "The Gubernatorial Coattails Effect: Federalism and Congressional Elections in Brazil." *Journal of Politics* 62, no. 1: 240–53.

———. 2003a. *Ambition, Federalism and Legislative Politics in Brazil.* New York: Cambridge University Press.

———. 2003b. "Fiscal Straitjacket: The Politics of Macroeconomic Reform in Brazil, 1995–2002." *Journal of Latin American Studies* 35:545–69.

———. 2004. "From Socialism to Social Democracy: Party Organization and the Transformation of the Workers' Party in Brazil." *Comparative Political Studies* 37, no. 9 (November): 999–1024.

———. 2006. "Sources of Mass Partisanship in Brazil." *Latin American Politics and Society* 48 (Summer): 1–27.

Sampaio, Augusto Luiz Duarte Lopes. 2004. "A ação afirmativa na PUC-Rio." In *Ação afirmativa na universidade, reflexão sobre experiências concretas—Brasil e Estados Unidos,* ed. Angela Maria de Randolpho Paiva. Rio de Janeiro: PUC.

Sani, Giacomo, and Giovanni Sartori. 1983. "Polarization, Fragmentation, and Competition in Western Democracies." In *Western European Party Systems: Continuity and Change,* ed. Hans Dalder and Peter Mair, 307–40. Beverly Hills: Sage Publications.

Sansone, Livio. 2003. *Blackness without Ethnicity: Constructing Race in Brazil.* New York: Palgrave Macmillan.

Santos, Fabiano. 1997. "Patronagem e poder de agenda na política brasileira." *Dados* 40, no. 3: 465–91.

———. 2003. *O poder legislativo no presidencialismo de coalizão.* Belo Horizonte: Editora UFMG.

Santos, Fabiano, and Lucio Rennó. 2004. "The Selection of Committee Leadership in the Brazilian Chamber of Deputies." *Journal of Legislative Studies* 10, no. 1: 50–70.

Santos, Fabiano, and Márcio G. Vilarouca. 2004. "Desigualdades e política partidária no Brasil contemporâneo." In *Imagens da desigualdade,* ed. Celi Scalon. Belo Horizonte: Editora UFMG; Rio de Janeiro: IUPERJ/UCAM.

Santos, Frei David Raimundo. 2004. "Cotas: Atos de exclusão substituídos por atos de inclusão?" In Paiva, *Ação afirmativa na universidade*.

Santos, Renato Emerson dos, and Fátima Lobato, eds. 2003. *Ações afirmativas: Políticas públicas contra as desigualdades raciais*. Rio de Janeiro: DP & A.

Santos, Gevanilda Gomes dos. 1992. "Partidos políticos and etnia negra." M.A. thesis, PUC–São Paulo.

Santos, Gevanilda, and Maria Palmira da Silva, eds. 2005. *Racismo no Brasil: Percepções da discriminação e do preconceito racial no século XXI*. São Paulo: Editora Fundação Perseu Abramo.

Santos, Hélio. 1998. "O Grupo de Trabalho Interministerial para a Valorização da População Negra e a ação afirmativa no Brasil." In *Populacão negra em destaque*, ed. Antonio Sérgio Alfredo Guimarães and Lynn Huntley. São Paulo: CEBRAP.

———. 1999. "Politicas publicas para a população negra no Brasil." In *Observatorio da Cidadania*, no. 3, 147–57. Rio de Janeiro: Ibase.

———. 2000. "Uma avaliação do combate as desigualdades raciais no Brasil." In Guimarães and Huntley, *Tirando a máscara*, 53–74.

———. 2001. *A busca de um caminho para o Brasil: A trilha do circulo vicioso*. São Paulo: Editora Senac Sao Paulo.

Santos, Ivair Augusto Alves dos. 2006. *O movimento negro e o estado (1983–1987): O caso do conselho de participação e desenvolvimento da comunidade negra no governo de São Paulo*. Sao Paulo: Coordenadoria dos Assuntos da População Negra/Prefeitura da Cidade de São Paulo.

Santos, Paulo Roberto dos. 1986. *Instituições Afro-Brasileiras*. 2 volumes. Rio de Janeiro: Centro de Estudos Afro-Asiaticos–CEAA, Conjunto Universitario Cândido Mendes.

Santos, Sales Augusto dos, ed. 2005. *Ações afirmativas e combate ao racismo nas Americas*. Brasília: Ministerio da Educação, Secretaria de Educação Continuada, Alfabetização e Diversidade.

———. 2007. "Movimentos negros, educação e ações afirmativas." PhD diss. Universidade de Brasília.

Santos, Ivanir, and José Geraldo da Rocha, eds. 2007. *Diversidade and ações afirmativas*. Rio de Janeiro: CEAP.

Santos, Wanderley Guilherme dos. 1987. *Crise e castigo: Partidos e generais na política brasileira*. Rio de Janeiro: Vértice/IUPERJ.

Schamis, Hector E. 2006. "Populism, Socialism, and Democratic Institutions."*Journal of Democracy* 17, no. 4: 20–34.

Schattschneider, Elmer Eric. 1935. *Politics, Pressures, and the Tariff*. New York: Prentice-Hall.

Schmitt, Rogério. 2000. *Partidos políticos no Brasil (1945–2000)*. Rio de Janeiro: Jorge Zahar.

Schreurs, Miranda A. 2003. *Environmental Politics in Japan, Germany, and the United States*. Cambridge: Cambridge University Press.

Schmitter, Philippe C. 1992. "The Consolidation of Democracy and the Representation of Social Groups." *American Behavioral Scientist* 35:422–49.

Schneider, Ben Ross. 1995. "Democratic Consolidations: Some Broad Comparisons and Sweeping Arguments." *Latin American Research Review* 30:215–34.

Schumpeter, Joseph. 1942. *Capitalism, Socialism and Democracy*. New York: Harper.

Schwarcz, Lilia Moritz. 1999 [1993]. *The Spectacle of the Races: Scientists, Institutions, and the Race Question in Brazil, 1870–1930*. New York: Hill and Wang.

Secretaria Especial de Promoção da Igualdade Racial. 2003. *Político nacional promoção da igualdade racial.* Brasília: SEPPIR.

Seligman, Adam B. 1992. *The Idea of Civil Society.* New York: The Free Press.

Sheriff, Robin E. 2001. *Dreaming Equality: Color, Race, and Racism in Urban Brazil.* New Brunswick, NJ: Rutgers University Press.

Silva, Cidinha da, ed. 2003a. *Ações afirmativas em educação: Experiências brasileiras.* São Paulo: Summus.

———. 2003b. "A união dos homens de cor: Aspectos do movimento negro dos anos 40 e 50." *Estudos Afro-Asiáticos* 25, no. 2: 215–35.

Silva, Maria Auxiliadora Gonçalves da. 1994. *Encontros e desencontros de um movimento negro.* Brasília: Fundação Cultural Palmares.

Silva, Nelson do Valle, and Carlos A. Hasenbalg. 1992. *Relações raciais no Brasil contemporaneo.* Rio de Janeiro: Rio Fundo Editora.

Silva, Luiz Inácio Lula da. 2005 [2002]. "Carta ao Povo Brasileiro." http://www.iisg.nl/collections/carta_ao_povo_brasileiro.pdf (accessed March 9, 2005).

Silva, Sidney Jard da. 2001. "Companheiros servidores: O avanço do sindicalismo no setor público na CUT." *Revista Brasileira de Ciências Sociais* 16 (June): 130–46.

Silveira, Flavio Eduardo. 1998. *A decisão do voto no Brasil.* Porto Alegre: EDIPUCRS.

Singer, André. 1999. *Esquerda e direita no eleitorado brasileiro.* São Paulo: EDUSP.

Skidmore, Thomas. 1993. *Black into White: Race and Nationality in Brazilian Thought.* Durham: Duke University Press.

Sniderman, Paul M., and John Bullock. 2004. "A Consistency Theory of Public Opinion and Political Choice: The Hypothesis of Menu Dependence." In *Studies in Public Opinion: Attitudes, Nonattitudes, Measurement Error, and Change*, ed. Willem E. Saris and Paul M. Sniderman. Princeton: Princeton University Press.

Sniderman, Paul M., Richard A. Brody, and Philip E. Tetlock. 1991. *Reasoning and Choice: Explorations in Political Psychology.* New York: Cambridge University Press.

Soares, Fábio Veras, Sergei Soares, Marcelo Medeiros, and Rafael Guerreiro Osório. 2006. "Programas de transferência de renda no Brasil: Impactos sobre a desigualdade." *IPEA Texto para Discussão* 1228 (October).

Soares, Gláucio. 1973. *Sociedade e política no Brasil.* São Paulo: Difel.

Soares, Gláucio Ary Dillon, and Lucio R. Rennó. 2006. *Reforma política: Lições da história recente.* Rio de Janeiro: Editora FGV.

Soares, Luiz Eduardo. 2000. *Meu casaco de general: 500 dias no front de segurança pública do Rio de Janeiro.* São Paulo: Companhia das Letras.

Souza, Jessé de. 1999. "A ética protestante e a ideologia do atraso brasileiro." In *O malandro e o protestante: A tese weberiana e a singularidade cultural brasileira*, ed. Jessé de Souza, 17–54. Brasília: Editora Universidade de Brasília.

Souza, Mario do Carmo Campello de. 1992. "The Contemporary Faces of the Brazilian Right: An Interpretation of Style and Substance." In *The Right and Democracy in Latin America*, ed. Douglas Chalmers, Maria do Carmo Campello e Souza, and Atilio Borón, 99–127. New York: Praeger.

Souza, Neusa Santos. 1983. *Tornar-se negro: As vicissitudes da identidade do negro brasileiro em ascenção social.* Rio de Janeiro: Edições Graal.

Spanakos, Anthony, and Lucio Rennó. 2006. "Elections and Economic Turbulence in Brazil: Candidates, Voters, and Investors." *Latin American Politics and Society* 48, no. 4: 1–26.

Stédile, João Pedro. 2004. "Globalization and Social Movements: A Brazilian Perspective." CERLAC colloquia paper, York University.

Steil, Carlos Alberto. 2006. *Cotas raciais na Universidade: Um debate.* Porto Alegre: Editora UFRGS.

Stepan, Alfred. 1988. *Rethinking Military Politics: Brazil and the Southern Cone.* Princeton: Princeton University Press.

Stokes, Susan. 2001. *Mandates and Democracy: Neoliberalism by Surprise in Latin America.* Cambridge: Cambridge University Press.

Suplicy, Eduardo M. 2002. *Renda de Cidadania: A saída é pela porta.* São Paulo: Cortez.

Tafner, Paulo. 1997. *Proporcionalidades e exclusão no sistema político-partidário brasileiro.* Master's thesis, IUPERJ.

Telles, Edward E. 2004. *Race in Another America: The Significance of Skin Color in Brazil.* Princeton: Princeton University Press.

Thomas, Clive S. 2001. "Toward a Systematic Understanding of Party-Group Relations in Liberal Democracies." In *Political Parties and Interest Groups*, ed. Clive S. Thomas. Boulder: Lynne Rienner.

Tocqueville, Alexis de. 1966 [1835]. *Democracy in America.* Translated by George Lawrence. New York: Harper and Row.

Tulchin, Joseph, and Meg Ruthenberg, eds. forthcoming. *Towards a Society under Law: Citizens and Their Police in Latin America.* Washington, DC: Woodrow Wilson International Center for Scholars.

Twine, France Winddance. 1998. *Racism in a Racial Democracy: The Maintenance of White Supremacy in Brazil.* New Brunswick: Rutgers University Press.

Ungar, Mark. 2002. *Elusive Reform: Democracy and the Rule of Law in Latin America.* Boulder: Lynne Rienner.

United Nations Human Settlements Programme. 2003. *The Challenge of the Slums.* London: Earthscan Publications Ltd.

Valladares, Licia. 2003. "Sistema urbano, mercado de trabalho e violência no Brasil e no Rio de Janeiro." Center for Migration and Development Working Paper Series, Princeton University.

Ventura, Gustavo, and Vilma Bokani. 2004. "Sociedade: Discriminação racial e preconceito de cor no Brasil." *Revista Teoria e Debate* 59. http://www2.fpa.org.br/portal/modules/news/article.php?storyid=2456 (accessed January 28, 2007).

Verba, Sidney, Key Lehman Schlozman, and Henry Brady. 1995. *Voice and Equality: Civic Voluntarism in American Politics.* Cambridge, MA: Harvard University Press.

Von Mettenheim, Kurt. 1995. *The Brazilian Voter: Mass Politics in Democratic Transition, 1974–1986.* Pittsburgh: Pittsburgh University Press.

Wampler, Brian, and Leonardo Avritzer. Forthcoming. "Participatory Publics: Civil Society and New Institutions in Democratic Brazil." *Comparative Politics.*

Wellford, Charles, and James Cronin. 2000. "Clearing Up Homicide Clearance Rates." *National Institute of Justice Journal* 243 (April): 1–7. http://www.ncjrs.gov/pdffiles1/jr000243b.pdf (accessed Dec. 6, 2007).

Weyland, Kurt. 1996. *Democracy without Equity: Failures of Reform in Brazil.* Pittsburgh: University of Pittsburgh Press.

Wibbels, E., and M. Arce. 2003. "Globalization, Taxation, and Burden-Shifting in Latin America." *International Organization* 57:111–36.

Williamson, John, ed. 1990. *Latin American Adjustment: How Much Has Happened?* Washington, DC: Institute of International Economics.

———. 2002. "Is Brazil Next?" Policy Brief 02-7, International Institute for Economics.

Wittman, D. 1995. *The Myth of Democratic Failure: Why Political Institutions Are Efficient.* Chicago and London: The University of Chicago Press.

World Bank. 2001. *Assessment of the Bolsa Escola Program.* Report no. 20208-BR. Washington, DC: The World Bank.

———. 2002. *Brazil Municipal Education Resources, Incentives, and Results.* 2 vols. Report no. 24413-BR. Washington, DC: The World Bank.

———. 2003. *Argentina—Crisis and Poverty 2002 A Poverty Assessment.* Vol. 1. Report no. 26127-AR. Washington, DC: The World Bank.

———. 2004. *Project Appraisal Report for the Bolsa Familia Project.* Report no. 28544-BR. Washington, DC: The World Bank.

Zaller, John R. 1992. *The Nature and Origins of Mass Opinion.* Cambridge: Cambridge University Press.

———. 2004. "Floating Voters in U.S. Presidential Elections, 1948–2000." In *Studies in Public Opinion: Attitudes, Nonattitudes, Measurement Error, and Change*, ed. Willem E. Saris and Paul M. Sniderman, 166–212. Princeton: Princeton University Press.

Zaverucha, Jorge. 2003. *Polícia Civil de Pernambuco: O desafio da reforma.* Recife: Editora Universitária UFPE.

———. 2005. *FHC, forças armadas e polícia: Entre o autoritarismo e a democracia.* Rio de Janeiro: Editora Record.

Contributors

Barry Ames is the Andrew Mellon Professor of Comparative Politics and chair of the Department of Political Science at the University of Pittsburgh. He is the author of *Political Survival: Politicians and Public Policy in Latin America* and *The Deadlock of Democracy in Brazil*. He is working on a study of mass politics in contemporary Brazil together with Andy Baker and Lucio Rennó.

Alberto Carlos Almeida is a professor at the Federal University Fluminense and holds a Ph.D. in political science from IUPERJ. He has been a visiting researcher at the London School of Economics and coordinated electoral and public opinion research for DataUFF and for the Getúlio Vargas Foundation. He is currently a columnist for the newspaper *Valor Econômico* and director of planning for Ipsos Public Affairs, where he is responsible for "Brazil Pulse," a monthly report on consumption, the economy, and politics. He is the author of *A cabeça do brasileiro* (Editora Record, 2007), *Por que Lula?* (Editora Record, 2006), *Como são feitas as pesquisas eleitorais e de opinião* (Editora FGV, 2002), and *Presidencialismo,parlamentarismo e crise política no Brasil* (Eduff, 1998).

Aline Diniz Amaral, specialist in public policy and public administration, is a graduate of the Federal University of Minas Gerais (1996) in administration and has an M.A. in political science from the University of Brasília (2000). She has been a research fellow with IPEA (Institute for Applied Economic Research) and an adjunct professor in the political science department of the University of Brasília. Currently, she is the coordinator of the Unified Registry of Social Programs for the Ministry of Social Development and a research associate of the Center for Advanced Studies of Government and Public Administration of the University of Brasília. She is the author, with Paulo Calmon, of a number of papers on the regulatory experience in Brazil.

Andy Baker is assistant professor of political science at the University of Colorado at Boulder. He conducts research on Latin America, mass political behavior, and international political economy. He has a forthcoming book manuscript with Cambridge University Press on the nature and causes of citizens' attitudes towards free-market policies in seventeen Latin American nations. He has also published articles in the *American Journal of Political Science, World Politics,* and *Electoral Studies*. His current research focuses on the social and interpersonal causes of voting behavior in Brazil.

Kathryn Hochstetler is professor of political science at the University of New Mexico. Her most recent book is *Greening Brazil: Environmental Activism in State and Society* (Duke University Press, 2007, coauthored with Margaret Keck). She has published numerous articles and book chapters on civil society actors in Brazil, Mercosur, and the United Nations.

Wendy Hunter is an associate professor of government at the University of Texas–Austin. Her early work focused on Latin American militaries during the transition from authoritarianism. More recently, she published several articles on social policy decision-making and human capital formation in Latin America. Currently, Professor Hunter is writing a book on the growth and transformation of the Workers' Party in Brazil from 1989 until the present.

Ollie A. Johnson III received his B.A. in Afro-American studies and international relations and a M.A. in Brazilian studies from Brown University. He later earned a M.A. and Ph.D. in political science from the University of California, Berkeley. His first book, *Brazilian Party Politics and the Coup of 1964*, was published in 2001. He coedited *Black Political Organizations in the Post-Civil Rights Era* in 2002. Professor Johnson has conducted research on the Black Panther Party, the National Association for the Advancement of Colored People, and other black political groups in the United States. He has also lectured on African American politics in Brazil, Colombia, Ecuador, and Japan. His current research focuses on Afro-Brazilian and Afro–Latin American politics.

Peter R. Kingstone is associate professor of Political Science at the University of Connecticut. He received his Ph.D. from the University of California, Berkeley. He is the author of *Crafting Coalitions for Reform* (Pennsylvania State University Press), coeditor (with Timothy Power) of *Democratic Brazil: Actors, Institutions, and Processes* (University of Pittsburgh Press), and editor of *Challenges to Democratization: Readings in Latin American Politics* (Houghton Mifflin). He has also published a number of articles on various aspects of the politics of economic reform in journals such as *Comparative Politics, Comparative Political Studies, Latin American Politics and Society*, and *Latin American Research Review.* He is currently at work on a comparative study of privatization and pension reforms in Argentina, Bolivia, Brazil, and Venezuela.

Jonathan Krieckhaus is an associate professor at the University of Missouri and conducts research on the politics of economic growth. His work has appeared in the *British Journal of Political Science* and *World Development.* He recently completed a book, *Dictating Development: How Europe Shaped the Global Periphery*, on the role of colonialism in determining long-run economic growth, based on an analysis of ninety-one countries, along with case studies of Mozambique, Brazil, and South Korea.

Marcus André Melo is currently a professor of political science at the Federal University of Pernambuco, and he has been a Fulbright Fellow at the Massachusetts Institute of Technology. He is the author of three books in Portuguese and many articles in English appearing in *Political Research Quarterly, Latin American Politics and Society, International Political Science Review*, the *Quarterly Review of Economics and Finance* and elsewhere. He has published a coauthored book, *Regulatory Governance in Infrastructure Industries* (The World Bank Press), and numerous book chapters, including a recent contribution to Pablo Spiller and Mariano Tommasi's *Political Institutions, Policy-making Processes and Economic Policy in Latin America.*

Anthony W. Pereira received his Ph.D. from Harvard University in 1991 and is a professor of political science at Tulane University. His research interests include the politics of military rule and changes in patterns of state coercion in Brazil. He is the author of *Political (In)justice: Authoritarianism and the Rule of Law in Brazil, Chile, and Argentina*

(University of Pittsburgh Press, 2005) and a chapter in Tom Ginsburg and Tamir Mustafa, eds., *Rule by Law: The Politics of Courts in Authoritarian Regimes* (Cambridge University Press, 2008). He received Fulbright and Fulbright-Hays fellowships in 2005–6 to carry out research on the reform of public security policy and policing in contemporary Brazil.

Janice E. Perlman recently completed her new book, *Favela: The Dynamics of Urban Poverty in Rio De Janeiro, 1968–2005* (Oxford University Press, 2008) based on her longitudinal study following four generations. She is the winner of several awards, including the Guggenheim Award, Fulbright Award, the Chester Rapkin Award (from American Collegiate Schools of Planners), and the C. Wright Mills Award, for her earlier book, *The Myth of Marginality: Urban Politics and Poverty in Rio de Janeiro* (University of California Press, 1976). She was a tenured professor in the Department of City and Regional Planning at the University of California, Berkeley, and has taught at the University of California, Santa Cruz, New York University, Hunter College, Columbia University, Trinity College, and various universities in Brazil. In addition to her academic positions, Dr. Perlman is the president and CEO of The Mega-Cities Project, a transnational nonprofit which she founded in 1987. Dr. Perlman holds a B.A. in anthropology from Cornell University and a Ph.D. in political science from the Massachusetts Institute of Technology.

Timothy J. Power is the director of the Latin American Centre and a fellow of St. Cross College at the University of Oxford, where he is also a member of the Department of Politics and International Relations. His research interests include political parties, elections, and executive-legislative relations in Brazil, and he is coeditor (with Nicol C. Rae) of *Exporting Congress? The Influence of the U.S. Congress on World Legislatures* (University of Pittsburgh Press, 2006). From 2004 to 2006, Power served as president of the Brazilian Studies Association, and he is currently an associate fellow of the Latin American and Caribbean Research Project at Chatham House, London.

Lucio R. Rennó received a Ph.D. in political science from the University of Pittsburgh in 2004. He is an associate professor of Latin American politics in the Research Center and Graduate Program on the Americas, CEPPAC. His main research areas are legislative studies and public opinion, and he has published in the *American Journal of Political Science, Latin American Politics and Society, Journal of Politics, Journal of Latin American Studies, Journal of Legislative Studies, Electoral Studies, Dados: Revista de Ciências Sociais,* and *Opinião Pública.* He is coeditor of *Reforma politica: Lições da história recente* (Editora da FGV, 2006).

Fabiano Santos has a Ph.D. in political science (IUPERJ - 1994) and is permanent professor at IUPERJ. He is the author of *O Poder Legislativo no presidencialismo de coalizão* (UMFG, 2003). He is the coauthor, with Octavio Amorim Neto, of "The Inefficient Secret Revisited: The Legislative Input and Output of Brazilian Deputies," *Legislatives Studies Quarterly,* which won the Jewell-Loewenberg Award of the Legislative Studies Section (APSA) for the best article published in *Legislative Studies Quarterly* in 2003.

Márcio Grijó Vilarouca has a Ph.D. in political science from Rio de Janeiro's Graduate Institute of Research (IUPERJ). At present, he is conducting research on political institutions, political parties, executive-legislative relations, and bicameralism at the Nucleus of Congressional Studies (NECON).

Index